W9-ADS-547

The Art of ILLUSTRATION

The Art of
ILLUSTRATION

by Michel Melot

© 1984 by Editions d'Art Albert Skira S.A., Geneva

Reproduction rights reserved by A.D.A.G.P. and
S.P.A.D.E.M., Paris, and Cosmopress, Geneva

Published in the United States of America in 1984 by

RIZZOLI INTERNATIONAL PUBLICATIONS, INC.
712 Fifth Avenue/New York 10019

All rights reserved. No part of this book may be
reproduced in any manner whatsoever without permission of
Editions d'Art Albert Skira S.A.
89 Route de Chêne, 1208 Geneva, Switzerland

Translated from the French by James Emmons

Printed in Switzerland

Library of Congress Cataloging in Publication Data

Melot, Michel.
The art of illustration.
Translation of: L'art de l'illustration.
Bibliography: p.
Includes index.
1. Illustration of books. 2. Illumination of books
and manuscripts. I. Title.
NC960.M413 1984 741.64 84-42752
ISBN 0-8478-0558-1

Contents

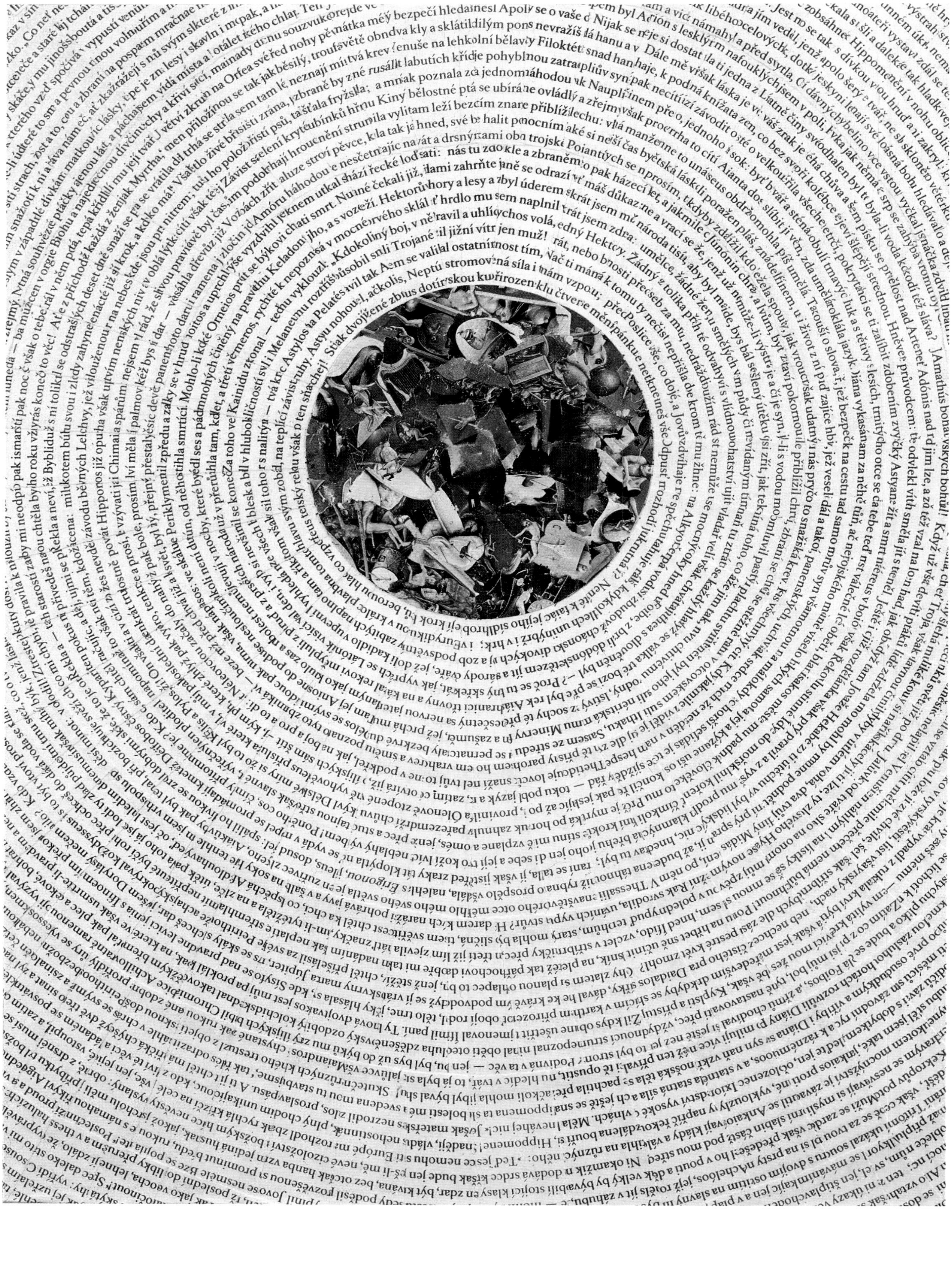

INTRODUCTION

Writing and Picturing

Writing may at times appear chilly and aloof. Speech is alive and responsive. Writing, however, can make its way across time and distance. To the evanescence of speech it adds the weight of permanence, for it is speech in objective, immutable, reproducible, transportable form. Convenience and permanence, then, in this double reduction of the thing to a sound, and the sound to an alphabet, but the consequence is a double remove from reality; and the widespread grafting of pictures onto writing may have its initial motive here.

Yet the abstraction of writing which classifies, orders and synthesizes has irresistible advantages over picturing, which is bound to the concrete aspect of things. Swift turned this truth into a satirical fable in *Gulliver's Travels*, where in the "Voyage to Laputa" he describes a "Scheme for entirely abolishing all Words... For, it is plain, that every Word we speak is in some Degree a Diminution of our Lungs by Corrosion; and consequently contributes to the shortning of our Lives. An Expedient was therefore offered, that since Words are only names for Things, it would be more convenient for all Men to carry about them, such Things as were necessary to express the particular Business they are to discourse on... [but] if a Man's Business be very great, and of various Kinds, he must be obliged in Proportion to carry a greater Bundle of Things upon his Back, unless he can afford one or two strong Servants to attend him." Here the limits of illustration may be seen at once. Another borderline case is reached with messages made up of symbolic objects, like the message of Darius who, according to Herodotus, sent his enemies a bird, a frog, a mouse and some arrows, meaning: "Unless you fly like the bird, unless you dive like the frog, unless you vanish into a hole like the mouse, you will be transfixed with these arrows." Here again it is clear that, while the abstraction

▲ Italian treatise on penmanship: *Tratteggiato Da Penna...* by Francesco Pisani, Genoa, 1640.

◄ Jiří Kolář: Pitiless Sun, 1981. Collage.

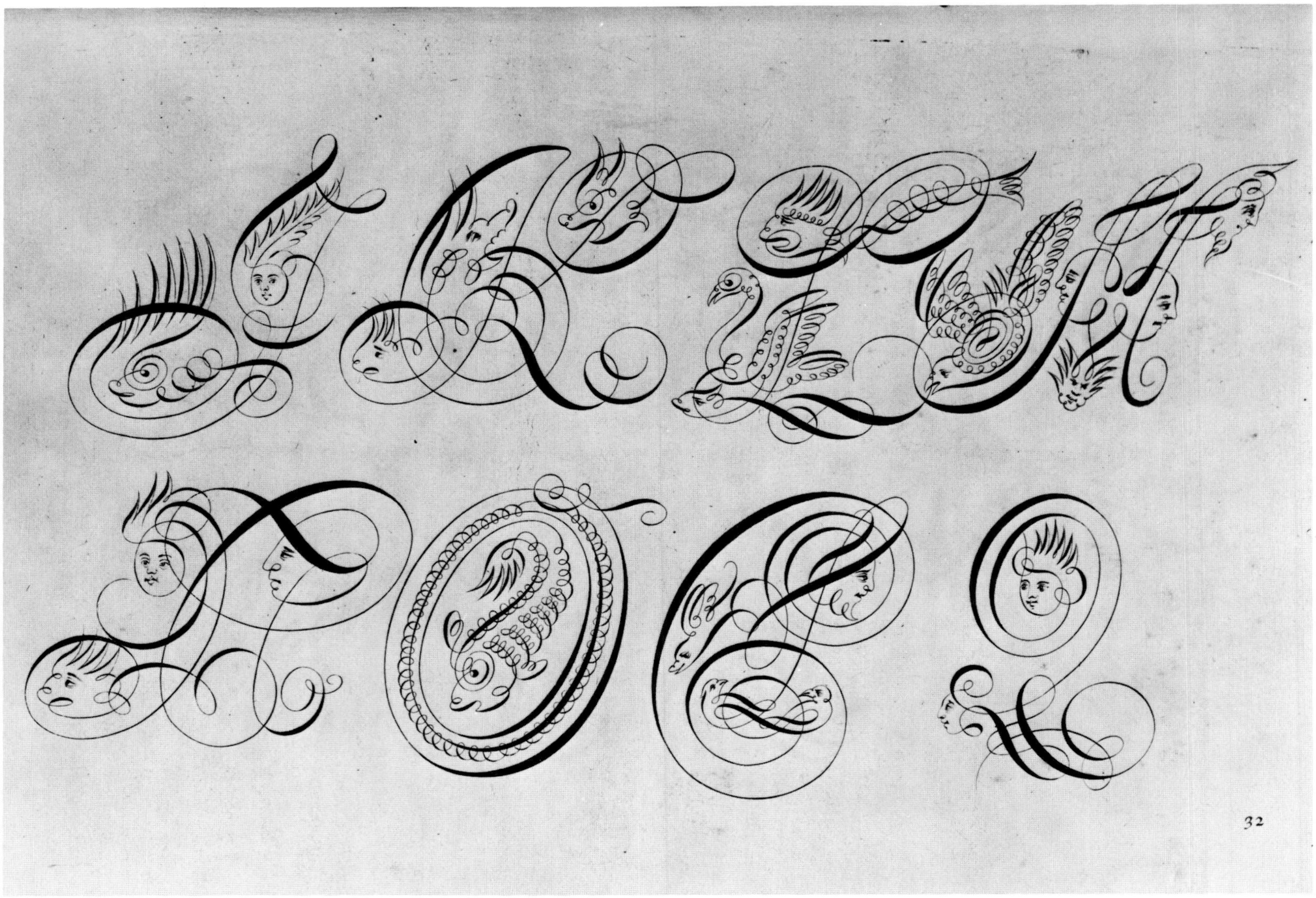

Fancy alphabet from *The Pen-Man's Paradis, Both Pleasant & Profitable*, by John Seddon, London, 1695.

always misses the essential of the message, picturing alone does not permit communication. So we are confronted by two equally unacceptable systems. Using them together may palliate the inadequacies of both, and that is why there are so many forms and examples of the use of illustration.

So natural is the combination of picture and writing that men of many times and places have believed the picture to be consubstantial with the thing or being that it represents. The picture, the sign, was not considered a thing distinct from reality but a mode of existence of that reality. Onomatomancy, the false science which claims to know things through their name, goes back to the very beginnings of writing. And one reason why men resisted the use of the alphabet instead of pictograms seems to have been their rooted belief in the identity of the image with its content. With no image beside it in which the reality seems anchored, writing is no more than the token of absence, no more than thought drained of vitality and governed by a system totally alien to it, imposed from without. The combination of pictures and writing, on the other hand, introduces into the sign system a tonic and indeed fruitful incoherence, for it confronts the reader with this truth, "that the sign may be more or less likely, more or less remote from what it signifies, that it may be natural or arbitrary, without affecting its nature or value as a sign—all this showing clearly that the relation of the sign to its content is not certified in the order of things themselves" (Michel Foucault, *Les Mots et les Choses*).

Ornamental letter from *Il Perfetto Scrittore* by Giovanni Francesco Cresci, Rome, 1570.

Writing and picturing cannot be considered as two radically distinct systems, for materially speaking their frequent union is only made possible by their common configuration. Both are line drawings, and even if sometimes the techniques of one progress more quickly than those of the other (printing in one case, photography in the other), they are bound to be produced and diffused together. Even today when a chasm divides them, moves from one towards the other vouch for their underlying contiguity.

Writing, and here lies its ambiguity, necessarily sketches out a figure of some kind; its patterns cannot help having connotations unconnected with the code which they denote. Calligraphers, typographers, graphic designers, graphologists, know that writing is as expressive as a picture. This concordance is not something marginal: it underlies the whole art of Oriental calligraphy in which writing is judged more by the flow and responsiveness of the line, the harmony of the intervals, the equilibrium of the letter stems, than by the word content. Nothing of this in Western calligraphy, concerned as it is first of all with legibility. It is a matter of order: to know how to write, in classical terms, means being a good secretary. It is an additional code permitting the most effective standardized reproduction of letters. It arose in places where much writing was done: in the Roman chancellery, in Dutch office-shops. This is the opposite of Oriental calligraphy, since the latter could be carried to the limits of legibility and was a matter of sensibility, not technique.

◀ Taoist talisman with a magic formula and the god of longevity. Chinese painting from Lung-men, Honan.

Unlike the alphabet, a phonetic system which thus became a figured system, we find figural images which do no more than record phonemes and act as phonograms of the objects figured, and so being able to designate homophonous objects: such is the rebus. It may exist even before the making of images. Thus the Incas are said to have sent to the Spanish viceroy Abascal, governing Peru, three packages containing respectively salt, beans and lime, which could be "read" phonetically as *sal, abas, cal*, meaning "Go, Abascal!" It is significant that since the Renaissance, when it was a widely practised game, the rebus has always been considered as a debasement of thought, too riddling and perverse for anything but smutty or anticlerical pleasantries. As opposed to it, the game of hieroglyphics came into fashion around 1500—the "figured" writing attributed to the Egyptians, in which a word is replaced by the picture of a symbolic object (some elegant examples are to be found in the *Dream of Polyphilus* of 1499). Such word games became popular about that time, when the written sign was being desacralized and a whole school of philosophy was desperately seeking out the spiritual emblems behind words. In the classical age, to the speculative efforts of philologists to establish the status of signs answered for example the games of concordance, the sound of words being acrobatically converted into puns, spoonerisms, anagrams, rebus devices, etc. Writing and picturing, then, went to form a new pair, distinct from the sum of its two components. And yet its new aptitudes can by no means be described as structural. Their history, if they can be said to have any common history, is only that of their interaction, for neither was determined by the other, and their relations were never at any time codified or fixed. Unlike speech, writing is not a universal phenomenon going back to time out of mind. It is a recent

b

Lequale uetuſtiſſime & ſacre ſcripture penſiculante,cuſi io le interpretai.

EX LABORE DEO NATVRAE SACRIFICA LIBERA LITER, PAVLATIM REDVCES ANIMVM DEO SVBIECTVM. FIRMAM CVSTODIAM VITAE TVAE MISERICORDITER GVBERNANDO TENEBIT, INCOLVMEMQVE SERVABIT.

c

Renaissance game of "hieroglyphics," woodcut illustration from Francesco Colonna's *Hypnerotomachia Poliphili*, Venice, 1499.

One of the earliest books of riddles: *Rébus de Picardie*, paintings on paper, a series of 151 rebus devices, composed about 1500 in the form of armorial bearings.

and artificial invention which, starting from a few specific points, gained currency and spread among the educated class of all countries. As for picture writing, its initial characteristic is that of being infinitely variable and flexible. Written speech and pictured speech, each representing one type of knowledge, have been very selectively used by the different authorities—religious, political, educational or familial. Their history is that of an unrelenting struggle between them, each trying as it were to arouse the bad conscience of the other. Historians of book collecting are apt to consider the illustrated book as a place of harmony, but it was more often a place of contention and rivalry.

In these combats there were several types of strategy. The quarrel over iconoclasm in Byzantium was the most famous and the most highly theoretical. The image, as being too close to reality, seemed likely to be confused with it. For the defenders of the image, the refusal of it was tantamount to refusing the divine incarnation and the duality based upon it, which the image alone could unify in abstract form. The condemnation of images in favour of Scripture is common to the Old Testament, some Islamic texts and many writings by the Reformers. The religion for which reality is only an image naturally despises the image of that reality. Distrust of images was and is widespread among intellectuals labouring to transmit knowledge, in order to preserve a tradition. The use of images here is not contradictory when they are controlled by the religious or educational authority for the benefit of the lower orders or children, whom they are supposed to reach more easily. But the image was always felt to be a dangerous thing to handle and of questionable utility. The code composed of writing was better suited to upholding the hierarchy. It could be taught to a chosen few;

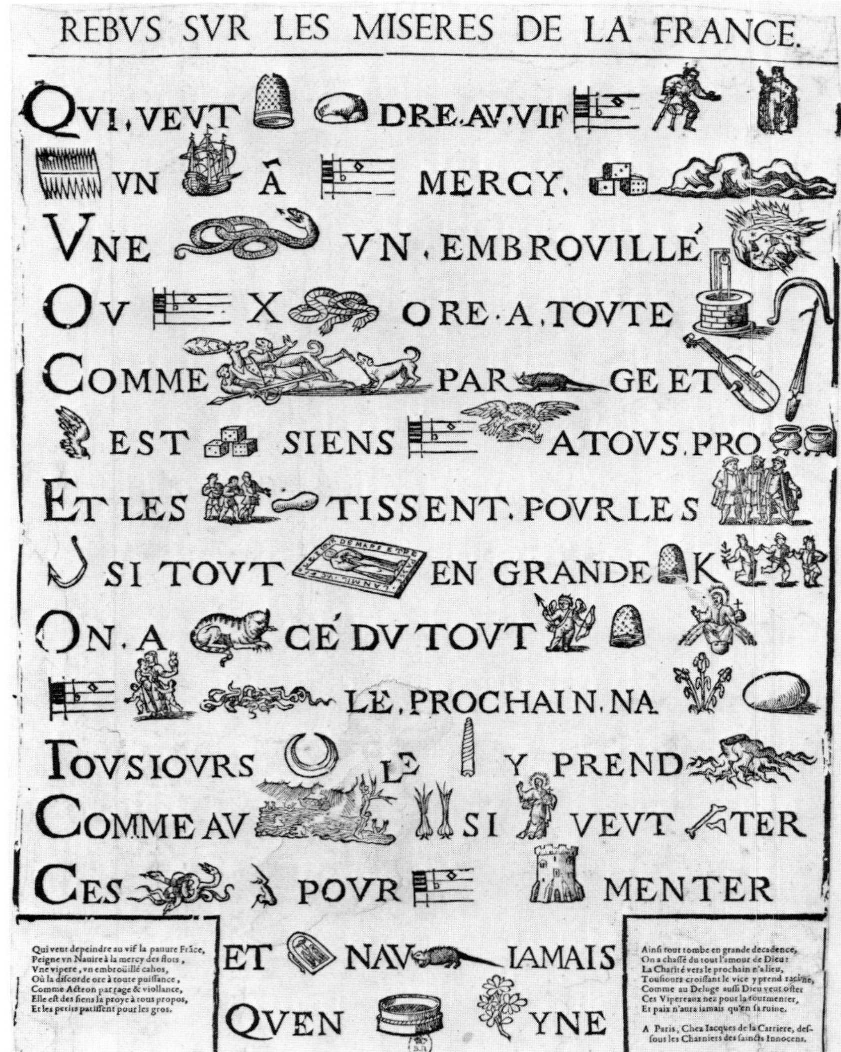

Rebus by Grandville in *Un Autre Monde*, 1844: "A-croix mois A mi-lecteur neuf fées pâque homme sept imbécile qui se casse la tête pour me deviner" (Ah! crois-moi, ami lecteur, ne fais pas comme cet imbécile, etc.: Ah, believe me, friend reader, don't do like this imbecile, who breaks his head trying to guess my meaning).

Rebus on the Miseries of France, woodcut broadsheet, Paris, 1592.

it was an instrument of teaching but also of concealment, and from the first centuries of writing scribes made up secret codes from it, and this in fact was its initial usage. Applied to a text whose code is controlled and which may therefore "officially" transmit the meaning, the image may appear as a wild vehicle authorizing as many meanings as there are interpreters. Illustration, which seems to keep to reality, drains off the idealism which fills the sign. Supposedly, anyhow, for an ideal significance is always reintroduced into it, and even into the mirror.

Instead of trying to destroy the image, the classical theories attempted to channel it, to reduce it to speech, to codify it by various devices: emblems, iconologies, allegories, physiognomies, etc. Finally, a third tactic consisted in containing it within a framework regulated by typography. But this was obviously the outcome of a clearing of the ground. Writing gradually moved away from the territory of the image, while leaving the image enclosed in it. In eighteenth-century Europe the scientific spirit of empiricism, by taking reality as an absolute reference, reversed the situation in favour of the image, and in our time the television screen has imposed its space on writing, and words here simply cannot keep up with the image.

One of the final consequences of this distrust of illustration is that no history of it has been written. What go by the name of "histories of illustration" are in fact no more than anthologies. And they are anthologies of book illustration, at the expense of everyday illustration; giving pride of place to the literature of fiction, they neglect scientific and technical illustration; and the pictures are usually considered independently of the text, even on the formal plane where illustration then becomes a category of the print. The present book makes no pretence to filling this immense void. Nor does it claim to trace out the main lines of a "history" of illustration, an impossible task, for the many-sided realities pictured here cannot be said to have any underlying unity. This study does no more than reflect a moment of time when, on all sides, the problem arises of treating illustration in relation to the writing around it, which it does not translate or transpose, but which rather it complements and competes with. To do this, it was necessary for both systems to be conceived of in terms of a single theory. Now it is not very long since semiotics came into existence. As long as the designation "sign" is reserved for a coded system (which was and remains the position of many linguists), illustration is not open to analysis. But semiotics extended to any object susceptible of falling into "significance"—the latter being conceived as an occasional, historical state, and not as the intrinsic quality of certain forms—permits us to think in terms of two articulated systems of different signs. The image then is no longer an appendix, ornament or redundance of the text. It is simply a different technique for the conveying of knowledge.

If any history is sketched out here, it is rather a history of the fashions and uses of illustration than that of the images themselves. Not so much because of the subject's diversity and abundance, which makes any synthesis difficult, but because it must be realized that the image always comes as a challenge to writing, and that any writing about pictures is limited to what words can say about them.

René Magritte: The Empty Mask, 1928-1929. Oil on canvas: "Sky, human body (or forest), curtain, house front."

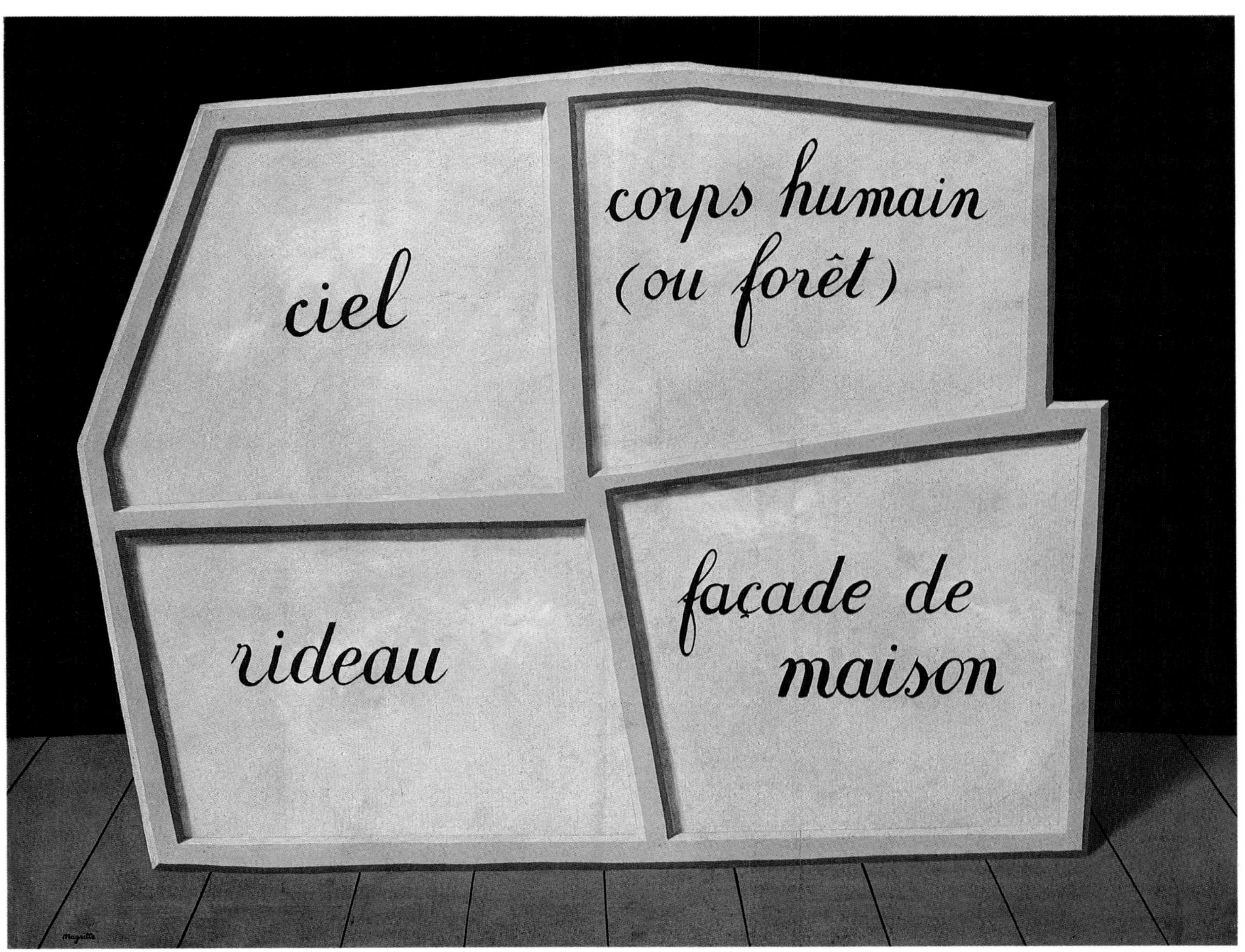

I

The Ambiguities of Line

FROM PICTOGRAM TO ALPHABET

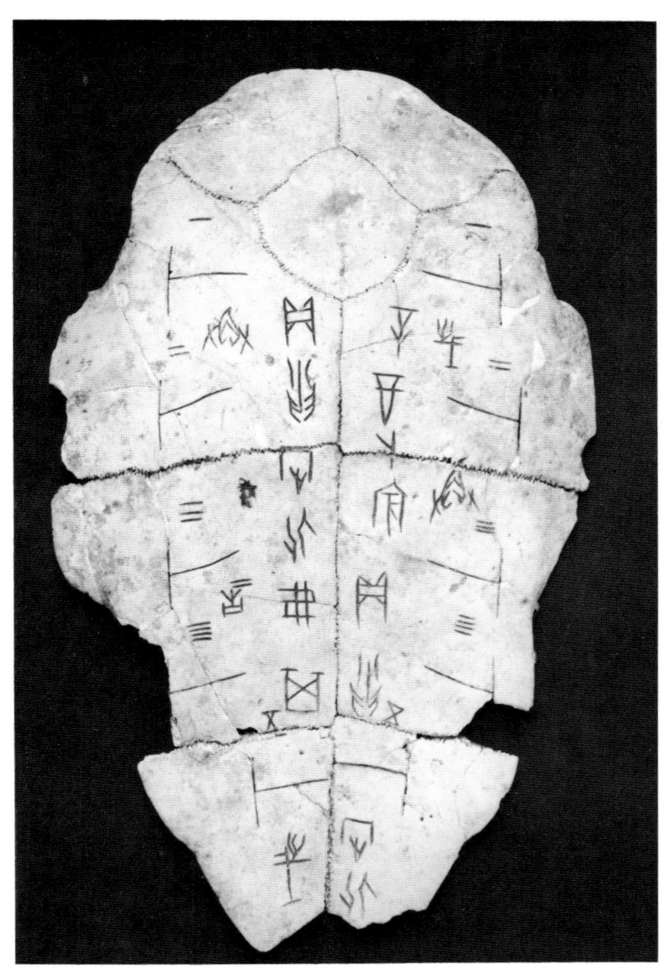

▲ Chinese oracle bone (engraved tortoise plastron). Shang-Yin dynasty, c. 1339-1281 B.C.

◄ An undeciphered script on a wooden tablet from Easter Island: entire and detail.

Since illustration only exists in the relation of the image to the text, it must first be seen how these two are to be distinguished from each other and whether this distinction is a radical one. Apparently it is not in the case of such figures as pictograms, where the two seem to have merged together.

It is difficult to conceive of any writing composed of images alone. For the pictogram seems to lose its figural character in proportion as the systems of primitive writing take form and a verbal code is worked out. It is often said that writing was figural to begin with, that the pictograms were then transformed into ideograms, and these into phonograms. This view is seen to be naive as soon as it is put to the test of archaeological discoveries.

The fact is that these different types of signs have always coexisted and often merge. The signifier (the form taken by the sign) tells us nothing about the signified (does not tell us whether this form refers to an image, a word, a sound or even a gesture or whatever). Now it is from the signified that arises the distinction between picture and writing, anyhow in the primitive systems. So it is a delicate point to say whether we are in the presence of simple picturing or of rudimentary writing, even when, as in the Easter Island tablets, the organization of the signs seems already perfectly coded. Thus, for example, chiefly among the North American Indians, narratives were set forth in pictures, and in the latter can be observed an order and rhythm comparable to that of writing. These are descriptive images, to which a name can be attached, but their syntax, which orders the narrative, calls for an oral commentary without which the narrative remains unintelligible. These "phrasograms" are akin to pictograms, but they cannot be said to amount to autonomous writing, and autonomy is one of the essential conditions for any writing. Likewise in the cave art of 15 or 20,000 years ago, prehistorians can single out structured groupings, whose arrangement and sequence no doubt had some precise significance. But the scenes represented must have been connected with an oral context, with some narrative or formula, which would relate them rather to our modern "illustrations" than to pictograms. It must further be noted that the pictograms of the North American Indians are a much later development than our own writing; far from being an earlier model of the latter, they appear to be no more than a figured or disfigured copy of it.

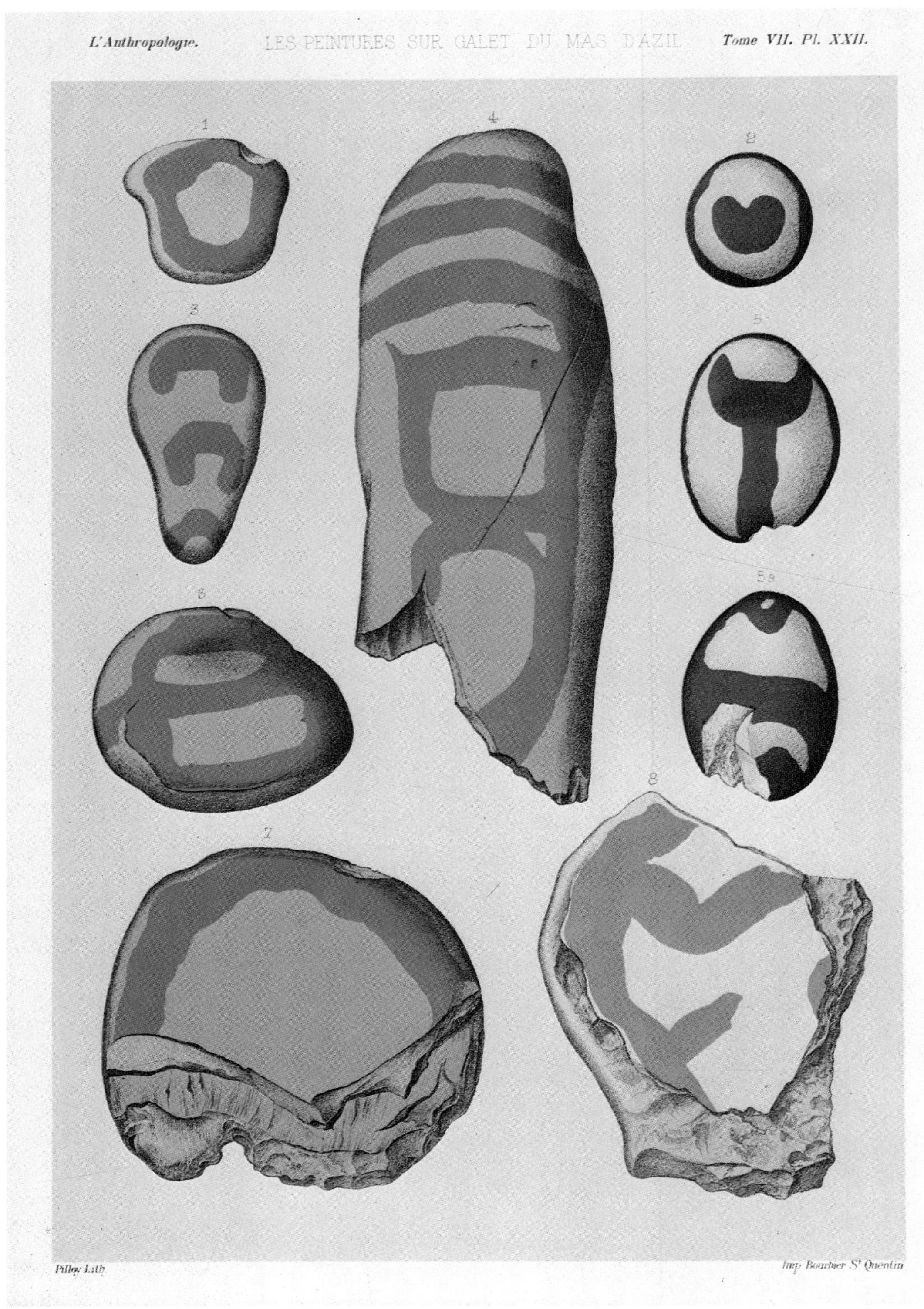

Coloured prehistoric river-pebbles from Mas-d'Azil (Ariège) in the French Pyrenees: ornaments or messages? Magdalenian period, c. 9000 B.C.

While there is no writing without picturing, one may also say that there is no picturing without speech. For Leroi-Gourhan *(Le Geste et la Parole)*, there can be no doubt that "figurative art at its origin was directly connected with speech and much closer to writing in the broadest sense than to the work of art." And he goes on: "Four thousand years of linear writing have made us separate art from writing... The achievement of writing lay precisely in this, that by way of the linear arrangement it completely subordinated graphic expression to phonetic expression. On the level where we still stand now, the connection of speech with graphic expression is one of coordination and not subordination." Arguing on the basis of palaeontological time-spans, Leroi-Gourhan considers that the discontinuity between the two languages, that of the hand, connected with sight, and that of the face, connected with hearing, is a recent development, and only appears with "agricultural settlement and the first forms of writing... But what seems, from the time when an agricultural economy arose, to be two divergent ways, is in reality only one."

In looking for the origins of writing, one meets with all kinds of sign systems in which, being ignorant of the signified, we cannot say to what extent the language is directly implied by them. So one may decide that certain figured systems, like maker's marks on prehistoric pottery, ownership seals, identifying emblems, totems or even divinatory signs, whether natural or provoked, are tan-

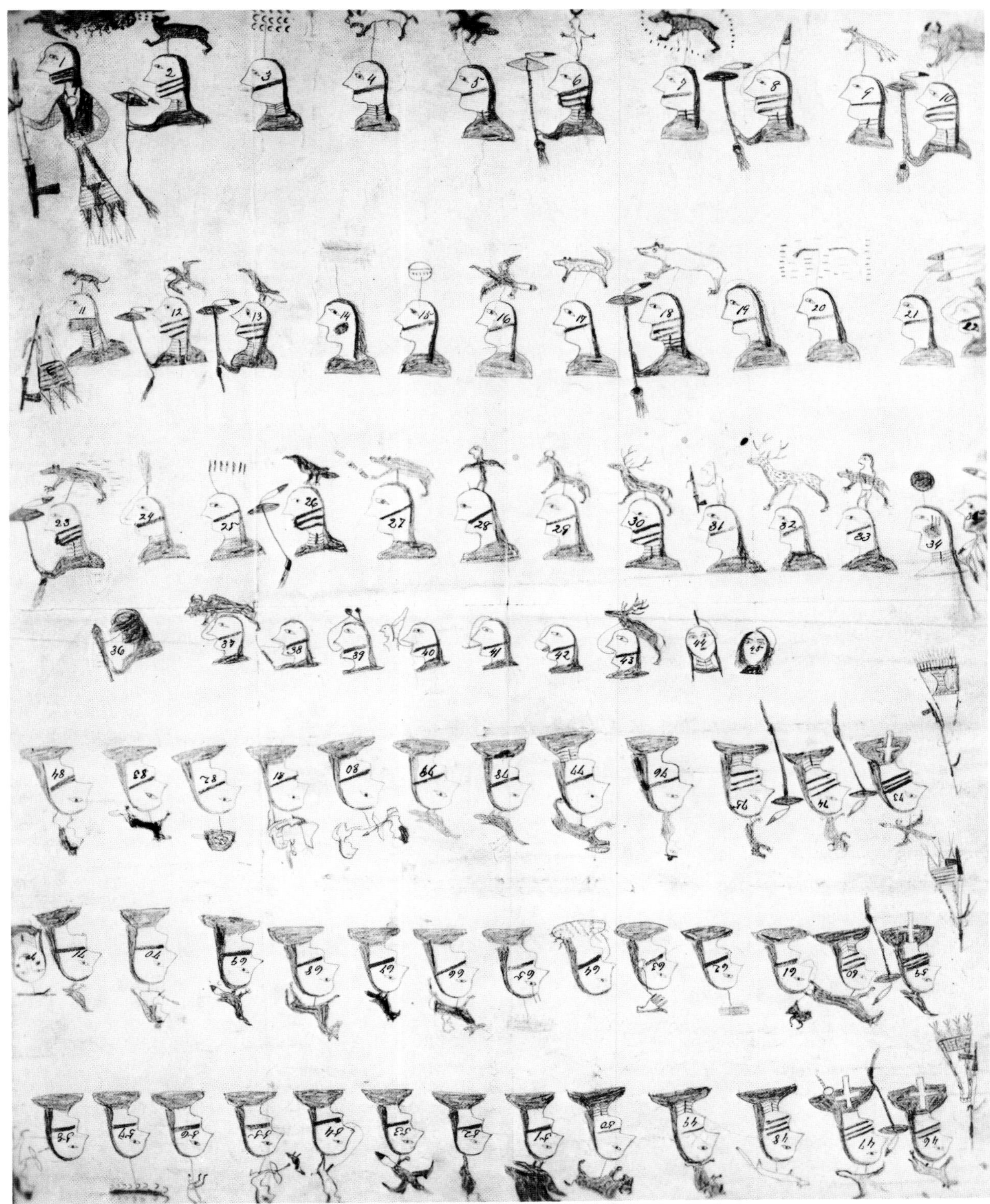

Pictographs of North American Indians: Pictorial roster of heads of 84 families in the band of Big Road, Oglala tribe, Dakota, before 1883.

tamount to writing. One may then, if one likes, go back beyond such marks to the traces with which men and beasts stake out their territories and chart their itineraries. The first marking systems known to us, by notches, still in use today, or the geometric ornaments on prehistoric river-pebbles from Mas-d'Azil (Ariège) which may have served for the transmission of messages, or the systems of coloured knots *(quipus)* used in complex ways by the Incas—all these marking and counting systems are not descriptive figures but signs referring to an abstract idea: authority, ownership, numbers. Consequently, without being directly connected with language, they may be said to prefigure writing. The origins of Chinese writing have been looked for now in the system of knots, now in the divinatory practices accompanying the signs provoked by the cracking of bones or tortoise shells worked with an iron point, and more recently in the marks incised on pottery found at Xian and dated to 5000 B.C. Unfortunately no historical link can be established between these various signs and the appearance of the first ideograms about 1400 B.C.

The Chinese language, once constituted as writing, appears from the first as a complex system of signs going from the ideogram to the phonogram, and referring either to the idea, to the sound, or to a classificatory determinant. The picturing behind it is so highly stylized that it is impossible for an illiterate person to recognize an image with any certainty.

Pictographic signs on a clay tablet in Sumerian cuneiform script, c. 3000 B.C. *Enlarged.*

Pictography, then, may be regarded as a morphological aspect of writing, but there is nothing to prove that it acts as an image and even less that it forms an intermediary stage between the image and writing.

Likewise, in Sumer, as soon as the appearance of writing can be detected, the pictograms have already lost much of their figural value. It is obvious that a Sumerian pictogram cannot be read unless one has the code behind it. Since they are not quite pictures any more, the schematic figures composing them are therefore already provided with a signified other than the visual memory which may be conceptual (numbers, marks), gestural (divinatory or ritual signs) or more probably verbal. So it is not a matter of finding out to what extent the first written signs borrowed their form from repertories of figural signs, such as may already have been known in decorative art. The relevant distinction between picture and writing was made when the verbal signified was substituted for the visual signified; that is, when the signs, whatever their form, proved capable of referring to something more than identifiable objects.

It may be asked then whether there was a rupture between these two conceptions or whether there may have been an evolution from one to the other.

For some Sumerologists, the rupture goes back to the beginning. They see proof of this in the fact that the ear-

Clay tablet with Sumerian pictographic script, Proto-Urban period, Uruk phase III, c. 3000 B.C. *Enlarged.*

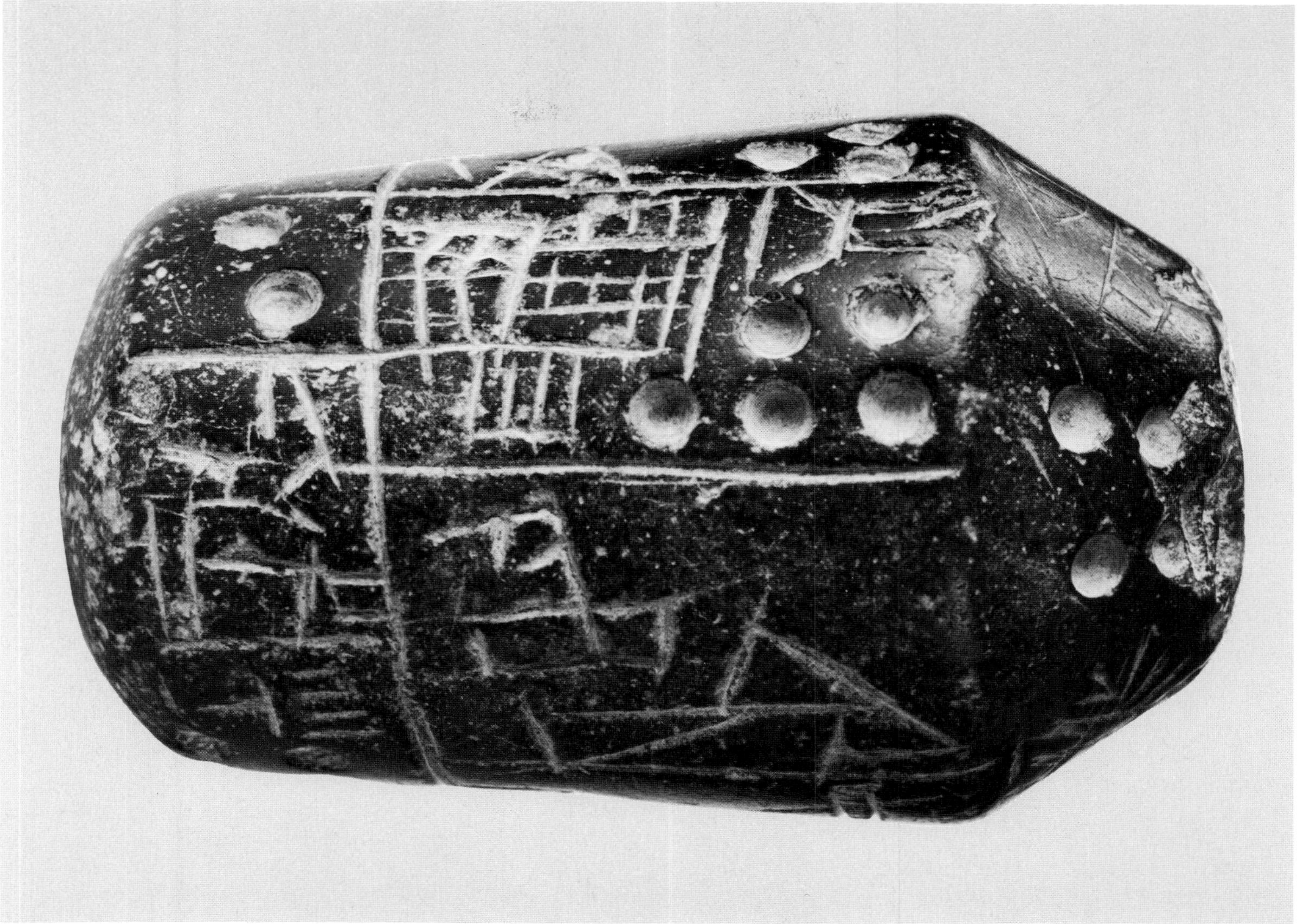

Sumerian cylinder seal in diorite with numerical and pictographic signs, late 4th millennium B.C. *Enlarged.*

liest Sumerian writing, found at Uruk and dating to 3300 B.C., is wholly abstract. This writing doubtless derived from a system of numbering with counters, associated with the designation of products and owners, worked out in the earliest merchant societies. In the vaguely figural drawings of Sumerian writing, which developed into the cuneiform script, abstraction is the rule throughout. But here we remain on the level of the signifier, which alone is accessible to us, and it cannot be otherwise. In the very principle of writing there are categories of determinants and inflexions incompatible with the empiricism of figural representation. Confusion between image and language may therefore occur in the signifier when the pictogram refers simultaneously to both. But the signifieds remain as foreign to each other as sight is distinct from hearing or gesture. The difficulty, indeed the false problem, of finding out how the image is to be distinguished from writing lies then in the fact that this distinction is at once impossible in its form and ineluctable in its substance–which understandably determines all the force of the relation between text and image which today we call "illustration." That relation may be stated as follows: a centripetal force constantly tends to bring text and image together by way of their common configuration, while a centrifugal force constantly tends to separate the function of each.

Sumerian diorite weight dedicated by Shu-Sin (2037-2029 B.C.), fourth king of the Third Dynasty of Ur.

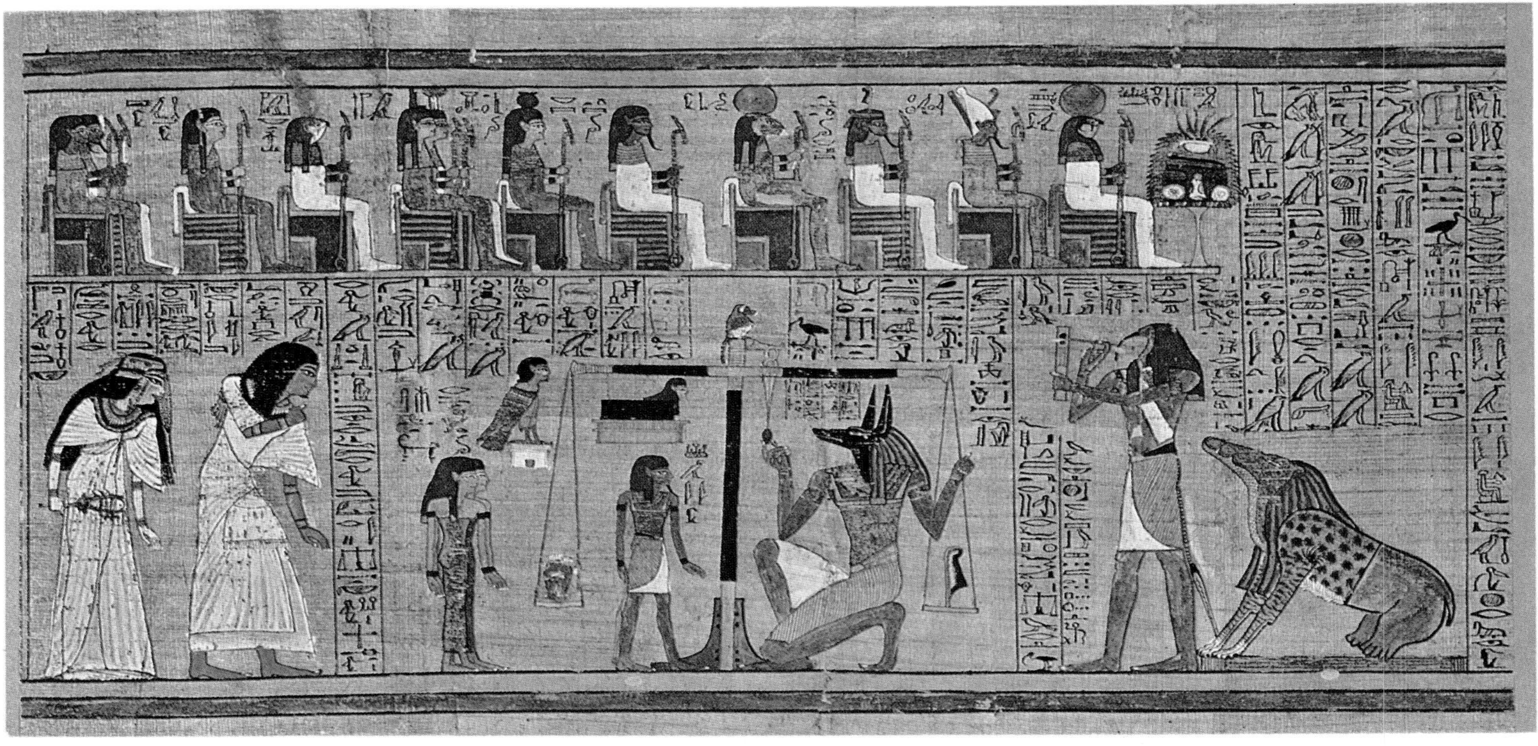

Things are made more difficult in primitive systems of writing, because abstraction still mingles indistinctly with figuration, both acting upon the text at once as image and as text. Their roles are not properly shared. The same sign may be provided with several values, either semantic or iconic or, more and more, phonetic, for the phoneme became the major but not exclusive signified of writing: it appears as early as 3000 B.C. This imprecision must even then have caused some problems of interpretation. For example, the pictogram schematically representing a foot could also mean, not "foot," but "walk" and at the same time "stand" (a similar but on occasion contradictory notion). This ambiguity had its advantages. Since the same signifier could refer to several signifieds, the scribe could write over several registers a "polyphonic" text, so to speak, in which the image was one of the melodies. The sign in a text designating an important person could be all at once enlarged in relation to the other signs, in order to convey the idea of his authority. An individual could be expressed by the outline of a head, the community by an abstract outline or an accumulation. Writing was still something of a game, and the rules were loose. The rebus device was then erected into a system of meaning which the scribes handled with virtuosity to convey parallel senses; punning too was a common device. The scribes also used these multiple meanings to devise secret forms of writing, whether ritual or strategic, and this of course enhanced their power.

Three centuries after Uruk, hieroglyphs appeared in Egypt. There may well have been some link between two countries so close, but none can be traced. As far back as we can go, we find the hieroglyphic system provided both with its own pictographic and also with phonetic signs (21 of the 24 alphabetic signs existing from the start), and it is impossible to retrace the path—or even to be sure there was one—which led from image to letter. Here again is that vacillation in the values of the signs, which go to enrich each other within the same signifier. And new meanings

The weighing of the dead man's conscience, after the Book of the Dead. Papyrus of the royal scribe Any (19th Dynasty, 1320-1200 B.C.), from Thebes, Egypt.

The Mistress of the Harem of Amun Here-Ubekhe, granddaughter of the High Priest Menkheperre, praying to the crocodile Geb. Papyrus from the hoard of the priests of Amun at Deir el Bahri, Egypt (21st Dynasty, c. 1085-950 B.C.).

are added by the figural level of the pictograms, above all by their size and sometimes by their orientation. "The subtlety arrived at in the arrangement of the inscriptions," writes Pascal Vernus *(L'Espace et la Lettre)*, "is due to the fact that they are not mere commentaries added to a scene and external to it. On the contrary, they are an organic part of the whole in which they figure, because there is no break between the representation and the hieroglyphic script, the latter remaining a combination of images as well as a combination of conventional signs." And he gives two examples: "In the funeral chambers, the hieroglyphs representing potentially dangerous creatures, whether men or animals, have to be neutralized in various ways: they are deleted, they are replaced by an innocuous sign, they are mutilated, they are pierced with arrows or knives." In a hieroglyphic inscription, a pictogram may be enlarged to act as an illustration without losing its semantic value in the text of which it is part. The human figures are usually all oriented in the same direction, but one of them may be turned round to show that he is addressing another. The idea of "being in" may be rendered figuratively by placing one sign "in" another, and so on. Certain values, then, can be represented spatially without the hieroglyph losing anything of its codification.

"The inclusion of the image in the writing bears out the widespread belief that the sign is consubstantial with the thing or being it designates," writes Pascal Vernus, who sees here, rightly no doubt, the reason why so unwieldy a system lasted so long, when the phonogram, the most discrete element in the notation of the language, had been known almost from the beginnings of writing. Hieroglyphs did die out nevertheless, belatedly, but retaining ever after the reputation of a sacred script giving access to a higher truth.

Writing was to be perfected by two inventions which carried it into the realm of abstraction, thus creating the gap which now separates it from illustration. One of course was the alphabet, which ruled out any attempt at figuration (though again at the Renaissance a wealth of ingenuity was expended on seeking out formal meanings in the shapes of letters). The other was linear writing, in which the sign no longer had any freedom of movement, being a necessary part of an irreversible chain. What occurred was a specialization of the signifiers according to the types of signifieds: for writing, languages; for pictures, reality. Here was created the landscape which from now on categorically opposed the space of the image to the space of the writing. Not only was the sign fixed and calibrated, but the sequence of signs was oriented. It took nearly three thousand years to explode the idea of the impossible marriage between picturing and writing. The picture, knowing nothing of syntax, inflexion, generalization, movement or abstraction, could have only the most superficial and occasional relations with the letter, particularly in Western civilization where language enjoys a fundamental cultural primacy. Word and picture thus became rivals. They have often been combined, but remain distinct, as unmixable as oil and water.

Greek papyrus roll with magical formulas invoking demons, from the Fayum, Egypt, fourth century A.D.
Left: Typhon-Seth with head of a sparrow-hawk, holding a thunderbolt.
Right: Stethocephalic monster with eyes in his breast.

1

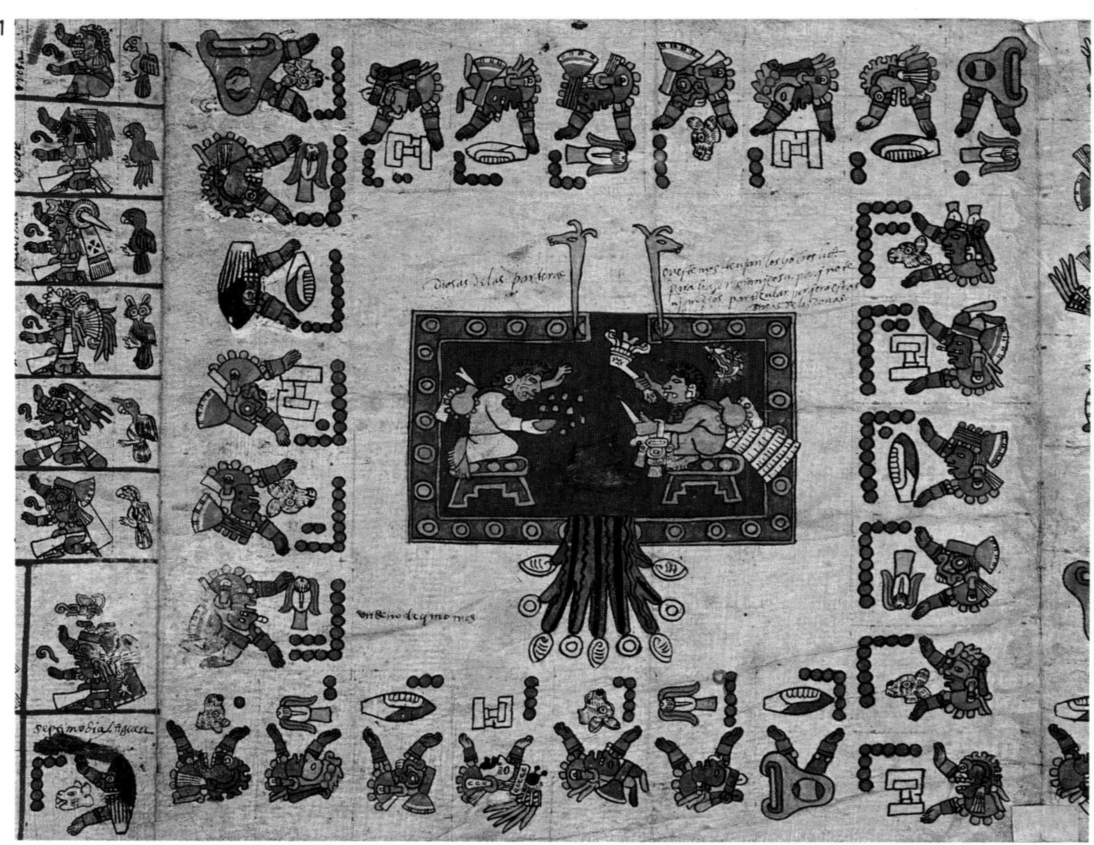

The "Codex Borbonicus"

3

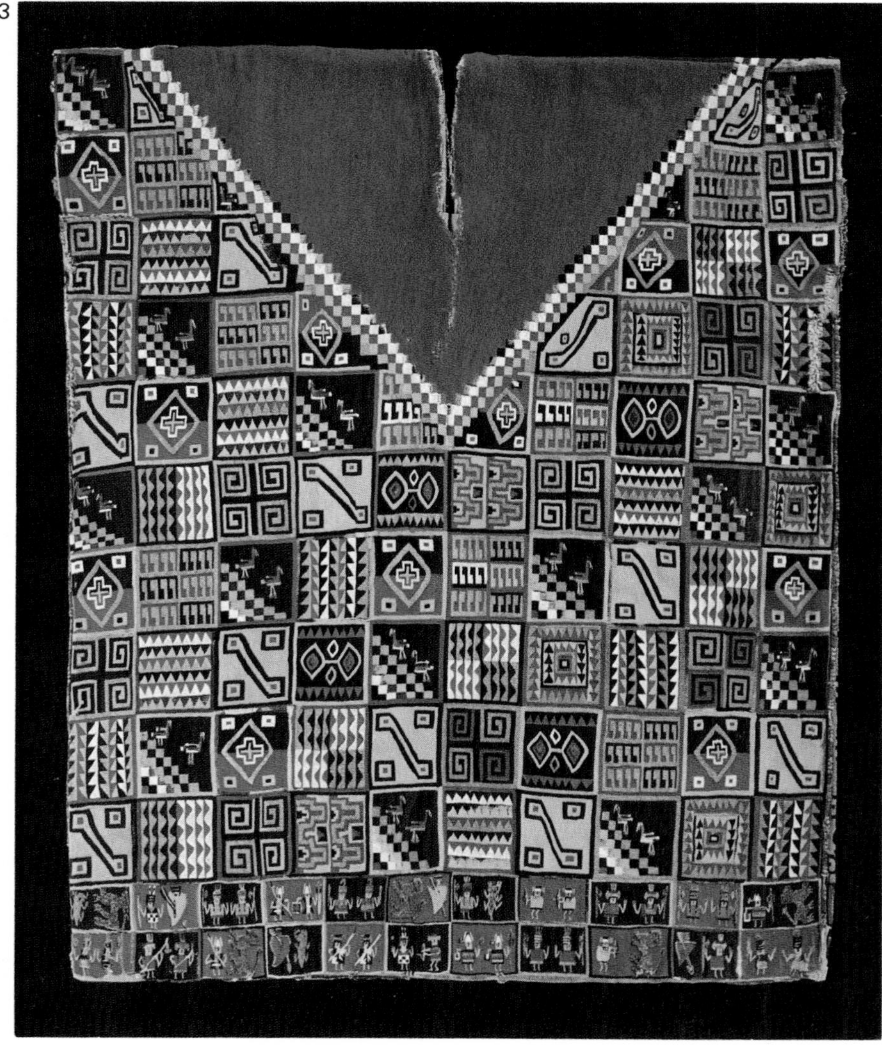

Among the painted manuscripts which survived the conquest of Mexico by Cortés, the *Codex Borbonicus* is one of the most richly illustrated. So named because it is now preserved in the Bibliothèque de l'Assemblée Nationale in Paris (Palais Bourbon), it consists of 38 leaves (of a paper made from *ficus benjamina*) entirely covered with paintings. Aztec manuscripts are often picture stories, veritable pictograms closely akin to our comic strips. Setting forth the chronicles, and particularly the migrations of the peoples of ancient Mexico, the Aztec writing, like many other primitive scripts, completes the figural pictograms with "determinating" signs (often another pictogram) having the value of a phonogram; these go to specify the meaning of the image, particularly as regards proper names, animal species, place names, etc. Another category of manuscripts is made up of the *tonalamatl*, calendars of great complexity representing the elaborate astrological cycles on which the Aztecs based their belief in a cyclic order of the universe. It is to this category that the *Codex Borbonicus* belongs. The first twenty leaves correspond to twenty "thirteeners," a cycle of 260 days used to calculate the dates of the festivals, ceremonies and sanguinary sacrifices by which the many divinities of the Mexican pantheon were appeased. On each leaf figures the cohort of gods corresponding to the period in question, accompanied by their symbols and attributes. Then two leaves evoke in pictures the creation and reform of the calendar, featuring the gods taking counsel together and dancing in a cave. The final leaves show the ritual of the feast days. In the fifteenth century the system of astronomical computation for determining these feast days had become so complex, and the number of divinities so great, that an attempt was made to unify the practices and many books were destroyed. For the Maya civilization, only three manuscripts survive, in Paris, Dresden and Madrid, and the Maya script remains largely undeciphered. ■

THE APPEARANCE OF THE DIAGRAM

▲ Shred of papyrus with uncoloured line drawing, c. fourth century A.D.: Briseis led away from Achilles by the two heralds Talthybius and Eurybates (*Iliad*, I.347ff.).

◀ *De materia medica* of Dioscorides: full-page plate of twenty-four birds. Illumination on vellum, c. A.D. 512.

Writing, in the civilizations of Greece and Rome, did not have the transcendental value which attached to the sacred texts, as the basis of faith, in the Jewish, Christian, and Islamic civilizations. In monumental art, in stelae and sarcophagi, illustration could continue to participate in the religious rite. In the text scrolls of antiquity it had an informative value more akin to our present-day conceptions. "Book illumination," writes Kurt Weitzmann, "was invented to facilitate the comprehension of a written document by the addition of diagrams for scientific treatises, and of illustrated scenes for literary texts." He adds: "The illustrations are physically connected with the text, whose content the illustrator wishes to elucidate by graphic means, and the understanding of them accordingly rests on a clear conception of that relation with the written word." The manuscript in fact lent itself better than the printed book to the inserting of pictures, which there fit into the text without the rigid framework later imposed by typography. The image is set in the same space as the writing, while being quite distinct from it.

The book as we know it, made up of gatherings of leaves folded and bound together to form pages, appeared under the name "codex" at the end of the first century A.D., when the sheet of vellum replaced the papyrus scroll. Illustrations are to be found on papyrus scrolls, and great numbers of them, those in particular which went to ornament the *Books of the Dead,* executed in specialized workshops of the Egyptian Middle Kingdom. The earliest known illustrated papyrus is a ceremonial piece executed for the Pharaoh Sesostris I about 1980 B.C.

In classical Greece papyrus was still scarce, and there is little likelihood of any illustration apart from bas-reliefs and vase paintings. It was from Alexandria, founded in the late fourth century B.C., that the Greeks learned about papyrus and began importing it. This had no effect on the development of illustration, but it was a prerequisite, another being the desire to spread knowledge, for outside its ritual roles the image had no other purpose here but to facilitate the approach to the text. These two conditions were met in the Hellenistic period, and Greek illustration made its appearance in the form of diagrams, as a scientific and pedagogical adjunct to books on mathematics and astronomy. It was treated like a script: in the oldest papyrus scroll illustrated with geometric figures (first century B.C., Nationalbibliothek, Vienna), the scribe left blank

De materia medica of Dioscorides: text page with plant (Thymellia). Illumination on vellum, c. A.D. 512.

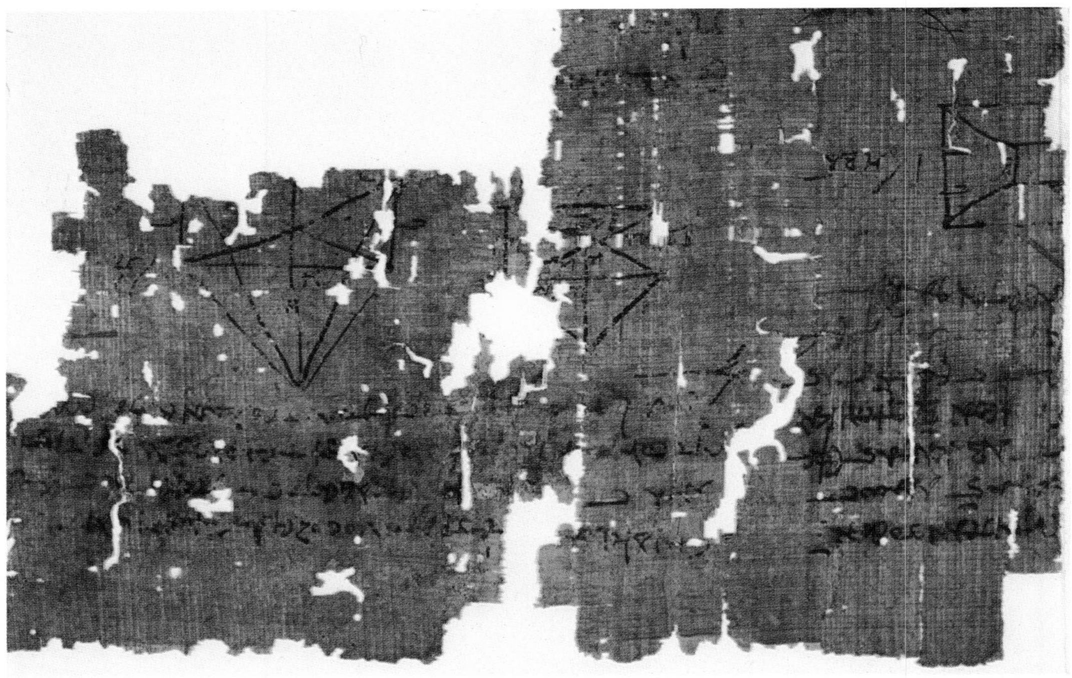

The oldest extant geometric figure, painted on papyrus, from a treatise on mathematics, first century B.C.

spaces for the diagrams to be added afterwards. But the oldest extant illustrated Greek papyrus is an astronomical text (second century B.C., Louvre, Paris), with, not a mere diagram, but a representation of Osiris figured as Orion and a scarab, the Sun. Maps, charts and mechanical devices called for illustrations, and so did two subjects much written about in antiquity, siegecraft and the construction of automata. From the early sixth century A.D. date some illustrations of living things, in texts on botany, then assimilated to medicine, such as the famous Dioscorides manuscript in Vienna, containing 400 plates facing the text on the opposite page. From then on, scenes of everyday life make their way into the diagram: soldiers in the texts on siegecraft, a girl picking flowers in a botanical treatise, or the young man frightened by snakes in an eleventh-century copy of Nicander of Colophon's *Theriaca* (Bibliothèque Nationale, Paris); and animal pictures range from fabulous beasts represented symbolically to the scientific illustrations in books on farriery, such as have come down to us in Byzantine copies.

Illustration also goes to complement the text in works of fiction, where it seems to have been used to emphasize certain paragraphs and to add helpful pictures for the non-scholarly reader. No useful distinction can be drawn between scientific and literary illustration at this time, for even reputedly literary texts were felt to call for pictures because of their educational and moralizing character: such were Hesiod's *Works and Days* in a much later manuscript with purely schematic illustrations (fourteenth century, Cambridge), or Virgil's *Georgics*, whose illustrations gradually evolve from agricultural information to lyrical views of landscape. When used as a demonstrational device to "interpret" the text, illustration may also be likened to the expressive language of the comic actor or the mime. Possibly the oldest literary illustrations are those of comic scenes from Euripides on a

Theriaca (poem on venomous animals) by Nicander of Colophon: Man frightened by snakes. Illumination on vellum, eleventh century.

papyrus anterior to the third century A.D. (Florence). But in practice, as one might expect, it was the most popular books, aimed at a non-scholarly public, that were most often illustrated. The *Iliad* first of all, the *Odyssey*, commentaries on both, and to a lesser degree the *Aeneid*, these were by far the most frequently illustrated texts of antiquity. A papyrus of the fourth century A.D. (Munich) has fragmentary illustrations of the *Iliad*; and a fifth-century codex (Milan) has preserved 58 miniatures. But four centuries earlier the many *tabulae iliacae* were already being made, out of marble dust: these were reliefs picturing comparable scenes. And even earlier the *Iliad* and *Odyssey* provided subject matter for paintings on vases and terracotta cups. Three Homeric frescoes survived at Pompeii alone.

In this ancient period, as again in modern times, the illustration was sharply distinguished from the script and played a different part from that of the text. And in antiquity were established the formats in which this type of illustration had to evolve in order to emphasize this distinction of purposes and means. Illustrations could be inserted in the text with more or less of regularity, and more or less of distance or closeness, each of these relations answering to a particular conception of their significance. In the early literary illustrations, the image alternates with the text, unframed and irregularly placed, in the same column with it. The unstandardized format of the papyrus discouraged any very strict layout. When, at the end of the first century A.D., the leaves were gathered up in a codex, the illustrator felt called upon to utilize the full page or geometric subdivisions of the page or columns, even if he had to divide up the full page (as a comic strip is divided up) in order to fit in several pictures: such is the case with the Vienna *Dioscorides.* The addition of a painted frame regularizing the size of the image, whether in the text or on a page by itself, contributed further to isolate

Vergilius Vaticanus: Aeneas founding the town of Thrace (*Aeneid*, III.13-22). Illumination on vellum, fourth-fifth century.

Ilias Picta: Illumination on vellum illustrating Homer's *Iliad*, fifth century. XVI: Diomedes, helped by Athene, wounds Phegeus (V. 4-8, 19). XVII: Athene keeps back Ares from the fight. Pandarus wounds Diomedes (V. 35, 95).

image and text from each other. The frame set the illustration apart, on a level of its own, independent of the text, in a hierarchical relation with it which reflected the relations then being assigned to these different types of approach to knowledge. The framed full-page illustration seems to have been "expelled" from the text, with the idea of preserving the latter's "dignity." It thus became a self-contained work, which could be divided up and treated for its own sake: such was the case with explanatory medical plates, geographical maps and calendars.

In the following chapters, some emphasis will be laid on the specific nature of the illustrations in sacred texts, both Christian and Moslem, after the sixth century. But outside the religious domain it is significant that the ancient formulas were neither renewed nor abandoned. On the one hand, they lingered on in secular and scientific literature, now in a minority; and on the other they reappeared in periods when the "Empire" ideology was revived and the ancient culture was appealed to, as in the Carolingian "Renascence" in the ninth century and the Byzantine "Renascence" in the tenth. Some formulas were never lost; for example, the galleries of famous men, widespread in antique illustration. The 1,300 medallions to be found in the *Sacra Parallela* of John of Damascus (ninth century, Bibliothèque Nationale, Paris) seem to answer to the invention attributed to Varro for the serial illustration of his biographies of famous men. But Varro (first century B.C.) knew nothing of the codex, though portraits on papyrus had existed from classical antiquity, when a text was commonly accompanied by an author portrait. The latter occurs frequently in medieval manuscripts, until superseded by the popular dedication scene, in which the author is portrayed symbolically offering his book to the dedicatee. This conventional representation has a place apart in the history of illustration, for it is not in fact a text illustration but rather a cover intended to safeguard the work by glorifying its patron. Other pictorial formulas devised in antique illustration survived Christianity in secular works of the Middle Ages, just as some more general themes also survived, over and above the formulas. The

Romance of Alexander, written about A.D. 300, figured largely in the literature of chivalry and only really found its illustrators in the thirteenth and fourteenth centuries. The same phenomenon can be observed, though less clearly, with Aesop's *Fables,* of which no illustrations are known until its medieval adaptations had been made. Among the complete readaptations is the late twelfth-century paraphrase of the *Aeneid* by Heinrich von Veldeke, illustrated in the medieval Germanic style at the beginning of the thirteenth century.

Quite apart from its themes, the fairly realistic style of antiquity—which the Middle Ages departed from in favour of a hieratic graphic style, both in pictures and script—was revived in the schools where these "Renascences" arose. In Byzantium the political heritage of the idea of Empire also preserved the realistic tradition of representation, which shaded faces and modelled drapery in the "Greek" manner. But the most remarkable difference of style with medieval blazonry occurs in the illuminations of the Carolingian Renascence, where the figures are once more given relief and movement, and even agitation, though significantly enough they move in a space by now become ethereal and unreal.

Finally, to complete this brief memento of the sub-antique features to be found here and there in medieval art, it must be emphasized that the medieval scientific texts remained indebted to antique formulas down at least to the Carolingian Renascence of the eighth and ninth centuries and, frequently, even down to the philosophical movement of the thirteenth century. Fritz Saxl has shown that English illuminated manuscripts on astronomy of the tenth, eleventh and twelfth centuries were, "like those on the continent, wholly based on the classical heritage." Likewise the extant illustrations of Hrabanus Maurus's *De Universo* (Monte Cassino, 1022-1023) seem to prove that, by way of hypothetical illustrations for Isidore of Seville's *Etymologiae* (an encyclopaedia based on Latin models), the antique representations, for example of the Planets or the Months, were repeated down to the Carolingian period.

The "Sacra Parallela"

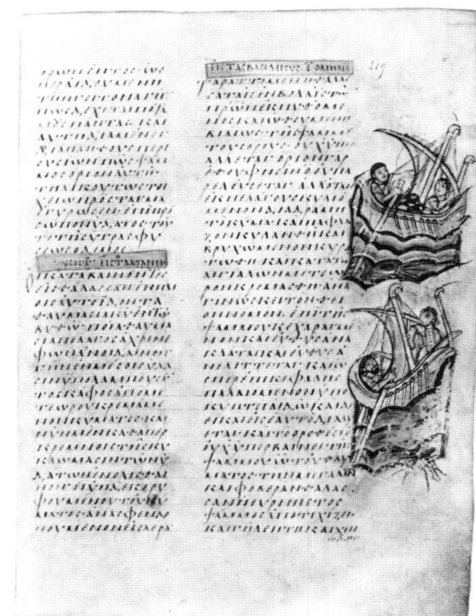

# of St John of Damascus

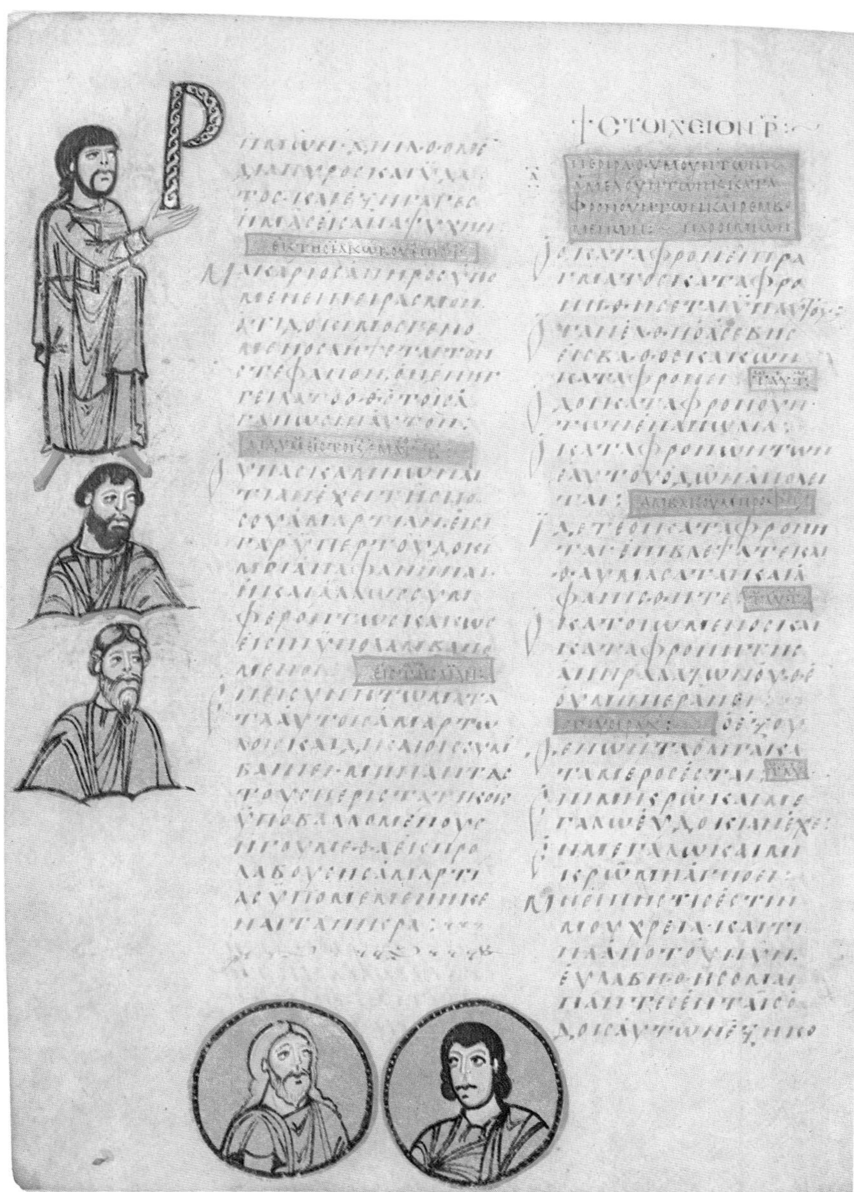

Greek manuscript 923 in the Bibliothèque Nationale, Paris, is a landmark in several respects. Of all known Greek manuscripts, it is the most extensively illustrated, containing 1,658 miniatures (402 figure scenes and 1,256 portraits) on its 392 pages written in two columns. Brought back from Constantinople in 1730 by Abbé Sevin, it is an anthology of mostly moralizing texts, assembled under alphabetical headings and taken from the Bible and the Fathers of the Church. It is known as the *Sacra Parallela*, the title given to the first Greek edition of the work, printed in 1712. Some thirty manuscripts of it have come down to us, but none of the others is illustrated. It was made, so far as we know, by John of Damascus (Johannes Damascenus), a priest of the Eastern Church who died about 749 at the monastery of Mar Saba near Jerusalem, and who, among a wealth of writings, made the most ardent plea in favour of image worship, at the time of the first quarrel over Iconoclasm (726-787). Palestine was then Moslem territory, and working there, out of the range of persecution, John of Damascus could safely raise his voice against the imperial churchmen of Byzantium who were intent on banning images.

The amazing thing about this manuscript is the extent to which the illuminator made the most of narrative passages in order to introduce an exuberant imagery. In addition, with a series of expressive, realistic portraits keeping to antique norms, he systematically portrayed all the authors in medallions or full-length, and sometimes even went on to illustrate scenes not included in the extract given. As shown by Kurt Weitzmann's study of it, it seems certain, on the evidence of some flagrant errors and omissions, that this manuscript is a copy of a lost prototype. From its kinship with South Italian frescoes, some scholars assign it to an Italian scriptorium. But Weitzmann points out other similarities with Syriac objects of art, which also make use of gold, and with icons from Mount Sinai, his conclusion being that this version of the *Sacra Parallela* was probably made at Mar Saba itself, soon after the author's death, in the first half of the ninth century during the second period of Iconoclasm (815-843). The profusion of illustrations would then take on a provocative air: not only would it represent the "largest known illustrated Greek manuscript," but "one feels behind this undertaking a mind preoccupied—one might even say obsessed—by the propagation of images as a powerful didactic instrument" (Weitzmann). Palestine continued to produce icons throughout the Iconoclast period, and so it may be that St John of Damascus, author of a treatise in favour of image-worship, deliberately made use of the illustrated book as a weapon and a challenge. ■

Illuminated vellum leaves from the Sacra Parallela *of St John of Damascus, ninth century.*

The Joshua Roll

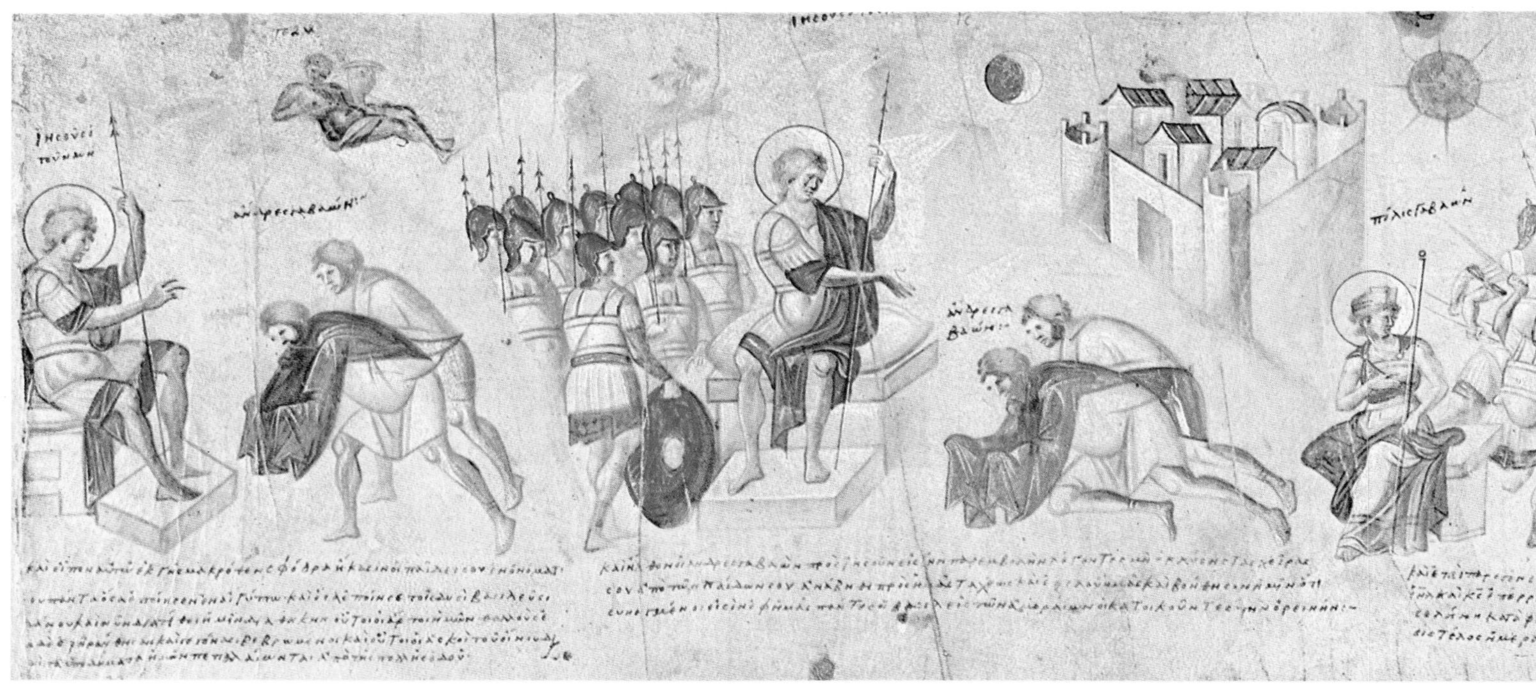

This extraordinary manuscript in the Vatican Library is made up of vellum sheets sewn end to end, forming a scroll over thirty feet long. Text and images are closely interlocked, almost like a strip cartoon, and give us the first twelve chapters of the Book of Joshua, relating the conquest of the Promised Land by the Jews. The dating of this Byzantine manuscript is a matter of controversy, ranging from the fifth to the tenth century. The text appears to have been written in the tenth century, but the scroll form, which had existed alongside the codex only from the second to the fifth century, had by then been abandoned, and some have supposed that the text was written around an earlier set of illustrations. Weitzmann prefers to assume that the illustrations too date from the tenth century, and that the scroll form, so unusual at that time, is to be accounted for by the content and purpose of this narrative. For him, this story of conquest and victory may be plausibly assigned to a period when Byzantium was waging victorious wars against the Bulgarians and the Arabs. This long scroll would then refer back to the traditional forms of pictorial narrative unfolding in a spiral around the Roman triumphal columns: the most famous of these is Trajan's Column in Rome, but two other examples, the column of Theodosius and the column of Arcadius, then stood in Byzantium. This form, admirably suited to a narrative sequence, was also used in the eleventh century in similar circumstances for the famous Bayeux Embroidery, relating the Norman conquest of England. So the *Joshua Roll* may be seen as an exceptional "monument" designed to integrate the classical tradition into the most brilliant period of Byzantine history, sometimes known as the Byzantine Renaissance, during which, after the Iconoclast period, the "Macedonian" emperors (867-1081) revived the antique tradition of the arts and letters. The moving spirit behind this manuscript might have been the Emperor Constantine Porphyrogenitus himself; indeed, he may have been its maker, for this scholarly emperor, who maintained a large scriptorium in his palace and wrote a treatise on farriery, is known to have been a talented painter as well. ■

Illuminated vellum leaves from the Joshua Roll, *tenth century.*

AST·SOBOLES·DOMINI·ET·DNS·DOMINANTIUM·UBIQ·HIC
EXPANSIS·MANIBUS·MOREM·FORMANTIS·HABENDUM·EN
PERDOCET·HUNC·UNUM·GREX IUSTIFICAT·COLIT·ATQE
ET·SIC·MORE·FATIGANT·IHC·XP·UCE·NAM·SUA·MEMBRA·HAC
RITE·PROBANT·PLEBES·TUR TIS·SPONDETQE·PARENTEM
NA·HUNC·SCRIPTURA·E ALTERUM·CULMINE·IESUM
ET·PROBO·QUOD·REX·ASTIVIA·INVENTA·MALORUM·EST
QA·E·OCCIDIT·REGEM·I·SU·SANCTA·MEN·ATQE·POTENTER
TELA·RUPIT·UAH·MARTI·ID·DOGMATA·CONPLENS
PRIMUM·NOS·SIMUL·ALACRE BITET·MALE·QUIS·Q·HINC
AETERNU·DOMINU·TACET·O·AUCTOR·SANCT·HIC·OR·BEST
TRADIS·SUMMI·CUNCTA·DECENT·QUIA·SANGUINE·DEMTA
DEXTERA·DERIPUIT·PRAEDAM·PROBA·SANCTA·PROFUN
IN·CRUCE·SIC·POSITUS·DE ERAT·DEUS·ARCE·CORS
PRINCIPIUM·HIC·DEUS·EMMANUEL·AC·FINIS·ORIGO·EST
LUX·ET·IMAGO·PATRIS·OS·SPLENDOR·GLORIA·CRISTUS
HOMOYSION·PATRI·ZOLUERBUM·EX·LUMINE·LUMEN·CUM
AEQUA·MAN·DOMINI·SEU·UIRTUS·DUX·QE·PROPHETA·EST
QUE·MUNIGENA·MIUSTE·QE·M·PRIMIGENA·ORE·FATEMUR
NAZAREUS·QUUM·OFFENSIO·FIT·AC·SCANDALI·INIQUIS
ANGULU·ATQUE·LAPIS·ESCANS·UR·O·HINC·IANUA·MUNDO
INDUTA·EN·UERITAS·UESTE·QUID·DOGMATE·CHRISTUS
INDICET·EXPONA·LEGEM·PARUA·HAEC·QUOQUE·UESTIS
SIGNIFICAT·NAMQE·HIC·TEGITUR·IN·GRAMMATE·RARO
SUMMIPOTENS·AUCTOR·QUI·CONTINET·OMNIA·RECTOR
ATQUE·M·MUNDUS·PERTINET·ASTRA·AC·PONT·ET·AETHER
NOSTRA·Q·NATURA·ARTATQUE·SOCIATA·CREANTI·EST
NAM·AUCTORE·HAEC·ILLUM·PALMO·QI·CLAUDIT·ET·ARUA
OBTEGIT·HUMANO·AUT·CLAUDIT·UISU·ECCE·POTENTEM
IPSE·TAMEN·OSTENS·UBIQ·ESUOS·T·OPERE·ORBI·HUIC
ANGELUS·HUIC·SPONSUS·ET·EST·DEUOTI·O·PLEBI·ET
ATQ·DOCENS·SAPIENTIA·PACIFICUS·QUOQUE·CUSTOS
FONS·BRACHIUM·ET·PANIS·DIUINA·Q·PETRA·MAGISTER
STELLA·ORIENS·QI·ET·CURA·POTENS·INTENTA·MEDELA
CLAUIS·ET·HIC·DAUID·LAETA·UIA·ET·AGNUS·HONESTUS
SERPENS·SANCTIFICANS·INLUSTRIS·FIT·MEDIATOR
UERMIS·HOMO·IS·QE·RETRAXIT·AB·HOSTE·UITA·RAPINA
MONS·AQUILA·PARACLYTUS·SIC·LEO·PASTOR·ET·EDUS
FUNDAMENTUM·OUIS·ACREDENS·PIE·UOTA·SACERDOS
MELCHI·PONTIFICIS·SADE·CHUINUM·QUOQUE·PANEM·ET
QI·UITULUS·ARIES·CARNE·DE·QUA·EST·SACRA·FINCTUS
UICTIMA·PATRE·Q·CU·BENE·SITISATUS·ABSQUE·CADUCO
QI·DAMPNA·SENSIT·ET·LUGNE·QUI·OMNIBUS·ANTE·EST
QI·ASTRA·EST·SIDERE·DEDIT·U·OMNIA·LUCIFER·UANTE
UIRGINE·HIC·EST·NATUS·MATRE·RUM·TEMPORE·IN·ARTO
ATQUE·HOMINEM·UT·SERUARET·ADORA·HIC·CRUCIS·LUIT
QUI·EST·SATOR·AETERNUS·XPS·BENEDICTUS·IN·AEUUM

THE WORD APPEARS

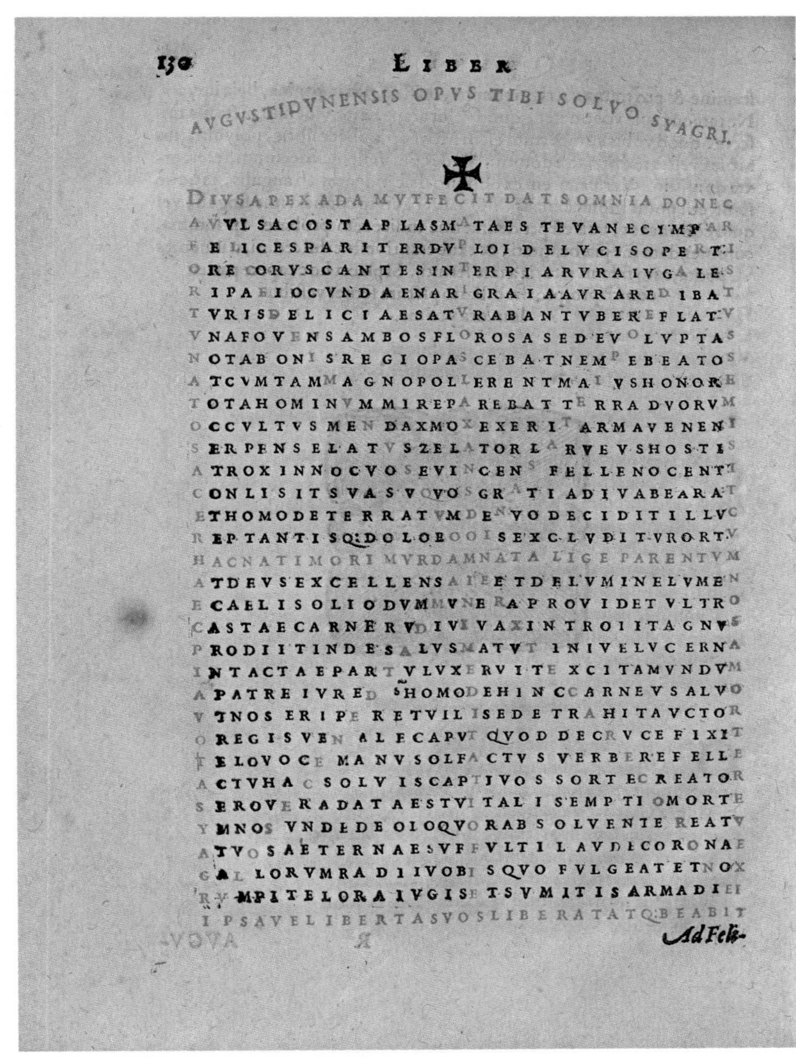

▲ Figured poem by Fortunatus, Bishop of Poitiers in 599-c. 609, printed edition of 1603.

◄ Figured poem from the *De laudibus Sanctae Crucis* by Hrabanus Maurus. Illuminated vellum manuscript, early ninth century.

In speaking of *illustrations* of sacred texts, it is necessary to be clear. They correspond to different realities from those behind our present-day notion of illustration as something which both complements the text and contradicts it. The text, in these two cases, does not have the same value, and our conception of illustration could only arise as the text came to be seen as a human and not a sacred production. This process of secularization, now completed for the text, is still incomplete for the image, which is often thought of as invested with an absolute and unquestionable meaning, especially when it refers to reality. Just as one is apt to suppose that a photograph in some way identifies with reality, so the script in Christian and Arab illuminations identifies with its representation. This illuminated rather than illustrated script is radically different from others, for the word it sets down is not an ordinary word: it is the word of God, which has never been spoken, and which has been and can only be solemnly reiterated, proclaimed, uttered, intoned. It is this solemnity that the illumination imparts to the sacred text which, inasmuch as it can never be heard from the very mouth of its author, has to be made visible. Illustration here, then, is not something added to the text: it is the manifestation of the text itself, in its divine beauty, as an apparition.

This fusion of the script, as both vehicle of meaning and signifying form, attains its highest pitch in Islamic art. The dogmatic reasons often invoked, that is the ban on imagery laid down by certain religious texts, by no means accounts for the wealth and refinement achieved in the abstract decoration of Koranic texts. First of all, because this ban is not explicitly set forth in the Koran, but only indirectly in texts which never had the force of authority. Secondly, because the essential point was to prevent idolatry and not figural representation itself, in terms analogous to the Biblical texts and no more stringently than in the commandment in Exodus (xx.4): "Thou shalt not make unto thee any graven image, or any likeness of any thing that is in heaven above, or that is in the earth beneath, or that is in the water under the earth." The Koran, on the other hand, much more than the Hebrew texts, is fascinated by the power of writing. One of the revelations made to the Prophet was: "Thy Lord is the Very Generous One who has instructed man by means of the quill and has taught him what he did not know" (Koran, xcvi.1-5). The sacredness of writing from the beginning, as gesture and as form, is to be explained by the importance attached to it in a civilization only barely acquainted with it, where all traditions were oral, and writing was "imported" only to the small extent that it proved indispensable. The so-called Arab script then, instituted on a wholly religious basis, was kept aloof from foreign practices. Indeed it was not really a script: it was the figuration of the divine word revealed to the Prophet, and as such it was an object of worship. This script, like others no doubt in earlier civilizations, had but one purpose: to enshrine a single text, the Koran, in superb forms, bringing it before the eye and preserving it in the memory.

Islamic calligraphy is not a "model" of writing. Rather, it is a liturgical gesture, and in principle—but not in reality—it knows nothing of that irreversible drive towards simplification and codification which carried Western lettering forward. But it gave rise to a profusion of complex forms which enriched it, and to monumental applications in stucco and ceramics which in Biblical texts have no parallel to this degree. It also shows a multiplicity of styles according to region, period and usage, ranging from the grandiloquent and solemn form of Kufic writing to the cursive signs of Nastaliq; and several systems could be used in perfect harmony on the same page, like a polyphony of scripts. Islamic calligraphy, with its open forms which the scribe enriched with graphic inventions, passes almost imperceptibly into the arabesque patterns that are often found intermingled with it. And yet one radical difference separates them: the letter remains a conventional sign and the decoration a sign with no explicit referent, but their forms merge into one another. The fusion between them becomes almost complete in the complex patterns of virtuoso calligraphers. In the case of geometric Kufic, for example, the extension of certain stems and the symmetrical arrangement of the letters conceal them almost completely from profane eyes within an abstract pattern. Conversely, in the case of *tughra*, the exuberant initials of the Ottoman Sultans, the scribe so pointedly emphasized the form of the signs and so embellished them with flourishes in ink and gold powder that the letter takes on the style of an oriflamme and becomes both an inimitable token of authenticity and an absolute sign.

The ban on figural representation in Moslem art was only justified afterwards on dogmatic grounds. Actually figuration occupies a privileged place in the illustration of Arab texts, but generally outside the sacred domain. Here, in the absence of any tradition of its own, it was more indebted to foreign influences, which varied from one area to another of the immense Islamic empire. Byzantine

Koran of Arghûn Shâh: Decorative page. Egypt, c. 1368-1388.

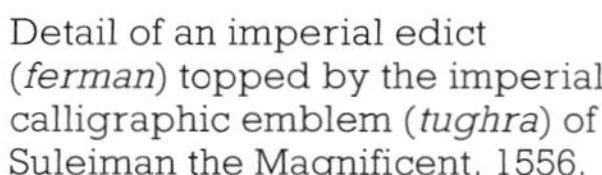

Detail of an imperial edict (*ferman*) topped by the imperial calligraphic emblem (*tughra*) of Suleiman the Magnificent, 1556.

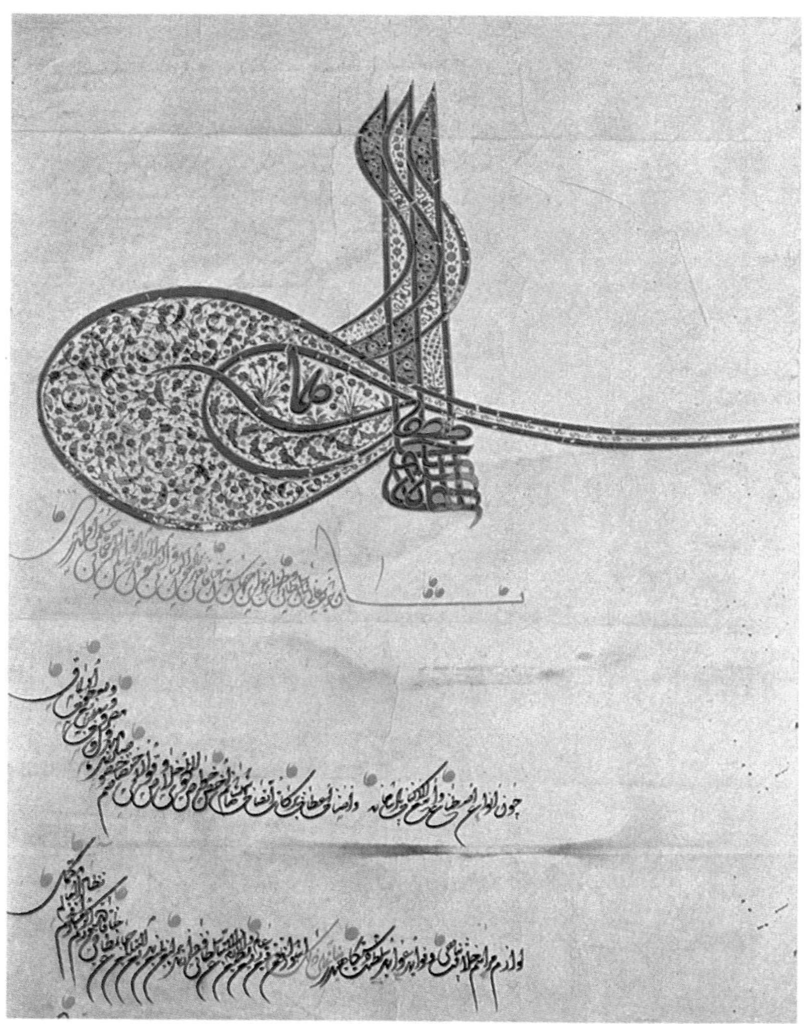

Calligraphic drawing of a lion, composed of the introductory prayer from the *Gulistan* of the poet Sa'di, Persia, eighteenth century. Drawing signed by Mirza Darabakht vati-'ahd Bahadur.

miniatures left their trace on it, and also, to a lesser degree, the Indian miniature. These illuminated Arab manuscripts differ much in their place of origin and the usages they observe. This was a court art, ostentatious and vying with the foreign style. These works had their place in the caliph's library, just as the mural paintings with figure scenes had theirs in the harem and the baths. The representation of plant life, then of animals, appears timidly even in the mosques of the seventh century. But it was in the illuminating of secular texts, in the twelfth and thirteenth centuries, that illustration in our sense of the term found full scope, particularly in the very popular *Maqâmât* (Assemblies), a story of picaresque adventure, in the love romance of *Bayâd and Riyâd*, and in didactic and scientific works such as the Arab versions of the *De materia medica* of Dioscorides. It must, however, be noted that in two of the three finest copies of the *Maqâmât* (Istanbul and Leningrad) the figures were mutilated by iconoclasts. In the first, the faces were scraped out; in the other, the heads were symbolically cut off with a stroke of the pen. But such practices also occurred in the Christian West: in the Cistercian manuscript of the *Moralia in Job* at Dijon some scenes, thought no doubt to have been handled too freely, were effaced by sticklers for orthodoxy.

To the superstitious mind the sign is directly assimilated to its referent, and where this is the case such interference is frequent. It justified the fears entertained about idolatry, which was much more likely to be inspired by the image than by the text. The interesting thing about the Islamic script is that it shows us words provided with a representational value without losing their conventional meaning. Since they are words and shapes at once, it was to be expected that they would be carried one step further and turned into words and figures at once, as a kind of perfect, self-contained illustration. This occurred later by the use of the word-image in which the formula *Basmalah*, which opens the verses of the Koran, takes the form of a bird. The word as figured sign, together with the underlying idea that signs are undifferentiated and that a secret harmony may connect them, finds here an open field of action, such as the Western alphabet has never enjoyed, being too closely bound up with secular functions.

Yet, at the time when Islam was on the rise, between the sixth and eighth centuries, figure compositions incorporating letters and forming words were also being devised in the Christian world. There was a vogue for them, from the geometric poem of Fortunatus, Bishop of Poitiers

1

in the sixth century, to the *De Laudibus Sanctae Crucis* of Hrabanus Maurus, written about 840, which marks the end of it. The illustrations are composed by the text itself: certain letters irregularly singled out in the page, while forming a new sentence, design the contour of the image which they evoke. It is difficult now to say how much this procedure owes to the sophisticated experiments of a literature at the end of its resources (like the poems in the form of an altar or pan-pipes composed by the mannered Hellenistic poets) or to the mystical mentality of believing Christians who, like the Moslems, wished to suggest that the divine word is the generating principle of all form. The two are not contradictory and may have gone hand in hand. True semantic fascination with the latter as a generator of forms also occurs in Christian art, but rather in the development of decorative initials than in these word games which concern the writer more than the scribe. In Anglo-Saxon manuscripts contemporary with these "calligrams," arabesques are deployed exuberantly and systematically in spaces which they fill up entirely, forming what are designated by comparison with Oriental art as "carpet pages." Alongside these patterned spaces, the initial letters show the same ambivalence of form and sign, as if the scribes were reluctant to assume the super-natural origin of the text and wished to turn a humble

2

1. Swan calligram from the *Phenomena* of Aratus, a poem of the third century B.C. Illumination on vellum, eleventh century.

2. Lindisfarne Gospels: Carpet page. Illumination on vellum, late seventh century.

3. Gospel Book from the Abbey of Saint-Bertin at Saint-Omer: Evangelist portrait. Illumination on vellum, early eleventh century.

3

instrument of reading into a glowing reflection of the Word. The explanation of so surprising a phenomenon again lies in the relation of the script to the words, the point here being to refer to something other than the voice. The text, as an object of contemplation, had to be beautified, for it was designed to be seen as well as heard, while in antiquity it was chiefly meant to be read aloud. Today we are so used to the independent existence of writing and the practice of silent reading that we have to exert ourselves to retrieve the direct relation of writing to the voice, and to realize that writing has first of all to be pronounceable. The image is not pronounceable and Merovingian decorative letters are pressed to the very limits of legibility, for which the scribe seems to care little. He takes the opposite course to ours: out of an essentially vocal sign, he has to make a spectacular object endowed with permanence and real existence. From the seventh to the twelfth century, the text was embodied in the decorative letter, blending indistinguishably the vehicular role of the word and the demonstrative role of the image. But soon, even in those fabulous exercises of the Irish calligraphers, legibility regained its rights, and legibility meant standardized letters. After a few more stately initials the trend continued towards a normal alphabet, with smaller letters and smaller pictures. The ornamental initial situates the text at once in an unchanging, supernatural realm, from which the common or individual reading may descend and proceed.

Hebrew Micrography

2

1

Among the many kinds of relation that the script maintained with the sacred image, micrography remains a speciality of Hebrew manuscripts. Perhaps it should be seen as a curious compromise between the ban on images—less sweeping than in Islam, but more so than in Christendom—and the power of scriptural reference in the Jewish world. Certainly the taboo on any representation of the divine image was everywhere present in Judaism and may have damped the imagination of the scribes. But, as with Islam, the rule was not wholly respected. Micrography may have been one way of eluding it, the writing acting as an alibi for the image which is made to appear wholly subsidiary. Here, as in the "calligrams," it is the script itself which forms the image. So while remaining akin to the word games of sacred calligraphy, Hebrew micrography is quite distinct both from the superb patterning of the Koran and the Christian *carmina figurata.* Owing no doubt to Islamic influence, the earliest micrographed manuscripts do not include animal or human forms, but keep to decorative motifs based on abstract designs or plant life. The oldest of these Hebrew manuscripts, a codex from Tiberias containing the text of the Prophets, dates from 895. By way of lines of minute script, it reproduces a luxuriant pattern of rosettes. The Pentateuch was of course also copied in this micrographed script, but it was in the texts of the Masora (a collection of prayers sometimes likened to the Catholic breviary) that micrography was used in an increasingly pictorial manner, that is in complex patterns representing animals or the seven-branched candlestick, for example, well into the Middle Ages (fourteenth century), particularly in Germany. ■

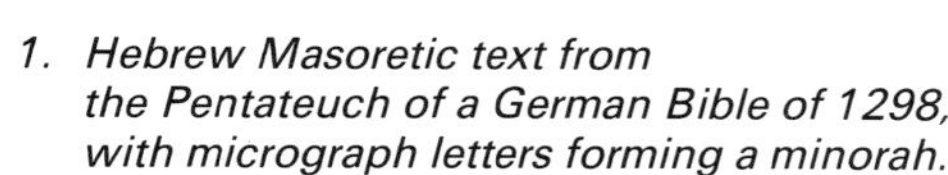

1. *Hebrew Masoretic text from the Pentateuch of a German Bible of 1298, with micrograph letters forming a minorah.*
2. *Micrograph carpet page from the Pentateuch of a Hebrew Bible of 1469.*

Hebrew Pentateuch decorated by the scribe Moses of Ebermannstadt, early fourteenth century: Micrograph frontispiece of Leviticus.

The Book of Kells

2

1

In the sixth century the monastic ideal coming out of Egypt reached Europe, and it was in the monasteries that the traditions of Latin culture and the practice of letters and writing were perpetuated, thanks to two institutions housed there: school and scriptorium. The latter was a necessity in a monastery, where the sacred texts were preserved and had to be continually recopied to meet the needs of the community. Being particularly vigorous, English and Irish monasticism spread over the continent to St Gall and Lombardy. But the great English monastic centres of Lindisfarne, Jarrow and York declined under the impact of the Scandinavian invasions of the late eighth century. The monastery of Kells, in the centre of Ireland, was not the largest one, but it served as a refuge in 806 for monks from the mother house founded by St Columba in the island of Iona and it then assumed great importance. The *Book of Kells* may have been made there at this time, or it may have been brought from Iona or another monastery by the refugee monks. Nothing is known of its history except that it was stolen in 1007 and found again. It was given to Trinity College, Dublin, by Henry Jones, who became Bishop of Meath in 1661. As we have it today, it consists of 340 pages (there may have been 370 originally), all illustrated except two, and bound in four volumes (after many restorations, the last in 1953). It contains the four Gospels and several canonical texts in the Latin vulgate version. From its elaborate beauty one can only infer that it was rather an object of ceremony than of study. The cosmopolitan character of monastic culture makes it impossible to sift out the traditions that went into it, including both Anglo-Saxon and Irish; and impossible to trace the origin of the influences at work on the scribes. The only light we can get on such points is by comparison with the other great examples of this original art: the Gospels of Lindisfarne, Echternach (late seventh century), Durham, Lichfield (late eighth century), and the Books of Durrow (seventh century) and Armagh (807). Nothing is known of the makers, nor can it be said whether the scribes responsible for the fine half-uncial writing were also the illuminators. Interestingly, a report of 1665 describes the book as being written in Irish, in characters "that no one today can read." Writing ornamental to this degree passed—in the words of an eleventh-century chronicler—for being "the work of an angel," something indecipherable and mysterious. Such was one of the roles that illumination was meant to play in the wondering eyes of the lay spectator. ■

3

The Book of Kells, illuminations on vellum, eighth century:

1. *Opening of St John's Gospel, "In principio erat Verbum et Verbum."*
2. *Opening of the "Breves causae" and "Argumenta" (i.e. chapter headings and summaries of the four Gospels).*
3. *Opening of St Matthew's Gospel, "Liber generationis."*

VO
NIAM
QUIDE
MVLTI
CONATISVNT
ORDINARE

ILLUMINATION OF THE TEXT

▲ St Gregory's *Moralia in Job* from Cîteaux, 1111: Ornamental initial with monks chopping wood.

◀ Carolingian Gospel Book from the Abbey of Saint-Martin, Tours, c. 857-862: Ornamental initial and opening of St Luke's Gospel: "Quoniam multi conati sunt ordinare" (Forasmuch as many have taken in hand to set forth in order...)

Medieval illumination is often characterized by its love of ornament. To us the latter seems a superfluous luxury, something uncalled for, having nothing in common with the ornamentation developed around cult objects. But at that time it was part of a ritual and, properly speaking, went to "represent" the sacred. Ornament was inseparable from the object in its religious function and, in the case of illuminated manuscripts, it sacralized the Scripture. It breathed a life of its own into the writing of the scribe, worked upon it, amplified it, and indeed could stifle it when carried to a point where spirituality was lost sight of. So this ornamentation was neither a game nor an accident: it had a purpose and took on its full meaning in the religious practice which it contributed to fortify. Or practices, rather, for they varied according to period and place, and to understand the art of illumination each work has to be seen in terms of the particular practice to which it belongs.

During the Middle Ages ornament gradually lost ground, giving way to figure scenes. To sum up the evolution of ten centuries in a few words, one might say: the image drew away from the script. The more the text was conceived of as the work of human hands, the more burdensome and indeed indecorous the ornament became. Imagery was by no means pointless or out of place, but it was detached from the script, ejected from the text like a foreign body. What happened, in effect, is that Scripture became writing again. Ornament, serving a sacerdotal purpose, departed from it to rejoin the image which filled another religious function: the representation of "vision." As such, the image was no longer of the same nature as the script, an arbitrary system of signs which could only come from the divinity. The role of the historian would then be to single out those features which connect the form taken by the illuminations, in their relation to the text, with the form of the beliefs in their relation to the signs, and with the practices that made up those beliefs. To understand this relation between faith and forms, arrived at through the value conferred on the sign, one has to distinguish between the uses made of different texts and different rituals. Obviously there is nothing in common between the Gothic psalters designed for the private devotions of noble ladies and the Romanesque Gospel books of a liturgical character. What separates them (including their mode of illustration) is the way they were read. One was

Godescalc Gospels, Palace School of Charlemagne, Aachen, 781-783: Frontispiece with Fountain of Life, and opening page with two interlace initials ("IN").

an object of silent daily reading; the other, a monumental object whose writing came from God and went back to Him. Among the giant Bibles, one thinks of the *Gigas Codex* (Royal Library, Stockholm), which required two people merely to turn over the pages. When Charlemagne ordered a Gospel book from Godescalc for the christening of his son Pepin in Rome in 781, it was meant to celebrate an event and the manuscript played the part of a stele or a Te Deum. Between these two extreme cases, one may situate all the different kinds of reading, public or monastic. Some schools, and the early Middle Ages in general, gave the preference to liturgical books: sacramentaries or lectionaries, designed to be read aloud on solemn occasions, their illustrations enshrined in the text as the host in the monstrance. The sumptuous ornamentation of the letters held the public in awe; the gorgeous beauty of the miniatures, achieved through the painstaking virtuosity of the illuminator, kept the public at a respectful distance from the text.

Sometimes the purpose of the illustration was more explicit, as when it was deliberately carried to a spectacular pitch in the antiphonaries, which stood on the lectern and had necessarily to be deciphered from a distance; or when the purpose was pedagogical, as in the Exultet Rolls of South Italy, which the preacher unrolled from the ambo in the course of his reading, bringing before the eyes of the faithful the pictures illustrating the text: the first audiovisual medium. But this didactic use of pictures as the "text of the illiterate" long remained marginal in the history of illumination. Other uses are more mysterious—that, for example, of the Apocalypse manuscripts common in south-western France and in Mozarabic art. Their figures and colours are impressive: were they similar to Gospel books or, as has been suggested, to encyclopaedias giving in condensed form the Summa of the world? From the books with Lives of the Saints, which were shown in the refectory of the monastery, to liturgical books placed on the altar, the power of the image and indeed its very nature varied with the purpose of the book.

These distinctions have to be carefully made. Others, drawn arbitrarily in terms of modern preoccupations and modern views of art history, are misleading. In its styles, illumination is only one area of religious art; and on the formal level there is much more difference between the pictures in a book placed in the hands of a princess and those in a book placed on the altar, than there is between this same liturgical book and the other cult objects around it. Carl Nordenfalk goes so far as to write that "in the course of its evolution the Merovingian miniature made increasingly frequent borrowings from other art techniques." And further: "All things considered, we get the impression that Romanesque book illumination had become a derivative art whose style, in the last analysis, depended on achievements in other fields." The relation to the text, which had determined the specific nature of illumination, had become no different from the relation with any other sacred object: so illumination then was hardly to be distinguished from enamels, goldwork, ivories and even less from the tooled cover of the binding which,

◄ Gold and ivory cover, set with precious stones, of the Psalter of Charles the Bald, ninth century.

Two scenes from an Exultet Roll, South Italy, eleventh century: Above, priest reading from the roll, whose pictures, upside down with respect to the text read by the priest, appear right side up to the congregation. Below, the earth in summer dress.

First Bible of Charles the Bald (Vivian Bible), Tours, c. 846: Scenes from the life of St Jerome, illumination on vellum.

Second Bible of Charles the Bald, Franco-Saxon School, ninth century:
Ornamental initial E ("Et factum est post mortem Moysi..."), opening the Book of Joshua.

when the book was closed, integrated it among the other cult objects. Likewise, in its didactic function, the style of the book illuminations was indistinguishable from that of the frescoes which served the same purpose, and which in some cases were apparently painted by the same artists. The sculptor, called on to adorn the church, faced the same problems as the illuminator called on to adorn the service book: the same interlaces and the same creatures are to be found on the column capitals and on the letter stems. The church thus carved, thus provided with illustration, has often been likened metaphorically to a book, since it had the dual mission of revealing the celestial forms (the Christs in majesty in Romanesque apses are identical with those painted on full pages) and instructing the unlettered (the Old Testament scenes at Saint-Savin-sur-Gartempe might just as well have been painted in a book). It has even been noted that the interlace patterns, which have made Irish manuscripts so famous, did not in all likelihood originate in religious art, but in the ornamentation of weapons. These interlaces, coming from pagan weaponry, returned to it after being abandoned in religious art, but there continued to play a similar role.

1

The transition from pure ornament to pure figuration was made between the eleventh and the fourteenth century. Doubtless the figural art of antiquity had not been soon and everywhere forgotten. Its lessons, at the time of the Carolingian Renascence, provided a form of illumination unusual in the Middle Ages for its knack of representing the third dimension and above all movement. But the realism that was to triumph at the end of the Middle Ages had its source rather in the script itself. It is in the initials overloaded with ornamental motifs that we find the first examples of the trivial, anecdotal picturing of plants, animals, and more rarely humans. From the eleventh century on, these initials provide the locus for genre and historical scenes—concealed in them at first, then filling them and finally projecting beyond them. Here it was the letter that imposed its space on the representation of the world. It was the setting, then the frame, and finally a mere accessory, thanks to which the figures were shaped and worked out, as hybrid monsters first of all, then small personages, and finally animated figure scenes, known as historiated letters: these became a prominent feature of manuscripts and continued so in the initial letters of printed books. During the twelfth century, these figures spawned by the letter departed from it and took on a life of their own, moving beyond the text and into the margins.

The development of historiated decorations and the abandonment of carpet pages were only the beginning of a movement towards figural and documentary imagery. This movement can be seen too in the timid reappearance of modelling, perspective and individualized figures, if not yet in their expressiveness. This period seems more alive to the fact that a book is the result of human labour, an object ordered, handmade and offered. And so in Romanesque manuscripts appear self-portraits of scribe-illuminators, discreetly sharing a privilege formerly reserved for the patron or dedicatee. Realistic imagery may also have been required by the necessity, keenly felt by the Church, to convince people by appealing to their reason and imagination. It came at the time when decoration was being condemned by St Bernard of Clairvaux, who spoke out against the gilt initial letters of manuscripts as an unnecessary and overweening luxury, precisely because they could no longer be seen as forms offering men a divine vision, but as human handiwork offered to God. But of course the Cistercians also possessed illuminated manuscripts, and one of them, antedating St Bernard's condemnation of them, is the four-volume *Moralia in Job* of St Gregory (Bibliothèque Municipale, Dijon): it is remarkable for containing some of the earliest realistic and indeed, apparently, satirical scenes of monastic life, with reference to the handicrafts which formed part of daily life in Cistercian monasteries.

In the extraordinary encyclopaedia of Abbess Herrade of Landsberg, compiled in the latter half of the twelfth century (and unfortunately destroyed in 1870 during the siege of Strasbourg), this evolution in the status of the image was evidenced. First, by the very subject of the book: only one other encyclopaedia then existed (apart from Isidore of Seville's *Etymologiae* and its rearrangement by Hrabanus Maurus), that of Lambert compiled fifty years earlier. Next, by its size: its 650 pages included 636 miniatures, and these in turn included over 9000 figures. Finally, by the placing of the pictures: no longer accompanying the text as in Lambert, the pictures (as Fritz Saxl has shown) were the leading feature, which the text did no more than explain and develop on particular points. The language of pictures came first, that of words second. And so we find, in this closing phase of the Romanesque period, that the space of the image had ceased to be subordinate to that of the script.

2

3

1. Ornamental initials from the Sacramentary of Limoges, twelfth century: "Te igitur."

2. Ornamental letter from the Luxeuil Gospel Book, copied and painted on vellum in the mid-eleventh century by Gerard, Abbot of Luxeuil.

3. Master and pupil: historiated letter from a book of medical texts of 1363 by Guy de Chauliac. Illumination on paper, 1469.

The Saint-Sever Apocalypse

1

2

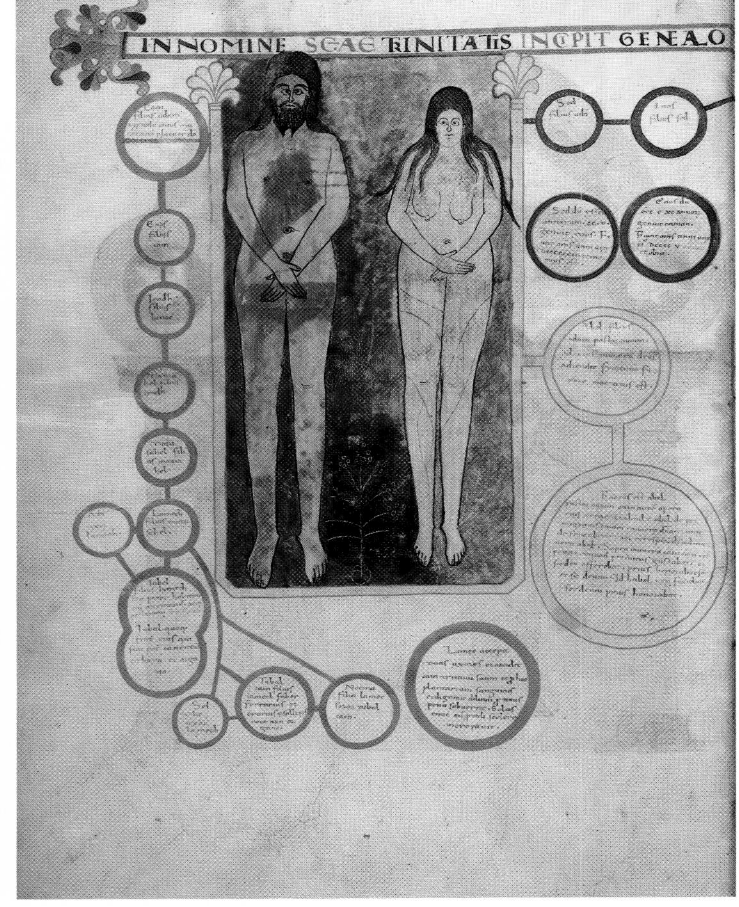

3

The celebrated manuscript known as the *Saint-Sever Apocalypse* (Bibliothèque Nationale, Paris) was executed in the monastery of Saint-Sever, in south-western France, between 1028 and 1072. It does not in fact contain the text of the Apocalypse of St John, but one of the most widely read commentaries on it, by Beatus of Liebana, together with a further commentary on the Book of Daniel. The Beatus commentary in this richly illustrated form, in which each part of the text is closely connected with a surprisingly forcible picture, is known in thirty other manuscripts dating from the ninth to the thirteenth century. One is therefore entitled to ask whether, in this particular text, the image does not play an organic, indispensable part. The text was originally directed against the Adoptianist sect, but its success long outlived the extinction of that heresy and the fascination of the illustrations may account for its popularity. Several scholars have seen in the Beatus commentary on the Apocalypse a theory of contemplation, written, as Beatus himself explains, for "the edification of his brethren"; and in fact all these Beatus manuscripts come from contemplative monasteries. The purpose of the pictures is to fix the monk's meditations and induce contemplation. The catastrophes of the Apocalypse are rendered with an expressive violence that must have answered to the liturgical chants hymning the terror of death before the Last Judgment: this has been shown by O.K. Werkmeister, who has also explained that "the illustrations, forming an integral part of the commentary from at least the second version of the text proper of Beatus in 784, if not from the original text, must have constituted a tool for a certain practice of reading... The painters who conceived and later developed these illustrations gradually translated the gist of the apocalyptic narrative into a very dense series of pictures, permitting the reader to verify visually the content of the text." These views have the merit of accounting perfectly for the scope and quality of the illustrations in this set of manuscripts, the most famous being the one preserved in Paris. So fine and original are these Apocalypse illuminations that they deservedly rank high in the history of illustration. ■

4

The Beatus Apocalypse *of Saint-Sever, illuminations on vellum, 1028-1072:*

1. *Ornamental design around the name of the Abbot of Saint-Sever, Gregorius Muntaner.*
2. *Beginning of the genealogy of Christ, with Adam and Eve.*
3. *Decorative composition with trees and birds.*
4. *"A stone was cut out without hands, which smote the image upon his feet that were of iron and clay, and brake them to pieces... and the stone that smote the image became a great mountain, and filled the whole earth" (Daniel, 2.34-35).*

Lambert's "Liber Floridus"

1

2

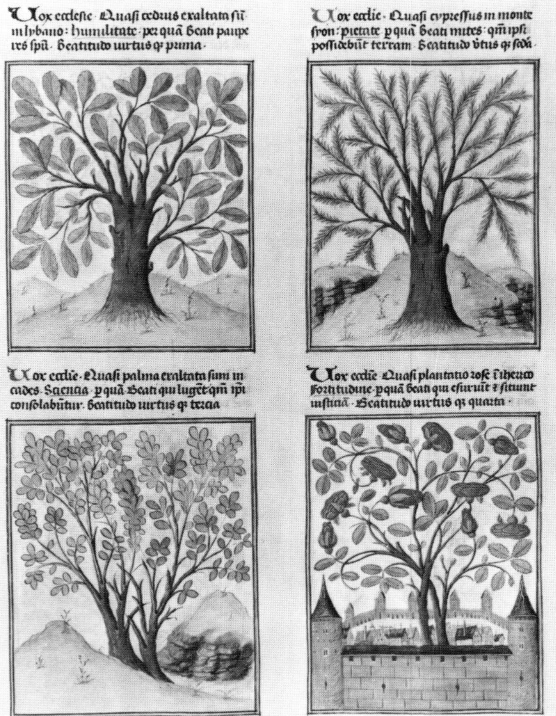

3

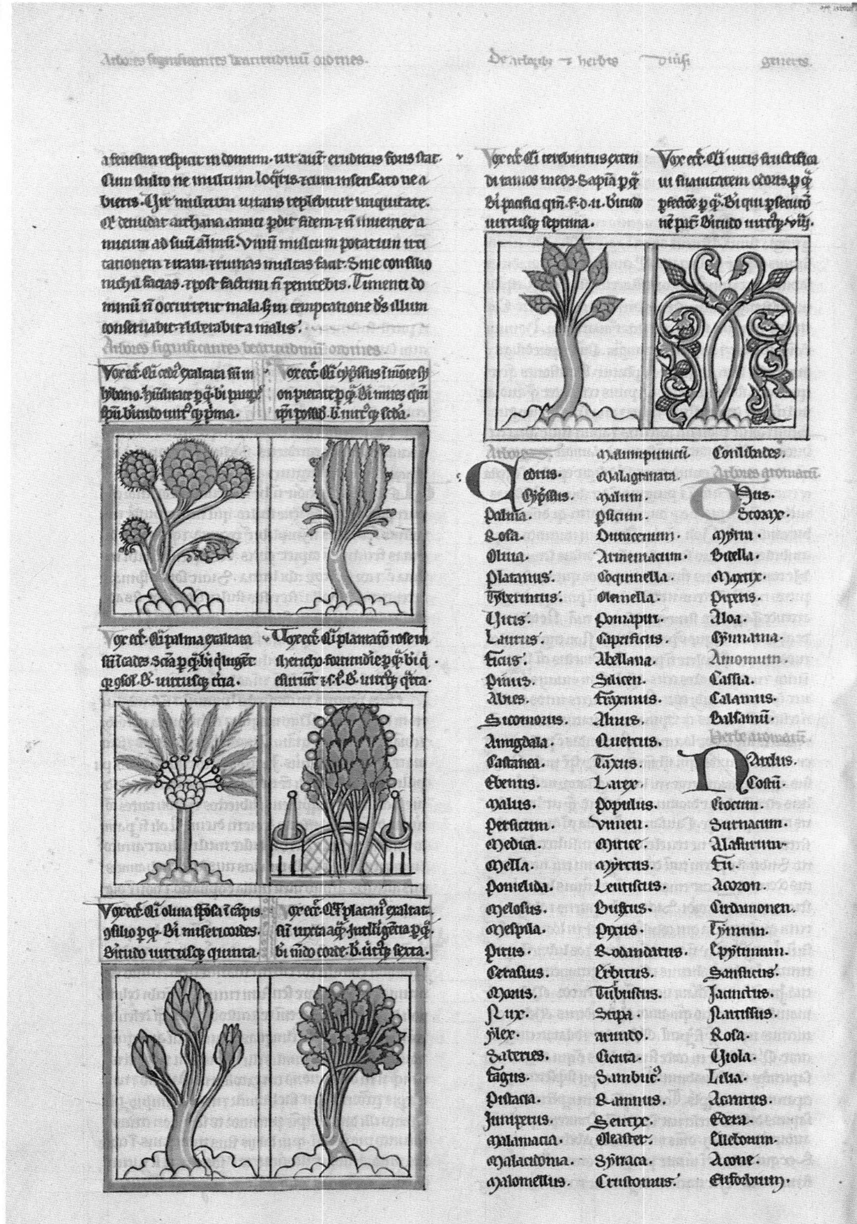

Compiled about 1120 by a canon named Lambert of the abbey of Saint-Omer, the *Liber Floridus* is one of the earliest tokens we have of the new scientific curiosity of the Middle Ages. At the time of the Crusades, when Aristotle was taken up into Western philosophy, the systems of knowledge rested largely on sub-antique models and the most recent encyclopaedia, Isidore of Seville's *Etymologiae*, was five centuries old. A patchwork medley of texts and pictures, the *Liber Floridus* strikes one at first as a step backward, lacking as it is in any systematic arrangement: historical genealogies turn up alongside cosmological observations, moral considerations and theological disquisitions. The order of the chapters seems equally arbitrary, and the many illustrations reflect this incoherence, both in their choice and in their relation to the text: sometimes they provide a concrete example or visual documentation (the Nile crocodile), sometimes an explanatory diagram (the labyrinth, the solar system). The same disorder appears in their relation to reality, now symbolical (Apocalypse plates), now realistic (portraits of Alexander, Charles the Bald and the author writing, map of Jerusalem, views of Rome and the Holy Sepulchre). It appears too in the very inclusion of illustrations in a text where they are neither distinct nor integrated. But rather than the disruption of philosophical thought, one may see here the appearance of a purely empirical mode of knowledge which also had its antecedents in antiquity (Pliny), and which was destined to follow a line of development down to Leonardo da Vinci and modern science.

It is clear, however, that the image here still fully plays its role as illumination, as an ornament sacralizing the writing. Clear too that Lambert's pictures are still wholly dependent on theological knowledge: trees materialize the virtues, and symbolic meanings attach to the lion, the lily, the palmtree. But the very abundance of the pictures (about sixty in the 287 leaves of the original manuscript, now in the University Library, Ghent) and their quality (including those in the copies preserved in the Bibliothèque Nationale, Paris, at Leyden and at Chantilly) mark a new approach to the documentary picture whose purpose now is not so much to enhance the text as to reflect it on another plane. Coming in the latter part of this same twelfth century, the *Hortus Deliciarum*, the now unfortunately lost encyclopaedia of Abbess Herrade of Landsberg, went deliberately in the same direction. ■

4

Lambert's Liber Floridus,
illuminations on vellum, Saint-Omer, c. 1120:

1. *The Constellations, copy of the late thirteenth century.*
2. *The Eight Trees of the Beatitudes, copy of the mid-fifteenth century.*
3. *The Eight Trees of the Beatitudes, copy of the second half of the thirteenth century.*
4. *Original manuscript of the* Liber Floridus*: The Mystical Palm-Tree.*

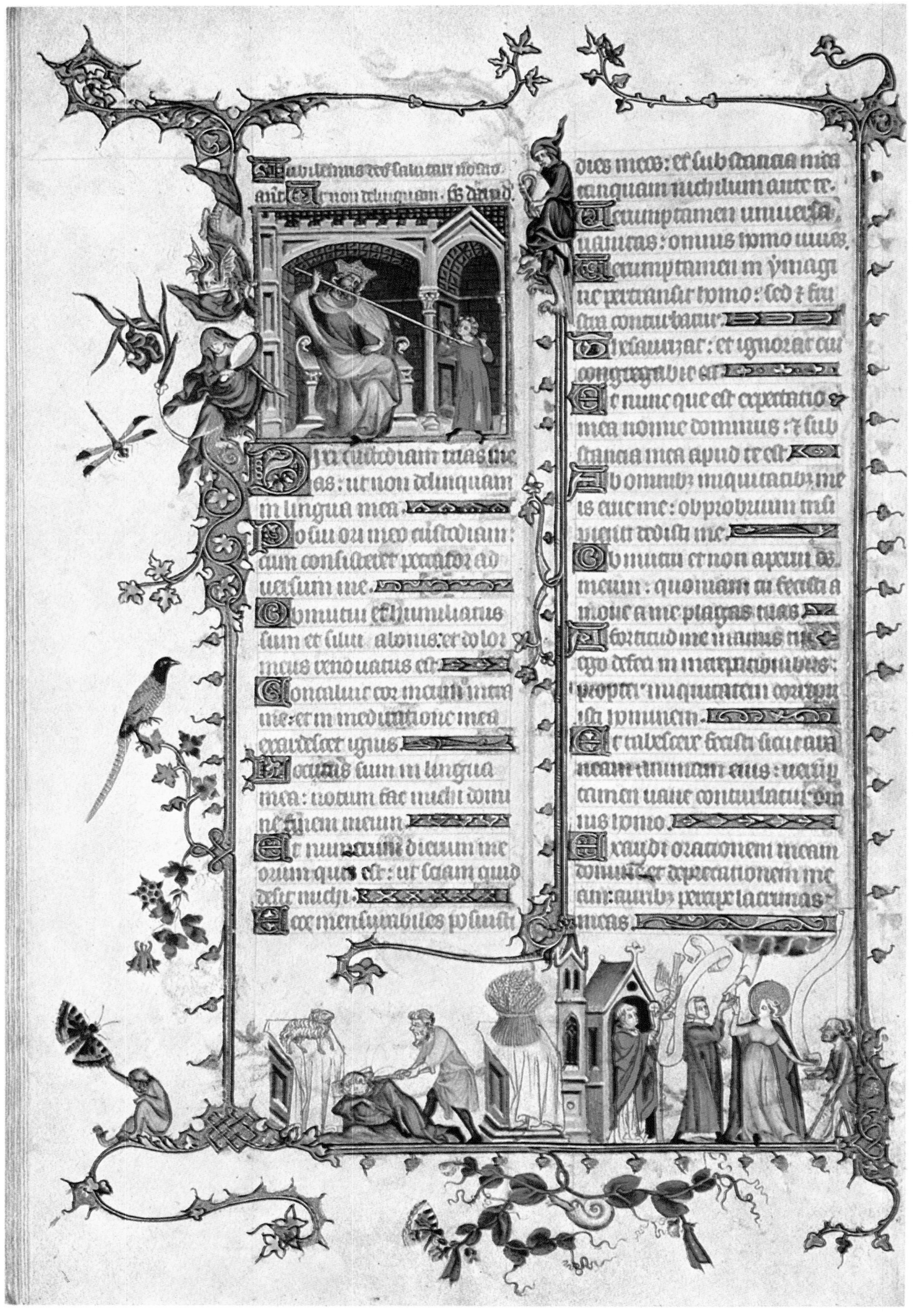

SECULARIZATION OF THE IMAGE

Illumination slowly moved towards naturalism. This was the necessary accompaniment of the movement which, in the thirteenth century, answering to new ideological needs, gradually shifted the basis of knowledge. St Bonaventure looked to nature as to a book whose interpretation led on to God; St Thomas Aquinas distinguished between faith and observation, between the attitude of the believer and that of the scholar; Albertus Magnus and Robert Grosseteste devoted a large part of their work to the study of the natural sciences. And no experimental science could exist without a secular conception of the image and a theory of figuration as objective representation—as token, symptom or reflection, but no longer as symbol. It comes as no surprise to find one of the boldest minds of this movement, Roger Bacon, turning his attention to astrology and divination (for which he was condemned by the Church) as well as to optics (on which the first treatise, by Witelo, was written about 1270). To find out something about the workings of the eye and the propagation of light could not help but undermine the idealistic conceptions of the image. This growing curiosity masked a growing distrust of dogmatic authority. The Church was losing its hold over pictures, as these moved closer to reality. This new movement of mind and inquiry meant a new approach to illustration. It may be too much to say, with Emile Bréhier: "There is much of Jules Verne in Roger Bacon." His inquiring outlook does, nevertheless, look forward to Leonardo da Vinci, and illustration began to be used as a medium of explanation and demonstration, a means of gaining knowledge and ensuring man's domination of nature.

Until the twelfth century, scientific illustrations were based on schemes and systems handed down from antiquity, occasionally renewed but never challenged. These traditional illustrations disappear in the mid-twelfth century, when they were seen to be unrelated to the questions being raised by the new philosophers. At the beginning of the thirteenth century they were replaced by designs inspired by direct observation of the visible world. The old allegorical or symbolical encyclopaedias had then to be renewed on the strength of fresh knowledge coming from the Arab philosophers, as in the *De proprietatibus rerum* written by Bartholomaeus Anglicus between 1225 and 1240. In the middle of the thirteenth century Vincent of Beauvais compiled his *Speculum majus*, whose influence

▲ Hours of Jeanne d'Evreux by Jean Pucelle, Paris, c. 1325: Christ before Pilate and the Visitation. Illuminations in grisaille on vellum.

◄ Belleville Breviary by Jean Pucelle, Paris, c. 1325: Illuminated page; in the initial, Saul casting the javelin at David.

on the "illustration" of the Gothic cathedrals was so fruitfully studied by Emile Mâle. The trend towards empirical observation thus made obsolete the heraldic style and the abstract conception of illustration: it oriented the image irreversibly towards the representation of concrete objects. It was anything but a rapid transition, and its results were only slowly secured; so slowly that for a long time to come, up indeed to our own time, we find schemes of imagery referring back to dogma and not to reality or, conversely, schemes inspired by reality which in turn became dogmas or anyhow "clichés."

Carl Nordenfalk has elucidated the evolution of forms brought about by this shift in values, by comparing three analogous miniatures illustrating the life of St Amandus in three different manuscripts (all three in the Bibliothèque Municipale, Valenciennes), dating respectively to the late eleventh century, to 1140 and to 1175. Modelling appears timidly in the faces, the figures are more and more individualized, and the setting has less and less in common with the ethereal space of realistic Carolingian miniatures: in the century covered by the three manuscripts, men and things gradually gain a volume and weight that brings them down to earth. Before, the illustration had acted rather as a device for making forms, and in particular the letters of the alphabet, escape from their terrestrial body. Now, little by little, it came to serve the contrary function of rooting the abstractions of writing in a concrete vision of things.

About the same time, from the late twelfth to the fourteenth century, the purpose and public of books, particularly of illustrated books, was diversified and broadened. From the early thirteenth century dates the vogue for psalters designed for high-ranking lay personages; for example, the *Psalter of Queen Ingeburge* (Chantilly). Illustration passed from ecclesiastical into aristocratic hands. Piety became an individual matter, and devotional reading a part of home life: breviaries, psalters, above all books of hours, were made for the devotions of laymen. It was here that realistic pictures found their most favourable ground, answering to didactic and moral purposes, also to the desire for luxury and entertainment. Such were the first books whose illuminations, painted on realistic lines, were meant to attract rather than to awe, and they were the work of the earliest illuminators whose personality stands out recognizably, the prototype being Jean Pucelle, active in Paris around 1320-1334, who illuminated the *Belleville Breviary* and the *Hours of Jeanne d'Evreux*. Such books, designed at first for women's hands, passed in the mid-fourteenth century into the library of princes, for reasons both of ostentation and utility.

Hours of Saint-Omer, Northern France, c. 1350:
Two illuminated pages; in the initial, the Adoration of the Magi.

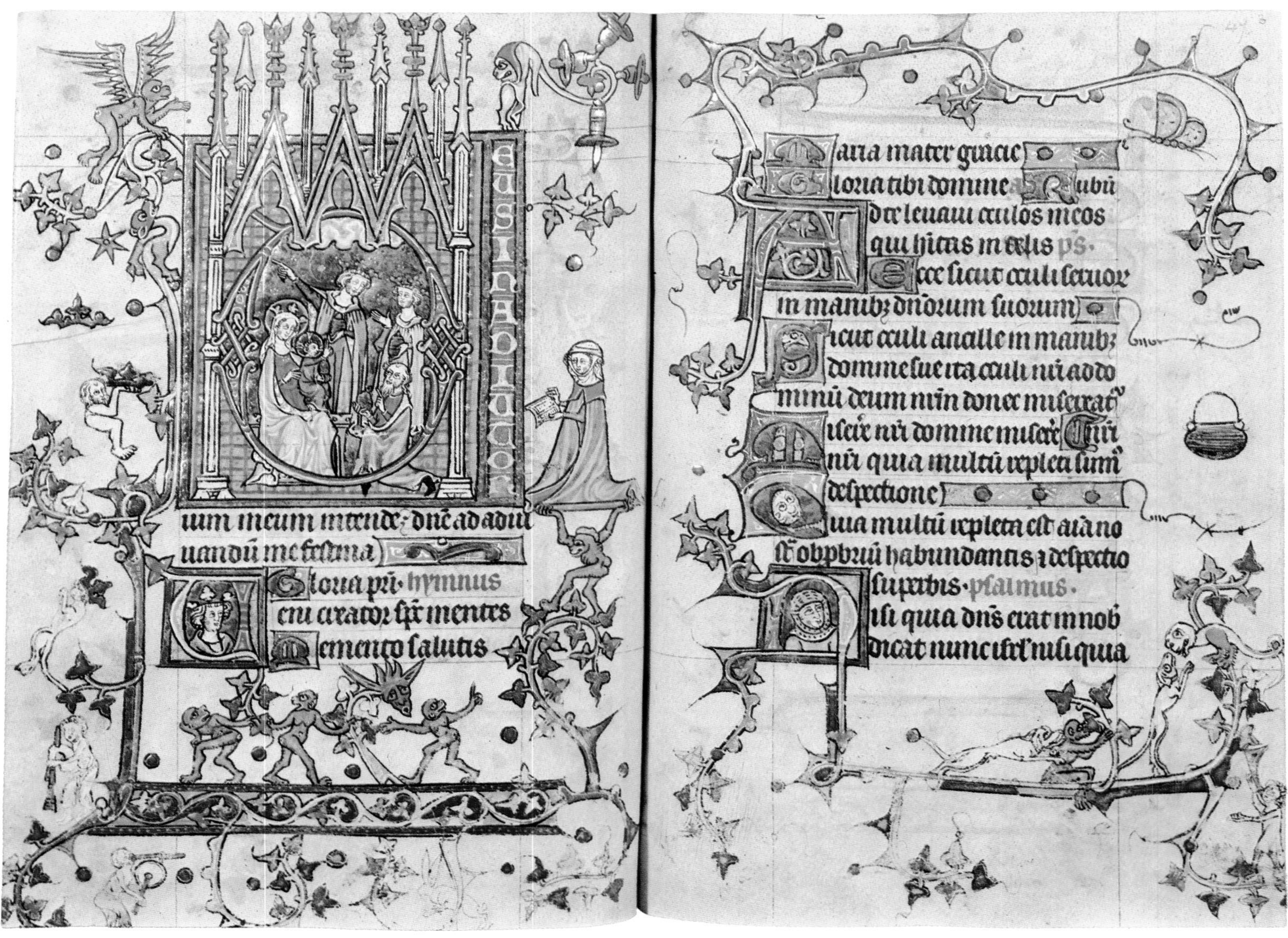

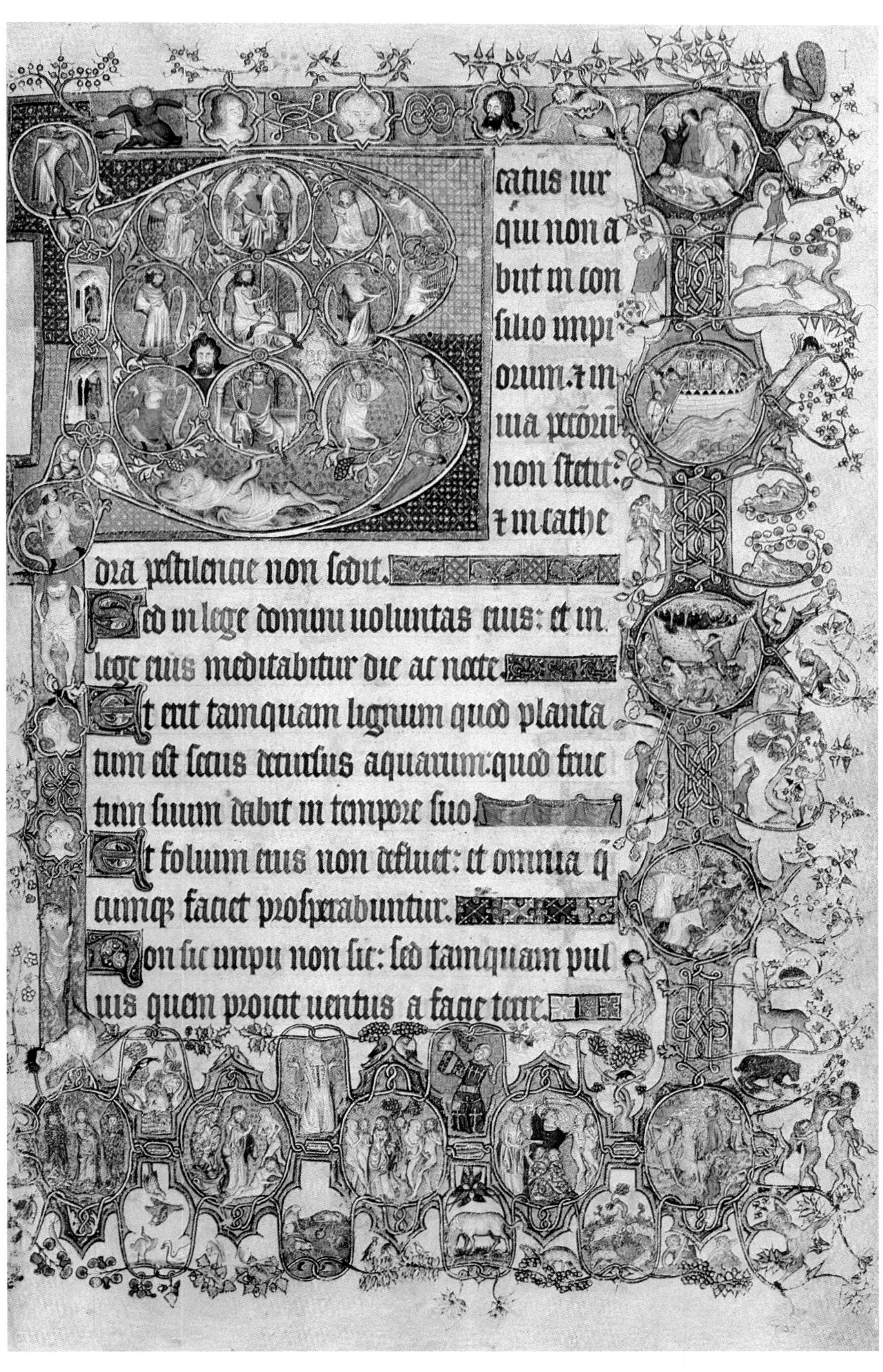

Saint-Omer Psalter, East Anglia, c. 1330:
in the initial, The Tree of Jesse.

The family of Charles V of France was famous for its love of fine books: Charles V himself, his brothers Philip the Bold, Duke of Burgundy, Louis of Anjou, and above all Jean, Duc de Berry. But well before this transition to the aristocracy, the trend towards secular imagery was already well marked, even in the monasteries, when the monks began illuminating their cartulary, the secular register book of their title deeds; the cartulary of Mont-Saint-Michel was illuminated as early as the twelfth century. Alongside the increasing number of profane illustrations for romances *(Romance of Troy, Romance of Alexander)* and books of satire *(Roman de Renart, Roman de Fauvel)*, we find a growing taste in the monasteries for the reading of saints' lives, which had an anecdotal appeal lacking in the liturgical books.

The ever growing and broadening demand for books was largely due to the rise of the universities. In their immediate neighbourhood, as around Saint-Séverin in Paris, sprang up in the thirteenth century the shops of lay scribes and illuminators. Their work, for these men, was not a prayer or hymn to God, it was a livelihood. Uncommitted to the iconographic programmes laid down by monks working in the seclusion of the scriptoria, they filled out their pictures with amusing or satirical motifs which spread over the margins of manuscripts. Such motifs, which had arisen from ornamental initials in the eleventh and twelfth centuries, often go to surround every column of text with garlands and a whole repertory of animal and vegetable forms. Lilian Randall has likened them to the *exempla*, the stories and anecdotes that preachers added

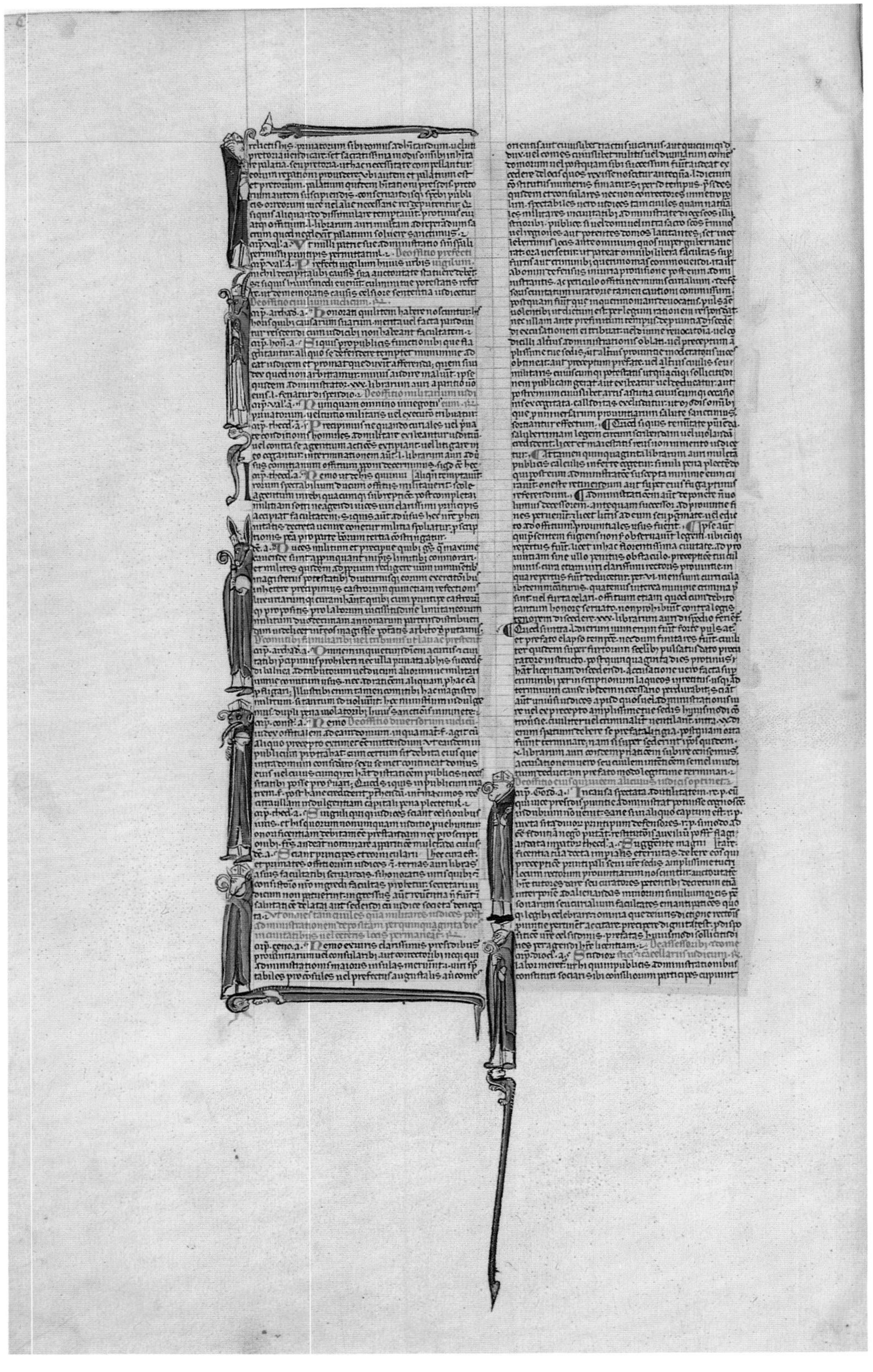

to their sermons to hold the attention of their public or to wake up the dozing. The comparison is justified by the exuberant fauna and flora that now appear, together with small figure scenes and caricatures of monks or Jews. In support of her view of this loosening of the ties of faith and morals, she quotes the satire of monks in Gautier de Coincy's *Miracles de Notre-Dame*—of monks who "En leur moustier ne font pas faire / Sitost l'image Nostre Dame / Com font Isengrin et sa fame / en leurs chambres ou ils reposent"—who, in a word, are more inclined to draw pictures of Isengrim, the wolf in the *Roman de Renart*, than of the Virgin. In the margins of these later medieval manuscripts appear the first genre scenes: games, craftsmen at work, beggars, fights, peasants and above all caricatures and satires of human folly, usually aimed at monks. It is difficult today to imagine the impact of these small pictures, stealthily or spiritedly introduced, or to judge the tone underlying them—corrosive, sarcastic or innocent? In any case, these illuminations break decisively with the mystical conception of early medieval imagery and have no further connection either with the form and style of the accompanying script or even, all too often, with its meaning.

This cleavage may be said to have occurred when the image lost its status as a conventional, symbolic representation, built up on plane, sharply delimited surfaces, and went to recreate the illusion of depth and movement. The devices of Byzantine art for executing "natural" folds or shading a face had gradually been forgotten, and in the fifteenth century naturalism had to be reinvented. First, by way of subjects taken from daily life, like the evocations of Parisian craftsmen and merchants that turn up in the illuminations of an early fourteenth-century *Life of St Denis*. Secondly, by way of the style deriving from the new procedures invented by Giotto and Duccio in Florence and Siena. Now appear in illustration some of the kinds of picture that were to be so prominent in the future: portraiture under Charles V, the first king of France whose features are well known to us from several illuminations; and landscape, pictured for its own sake in the illustrations to texts that describe the beauty of nature, like Guillaume de Machaut's *Remède de Fortune*. Jean Pucelle synthesized this new art and "brought three-dimensional space into French illumination," writes François Avril, who conjectures that Pucelle may also have practised easel painting.

For as soon as it ceased to have any more physical connection with writing, painting was ready to move onto other surfaces. And if Parisian illumination then held the field, it may be because those other surfaces were less developed than in the Italian merchant towns. Distinct now from the scribe, the illuminator became a painter and his work departed from the text with which at first it was connected. The illuminator who composed the unusually realistic dedication of the book presented to Charles V by Jean de Vaudetar took good care to sign his work. He was a Flemish painter, Jean de Bondol, and it was another Fleming, Jan van Eyck, that the Duc de Berry commissioned to complete his *Très Belles Heures de Notre-Dame*.

▲ Bible of Jean de Vaudetar illuminated by Jean de Bondol, Paris, 1371: Presentation of the volume to King Charles V by Jean de Vaudetar.

◄ *Corpus Iuris Civilis*, Northern France, late thirteenth century: In the margins, satirical drawings of animal-headed bishops.

The *Très Riches Heures du Duc de Berry* illuminated by Pol de Limbourg, early fifteenth century: The month of January, with the Duke of Berry at table surrounded by his friends.

Histoire de la destruction de Troye la Grant, c. 1500: Helen carried off by Paris.

Illumination was closely linked not only with the rise of easel painting, but also with the first illustrated printed books. Before the double version of certain works, one engraved, the other painted in a book, one may wonder whether the painting served as model for the engraver or whether it was not rather the engraver who created the model which was then diffused among illuminators, as was no doubt the case with the Master of the Playing Cards, one of the earliest copperplate engravers. There are many illustrated books whose engravings were hand-coloured after printing, and after the sixteenth century the term illumination often means no more than hand-colouring. So it is that we have two versions of the *Livre des déduis du roi Modus et de la reine Ratio*, the first illuminated in 1379, all the pictures being recopied by the engraver for the printed edition issued by Antoine Neyret in 1486. The illuminators were the chief victims—and did not fail to make their complaints heard—of the mechanical revolution wrought in the fifteenth century by the printing of pictures and their popularization. Illumination lingered on only as a luxury art, of marginal importance, its place being taken now by the coloured engraving.

For by the fifteenth century the miniature had become an actual picture whose inclusion in a book appeared more and more problematic: such is the case with the "spectacular" miniatures of Jean Fouquet. It is the miniature again that we find transposed into the monumental designs of the *Apocalypse* tapestries for the Duke of Anjou: these form a veritable spectacle in which the text now is no more than a subtitle. It is no surprise to find the stairway scene of Helen carried off by Paris, in the *Histoire de la destruction de Troye la Grant*, being compared with the Odessa steps sequence in Eisenstein's *Battleship Potemkin*. The fact is that the Troy manuscript was in the Hermitage library, and on display, at the time when Eisenstein was planning his film; and he was a careful planner if ever there was one, with a keen eye for classical models. But there is no need for bold conjectures, for it is clear that between the late medieval illumination and the modern cinema, there is no difference of kind.

The "Ars moriendi" and the Block Books

2

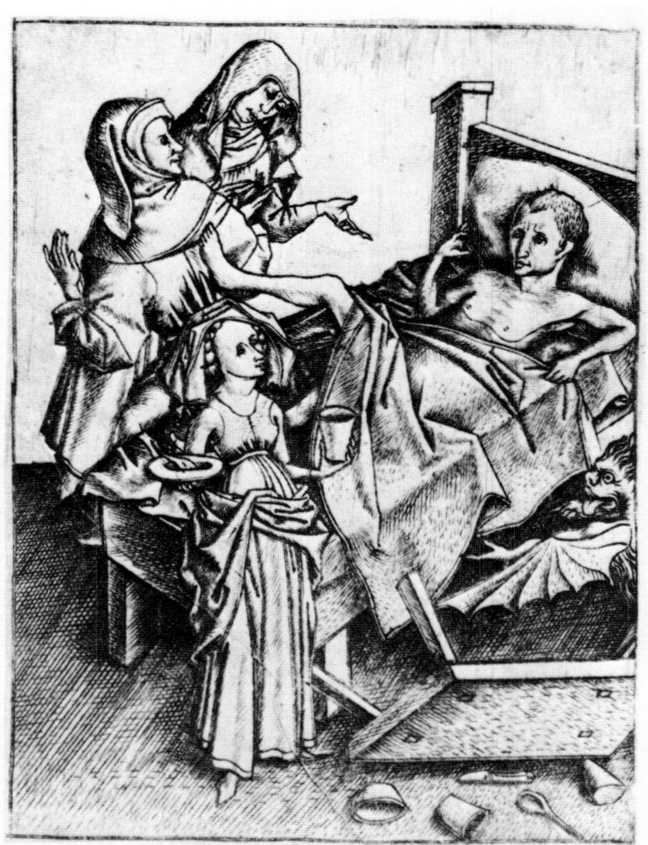

1

Hardly more than fifty years after Gutenberg's invention, pictures were already being printed from woodcut blocks. These latter also included text, the letters being cut in the same block with the illustration. Even after the invention of movable type, which freed the reproduction from the writing and set the image apart, there was still a large output of these small block books, as they were called, in which each page of text, or of text and illustrations combined, was cut in a single block. This production, designed for a wide public, reached its height in the Rhine valley between 1460 and 1480. The subject matter of these books, whether religious *(The Apocalypse)* or profane *(The Story of the Three Dead and the Three Quick)*, came straight from the popular culture of the Middle Ages. The texts themselves were condensed and adapted to the format, the number of leaves and the level of the readership. The *Ars moriendi* (Art of Dying) was a booklet containing eleven pictures and eleven commentaries, preceded by an introduction. Its French version, *Art au morier*, was one of the first books to be printed in French. Scholars have given a good deal of attention to it because of the skilful workmanship of the compositions, issued both as woodcuts (in thirteen versions) and as metalcuts (in three versions, one of them attributed to Master E.S.). The book was widely diffused and seems indeed to have appealed to people in all walks of life.

The *Ars moriendi* also shows the transition from manuscript to printed book: hundreds of unillustrated manuscripts of the text are extant, and there is one manuscript whose miniatures show the same layout as that taken over in the block books. Two of the versions with woodcuts are accompanied by a manuscript text; so originally was the sequence of copperplate illustrations. Later, in the sixteenth century, an edition was printed entirely from movable type. Questions then arise about the evolution of the text, its adaptation to the pictures, and the complex interrelation of the different versions. In a recent study of the book, Henri Zerner concludes that while, in the miniatures, the illustration still appears as "a figured script..., at the other end of its evolution... the situation has been reversed... The written page occupies the place of an image, it is the picture of an inscription. The effect of the book is chiefly visual, the text itself being seen before being read." ■

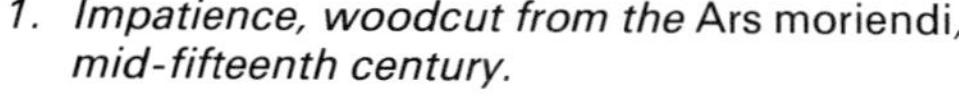

1. *Impatience, woodcut from the* Ars moriendi, *mid-fifteenth century.*
2. *Impatience, line engraving from the* Ars moriendi *of Master E.S., c. 1450.*

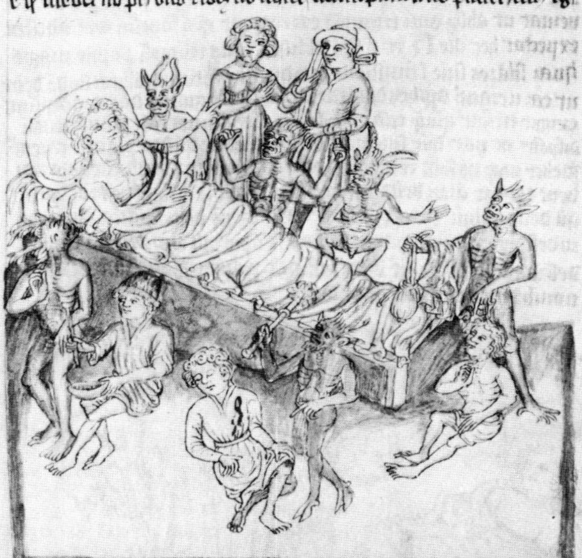

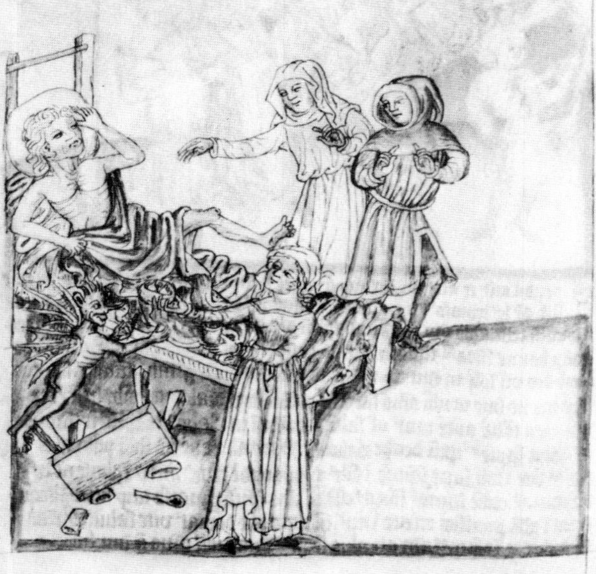

Illuminated manuscript of the Ars moriendi*, c. 1430.*

Around the Master of the Playing Cards

1

2

3

4

5

This small print of the *Three of Deer* belongs to a series made up of assembled motifs, some of them arranged like a pack of cards whose colours correspond to deer, wild men and asses; some of them, as here, having several motifs brought together on a single plate; and some with several plates printed on a single sheet (deer, bears, cyclamens, roses...). This printmaker is known as the Master of the Playing Cards, and his may be the earliest of all copperplate engravings. For several scholars have noted that these same motifs recur in a number of manuscripts dating to the 1450s, such as the *Livre des déduis du roi Modus et de la reine Ratio.* They are to be found in the margin of the large Bible of Mainz (1452-1453) and in various manuscripts of that region; so that it has been thought that Gutenberg himself may have overseen the making of these images with the idea of printing them. But they also figure in earlier manuscripts, at Turin, about 1443, and in the *Hours of Catherine of Cleves* of about 1435-1440. From the large number of manuscripts exactly re-employing these motifs in different contexts, and the fact that the miniatures face the same way as the prints, it is safe to say that it was the print which served as model. One may then imagine the use made of these small sheets, which not only served for some unknown game (one of them is mounted on cardboard) but also and above all as a set of models, diffused on a massive scale and used by illuminators. Here was one of the first and essential revolutions wrought in the field of illustration by the power of reproducing and diffusing models—a definitive break with the relative isolation of craftsmen. A recent study has shown that these prints did not spring up "spontaneously" but were themselves inspired by earlier naturalistic miniatures: the animals in the *Books of Venery* and perhaps even the miniatures in the *Hours of Catherine of Cleves* which either explain the engravings or are explained by them—it is not sure which. Here we witness a turning point in the history of the book and, as noted by Anne Van Buren and Sheila Edmunds, the popularity of this series, attested by so many engraved copies, vouches not only for the widespread taste for realistic art but also for the preoccupation of this period with techniques of reproduction based on high-quality type moulds which culminated in Gutenberg's invention of printing in the fifteenth century. ■

6

1. *Detail of a Book of Hours illuminated by the Bedford Master, 1422-1425.*
2. *Master of the Playing Cards: Three of Deer, German engraving, mid-fifteenth century.*
3. *Marginal detail from the Missal of Felice V, Turin, c. 1443.*
4. *Marginal detail from the Hours of Catherine of Cleves, c. 1435-1440.*
5. *Miniature from the* Livre de la Chasse *of Gaston Phébus, c. 1400-1410.*
6. Livre des déduis du roi Modus et de la reine Ratio, *c. 1450: Illuminated page with deer hunting.*

L.
INSIPIENS
SAPIENS
TE FACIMVS FORTVNA DEA CELOQVE LOCAMVS
FIDITE VIRTVTI FORTVA FVGATIOR VNDIS
FORTVNA
SAPIENTIA
SPECVLVM SAPIENTIE
SEDES FORTVNE ROTVDA
SEDES VIRTVTIS QVADRATA

THE IMAGE AS LANGUAGE

ORVS

Que c'eſt qu'ilz entendoient en paignant vne Eſtoille.

VNe eſtoille entr'eulx ſignifioit aucunesfois Dieu, aucunesfois la nuyt, aucunesfois le tẽps, & tellefois eſtoit l'Ame d'vn homme maſle.

Quoy

APOLLO. 50

Quoy par le petit d'vn Agle.

VN Aygleron ſignifioit auſſi aucuneſfois vn maſle, aucunesfois vne choſe bien ronde, & d'autresfois la ſemence de l'homme.

g ij

▲ First illustrated edition of Horapollo's *Hieroglyphica*, Paris, 1543. Woodcuts.

◀ Fortune and Wisdom, allegorical frontispiece of the *Livre de la Sagesse* by Charles de Bouelles, Paris, 1510.

For the medieval mind, man was the illustration of God. The whole world of forms was only an illustration, whose relations and meaning it was sometimes given to man to grasp. Between the image fashioned by the artist and the world created by God, there was no difference in kind. No difference, then, between the philosopher and the poet, between the poet and the painter. Knowledge of the world did not depend on knowledge of the right workings of the sign, of word and image, but on a right interpretation of them. The displacement of this problem, of the terms in which it was seen, beginning in the fifteenth century, shifted the evolution of the history of illustration. The sign wrought its Copernican revolution and a new venture began, a new endeavour to decipher the world.

In 1419, in the Aegean island of Andros, a Greek manuscript was discovered: the *Hieroglyphica* of Horapollo. Who this author was, and where the manuscript originated, will never be known. Its amazing popularity (the Greek text was reprinted as late as 1828, and a modern English translation appeared in 1950) shows that it came at the right time. It is a dictionary of pictorial signs. It was seized on by printers and the first illustrated edition was published in France in 1543, subtitled "On the meaning of the hieroglyphic notes of the Egyptians, that is the figures by which they write their sacred mysteries and holy and divine matters." Each page pictures a symbol accompanied by a verbal translation and a brief commentary. Here then the order of presentation is reversed: the image is given pride of place, and the text derives from it. Although these images were presented as being "divinely ordained," a whole science of symbol and metaphor was founded upon them. That these "Egyptians," even if imaginary, should have replaced the Creator as the divine source of pictorial signs marks a date: the image was integrated into the historical order of human productions.

This "science" of hieroglyphs (the word means sacred engraved writing) acted as one of the sources of that large body of literature in which, during the first two centuries of printing, the image tried to find its position in relation to the text. The century in particular from about 1550 to 1650 saw a spate of handbooks of emblems, mottoes, personifications and symbolic devices in which we find the premises of what today is known as semiotics. These repertories of pictured signs and symbols are usually small books of about a hundred pages. On each page a more or less complex image is combined with a maxim which it illustrates, together with an explanation in the form of a distich, a quatrain or a ten-line stanza which reveals or suggests their connection. This patchwork combination of text and image answers to the Italian fashion for the *concetto* or conceit, which came as the expression of a subtle relationship between things or as "an act of intelligence conveying the correspondence between objects" (Gracián)—an art or game of fanciful thought much appreciated by humanist intellectuals, and connected too with the literary genre of the portrait sketch or epigram. This close alliance of text and image has another source in the tradition of chivalry and heraldry, where a graphic sign or badge of recognition was in the fifteenth century associated with the "motto," which summed up the person carrying it, set his line of conduct and gave his moral portrait: it was his "inner concept," like the "Plus ultra" of the Emperor Charles V associated with the Pillars of Hercules or the "Cominus et eminus" of Louis XII of France combined with a picture of a porcupine (which hits its mark from "near and far"). The device or emblem, an inseparable combination of words and images, comes as a kind of individual appropriation of the sign.

The first emblem book was the *Emblemata* of Andrea Alciati, a Milanese jurist. Finished in 1521 and published in 1531, it was a great success. Translated throughout Europe, annotated and augmented, it went through more than 150 editions; the Padua edition of 1621 ran to a thousand pages. The mania for emblems spread through Italy, France, the Low Countries (where the Jesuits made great use of them) and England. In his bibliography of emblem books, Mario Praz lists over six hundred titles. This vogue was like an afterglow of the medieval philosophies. In the language of Christianity and Platonism, the pairing of text and image was often assimilated to the pairing of soul and body. Hence the importance for

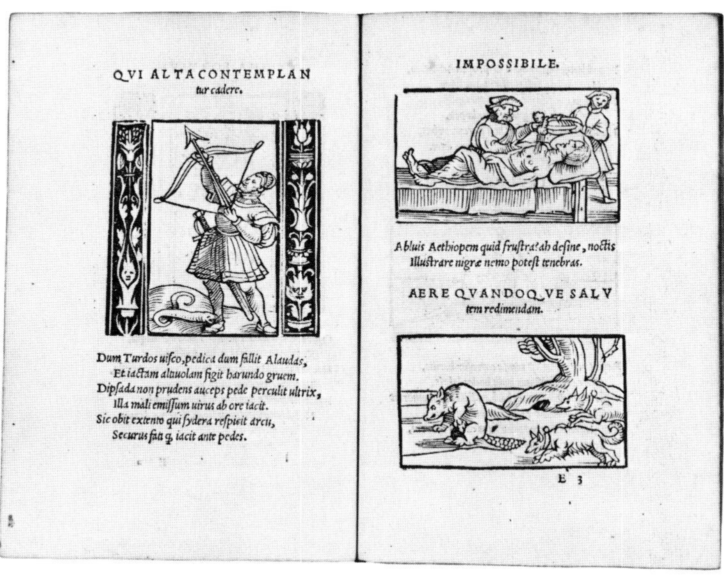

QVI ALTA CONTEMPLANtur cadere.

Dum Turdos uiſco, pedica dum fallit Alaudas,
Et iactam altuolam figit harundo gruem.
Dipſada non prudens auceps pede perculit ultrix,
Illa mali emiſſum uirus ab ore iacit.
Sic obit extento qui ſydera reſpicit arcu,
Securus fati q; iacit ante pedes.

IMPOSSIBILE.

Abluis Aethiopem quid fruſtra? ah deſine, noctis
Illuſtrare nigræ nemo poteſt tenebras.

AERE QVANDOQVE SALVtem redimendam.

E 3

Two illustrated pages from the first edition of Andrea Alciati, *Emblemata*, Augsburg, 1531.

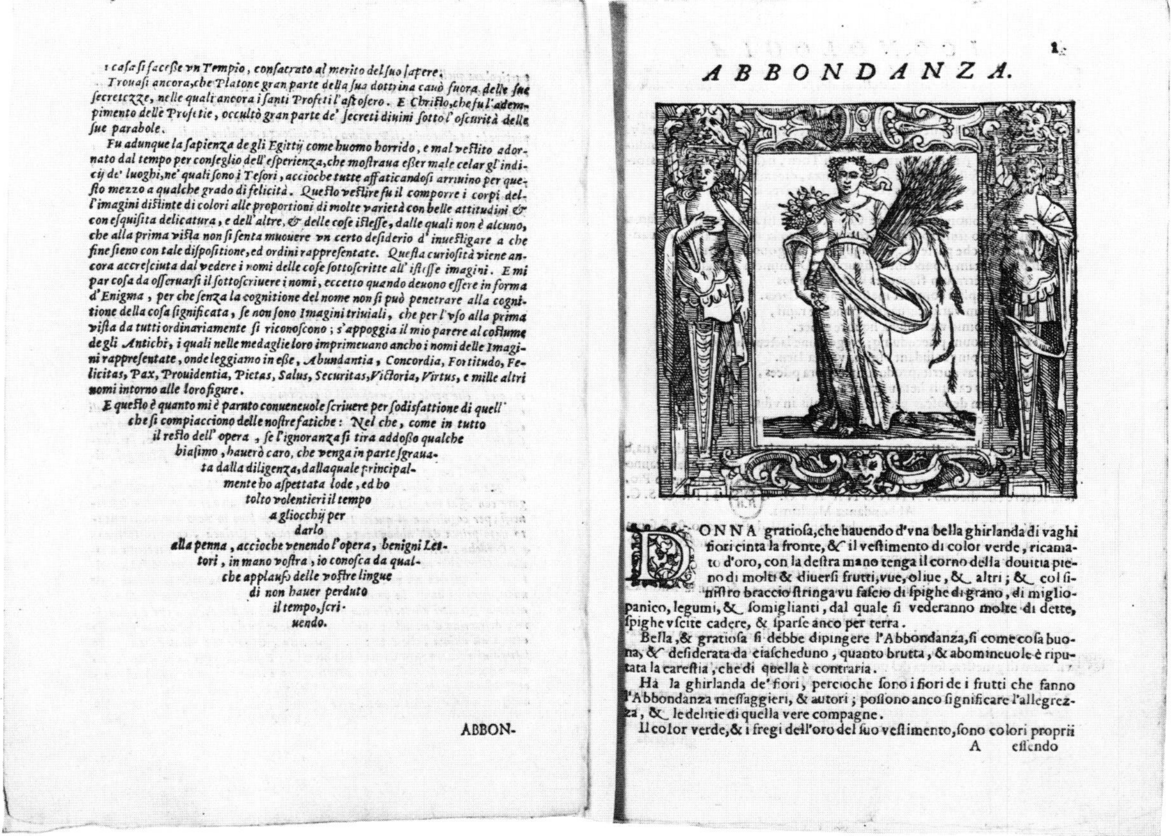

i caſa ſi faceſſe vn Tempio, conſacrato al merito del ſuo ſapere.

Trouaſi ancora, che Platone gran parte della ſua dottrina cauò fuora delle ſue ſecretezze, nelle quali ancora i ſanti Profeti l'aſtoſero. E Chriſto, che fu l'adempimento delle Profetie, occultò gran parte de' ſecreti diuini ſotto l'oſcurità delle ſue parabole.

Fu adunque la ſapienza de gli Egittij come huomo horrido, e mal veſtito adornato dal tempo per conſeglio dell'eſperienza, che moſtraua eſſer male celar gl'indicij de' luoghi, ne' quali ſono i Teſori, acciochè tutte affaticandoſi arriuino per queſto mezzo a qualche grado di felicità. Queſto veſtire fu il comporre i corpi dell'imagini diſtinte di colori alle proportioni di molte varietà con belle attitudini & con eſquiſita delicatura, e dell'altre, & delle coſe isteſſe, dalle quali non è alcuno, che alla prima viſta non ſi ſenta muouere vn certo deſiderio d'inueſtigare a che fine ſieno con tale diſpoſitione, ed ordini rappreſentate. Queſta curioſità viene ancora accreſciuta dal vedere i nomi delle coſe ſottoſcritte all'iſteſſe imagini. E mi par coſa da oſſeruarſi il ſottoſcriuere i nomi, eccetto quando deuono eſſere in forma d'Enigma, per che ſenza la cognitione del nome non ſi può penetrare alla cognitione della coſa ſignificata, ſe non ſono Imagini triuiali, che per l'vſo alla prima viſta da tutti ordinariamente ſi riconoſcono; s'appoggia il mio parere al coſtume degli Antichi, i quali nelle medaglie loro imprimeuano ancho i nomi delle Imagini rappreſentate, onde leggiamo in eſſe, Abundantia, Concordia, Fortitudo, Felicitas, Pax, Prouidentia, Pietas, Salus, Securitas, Victoria, Virtus, e mille altri nomi intorno alle loro figure.

E queſto è quanto mi è paruto conueneuole ſcriuere per ſodisfattione di quell' che ſi compiacciono delle noſtre fatiche: Nel che, come in tutto il reſto dell'opera, ſe l'ignoranza ſi tira addoſſo qualche biaſimo, hauerò caro, che venga in parte ſgrauata dalla diligenza, dalla quale principalmente ho aſpettata lode, ed ho tolto volentieri il tempo a gliocchij per darlo alla penna, acciochè venendo l'opera, benigni Lettori, in mano voſtra, io conoſca da qualche applauſo delle voſtre lingue di non hauer perduto il tempo, ſcriuendo.

ABBON-

1

ABBONDANZA.

DONNA gratioſa, che hauendo d'vna bella ghirlanda di vaghi fiori cinta la fronte, & il veſtimento di color verde, ricamato d'oro, con la deſtra mano tenga il corno della douitia pieno di molti & diuerſi frutti, vue, oliue, & altri; & col ſiniſtro braccio ſtringa vn faſcio di ſpighe di grano, di miglio, panico, legumi, & ſomiglianti, dal quale ſi vederanno molte di dette, ſpighe vſcite cadere, & ſparſe anco per terra.

Bella, & gratioſa ſi debbe dipingere l'Abbondanza, ſi come coſa buona, & deſiderata da ciaſcheduno, quanto brutta, & abomineuole è riputata la careſtia, che di quella è contraria.

Hà la ghirlanda de' fiori, percioche ſono i fiori de i frutti che fanno l'Abbondanza meſſaggieri, & autori; poſſono anco ſignificare l'allegrezza, & le delitie di quella vere compagne.

Il color verde, & i fregi dell'oro del ſuo veſtimento, ſono colori proprii

A eſſendo

Personification of Abundance from the first illustrated edition of Cesare Ripa, *Iconologia*, third edition, Rome, 1603.

Neo-Platonism of the problem of the pictorial sign: it appeared as the image of the soul giving form to matter. In the Aristotelian tradition, the practice of emblems raised a no less important problem, for it illustrated the crisis in the relations between the universal and the particular. The latter, which could be represented, became more than the particular when given the form of an image with a general meaning. Under the pressure of rationalism and empiricism, philosophers then sought to work out a logic of the image, building on the rules which the emblematists had drawn up for themselves.

In the mid-sixteenth century the types of relation that could exist between text and image were classified (long before Peirce's attempt to classify the relations of the image and its referent logically in broad categories of "resemblance," "clue" and "icon"). According to the first of these "legislators" of illustration, Paolo Giovio, the image and text of the emblem had to complete each other; that

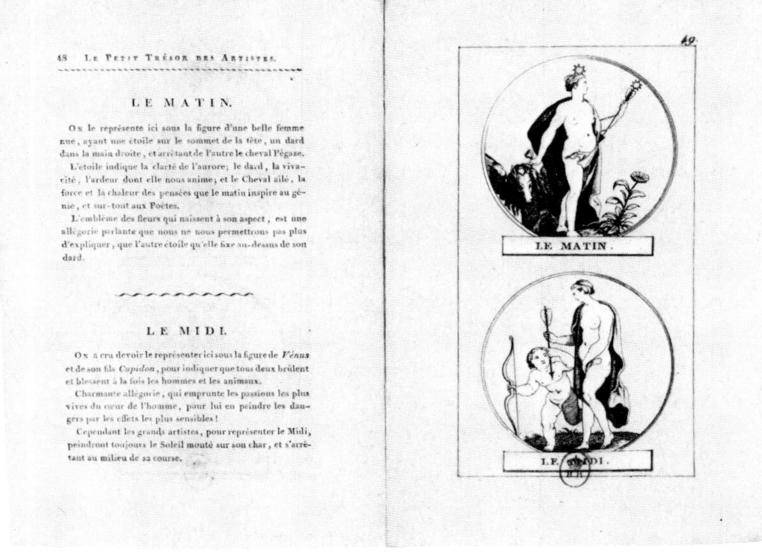
48 Le Petit Trésor des Artistes.

LE MATIN.

On le représente ici sous la figure d'une belle femme nue, ayant une étoile sur le sommet de la tête, un dard dans la main droite, et arrêtant de l'autre le cheval Pégaze.

L'etoile indique la clarté de l'aurore; le dard, la vivacité, l'ardeur dont elle nous anime; et le Cheval ailé, la force et la chaleur des pensées que le matin inspire au génie, et sur-tout aux Poëtes.

L'emblème des fleurs qui naissent à son aspect, est une allégorie parlante que nous ne nous permettrons pas plus d'expliquer, que l'autre étoile qu'elle fixe au-dessus de son dard.

LE MIDI.

On a cru devoir le représenter ici sous la figure de *Vénus* et de son fils *Capidon*, pour indiquer que tous deux brûlent et blessent à la fois les hommes et les animaux.

Charmante allégorie, qui emprunte les passions les plus vives du cœur de l'homme, pour lui en peindre les dangers par les effets les plus sensibles!

Cependant les grands artistes, pour représenter le Midi, peindront toujours le Soleil monté sur son char, et s'arrêtant au milieu de sa course.

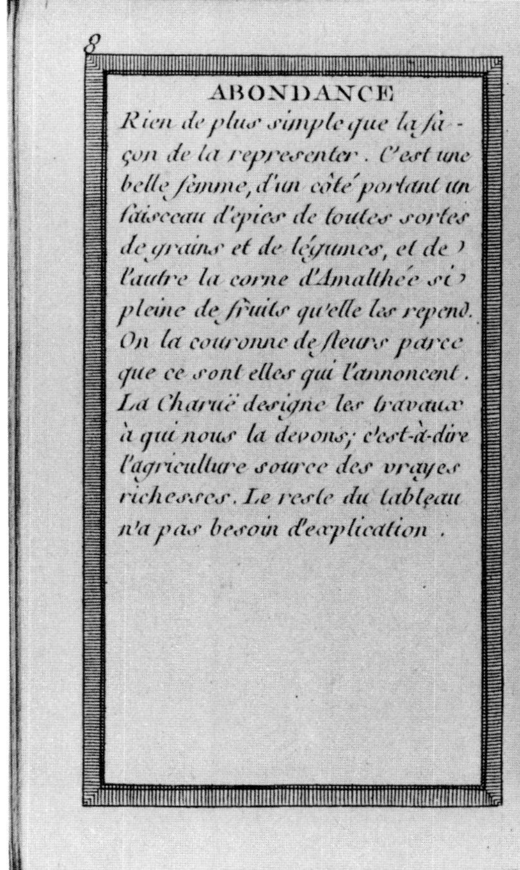
8

ABONDANCE

Rien de plus simple que la façon de la représenter. C'est une belle femme, d'un côté portant un faisceau d'épics de toutes sortes de grains et de légumes, et de l'autre la corne d'Amalthée si pleine de fruits qu'elle les répand. On la couronne de fleurs parce que ce sont elles qui l'annoncent. La Charuë designe les travaux à qui nous la devons; c'est-à-dire l'agriculture source des vrayes richesses. Le reste du tableau n'a pas besoin d'explication.

▲ Morning and Noon from *Le Petit Trésor des Artistes et des Amateurs d'Art, ou le guide sûr et infaillible des Peintres, Sculpteurs, Dessinateurs, Graveurs, Architectes, Décorateurs...*, Paris, Year VIII (1800).

◄ Figure of Abundance from Charles-Nicolas Cochin and Hubert-François Gravelot, *Almanach iconologique*, plate 8 of the year 1773, line engraving.

is, neither could have any sense without the other. But, for the purists, they also had to be neither an explanation of each other, nor an affirmation of one by the other, nor a comparison of one with the other. The human figure was generally excluded, just as from the text were banished proverbs, adages, apophthegms, precepts and riddles. The images were not to be taken in a metaphorical sense nor the texts in a figurative sense. Thus the image and its text maintained an almost mathematical relationship which might be accounted for in terms of "implication" or "wholeness." The guiding purpose was a logical coherence with the human judgment. What was the underlying sense of these strict requirements, if not to define a structural and indeed organic link between word and picture? At the time when men seized on signs and symbols, the great threat to knowledge lay in the anarchy of meaning. The important thing then was to replace God by Law, since images now were no longer felt to be messages written to man by God, but human inventions giving shape to man's thoughts.

The fashion for emblems waned in its acute form, but lingered on in the very degeneration of the spiritualistic philosophies of the symbol. Its by-products can be followed up in several fields. First of all, emblems served from the start as a repertory of motifs for artists and craftsmen, providing a wide range of conventional patterns. These were widely diffused in "standard works," the most famous of which was Cesare Ripa's *Iconologia* (1593). Such books were still appearing in the eighteenth and nineteenth centuries; for example, the *Petit Trésor des Artistes et des Amateurs d'Art...* Paris, Year VIII (i.e. 1800). They were compilations of allegories, no longer of emblems in the strict sense. Elsewhere we find the structure of the emblem in the medieval form of *exempla* (for which Ovid's *Metamorphoses* provided a rich store of imagery), in the "moralities in action" and popular prints where this or that maxim is illustrated by a concrete example, like the Good Boy in the *images d'Epinal.* Finally, the structure of the emblem can be readily detected in certain advertisements made up of a symbolic, idealized image, a brief slogan which would have no meaning apart from that image, and a short explanation of this slogan/image relationship which functions like a *concetto.* Slogan and picture are coupled and mutually reinforced in an ideal combination which still today has given rise to lively debate. Attempts to work out a "logic" of the image, renewed today by semioticians and publicists by way of enumerations of figure cases and distinctions, already have a long history behind them. At the end of the Middle Ages, up to thirty-two categories of figured signs were distinguished which, in addition to emblems, hieroglyphs, symbols, ensigns and representations, also included the signs of the zodiac and heraldic devices. A belated echo of them is to be found in Boudard's manual of *Iconology* (1759), whose purpose was to "enable our young students to distinguish Hieroglyphs from Emblems, Emblems from Attributes, and Attributes from Symbols."

This may be seen perhaps as the last episode in the "quarrel over universals" which, in the Carolingian period, divided philosophers on the question of the reality of abstractions. But in order to understand the Renaissance vogue for emblems, they have to be clearly distinguished from medieval symbols. What differentiates them from the latter is precisely the fact that they necessarily refer back to figural shapes, to concrete things. Form, in the Middle Ages, was an emanation of the soul, and as such entirely governed by abstraction. As it degenerated, the abstraction originally governing the sign was taken over by it, and the symbol, inflated with meaning, lapsed into a social amusement, into pictorial punning, rebus devices and the canting arms of heraldry. The normativity of emblematic literature has something desperate about it: no meaning can be pinned down, and the sign fails to hold together. Individualization ruins absolute values, as in the paintings of Bosch where the realism of the representation still serves a religious ideal: hell is given shape. Determined

LIBRO

ne di la morte del figliolo & ſcomincio aluminare el mondo:ma io hauẽdo cura di eſſo mondo riguardo per tuto el cielo:acio che non ſi fuſſe coſa diſordinata per caſone del fuoco che era ſtato. poi diſſeſe nela terra & gli fiumi bagno & gli arbori feze frondure & dete alla ſterile terra le ſemente & fata fertile.

Cap. XII.

Alegoria.

La tertia tranſmutatiõe e ſi come cigno diuẽne uciello:loq̃le alegoriçareõ ma lo uero di queſta fabula e cħ queſto Cigno fue re di lombardia & edifico piacemza. Queſta lõbardia e maxima ꝓuincia de Italia poſta nella europa: & cõ fina cõ gli mõti apenini:gliq̃li la ſera p in ſino alla marcha triuiſana & da leuãte a lo mare adriatico:queſta ſi ha molte citade uidelicet uerſo le alpe a Milão texino.piacenza & piu iſeriori uerſo el mare a adria da laqual fu dito driaticho:auinecia ale cõfine & aſſai altre cita de populi nobiliſſimi & molto fertile habundãte.&c.Queſto cigno ſi dolſe de la morte di Phetõte:cioe cħ egli ſi dolſe di la uanagloria cħ egli pdete e po cħl fue chaciato del regno & fugli tolta & guaſta piacẽza laquale poſedẽdo ne hebe grãde uanagloria.onde dice Ouidio che egli diuẽto cigno:che e ucielo uile adi mõſtrare cħ colui:cħ pde q̃lla coſa cħ ha aquiſtato cõ peccato e uile huomo:per che ſi dole del male & del peccato da lui poſſeduto.Apſſo dice cħ phebo ſi dolſe de la morte del figliolo & uno di ſtette che nõ alumino el mondo cioe ſignifica che.xii.hore ſta rinchiuſo loſdegno dentro dila mẽte humana.peroche mentre che altri e i ſdegno ſono morte i lui le.vii. operẽ dila miſericordia:& ſono adormẽtati gli .v.ſenſi del corpo.Ma lomnipotẽte idio luſenga & comanda cħ lhuomo retorni i priſtino ſtato.luſenga p cħ adopera il libero arbitrio a ſpinger el male & adoperare el bene:comãda p che ogni generation humana & ogni altra creatura e tenuta ſequire lordine & lo piacere del ſumo creatore.

Cap. XIII.

De Ioue & Caliſto.

ANdando cuſi Ioue procurando come di ſopra edito:ando per archadia prouincia dedicata & data a Diana: de laquale edito auãti & cui prouedendo uide una donna dita Caliſtone;& ſi come lauide gli piaque & fu di lei inamorato:& lei andaua con larcho & con le ſaete imperoche lei era nimpha: laqual uedendo Ioue puoſe larco & le ſaete ſopra uno bello ceſpo di arbore Iupiter cio uedendo diſſe & preſe forma di Diana dea: &

Page with woodcut illustration from Ovid's *Metamorphoses*, Venice, 1501.

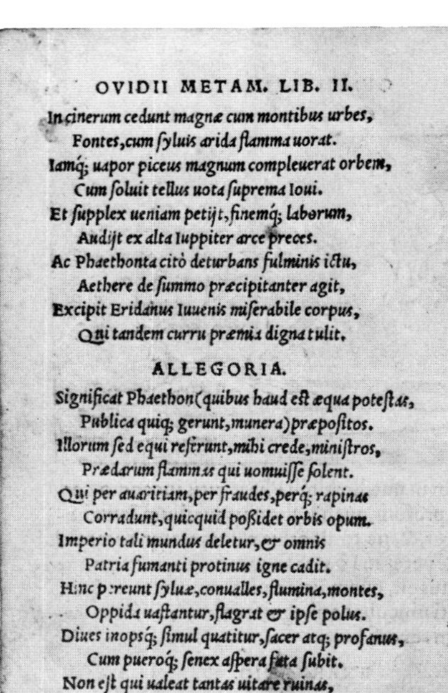

OVIDII METAM. LIB. II.

In cinerum cedunt magnæ cum montibus urbes,
Fontes, cum ſyluis arida flamma uorat.
Iamq; uapor piceus magnum compleuerat orbem,
Cum ſoluit tellus uota ſuprema Ioui.
Et ſupplex ueniam petijt, finemq; laborum,
Audijt ex alta Iuppiter arce preces.
Ac Phaethonta citò deturbans fulminis ictu,
Aethere de ſummo præcipitanter agit,
Excipit Eridanus Iuuenis miſerabile corpus,
Qui tandem curru præmia digna tulit.

ALLEGORIA.

Significat Phaethon (quibus haud eſt æqua poteſtas,
Publica quiq; gerunt, munera) præpoſitos.
Illorum ſed equi reſerunt, mihi crede, miniſtros,
Prædarum flammas qui uomuiſſe ſolent.
Qui per auaritiam, per fraudes, perq; rapinas
Corradunt, quicquid poßidet orbis opum.
Imperio tali mundus deletur, & omnis
Patria fumanti protinus igne cadit.
Hinc pereunt ſyluæ, conualles, flumina, montes,
Oppida uaſtantur, flagrat & ipſe polus.
Diues inopsq; ſimul quatitur, ſacer atq; profanus,
Cum pueroq; ſenex aſpera fata ſubit.
Non eſt qui ualeat tantas uitare ruinas,
Sic cum rege cohors ſubdita ſæpe perit.

Heliades

OVIDII METAM. LIB. II. 23

Heliades in arbores. IIII.

SOrores Phaetontis Heliades, miſerabilem fratris ſui caſum deflentes, Deorum benignitate ac miſericordia, in arbores populeas mutatæ, lachrymæ autem earum (ut & Heſiodus & Euripides fabulãtur) de ramis effluentes, atq; calore Solis induratæ, in Electrum conuerſæ ſunt. Item rex Lyguriæ Cygnus, Phaetonti propinquitate coniunctus, ad Pædi ripas, caſum amici deflens, in auem ſui nominis euaſit.

ENARRATIO.

INterea caſum Genitrix Phaethontis acerbum

◄ Phaëthon's sisters, the Heliades, transformed into poplars, from Ovid's *Metamorphoses*, Frankfurt, 1563. Woodcut by Johann Sprenger.

▼ Tomb of Phaëthon, with his sisters transformed into poplars and King Cycnus into a swan, from Ovid's *Metamorphoses*, Paris, 1767-1770.

Le Tombeau de Phaëton, auprès du quel ſes Sœurs furent changées en Peupliers, et le Roi Cycnus en Cygne.

MÉTAMORPHOSES. LIV. II. 121

FABLE III.

Les ſœurs de Phaëton métamorphoſées en arbres, & Cycnus en Cygne.

LES Nymphes de l'Heſpérie, après avoir rendu les derniers devoirs à Phaëton, mirent cette épitaphe ſur ſon tombeau :

Cy gît Phaëton qui conduiſit autrefois le Char du Soleil ſon père : malheureux dans l'exécution, la beauté d'une entrepriſe ſi noble & ſi hardie le juſtifie aſſez du mauvais ſuccès qui la ſuivit.

Cependant le Soleil, accablé de la douleur que lui cauſoit le malheur qui venoit d'arriver à ſon fils, ſe cacha ; &, s'il en faut croire la Tradition, il y eut un jour entier pendant lequel il n'éclaira point le Monde. L'embraſement ſervit de lumière, & ce fut le ſeul avantage que l'Univers tira de cet accident. Après que Clymène eut dit tout ce que la douleur inſpire dans des occaſions auſſi triſtes, elle s'arracha les cheveux, & courut de tous côtés pour chercher le corps, ou du moins les cendres de ſon fils. Enfin, ayant trouvé ſes os enſevelis ſur un rivage étranger, elle s'arrête près du tombeau qui les tient enfermés, mouille de ſes larmes le marbre où ſon nom étoit gravé, & tâche de l'échauffer en l'embraſſant. Les Héliades de leur côté font entendre leurs pleurs, leurs gémiſſemens, leurs cris, ſe meurtriſſent le ſein, & donnent toutes les autres marques de la plus vive douleur, (vaine & inutile conſolation pour ceux qui ne ſont plus !) Attachées jour & nuit au tombeau de leur frère, elles prononcent ſans ceſſe le triſte nom de Phaëton, qui ne peut plus entendre leurs regrets. Quatre mois s'étoient écoulés, & leur douleur, tournée en habitude, étoit encore auſſi vive que le premier jour, lorſqu'enfin Phaëtuſe, qui étoit l'aînée, voulant s'af-

Tome I. Q

attempts were made by late medieval churchmen to keep that reality from collapsing and impart to it for the last time some semblance of harmony. But the whole exercise proved in turn merely symbolic. What was the outcome of this breakdown of the old figuration? An ineluctable upsurge of figural realism on one side, but on another this battle had but one winner: the language. Bemused by the incredible variety of these emblems, extending to the genre aptly called "capriccio," many scholars have concluded that they were purely fanciful. This is only the fruit of our ignorance. This very variety had its point in the necessity for each individual to be able to interpret images in his own way. Each man became the arbiter of the signs and the image became polysemic. The emblem was meant to be obscure but not indecipherable; it was a game of hidden meanings. The emblem-maker had to press the image to the last degree of its possible meaning. The thread connecting the figure to its referent became ever thinner and snapped. The figure was then disfigured, set free from its terrestrial body; it still dreamed that it was a word. The universal was taken in tow by the particular. What was at stake in this crisis, contemporaneous with Mannerism, was the status of the sign and, beyond that, the status of the divinity who set it up.

Sebastian Brant's "Ship of Fools"

4
Der iſt eyn narr / der nit verſtot
So jm vnfall zů handen gat
Das er ſich wißlich ſchyck dar jn
Vnglück will nit verachtet ſyn

Verachtung vngfelles
Manchem iſt nit mit vnglück wol
Vnd ryngt dar noch doch yemer tol
Dar vmb ſoll er nit wunder han
Ob jm das ſchiff würt vndergan

1

3

2

The vogue for concrete, realistic representation in illustrating abstract moral precepts was not confined to the emblem books published mostly in Italy. The northern schools followed the same trend in the publication of books inspired by their own tradition. One of the most important was *Das Narrenschiff* (The Ship of Fools) by Sebastian Brant, first published at Basel in 1494 and soon followed by French, English and Latin versions. The theme of the "fool" provided abundant matter for the moral symbolism of the late Middle Ages, but it now took on a new dimension thanks to the expressive power of the woodcut illustration. The original German edition of Brant's book included 112 woodcuts, 73 of them attributable to Dürer, who worked for Brant at Basel in other ventures. As in the emblem books, each picture refers to a maxim, precept or proverb, which it sums up in concrete and particular terms. The picture contributes a realistic aspect, different from the universal, normative character of the text, which seems to have been much appreciated by the public. In contrast with Italy, these northern images seem to have been a didactic tool taking over directly from popular oral literature: they were intended for an unlettered public, which could be reached now by the woodcuts issued in their thousands. It was only later, with Erasmus's *Moriae encomium* (In Praise of Folly), that the theme was treated on a scholarly level for a public of intellectuals, but at first this famous book was not illustrated. The fashion for pictures prevailed, however, and the *Praise of Folly* found its illustrations, willy nilly, in the drawings which Holbein added in the margin of his copy of the book. ■

5

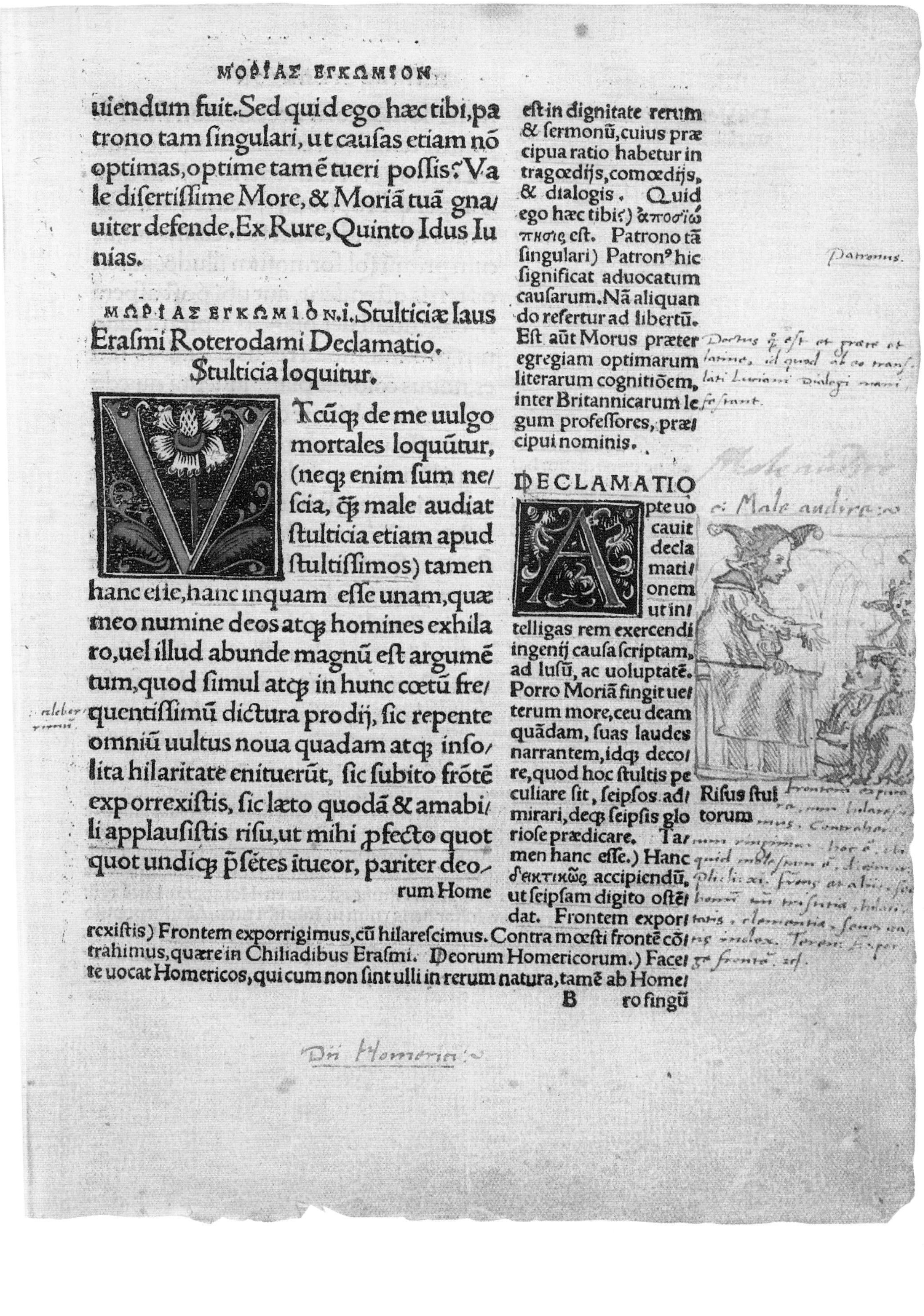

uiendum fuit. Sed quid ego hæc tibi, patrono tam singulari, ut causas etiam nō optimas, optime tamē tueri possis? Vale disertissime More, & Moriā tuā gnauiter defende. Ex Rure, Quinto Idus Iunias.

ΜΩΡΙΑΣ ΕΓΚΩΜΙΟΝ, i. Stulticiæ laus Erasmi Roterodami Declamatio.

Stulticia loquitur.

Tcūq; de me uulgo mortales loquūtur, (neq; enim sum nescia, q̄ male audiat stulticia etiam apud stultissimos) tamen hanc esse, hanc inquam esse unam, quæ meo numine deos atq; homines exhilaro, uel illud abunde magnū est argumētum, quod simul atq; in hunc cœtū frequentissimū dictura prodij, sic repente omniū uultus noua quadam atq; insolita hilaritate enituerūt, sic subito frōtē exporrexistis, sic læto quodā & amabili applausistis risu, ut mihi p̄fecto quotquot undiq; p̄sētes ĩtueor, pariter deorum Home

est in dignitate rerum & sermonū, cuius præcipua ratio habetur in tragœdijs, comœdijs, & dialogis. Quid ego hæc tibi?) ἀποσιώπησις est. Patrono tā singulari) Patron⁹ hic significat aduocatum causarum. Nā aliquando refertur ad libertū. Est aūt Morus præter egregiam optimarum literarum cognitiōem, inter Britannicarum legum professores, præcipui nominis.

DECLAMATIO

pte uocauit declamationem ut intelligas rem exercendi ingenij causa scriptam, ad lusū, ac uoluptatē. Porro Moriā fingit ueterum more, ceu deam quādam, suas laudes narrantem, idq; decore, quod hoc stultis peculiare sit, seipsos admirari, deq; seipsis gloriose prædicare. Tamen hanc esse.) Hanc δεικτικῶς accipiendū, ut seipsam digito ostēdat. Frontem expor

Risus stultorum

rexistis) Frontem exporrigimus, cū hilarescimus. Contra mœsti frontē cōtrahimus, quære in Chiliadibus Erasmi. Deorum Homericorum.) Facete uocat Homericos, qui cum non sint ulli in rerum natura, tamē ab Homero fingū

B

Sebastian Brant's Das Narrenschiff *(The Ship of Fools):*

1.2. *Strasbourg edition, 1512.*

3.4. *Basel edition, 1494.*

Woodcuts.

5. *Erasmus'* Moriae encomium *(In Praise of Folly), Basel edition, 1515, with Hans Holbein's marginal notes and drawings.*

1

HYPNEROTOMACHIE, OV

Diſcours du ſonge
DE POLIPHILE,

Deduiſant comme Amour le combat
à l'occaſion de Polia.

Soubz la fiction de quoy l'aucteur monſtrant que toutes choſes terreſtres ne ſont que vanité, traicte de pluſieurs matieres profitables, & dignes de memoire.

Nouuellement traduict de langage Italien en Francois.

A PARIS.
Pour Iaques Keruer à la Licorne, Rue S. Iaques.

M. D. LXI.

"The Dream of Polyphilus"

2

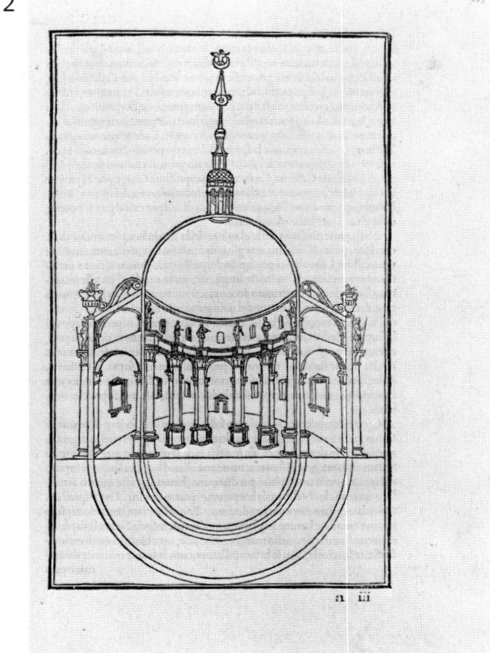

a iii

3

LIVRE PREMIER DE

Toute

4

POLIPHILE.

Il ne tarda gueres que le poure corps reuint entierement en ſon premier eſtat, & la coleur luy remonta au viſage. Mais ſur ces entrefaictes la Prieuſe du temple, qui (peut eſtre) auoit eſcouté mes plainctes, vint auec vne grãde trouppe de ſes religieuſes, leſquelles voyans noz priuautez illicites & interdictes en lieu ſainct, furent grieuement irritées, de maniere que à coups de baſton, accõpagnez d'iniures & reproches, elles deſmeſlerent & troublerent noz gracieux embraſſemens. Choſe qui me feit auoir peur qu'il ne m'aueint ainſi comme à Meduſe quand elle fut congneue de Neptune au temple de Minerue, ou cõme à Hippomanes & à s'amye Atalanta: leſquelz pour vn pareil cas furẽt trãſmuez en Lyons. A peine peuſmes nous eſchapper de leurs mains tant elles deſiroient à nous malfaire.

5

to optatiſſime carne ſentendo, nelle quale lalma ſua uigendo, ſe nutriua ſe euigiloe ſuſpirulante, & reaperte le occluſe palpebre. Et io repente audiſſima anhellando alla ſua inſperata reiteratione riceuute le debilitate & abandonate bracce, piamente, & cum dulciſſime & amoroſe lachrymule cum ſingultato pertractantilo, & manuagendulo, & fouente baſiantilo, præſentandogli, gli monſtraua il mio, Immo ſuo albente & pomigero pecto paleſemente, cum humaniſſimo aſpecto, & cum illici ochii eſſo ſécia uario di hora, riuéne nelle mie caſte & delicate bracce, Quale ſi læſione patito non haueſſe, & alquantulo reaſſumete il contaminato uigore, Como alhora ello ualeua, cum tremula uoce, & ſuſpiritti, manſuetamente diſſe, Polia Signora mia dolce, perche cuſi atorto me fai? Di ſubito, O me Nymphe celeberrime, me ſentiui quaſi de dolcecia amoroſa, & pietoſa. & exceſſiua alacritate il core p medio piu molto dilacerare, per che quel ſangue che per dolore, & nimia formidine in ſe era conſtricto p troppo & inuſitata lætícia, laxare le uene il ſentiua exhauſto, & tuta abſorta, & attonita ignoraua che me dire, Si non che io agli ancora pallidati labri, cum ſoluta audacia, gli offerſi blandicula uno laſciuo & muſtulento baſio, Ambi dui ſerati, & conſtrecti in amoroſi amplexi, Quali nel Hermetico Caduceo gli intrichatamente conuoluti ſerpi, & quale il baculo inuoluto del diuino Medico.

The *Hypnerotomachia Poliphili* or "Dream of Polyphilus" is unquestionably the most representative book of the humanist movement, both in its form and content. Published in 1499 by the great Venetian printer Aldus Manutius, it stands out first of all as a model of typography, for the elegance and clarity of its type and layout. It is the first book in which the printer seems to have had in mind the sensuous pleasure of the reader. The anonymous woodcut illustrations are designed in a spare, well-balanced, linear style, well suited to these architectural motifs and love processions. In them, the unknown artist evokes a lost paradise for which antiquity provided the ideal model, and there the reader wanders freely, among gardens, fountains, processions, amphitheatres, unfolding in a pagan ceremonial imbued with a mathematical grace. The text by the Dominican friar Francesco Colonna keeps to the tradition of symbolic journeys, combining in an overall harmony minute and frankly didactic descriptions (how to divide a circumference into twenty equal segments) with an erotic narration of charm and refinement (Polyphilus and Polia tied together by chains of flowers), carried sometimes to the point of sadism (naked girls cut to pieces and devoured by beasts). Imagination is enlisted in the service of science in fascinating accounts of architecture, where accuracy of description is combined with the idealized strain so characteristic of long passages of the story. At one point, as in science fiction, the door opens untouched by human hands, moved by a magnet and a mechanical device exactly described by the author. From this alliance of amorous allegory and geometry lessons arises an ambiguous fragrance of pleasure and necessity: never perhaps has the notion of sublimation been so attractively illustrated. ■

6

LIVRE PREMIER DE

Ainſi eſtoit accompagné Cupido triumphant,Polia & moy menez apres attachez à lyens de fleurs, & de cordes faictes de Roſes. Les Nymphes nous entretenoient de propoz amoureux,& courtoiſes parolles, en viſage ioyeux, accõpagné de bonne grace,comme pucelles humaines &gracieuſes.Finablemẽt en ce ſuperbe arroy &pompe magnifique marcha ce grand Seigneur,entre tant d'enſeignes de victoire ſuyuantes la banniere imperiale,au milieu de tant de muſique,parmy beaux roſiers,ſemé par deſſus des fleurs odorantes,& ſoubz la couuerture de tant de riches treilles, que nous peruimes àvne grãde place deuant la porte d'un excellent & merueilleux amphiteatre, tel qu'onques ne fut veu ſon pareil.C'eſtoit vn monſtre & prodige de ſtructure,&pluſtoſt ouurage diuin, que faict par mains d'ouuriers mortelz.Noſtre venue fut par la grand voye,au long de laquelle de chacun coſté y auoit des petitz tuyaux ſecretz qui iectoient inceſſamment eau muſquée, ſi perfecte que iamais plus doulce odeur ne fut ſentye. Quãd nous fumes arriuez à la porte de l'Amphitheatre,ie me prins à la contempler par le menu,pour deſcrire ſes particularitez.Elle eſtoit de pierre d'Azur: les baſes &les chapiteaux des colonnes de fin or eſpuré : l'architraue, la frize, la cornice,& le tympan du frontiſpice, de la meſme pierre d'Azur. Les coſtieres ou iambages qui ſouſtenoient l'arceau de l'ouuerture, d'Ophite : les colonnes miſes pour ornement aux deux coſtez, de Porphyre:& les ſuiuantes variées,aſauoir vne de pierre Serpentine,& l'autre de Porphyre.Les moyennes venant à plomb de celles de Porphyre, eſtoient d'Ophite:& les plus haultes de façon quarrées à la mode Athenienne, eſtoient

POLIPHILE. 122

eſtoient auſsi de beau Porphyre:diuerſifiant ainſi lesvnes au contraire des autres. Aux deux coſtez de la porte y auoit deux vaſes excellemmẽt riches, l'un de Saphyr,& l'autre d'Eſmeraude, entaillez par vn artifice admirable: qui me firent ſouuenir de ceux qui eſtoiẽt à l'entrée du temple de Iupiter en Athenes.

Lá deſcendit Cupido de ſon Char triumphant pour entrer en l'Amphitheatre ordonné en la maniere cy apres deduite.L'empietement, l'architraue, les baſes,les ſtylopodes,la frize, & les ceinctures faiſans le tour du baſtiment eſtoient de cuiure doré, & tout le reſte d'Albaſtre blanc & poly de nature,& par induſtrie.Il auoit par dehors deux ordres de colonnes, & deux voultures l'vne ſur l'autre. Les troiſiemes eſtoient pilliers quarrez, les voultures faictes en demycercle,auec addition d'une ſeptieme partie de leur largeur.Les colõnes appuyées à la muraille,ne ſortoient qu'a demy hors du maſsif, & eſtoient cannelées,& rudentées (c'eſt à dire à baſtons ou boudins) depuis le coleriz de leur aſsiette, iuſques à leur tierce partie. Les chapiteaux, baſes, & ſtylobates (autrement nommez piedeſtalz)eſtoient de cuiure doré. Aux angles d'iceux ſtylobates, ſpecialement au deſſoubz de leurs moulures, y auoit des teſtes de Mouton ſeiches auec leurs cornes ridées & rẽuerſées,eſquelles pendoient plusieurs beaux feſtons ou faiſſeaux de verdure, paſſans ſoubz vn rond faict au milieudu quarré rabaiſſé,& pareillement enclos de moulures, dedans lequel eſtoit taillé de demyboſſe vn ſacrifice Satyrique,ou auoit vn autel, & deſſus vn trepier,ſouſtenant vn vaſe d'Arain bouillant ſur le feu : & à chacun coſté de l'autel vne Nymphe nue ſoufflãt le feu auec vn petit tuyau. Aupres de l'au

X ij

1.3.4.6. *Francesco Colonna's* Hypnérotomachie ou Discours du songe de Poliphile *(The Dream of Polyphilus), Jacques Keruer, Paris, 1561. Anonymous woodcuts.*

2.5. *Francesco Colonna's* Hypnerotomachia Poliphili *(The Dream of Polyphilus), Aldo Manuzio, Venice, 1499. Anonymous woodcuts.*

II

The Order of the Text

O
D.II.

THE LANGUAGE OF TECHNICS

▲ Title page of Lorenz Stoer, *Geometria et Perspectiva*, Augsburg, 1567, with twelve woodcuts by Hans Rogel the Elder.

◄ Illustration from Wenzel Jamnitzer, *Perspectiva corporum regularium*, Nuremberg, 1568: Icosahedron, plate D.II.

Between the world of the manuscript and that of the printed book, the main revolution was not the invention of printing but the resulting shift in the status of the sign and its usage. Up to the sixteenth century, as pointed out by Michel Foucault (*Les Mots et les Choses*), the sign was still "natural": "Language is not an arbitrary system. It is deposited in the world and is a part of it both because things themselves conceal and manifest their enigma as a language and because words are proposed to men as a language to be deciphered." As we have seen, this irruption of the image into the book, imposing its meaning on the text, was due not only to a "semiotic" crisis but also to the ever more pressing need for pictures, in a world now coming under the control of empirical knowledge. The concrete world had to be made intelligible, things had to be described and delineated in order to be understood. By the seventeenth century this revolution was complete: "The sign did not silently wait for the coming of someone capable of recognizing it: it came into existence only by an act of knowledge" (Michel Foucault). The massive use of books as scientific tools—of books, compilations of signs elaborated by man and no longer the receptacle of revealed truths—meant the use not only of human speech but of explanatory figures and pictures. From an ornament, illustration became a necessity in order to know, to memorize, to produce. The spiritual content of the image was drained away, as it came to refer simply and solely to a coded reality. "Characteristically enough," writes Michel Foucault, "the first example of a sign given in the Port-Royal textbook on logic is not a word, not a cry, not a symbol, but the graphic representation of space—the drawing, as map or picture."

At a time when Latin was losing its privileged place as the universal language of scholarship, when knowledge was being spread mechanically by books and anonymously by the publishing business, illustration possessed one advantage over writing: it overleaped the language barrier. But what it offered above all was accuracy. It spoke the true language of empiricism and direct observation, and so it was made use of in books on mechanics (the first illustrated Italian book, Valturio's *De Re militari* of 1472, described engines of war), on optics, on astronomy. Accuracy with some illustrators was a mania. Thus, commenting on the illustrations he designed for his *Premier Tome de l'Architecture* (1567), Philibert Delorme complained of the distortions caused by the block-cutters who

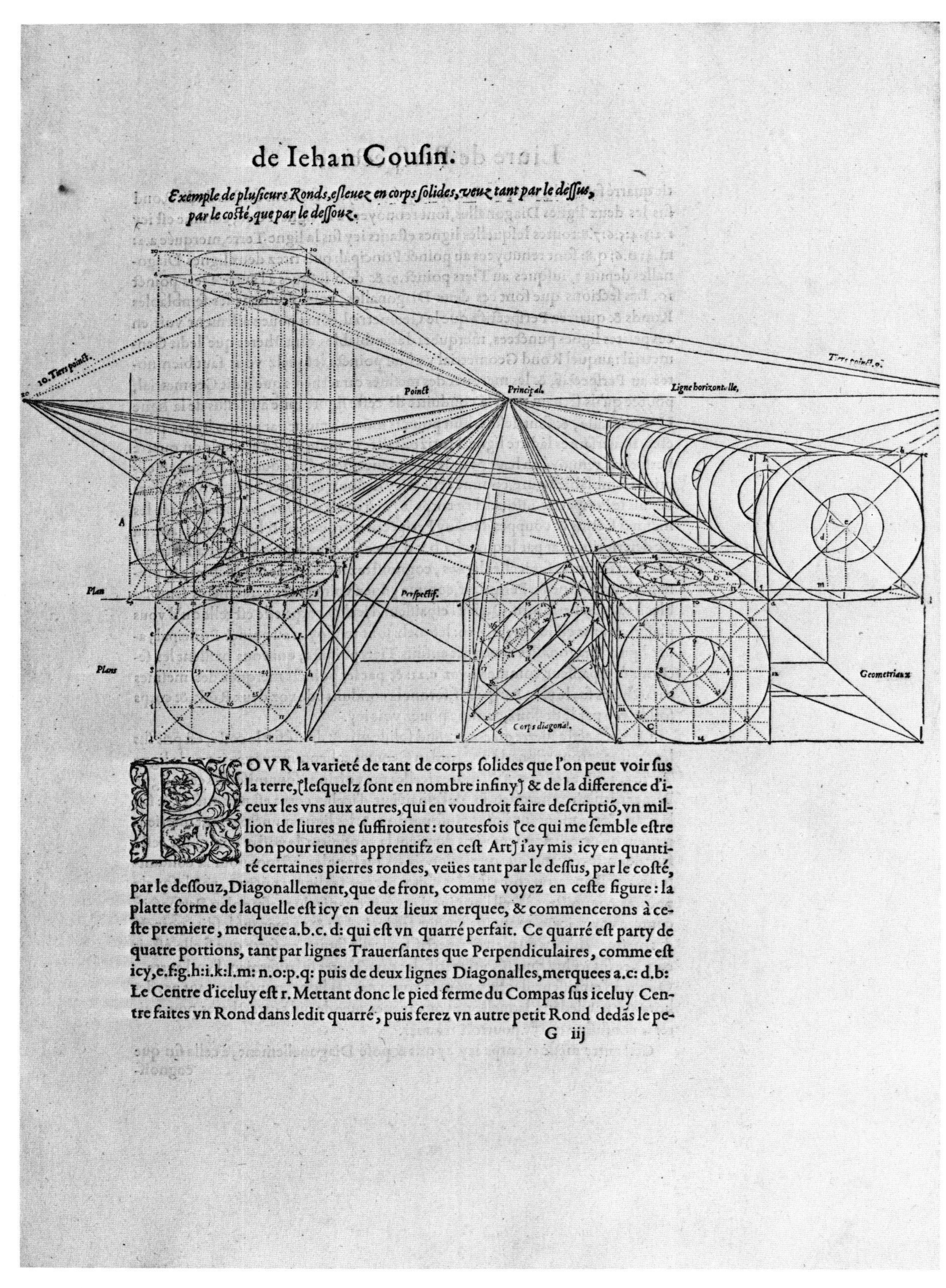

de Iehan Cousin.

Exemple de plusieurs Ronds, esleuez en corps solides, veuz tant par le dessus, par le costé, que par le dessouz.

POVR la varieté de tant de corps solides que l'on peut voir sus la terre, (lesquelz sont en nombre infiny) & de la difference d'iceux les vns aux autres, qui en voudroit faire descriptiõ, vn million de liures ne suffiroient : toutesfois (ce qui me semble estre bon pour ieunes apprentifz en cest Art) i'ay mis icy en quantité certaines pierres rondes, veües tant par le dessus, par le costé, par le dessouz, Diagonallement, que de front, comme voyez en ceste figure : la platte forme de laquelle est icy en deux lieux merquee, & commencerons à ceste premiere, merquee a.b.c. d: qui est vn quarré perfait. Ce quarré est party de quatre portions, tant par lignes Trauersantes que Perpendiculaires, comme est icy, e.f:g.h:i.k:l.m: n.o:p.q: puis de deux lignes Diagonalles, merquees a.c: d.b: Le Centre d'iceluy est r. Mettant donc le pied ferme du Compas sus iceluy Centre faites vn Rond dans ledit quarré, puis ferez vn autre petit Rond dedás le pe-

G iij

Jean Cousin the Elder, *Livre de perspective*, Paris, 1560: "Example of several rings, raised into solid bodies, seen from above, from the side and from below."

"wet and sometimes slightly seethe the paper of the initial design instead of pasting it on the block to guide them in their cutting." The basis of exact figuration was geometry, the science of proportions, and treatises on this subject number among the outstanding illustrated books of the sixteenth century. Luca Pacioli's *De divina proportione* (1509) and Dürer's *Vier Bücher von menschlicher Proportion* (1528) are landmarks. From this time on, when forms were reduced to the elements of the human body, itself systematically broken down into initial figures, there began to appear the masterworks of the mathematical illustrators of Nuremberg (capital of the transformation industry), of Hans Lencker, goldsmith at the court of Dresden, of Lorenz Stoer and his *Geometria et Perspectiva* of 1567, and—a piece of virtuoso work—Wenzel Jamnitzer's *Perspectiva corporum regularium* published at Nuremberg in 1568.

Illustration was also expected to spread the image abroad as a key to the text, permitting practical applications and imitations of it. It diffused designs and models

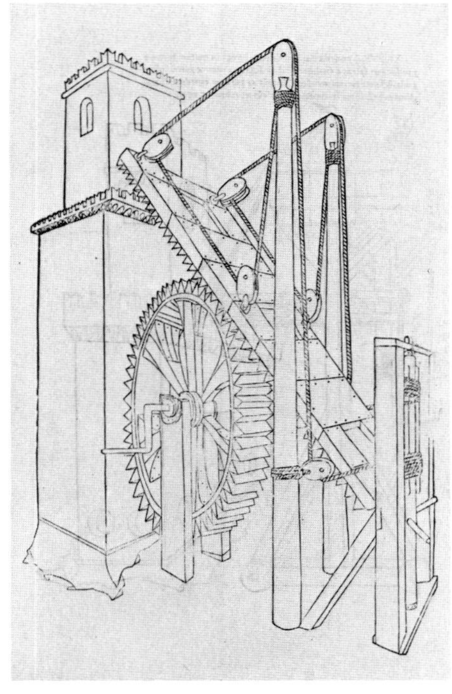

for the teaching of drawing and the generalized production of objects. One thinks for example of the astonishing output of books on linen drapery (114 of them in the Bibliothèque Nationale of Paris alone) by the Italian Federico di Vinciolo, who made them a speciality of his; or the pattern book on the same subject by the Italian Domenico da Sera, published in Paris by Jean de Marnef in 1584 with designs by Jean Cousin. The *Livre de pourtraiture* also by Jean Cousin, published in 1595, had gone through twenty-one editions by 1821; an abridgment of it by Bellay was published in Paris in 1930, by Delagrave, for the use of drawing classes. Ornament books covered a wide range of products, extending from geometric figures for illiterate embroiderers to sets of learned subjects for de-luxe tapestry cartoons. The illustrations of the *Dream of Polyphilus* provided designs for Bernini's obelisk in front of Santa Maria sopra Minerva, for the colonnade in the gardens of Versailles, for the bas-relief on a private house in Nantes, and for glazed tiles made at Poitiers.

Roberto Valturio,
De Re militari,
Verona, 1472, Book X:
Siege engine with cog-wheel,
woodcut by Matteo Pasti.

Lorenz Stoer,
Geometria et Perspectiva,
Augsburg, 1567,
woodcut by Hans Rogel
the Elder.

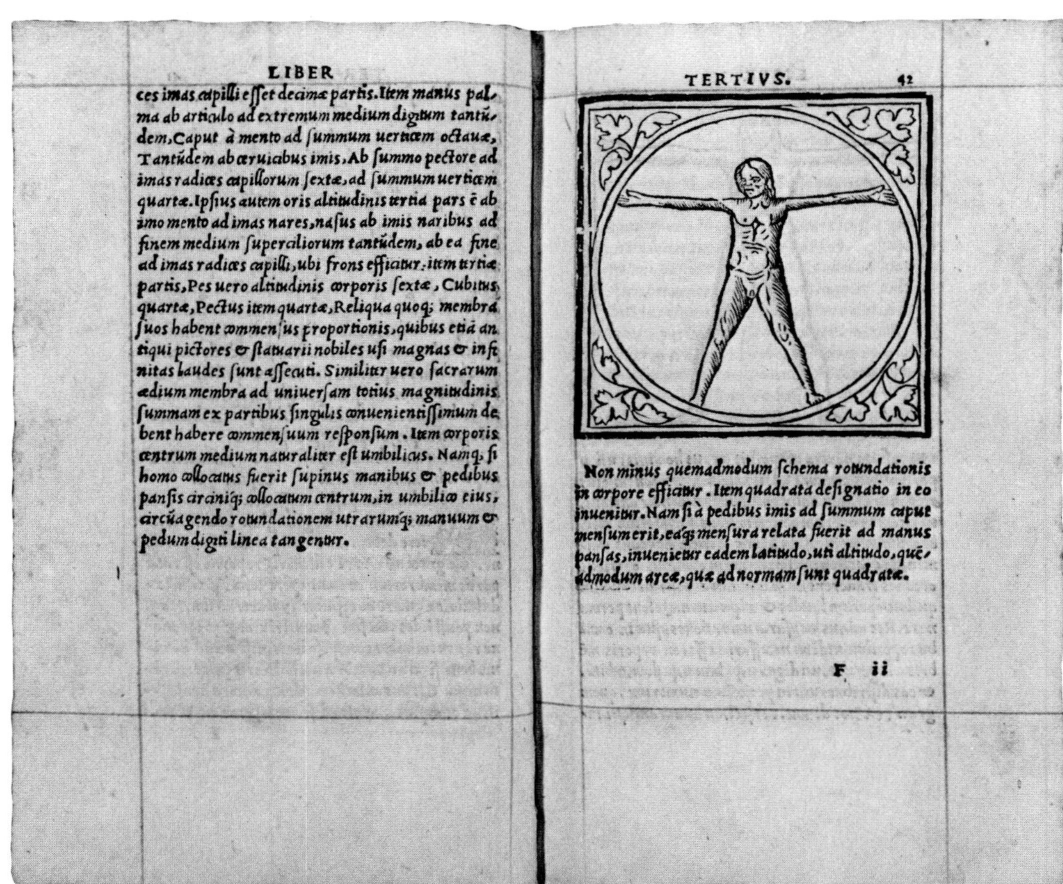
LIBER

ces imas capilli eſſet decimæ partis. Item manus palma ab articulo ad extremum medium digitum tantũdem, Caput à mento ad ſummum uerticem octauæ, Tantũdem ab ceruicibus imis. Ab ſummo pectore ad imas radices capillorum ſextæ, ad ſummum uerticem quartæ. Ipſius autem oris altitudinis tertia pars ẽ ab imo mento ad imas nares, naſus ab imis naribus ad finem medium ſuperciliorum tantũdem, ab ea fine ad imas radices capilli, ubi frons efficitur: item tertiæ partis, Pes uero altitudinis corporis ſextæ, Cubitus quartæ, Pectus item quartæ, Reliqua quoq; membra ſuos habent commenſus proportionis, quibus etiã antiqui pictores & ſtatuarii nobiles uſi magnas & infinitas laudes ſunt aſſecuti. Similiter uero ſacrarum ædium membra ad uniuerſam totius magnitudinis ſummam ex partibus ſingulis conuenientiſſimum debent habere commenſuum reſponſum. Item corporis centrum medium naturaliter eſt umbilicus. Namq; ſi homo collocatus fuerit ſupinus manibus & pedibus panſis circiniq; collocatum centrum, in umbilico eius, circũagendo rotundationem utrarumq; manuum & pedum digiti linea tangentur.

TERTIVS. 42

Non minus quemadmodum ſchema rotundationis in corpore efficitur. Item quadrata deſignatio in eo inuenitur. Nam ſi à pedibus imis ad ſummum caput menſum erit, eaq; menſura relata fuerit ad manus panſas, inuenietur eadem latitudo, uti altitudo, quẽadmodum areæ, quæ ad normam ſunt quadratæ.

F ii

Vitruvius, *De Architectura*, Florence, 1513, with woodcuts.

First French translation of Vitruvius by Jean Martin, Paris, 1547.

TROYSIEME LIVRE

eſtoien t tranſparentes & viſibles (comme Socrates le deſiroit) la flatterie ny l'ambition n'auroit plus de lieu: ains ſi aucuns peruenoient au ſouuerain degré de ſcience par extreme labeur & bonne conduitte, lon leur bailleroit de pleine volunté les ouurages a faire. Mais d'autãt que les fantaſies d'iceulx hommes ne ſont viſibles (comme dict eſt) ce qu'il me ſemble qu'elles deuroient eſtre: ie voy que les lourdaux ſurmontent les meilleurs ouuriers en grace & en faueur. Parquoy ie me reſoulz qu'il ne ſe fault amuzer a combatre ces groſſes beſtes, pour couuoytiſe de faire les ouurages, ains ayme trop mieulx par ces miens eſcriz faire apparoir quele eſt la vertu de ma ſcience.

En mon Premer liure (O Empereur) ie vous ay expoſé les proprietez de l'art, & dict les prerogatiues dont il doit eſtre accompagné: puis de queles doctrines eſt requis que l'Architecte ſoit muny: & ſi ay ſuradiouſté les cauſes pourquoy il fault qu'il ſoit ainſi. Apres ay diſtribué par partitions les diſcours du ſommaire d'Architecture, & l'ay determiné par diffinitions certaines. Conſequemment i'ay expoſé par quele induſtrie on peult elire des lieux ſalutaires pour y edifier: choſe qui eſt la principale & plus neceſſaire en ceſt endroict: & n'ay omis a dire quelz ſont les Ventz, & de queles contrees ilz ſoufflent, les repreſentant par pourtraict & figure. Oultre tout cela i'ay encores enſeigné par quel moyen ſe doyuent faire les diſtributions des places & des rues dedans l'enclos des murailles d'vne ville: et ainſi ay mis fin a mon dict Premier liure.

Au Second i'ay parlé de la matiere, & dict ſes vtilitez en baſtimés, meſmes queles ſingularitez la Nature luy a donnees: maintenant en ce Troyſieme ie traicteray des Temples conſacrez aux Dieux immortelz, donnant raiſon comment il les fault conduire pour venir a perfection d'ouurage.

DE LA COMPOSITION DES MAISONS *ſacrees, enſemble des ſymmetries du corps humain.* Chap. I.

LA compoſition des Temples conſiſte en ſymmetrie, delaquelle tous Architectes doyuent diligemment entendre le ſecret. Ceſte ſymmetrie eſt engendree de proportion, que les Grecz nomment Analogie.

Proportion eſt vn certain rapport & conuenance des membres ou particularitez a toute la maſſe d'vn baſtiment: & de ceſte la vient a ſe perfaire la conduitte d'icelles ſymmetries.

Or n'y a il ne Temple ny autre edifice qui puiſſe auoir grace de bonne ſtructure ſans ſymmetrie & proportion, & ſi la conuenance n'eſt gardee en toutes ſes parties auſſi bien qu'en vn corps humain perfectement formé.

CE corps humain a eſté compoſé de la Nature par vn tel artifice, que depuis le bout de ſon menton iuſques au plus hault de ſon front, ou eſt la racine de ſes cheueux, cela faict vne dixieme partie de ſon eſtendue. Autant en emporte la longueur de la main depuis le ply par ou elle ioinct au bras, iuſques a l'extremité du doy du mylieu. Toute la teſte a prendre depuis le bout du ſuſdict menton iuſques a la ſommité du teſt, contient vne huytieme partie: & autant en deuallant par derriere iuſques a la fin du col. Depuis le hault de la poytrine iuſques aux plus baſſes racines des cheueux, c'eſt vne ſixieme portiõ: & ſi lon mõte iuſques au plus hault du teſt, elle vault iuſtement vne quarte.

Quant a la

DE VITRVVE. 28

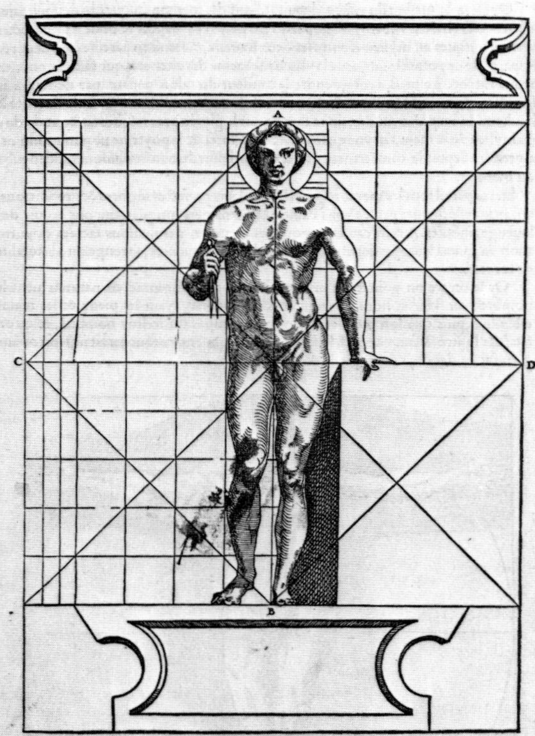

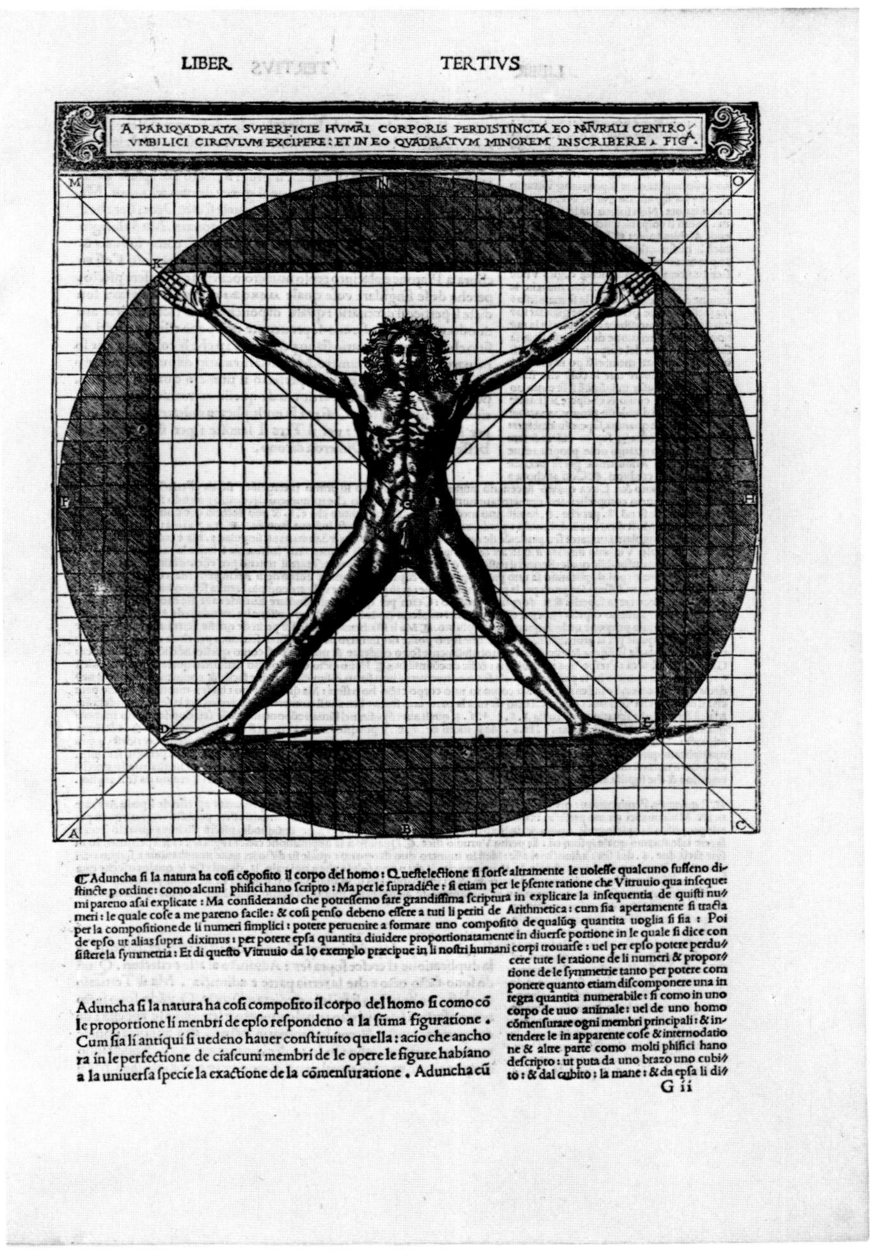

LIBER TERTIVS

A PARIQVADRATA SVPERFICIE HVMĀI CORPORIS PERDISTINCTA EO NĀTVRALI CENTRO VMBILICI CIRCVLVM EXCIPERE: ET IN EO QVADRATVM MINOREM INSCRIBERE. FIG. A.

¶ Aduncha ſi la natura ha coſi cōpoſito il corpo del homo: Queſte lectione ſi forſe altramente le uoleſſe qualcuno fuſſeno diſtincte p ordine: como alcuni phiſici hano ſcripto: Ma per le ſupradicte: ſi etiam per le pſente ratione che Vitruuio qua inſeque: mi pareno aſai explicate: Ma conſiderando che potreſſemo fare grandiſſima ſcriptura in explicare la inſequentia de quiſti numeri: le quale coſe a me pareno facile: & coſi penſo debeno eſſere a tuti li periti de Arithmetica: cum ſia apertamente ſi tracta per la compoſitione de li numeri ſimplici: potere peruenire a formare uno compoſito de qualūq quantita uoglia ſi ſia: Poi de epſo ut alias ſupra diximus: per potere epſa quantita diuidere proportionatamente in diuerſe portione in le quale ſi dice conſiſtere la ſymmetria: Et di queſto Vitruuio da lo exemplo præcipue in li noſtri humani corpi trouarſe: uel per epſo potere perducere tute le ratione de li numeri & proportione de le ſymmetrie tanto per potere componere quanto etiam diſcomponere una integra quantita numerabile: ſi como in uno corpo de uuo animale: uel de uno homo cōmenſurare ogni membri principali: & intendere le in apparente coſe & internodatione & altre parte como molti phiſici hano deſcripto: ut puta da uno brazo uno cubito: & dal cubito: la mane: & da epſa li di-

Aduncha ſi la natura ha coſi compoſito il corpo del homo ſi como cō le proportione li menbri de epſo reſpondeno a la ſūma figuratione. Cum ſia li antiqui ſi uedeno hauer conſtituito quella: acio che anchora in le perfectione de ciaſcuni membri de le opere le figure habiano a la uniuerſa ſpecie la exactione de la cōmenſuratione. Aduncha cū

G ii

First Italian translation of Vitruvius
by Cesare Cesariano, Como, 1521

The most direct and also the most sophisticated use of geometric figures is to be found in the books on architecture, which form one of the most attractive groups of sixteenth-century illustrated books. The first great Renaissance treatise on architecture, by Leon Battista Alberti (1485), was not illustrated in its initial Latin text; in its Italian translation by Bartoli, published sixty years later, it was. The same is true of the early editions of Vitruvius. But here the illustrations appeared sooner, figuring already in Fra Giocondo's Venice edition of 1511 and more notably in the first Italian translation by Cesare Cesariano, published at Como in 1521. It was not until the middle of the sixteenth century that illustration can be said to be organically integrated into the architectural treatise. For by then architecture had moved on from dogmatic theory to human practice. One finds indeed that, besides being more alive to illustration, architectural theorists were introducing practical recommendations. Thus in the books of Sebastiano Serlio (from 1545 on) the illustrations are closely associated with the text, which itself has taken a more concrete turn, allotting more space for example to private houses and showing an interest, in Book VI, in all social categories, with sixty-two plates (whose first state was recently rediscovered in Vienna). Then came the great undertakings: Jean Martin's French translation of Vitruvius, with lavish illustrations based on the plates of Fra Giocondo and Serlio; and after 1560 the books of Philibert Delorme. While illustrating them carefully and extensively, Delorme also takes up the human, social and moral problems of architecture, taking account, for example, of the client's status and the relations which the architect should maintain with him. Illustrations then were not only a means of achieving accuracy; they also stemmed from a practical, pedagogical and philosophical approach to architecture. The builder's techniques had to be worked out by man, for man, and the text figure eliminated whatever was vague or uncertain in the words. As such, illustration proved indispensable. The figures drawn by the humanist mathematicians are like maps drawn up by explorers: a reconquest of space by man.

This reconquest of space affected the actual tool of abstract knowledge, in the very place where it was set down: writing. There can be no understanding the passionate interest taken by the Renaissance humanists in Roman epigraphy, and the historical importance of their remodelling of the alphabet, if these things are seen merely as a matter of order and policing. True, the use of movable type called for standardized alphabets, and the book-reading public extending to ever wider circles called for easily readable type. But there was more to it than this: through the letter, through the printing type, the whole language was involved. Antique inscriptions fascinated scholars both as historical evidence and as graphic work. Compilations of Latin inscriptions were published very early (the first at Venice in 1489) and scholars such as Alberti and Fra Giocondo studied them as architects rather than historians. Pattern books explaining how to form these letters geometrically soon began appearing; the earliest is that of Felice Feliciano. Then came the theorists: Luca Pacioli and his *De divina proportione* in 1509, Sigismondo Fanti and his *Theorica et Practica* in 1514, and above all the *Champfleury* by a scholar of Bourges, Geoffroy Tory, published in 1529. This last was a compilation of elegant lettering: "In it are contained the art and science of the right and true proportions of antique letters and in common parlance roman letters, in relation to the human body and face." In spite of its flowery title (chosen "for the grace and sweetness of the name"), Tory's book is an abstract of Renaissance humanism and a tribute to Dürer, in which such names as Leonardo da Vinci, Euclid, Erasmus, Plato, Michelangelo and Pythagoras are also cited. It is also a "defence and illustration of the French language," an endeavour to rehabilitate accents and cedillas, nationalizing and rationalizing the language as against Latin and current jargons.

The importance of this book lies in the fusion it achieves between phonetics and geometry, at the only point where such a fusion was possible: the actual letter, as the work of both linguist and architect, when the language itself became architecture. The human mastery of this design and architecture went far to justify the conviction that man was master of his language.

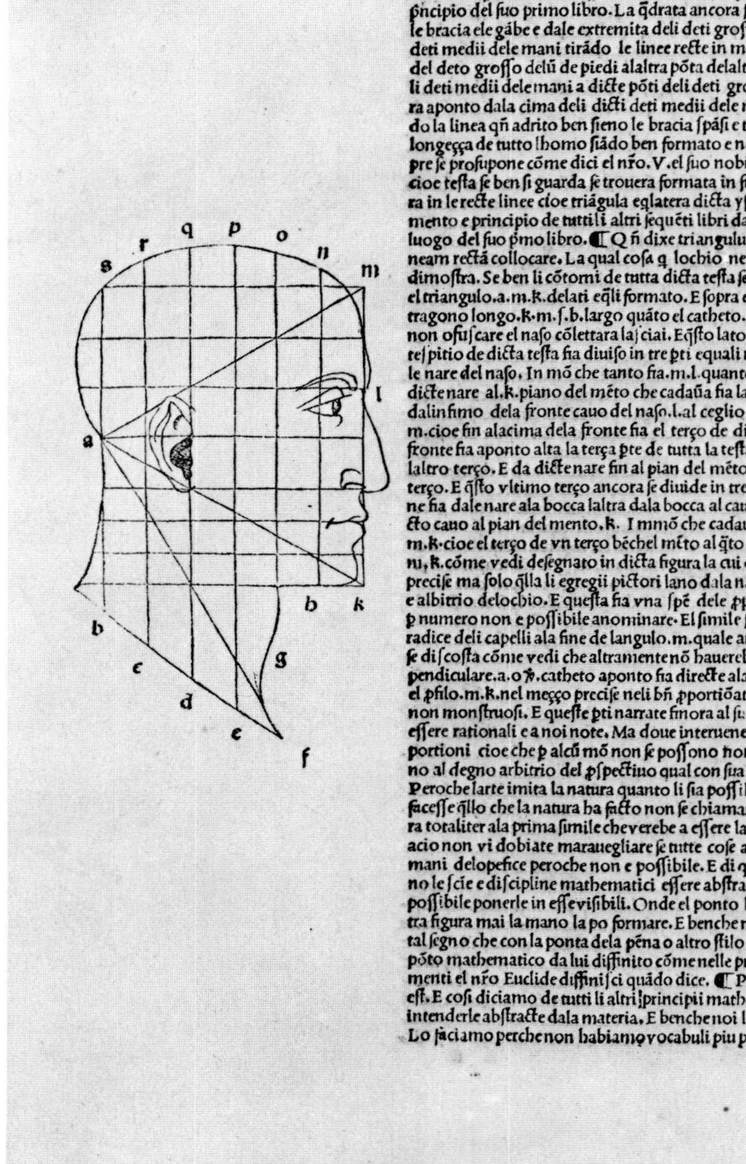

PARS

deli deti medii dele mani e quelle deli deti grossi deli piedi che sono cō
dictiōi reqsite ala vera diffinitiōe del cerchio posta dal nr̃o Euclide nel
ꝑncipio del suo primo libro. La q̃drata ancora se hauera spansi similmēte
le bracia ele gābe e dale extremita deli deti grossi de piedi ale ponti deli
deti medii dele mani tirādo le linee recte in mō che tanto fia dala pōta
del deto grosso delū de piedi alaltra pōta delaltro pede quāto dalacia de
li deti medii dele mani a dicte pōti deli deti grossi deli piedi e tāto anco
ra aponto dala cima deli dicti deti medii dele mani da luno a laltro tirā
do la linea qñ adrito ben sieno le bracia spāsi e tāto apōto fia lalteçça o ꝓ
longeçça de tutto lhomo siādo ben formato e nō mōstruoso che cosi sem
pre se prosupone cōme dici el nr̃o. V. el suo nobilissimo mēbro exteriore
cioe testa se ben si guarda se trouera formata in su la forma dela ꝑma figura in le recte linee cioe triāgula eqlatera dicta ysopleuros posta per fonda
mento e principio de tutti li altri sequēti libri dal nr̃o Euclide nel primo
luogo del suo ꝑmo libro. ¶ Q ñ dixe triangulum eqlateꝝ supra datam li
neam rectā collocare. La qual cosa q locchio nella pñte figura chiaro vel
dimostra. Se ben li cōtorni de tutta dicta testa se cōsidera. Cōme vedete
el triangulo. a. m. k. de lati eq̃li formato. E sopra el lato suo. m. k. fatto el te
tragono longo. k. m. f. b. largo quāto el catheto. a. ala basa. m. k. qual per
non ofuscare el naso cōlettara lasciai. Eq̃sto lato. m. k. qual fia tutto el frō
tespitio de dicta testa fia diuiso in tre ꝑti equali nel ponto. l. e termino de
le nare del naso. In mō che tanto fia. m. l. quanto dal. l. a dicte nare. E da
dicte nare al. k. piano del mēto che cadaūa fia la terça ꝑte del. m. k. Onde
dal infimo dela fronte cauo del naso. l. al ceglio fin ale radici de capelli.
m. cioe fin ala cima dela fronte fia el terço de dicto lato. m. k. siche la sua
fronte fia aponto alta la terça ꝑte de tutta la testa el naso similmēte ne fia
laltro terço. E da dicte nare fin al pian del mēto. h. o ꝓ. k. ne fia vnaltro
terço. E q̃sto vltimo terço ancora se diuide in tre altre ꝑti equali che luna
ne fia dale nare ala bocca laltra dala bocca al cauo del mēto la terça da di
cto cauo al pian del mento. k. Immō che cadauna fia el nono de tutta
m. k. cioe el terço de vn terço bēche el mēto al q̃to deuii dal ꝓfilo dela facia
m. k. cōme vedi desegnato in dicta figura la cui quantita a noi nō e nota
precise ma solo q̃lla li egregii pictori lano dala natura reseruata ala gratia
e albitrio delochio. E questa fia vna spē dele ꝓportioni irrationali qual
ꝑ numero non e possibile a nominare. El simile se dici dela distantia dala
radice deli capelli ala fine de langulo. m. quale ancora al quanto da q̃llo
se discosta cōme vedi che altramente nō hauerebe gratia alochio. E la ꝑ-
pendiculare. a. o ꝓ. catheto aponto fia directe ala tomba del naso e taglia
el ꝓfilo. m. k. nel meçço precise neli bñ ꝓportiōati e debitamēte disposti e
non monstruosi. E queste ꝑti narrate finora al suo ꝓfilo tutte vengano a
essere rationali e a noi note. Ma doue interuene la irrationalita dele pro
portioni cioe che ꝑ alcū mō non se possono nominare per numero resta
no al degno arbitrio del ꝓspectiuo qual con sua gratia le ha a terminare.
Peroche larte imita la natura quanto li sia possibile. E se apōto larteficio
facesse q̃llo che la natura ha facto non se chiamaria arte ma vnaltra natu
ra totaliter ala prima simile che verebe a essere la medesima. Questo dico
acio non vi dobiate marauegliare se tutte cose aponto non rñdano ale
mani delopefice peroche non e possibile. E di qua nasci che li sauii dica
no le scie e discipline mathematici essere abstracte e mai actualiter nō e
possibile ponerle in esse visibili. Onde el ponto linea superficie e ognal-
tra figura mai la mano la po formare. E benche noi chiamamo ponto q̃l
tal segno che con la ponta dela pēna o altro stilo si facia non e quello ꝑo
pōto mathematico da lui diffinito cōme nelle prime parolle deli suoi ele
menti el nr̃o Euclide diffinisci quādo dice. ¶ Pūctus est cuius pars non
est. E cosi diciamo de tutti li altri principii mathematici e figure douerse
intenderle abstracte dala materia. E benche noi li diciāo ponto linea &c.
Lo faciamo perche non habiamo vocabuli piu proprii a exprimer lor cō

Luca Pacioli,
De divina proportione,
Venice, 1509, fol. 25v.

1

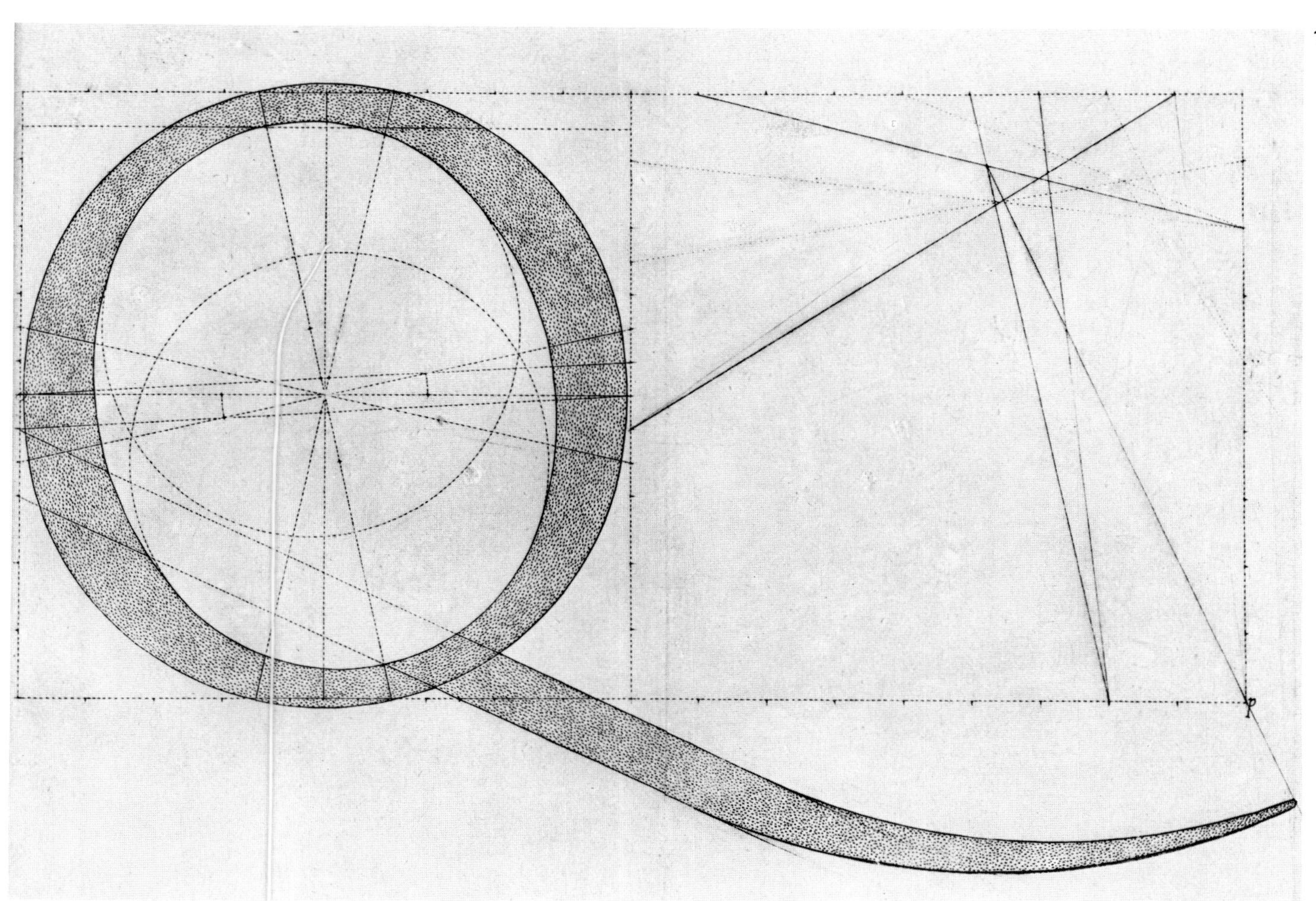

1. Shaping of the letter Q in Cesare Domenichi, *Delle Lettere Nominate Maiuscole Antiche Romane. Trattato Primo*, Rome, 1602.

2. Shaping of the letter Q in G.B. Verini, *Luminario*, Toscolano, 1527.

3. Shaping of the letter Q in Geoffroy Tory, *Champfleury*, Paris, 1529.

2

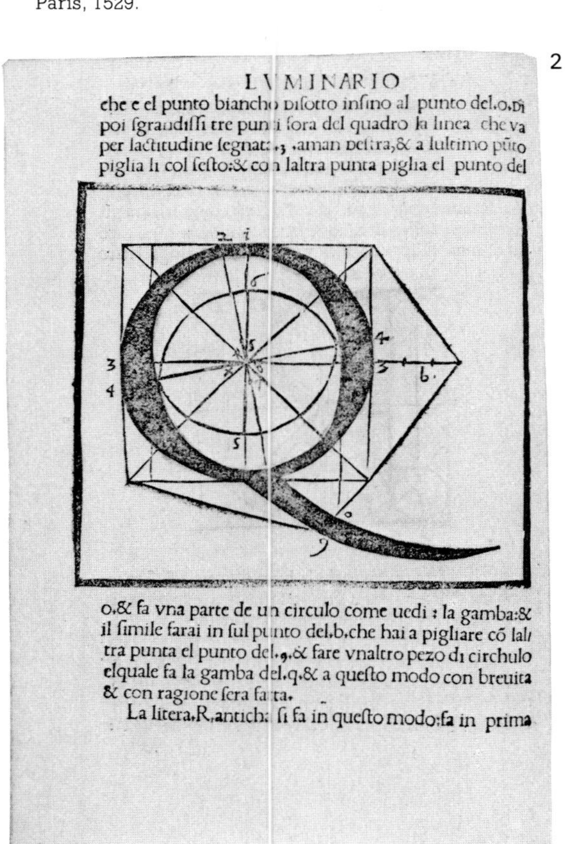

LVMINARIO

che e el punto biancho disotto insino al punto del.o.Di poi sgrandissi tre punti fora del quadro la linea che va per lactitudine segnata.3.aman destra,& a lultimo pũto piglia li col sesto:& con laltra punta piglia el punto del

o.& fa vna parte de un circulo come uedi : la gamba:& il simile farai in sul punto del.b.che hai a pigliare cõ lal/tra punta el punto del.9.& fare vnaltro pezo di circhulo elquale fa la gamba del.q.& a questo modo con breuita & con ragione sera fatta.

La litera.R.anticha si fa in questo modo:fa in prima

3

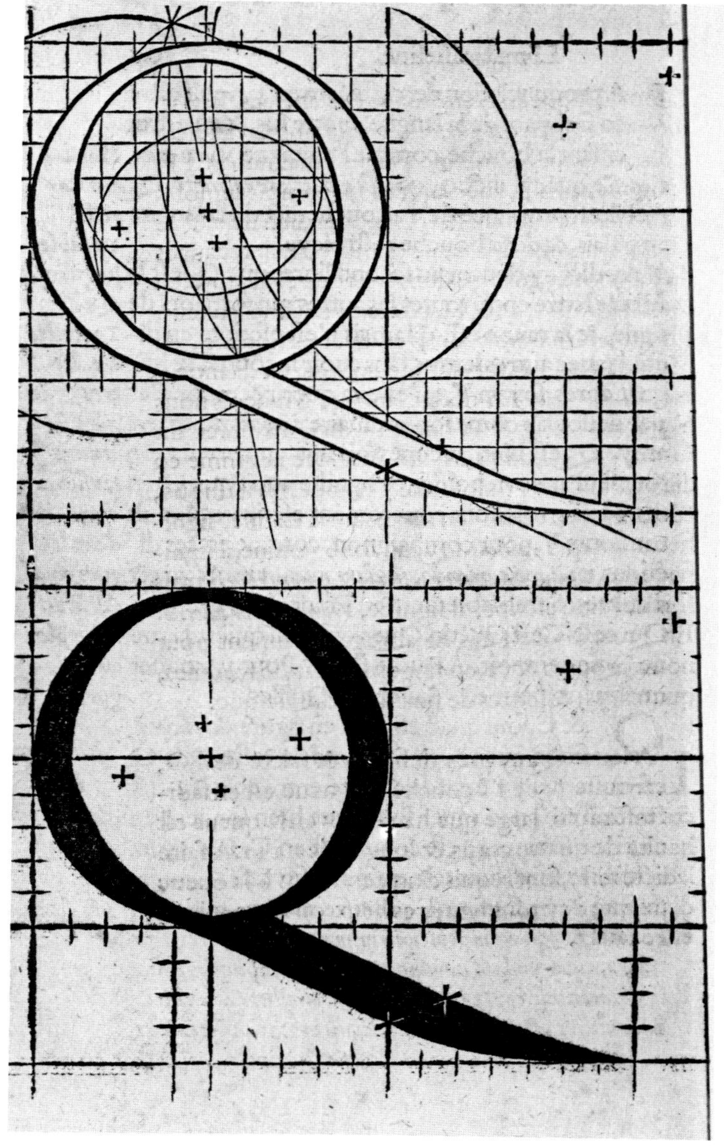

The "De humani corporis fabrica" of Vesalius

1

2

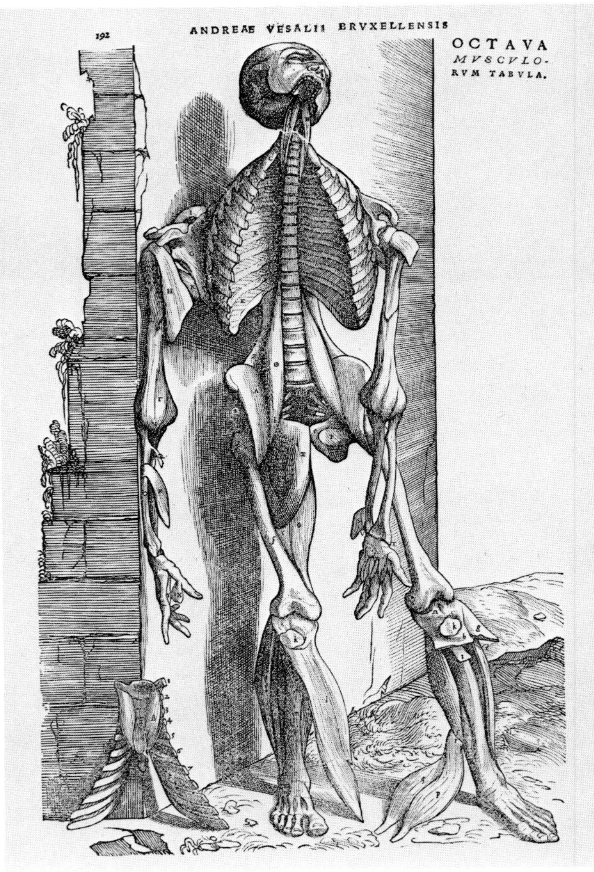

4

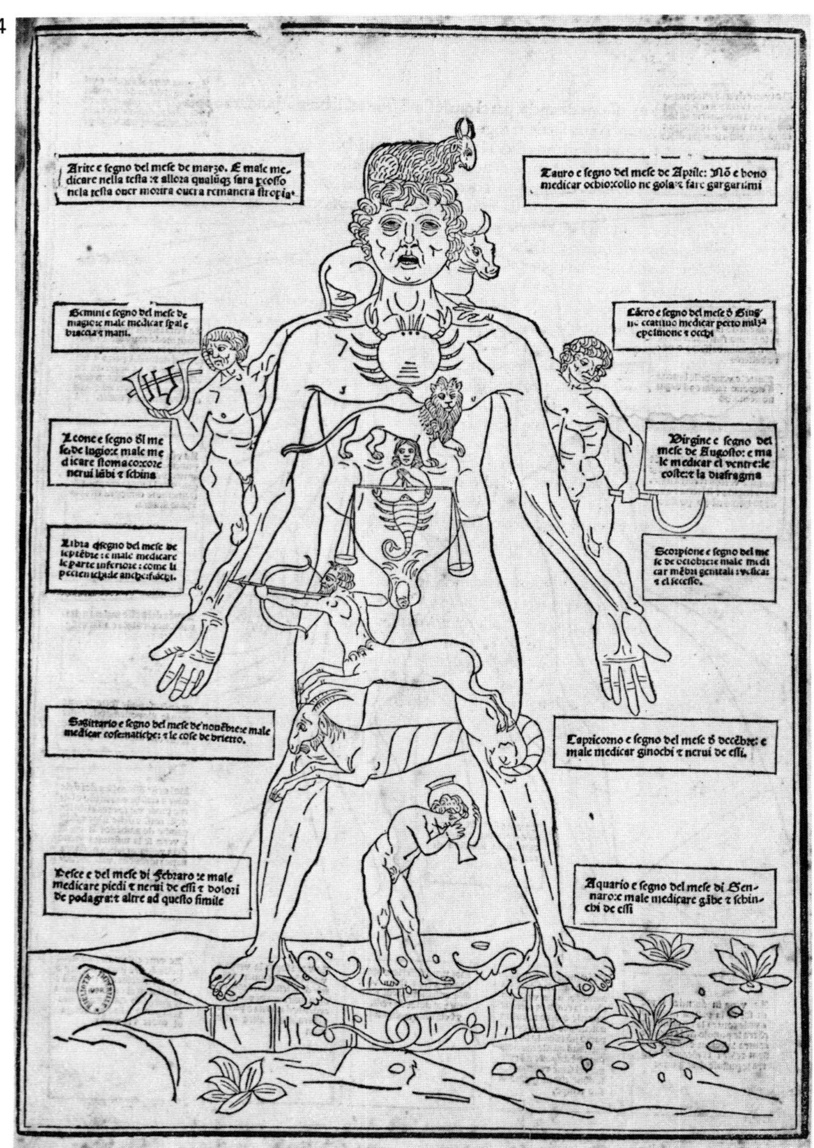

The illustration of medical books, as it evolved in the fifteenth and sixteenth centuries, shows clearly the radical shift that occurred in the role of the image, which changed its references completely. Medieval medicine, like all sciences at that time, was a matter of dogma. The human body was not studied for its own sake: it was seen as reflecting a pre-established cosmic harmony. Such for example is the diagram of the "zodiac man" which appeared in the first printed handbooks of Georg Reich and Joannes de Ketham (1491), and which to us now looks more like a figure of chiromancy than an anatomical study. But the anatomical theatre in Padua was opened in 1490 and the empirical study of the human body began taking over from earlier conceptions. No longer seeking to interpret the body by way of the Scriptures but simply describing what he saw, the surgeon needed realistic, empirical representations in which perspective played no less a part than in architecture. In this new order of things the great work on human anatomy was the *De humani corporis fabrica* of Andreas Vesalius (first edition, 1543; second edition with new plates, 1555). The surgeon, who before had preached from a pulpit, now came down to the operating table; and instead of listening, his students watched. The illustrations of Vesalius' book are so fine, so remarkable for the care and accuracy that went into them, that they were once attributed to Titian, then to his studio; actually they were designed by a Dutch pupil of Titian's, Stephan van Calcar.

But the artist and the doctor did not in fact speak the same language. Several prominent surgeons refused to make use of pictures, knowledge in this field being essentially tactile and at that time owing nothing to the practice of dissection. Such pictures therefore seem to have been used more by artists and scholars in other disciplines than by doctors themselves. This goes to remind us of the long prevailing symbolic character of the image, of any image, however realistic. The realism achieved through perspective was also a code, still beyond the grasp of many. ■

3

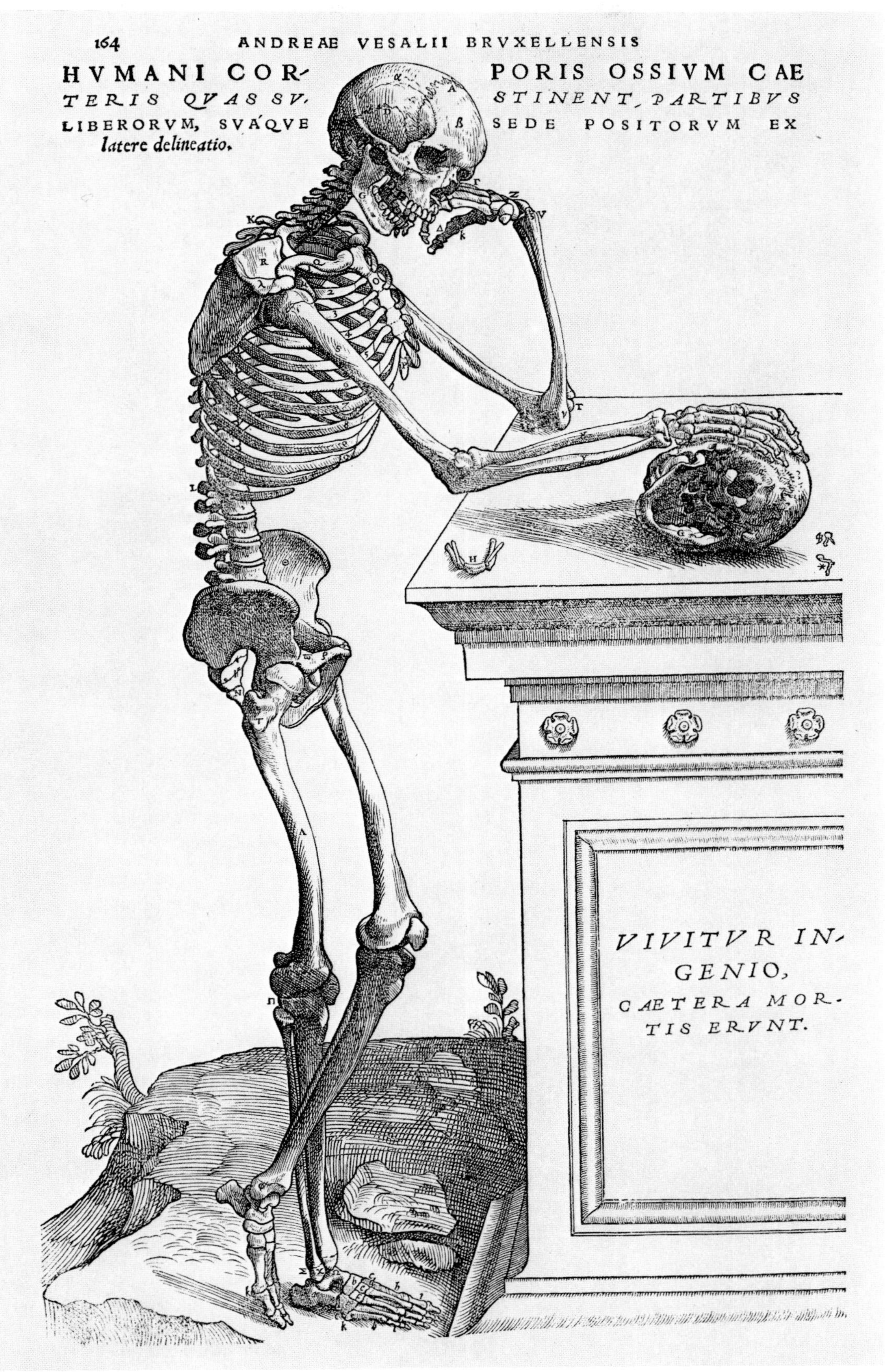

Andreas Vesalius, De humani corporis fabrica, *first edition, Basel, 1543, with woodcuts designed by Stephan van Calcar:*

1. *Title page.*
2. *Plate showing muscles.*
3. *Skeleton meditating on a skull lying on a funerary monument, with Latin inscription: "Man lives by his mind. The rest is doomed to death."*
4. *Joannes de Ketham,* Fasciculus Medicinae, *Venice, 1493 (first edition 1491): Zodiac man.*

The "Codex Atlanticus" of Leonardo da Vinci

1

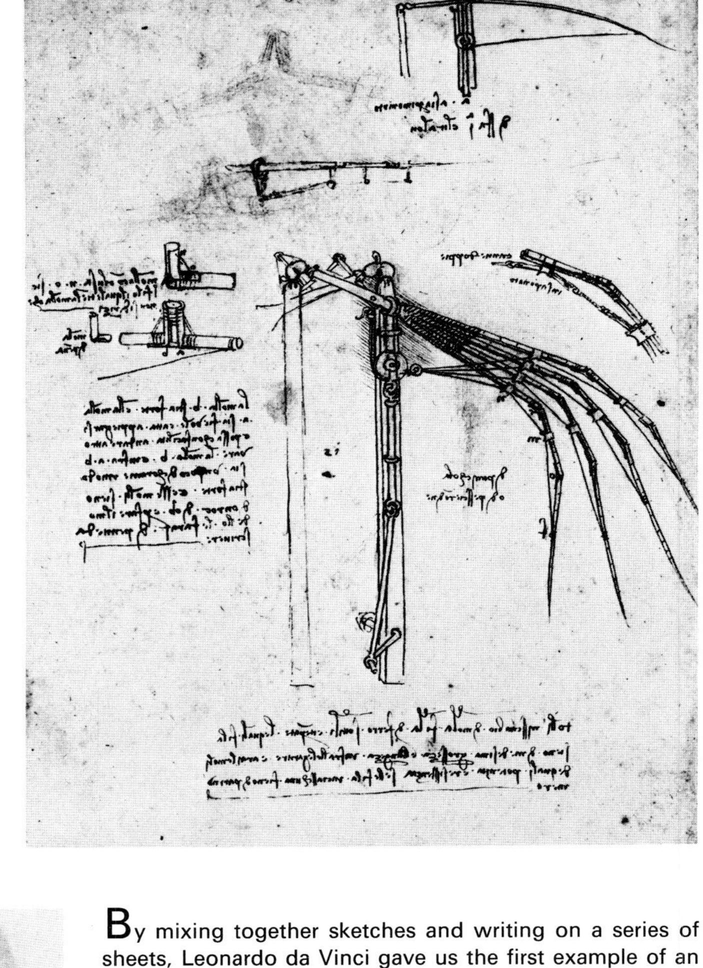

Leonardo da Vinci, Codex Atlanticus*:*

1. *Device with spring release, fol. 308 recto a.*
2. *Wire-drawing machine driven by a hydraulic wheel, fol. 2 recto a.*
3. *Drawings of pulleys, fol. 155 verso b.*
4. *Designs for a small fort, fol. 48 recto a.*

2

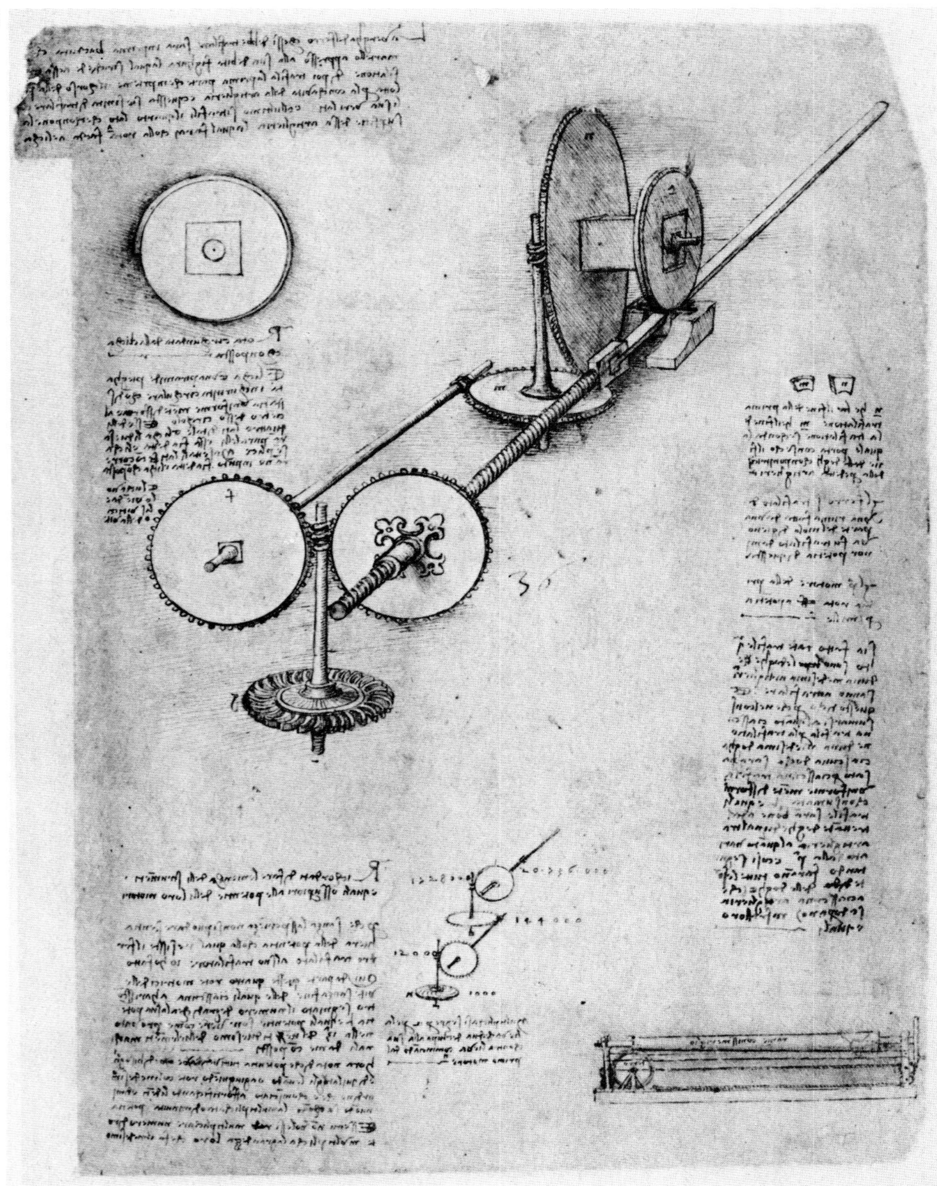

By mixing together sketches and writing on a series of sheets, Leonardo da Vinci gave us the first example of an "artist's notebook." He initiated his contemporaries into the method of visual and logical explanation which culminated in the modern encyclopaedia. He stands out from his time as an empiricist whose ultimate reference was always to reality. Observation, description and delineation were for him the indispensable groundwork of knowledge. His writings are scrupulously explanatory and he avoided philosophical speculation: "All it eternally gives us is a noise." He had little use for general ideas, and as a man of positive mind he considered things under their own peculiar aspect with a view to drawing practical conclusions from them. He studied smoke fumes hoping to make them turn a roasting spit; the fall of a leaf as a clue to flight; eddying water as a driving force to be used. For though he invented many of the mechanical devices of the modern world, he had no engine to drive them and his search for energy verged on an obsession. He only began to keep such notebooks at the age of thirty, during his stay in Milan, after 1482. The most extensive collection of them, the *Codex Atlanticus*, contains about four thousand sheets; thirteen further notebooks are in the library of the Institut de France, Paris, and further sheets are preserved in London, Tunis and at Windsor Castle; others were lost when Leonardo's manuscripts were dispersed by the son of Francesco Melzi, the friend and disciple to whom he had bequeathed them. Two further manuscripts came to light in Madrid in the 1960s. They are the work of an observer intent on accumulating ideas rather than classifying them, of a man with a mania for precision which, he found, could best be expressed by drawing. He was nevertheless a genuine writer. Witness this passage in which he compares the merits of drawing and writing and heralds the modern viewpoint that sees in any medium of knowledge a means of production: "If you historiographers, poets or mathematicians have never seen things with your own eyes, you will be hard put to it to set them forth in your writings. And if you, poet, depict a story with your pen, the painter represents it with his brush in a manner more satisfactory and less tedious to understand. As you call painting 'mute poetry,' so may the painter call the poet's art 'blind painting.' Consider then which is the greater affliction, being blind or mute?... Consider then what is most essential to man, his name or his image?" ■

3

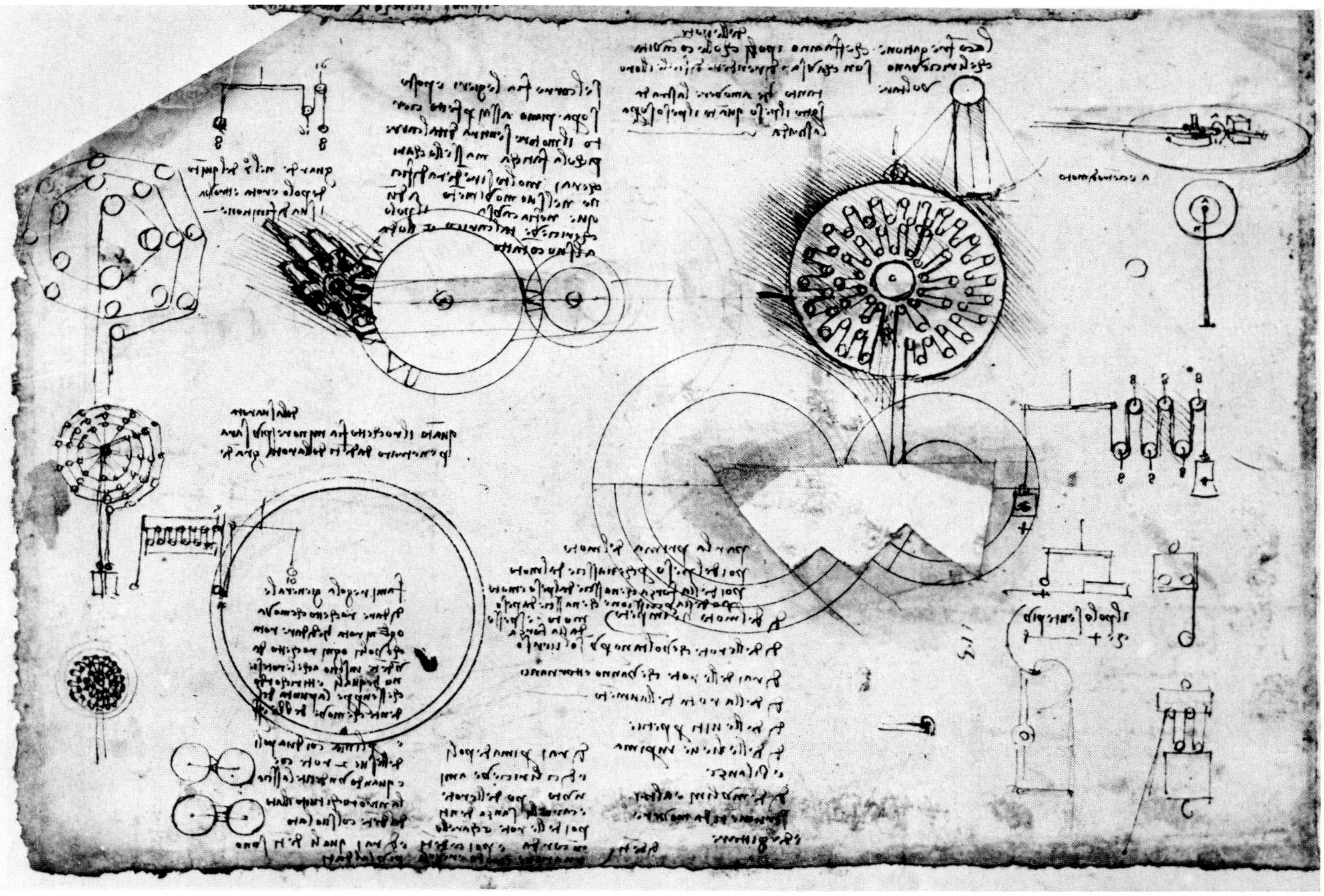

4

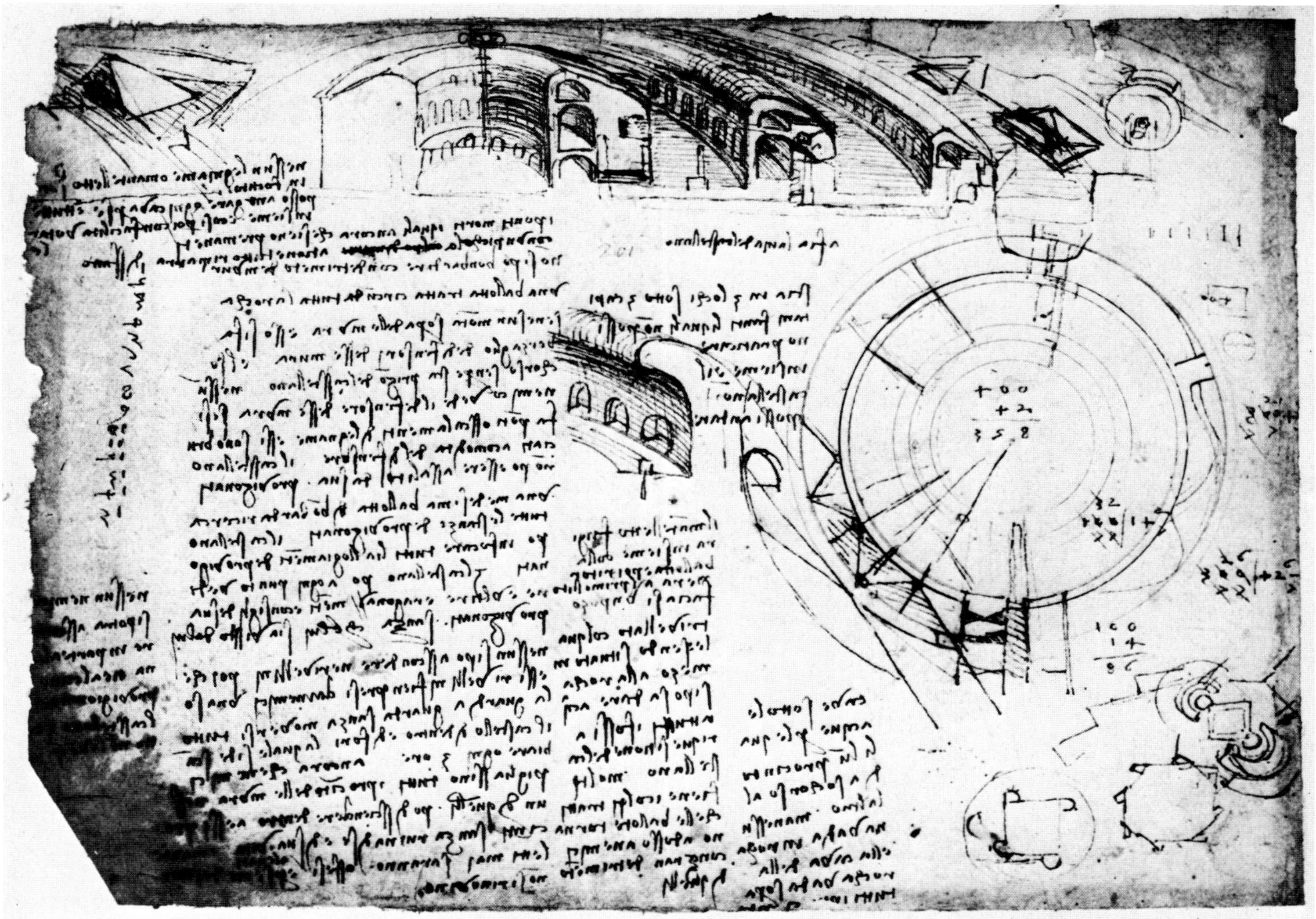

La sixiesme aage

Il constitua quen leglise de sainct pier
re et de sainct pol y eust vij prestres po'
ouir les penitentz et baptiser les nō ba/
ptisez. En oultre il fist. v. rues ou quar
tiers separez pour demourer les pstres
de la cite de rome. Le premier quartier
est a sainct pierre. Le ij^e a sainct pol. Le
tiers a sainct laurentz. Le quart a. S.
Jehan du latran. Et le ve a saincte ma
rie la maiour. Item il ordonna que nul
clerc ne recoiue inuestitures promotiō
ne degre par hōme laypque.

Lā xiij^e de son empire il fist et consti
tua son gendre nomme zenon maistre
et gouuerneur de tout orient.

Lā xvij^e de son empire ledit empere'
nōme leon le grand voyant sa mort a/
procher ordōna pour empereur le filz
de sa fille ariagne nōme leon le ieune.
et incōtinent mourust. Aprez la mort
duquel ne vesquist gaires le dit leon ij^e
mais couronna son pere zenon et le nō
ma empereur. Lors estoyt en affrique
vng qui se disoit empereur nōme basi/
liscus ayant vng filz appelle marc le/
quel il fist empereur Et sa femme nō/
mee zenobia fist sēblablemēt appeller
auguste et couronner emperiere. Ce
pendant zeno maistre de tout orient a
uec sa femme ariagne vint a la cite ca/
pitale de lempire ou il fust receu hōno/
rablement du peuple et du senat. quāt
ledit basiliscus entendist ces nouuelles
il sen fuyst en franchise en leglise auec
sa femme et par ainsy ledit zeno obtit
lempire.

Chapitre lvj^e de zeno lij^e empereur
des romains

Zenon y/
saurus gē
dre de lempere'
leō dessusdit fut
cree lij^e empere'
et tint sō empi/
re en occident.
Mays vng sien
nepueu gouuer
na lempire occi/
dental commen
cant regner lan du monde iiij^m iiij^c
xxxviij: De lolimpiade iij^c xiij lā iiij^e
De rome mil ij^c xxvij. De nostre sei/
gneur iiij^c lxxvj. Et de chilperich roy
des francois lan xviij^e. Et regna xvj
ans selond eusebe. Les autres diēt xvij
durant lesquelx il institua maintes
lois viles. Hugo floriacensis en sō
v^e liure dit que ledit zeno composa aul/
cunes escriptures contre la foy catholi
que. Il vsurpa et a soy appropria le roy
aulme de ytalie. Et affin que perpetu
ellemēt le dit royaulme luy peust de/
mourer. Il bailla ses filles en mariage
aux roys voisins cestassauoir lune au
roy des gothz nomme alaricus. La ij^e a
sigismund roy des bourguignons. Sa
niepce almerga au roy des turiges ap
pelle hermenfridus. En oultre pour a
uoir aliance aux francois Il espousa
la fille de Clouis Roy de France. ꝛ dō/
na sa ppre seur pour femme au roy des
vvandes. Il tint son siege a Rauenne
comme cite capitale de son empire. Il
estoit pollut de la secte et heresie arria/
ne parquoy auoit en cruelle hayne to'
bons catholiques.

Lan iiij^e de son empire le corps de. s.
barnabe apostre fust trouue en salami
ne cite de cipre auec leuangille de saint
Mathieu escripte en hebrieu par les
mains du dit euangeliste.

Lan v^e Auicus euesque de Vienne
acheua et acōplist son liure fait en vers
et touchant la condition du monde.

Sigibert dit quen ce temps flouris/
soyent de bon renom en France Saict
Remy archeuesque de Reins. Et sēbl
re Auicus euesque de Vienne. Sollen/
nis de chartres. Item en affrique Ful/
gentius rutspensis qui escript maints
beaulx liures. Et en ytalie Saint ger
main euesque de capue Et episenius de
pauie. Dudit Sainct germain parle
Vincent listorial ou xxj^e liure et chapi/
tre cent et iiij^e disant que Saint benoit
le glorieux confes vit son ame en la spe
re ꝛ haulte region du feu que les saictz
angles portoyent en la triumphante
gloire de paradis.

L'an huitiesme de
lempereur zenon
trespassa Chilperich iiij^e Roy des fran
cois aprez lequel fust couronne son filz
Clouis premier Roy chrestien. et v^e en
lordre total des rois de France Car gil
lon qui en lieu de Chilperich fust fayt
Roy nest point mis ou nōbre des Rois.
Ledit Clouis commenca regner lā de
grace iiij^c iiij^xx et iiij. Il espousa Clo/

THE THEATRE OF THE WORLD

Habiti dell'Asia, & dell'Africa.

DONNA NOBILE DELLA CHINA.

LE Donne del sopra posto ritratto sono di mediocre statura, et carnagione olinastre, et assai modeste, e continenti, che non si vedono mai alle finestre, nè alle porti delle loro case. Non mangiano mai à conuitto nessuno, se gli cõuitati non sono parenti, ò amici strettissimi. Nell'andare à visitare i loro padri si fanno portare da quattro huomini in vna Lettica serrata da tutte le parti di gelosie spessissime di fili di oro, e d'argento, ò di seta, per le quali vedono altri, e non sono vedute loro. Queste tali donne si dilettano di saper disegnare, e lauorare di rileuo, e d'intaglio, et dipingono eccellentemente. L'Habito delle sopradette dunque è simile alla prossima posta di sopra. L'acconciatura della testa è fatta à guisa di fiori con perle, e gioie nelle legature, e con alcuni ornamenti al collo con pietre pretiose. La ueste è di seta di colore lunga fino in terra, e cinta assai alta, e le maniche sono larghe assai con bellissimi lauori in capo di esse vicino alle mani, doue mostrano le maniche delle camice sottilissime. Et in mano portano alcuni fiori odoriferi à guisa di garofoli. Si profumano assai, e si dilettano di Musica, e di sonare di varij istromenti, molti à modo di citara. vsano bellissimi giardini con bagni odoriferi, e con arbori di molti, e diuersi delicati frutti, e molti da noi non conosciuti. vsano molti lisci, et belletti, et quasi di superfluo.

NO-

NOBILE CHINESE.

Ppp 3

▲ Cesare Vecellio, *Degli habiti antichi e moderni di diverse parti del mondo*, Venice, 1590: Costume of a noble Chinese lady.

◄ *La Mer des Hystoires*, Paris, 1488-1489: Christening of Clovis, first Christian king of France.

After the exact sciences, but with a certain time-lag, the need for illustrations was also felt in what today we might call the human sciences. Here the allegedly objective use of the image was a much more delicate matter, verging indeed on the sacrilegious, and it was only in the latter half of the sixteenth century that one can really speak of illustration in this field as an intended source of knowledge. Man's grasp of the outside world could only be secured with the help of pictures. Naive ones first of all, in collections of imaginary portraits inspired by medals, or of strange costumes acting as so many glimpses of other places. The first costume book, professing to be an objective repertory, that of François Desprez (1562), was still mixed with medieval fantasies. These disappeared from the more serious, better documented costume books of the late sixteenth century by Vecellio and Jean-Jacques Boissard. The humanist was intent on seeing the plain aspect of things, their external shape and features, apparently devoid of any meaning: he concentrated on the visible, picturing it in order to understand it, seeing before knowing, and showing before demonstrating. The illustrations are meant to be read, not deciphered as in the Middle Ages: they are accordingly governed by a syntax of their own, organized by man alone. It could not be anything but an elementary syntax: consisting of enumeration, of accumulation by analogy, which could however ramify into a complex classification. The resulting picture is still a microcosm, but one for which its maker alone was responsible, one which was shaped by him alone as a man might shape a tool designed to get a purchase on the world.

The earliest illustration of this kind was the map. Or rather, keeping to the book, we should say that it was the "panoramic view," a documentary and often a bird's-eye view, that of the city to begin with. And, first of all, *the* city: Rome. Already in the Middle Ages the description of Rome had almost become a literary form in itself. Its origins are to be found in the ninth-century Einsiedeln manuscript which names the ancient monuments as landmarks for pilgrims. But at that time it was the symbol, not observation, that determined the form of the city, which was generally circular, or sometimes lion-shaped. One of the first purposes of the printed image, in those block books of the later fifteenth century in which each text page and illustration were cut in a single wood block, was to

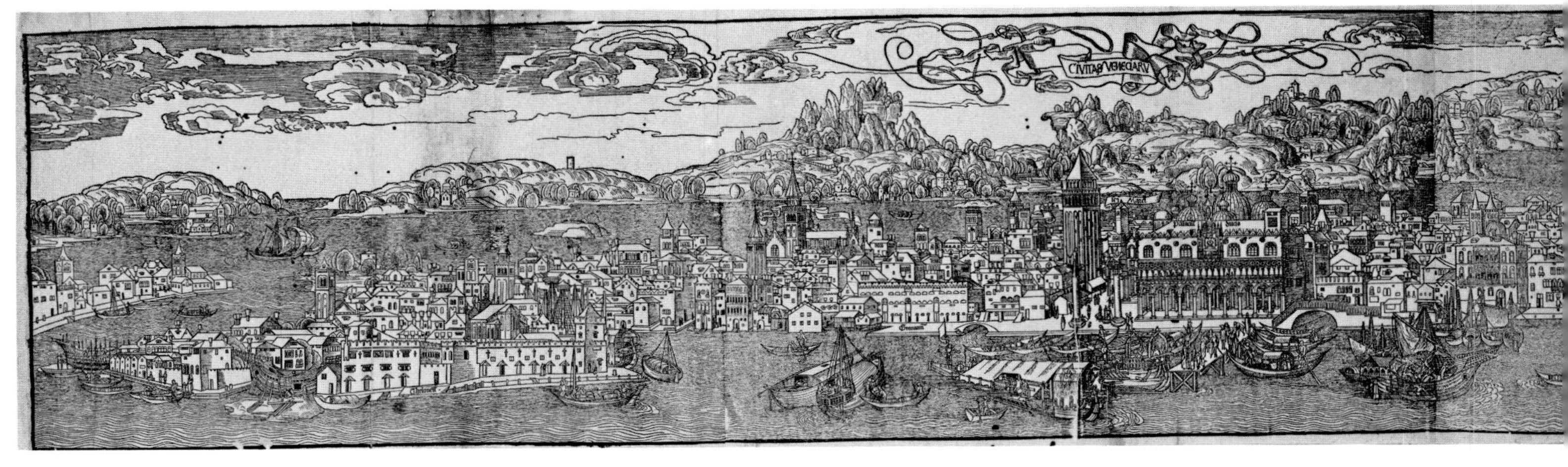
CIVITAS VENECIARV

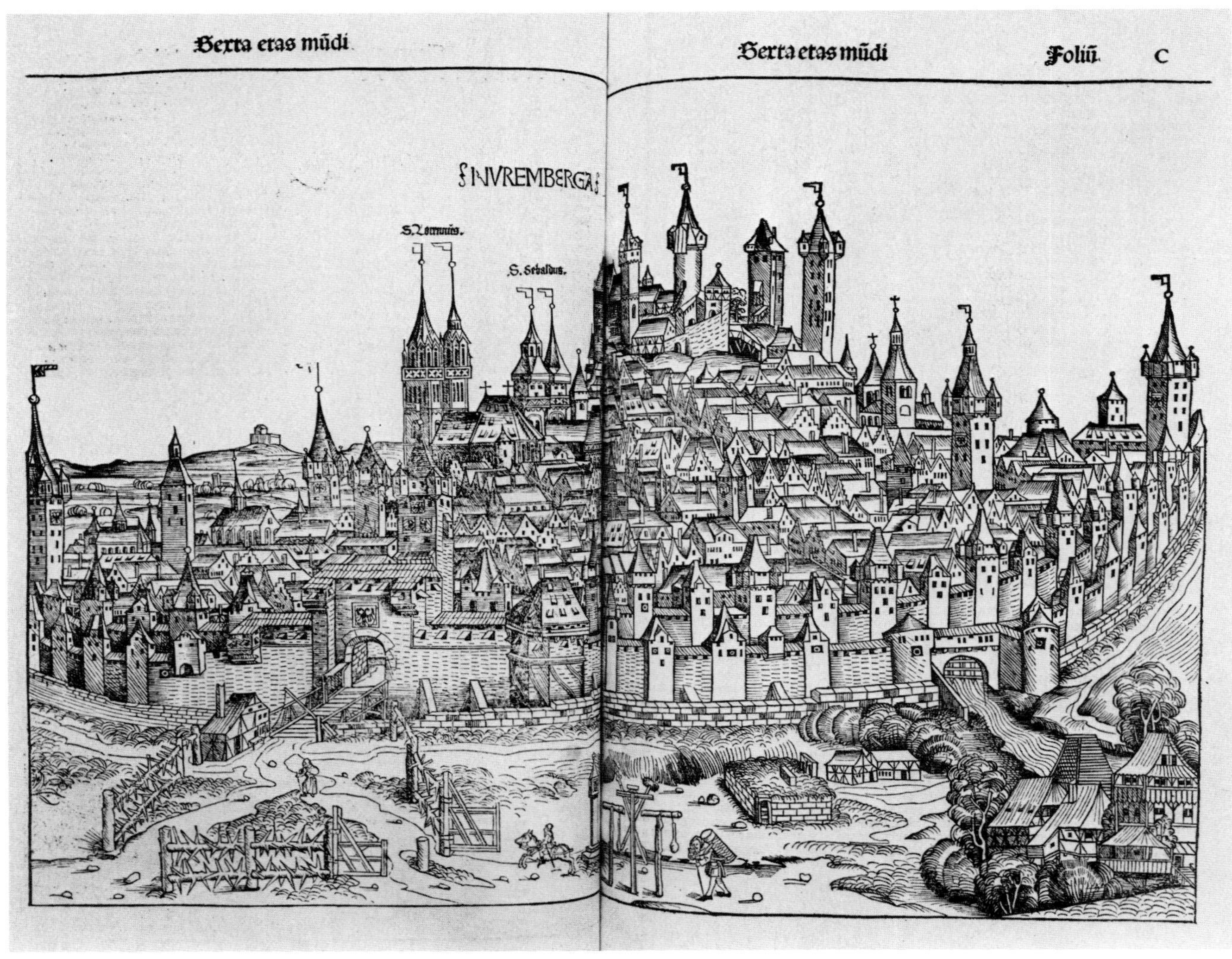
Sexta etas mūdi
Sexta etas mūdi
Foliū.
C
NVREMBERGA
S. Sebaldus.

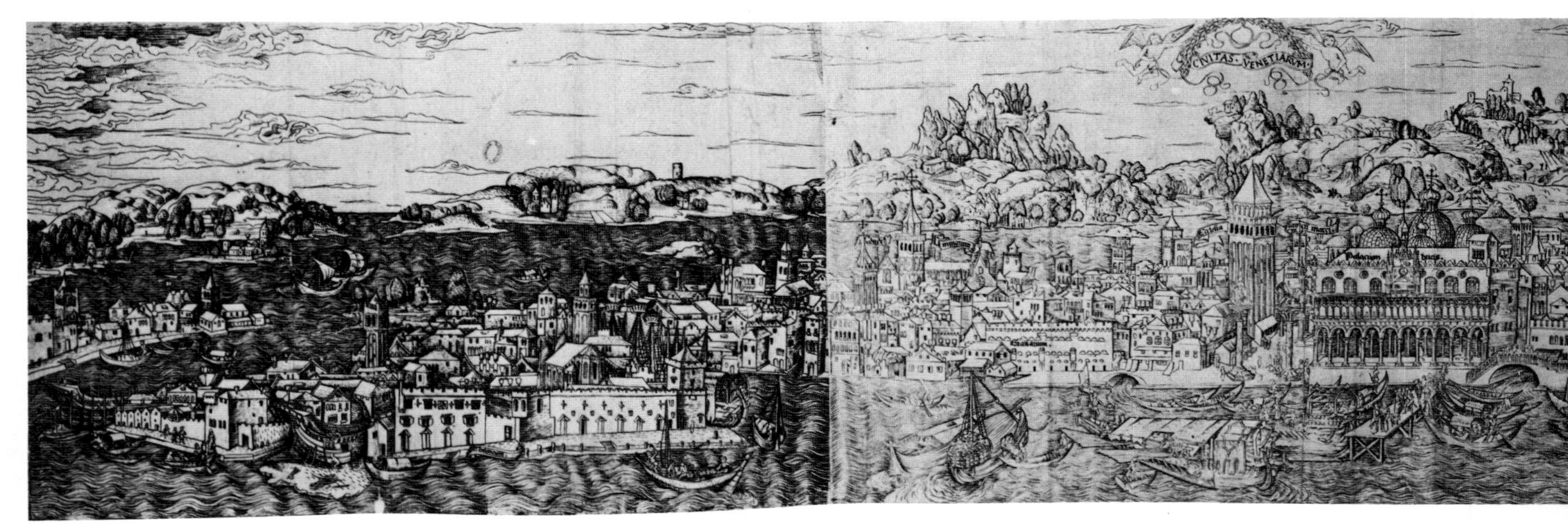
CIVITAS VENETIARV

Bernhard von Breydenbach,
Reise ins Heilige Land,
Mainz, 1486:
View of Venice, woodcut.

offer a delineation of Rome, no doubt for the use of pilgrims. Among the first books printed with movable type, we have some thirty copies of the *Mirabilia urbis Romae*, dating from 1484 to 1500. The first scientific view of it, by Alberti, has not come down to us and may have been an unexecuted project. These early *Mirabilia urbis Romae*, printed in large numbers in Nuremberg and Florence, were soon shown up for what they were, inaccurate and indeed fanciful, by the progress of archaeology and the demands of scholars. They were superseded by the *Opusculum novae et veteris urbis Romae*, which went through five editions from 1510 to 1523. But scholarly research was making steady strides. As early as 1472 Alessandro Strozzi had published a plan of Rome, and in 1500 the *Antiquaria prospectiche* appeared as an initial attempt at popularization. Andrea Fulvio's *Antiquitates Urbis* gives a view of Rome before the sack of 1527, and in 1544 an accurate plan was published in the second edition of Marliani's *Urbis Romae topographia*. By now, in the interval since the block books of the previous century, illustration had changed its system of reference. In the earliest woodcuts, specific cities like Padua, Munich and Vienna appear to be identifiable; certainly Venice is in 1470. Nuremberg figures in the famous *Nuremberg Chronicle* (1493), a monumental book fittingly published in the then capital of printmaking, and by its leading printer Anton Koberger, for the publisher Hartmann Schedel; containing two thousand woodcuts by Michael Wolgemut and Wilhelm Pleydenwurff, it was issued in both German and Latin. But the most interesting illustrated book in this field is the one known as *Breydenbach's Travels*, from the name of the author, who made the journey to Jerusalem and charted the daily stages on the way. The first edition, *Reise ins Heilige Land*, appeared at Mainz in 1486, illustrated with woodcuts.

The French edition of this book, *Les Sainctes Peregrinations de Jherusalem*, published at Lyons in 1488, is the earliest book illustrated with copperplate engravings; it was reissued in Paris in 1517 with forty-eight woodcuts and two fold-outs showing the city of Jerusalem.

◀ *Nuremberg Chronicle* or *Weltchronik*, Nuremberg, 1493:
Fold-out view of Nuremberg, woodcut by Michael Wolgemut and Wilhelm Pleydenwurff.

▼ Bernhard von Breydenbach,
Les Sainctes Peregrinations de Jherusalem, Lyons, 1488:
Fold-out view of Venice, copperplate engraving.

Johannes Theodorus de Bry, *Admiranda Narratio, fida tamen, de commodis et incolarum ritibus Virginiae*, from the *Collectiones Peregrinationum...*, Frankfurt, 1590: Indians of Virginia sacrificing their first-born children.

Primogeniti ſolennibus ceremonijs Regi ſacrificantur. XXXIIII.

MORIS apud illos eſt primogenitum maſculum Regi victimam offerre. Sacrificij autem die Regi ſignificato, locum adit ad id deſtinatum, ubi ſcamnum in quo ſedeat, & in media area truncus ligneus binos pedes altus, totidem craſſus: ante hunc pueri mater calcaneis inſidens, & manibus faciem tegens filij mortem deplorat. Cognatarum vel amicarum ejus primaria, puerum Regi venerabunda offert; deinde quæ matrem comitatæ ſunt feminæ in orbem conveniunt, & canendo ſaltant lætabundæ, mutuis manibus non apprehenſis: quæ puerum tenet, in medium illarum ſe infert ſaltans, & in Regis laudem quædam accinens. Interea ſex Indi ad id munus delecti ſeparatim in areæ quadam parte ſtant, & inter eos medius ſacrificus cum magnificentia quadam clavam tenens. Peractis ceremonijs, ſacrificus infantem capiens, Regi, coram omnibus, in ligneo illo trunco mactat. Nobis præſentibus ſemel peracta eſt ſimilis victima.

Bernard Picart, *Cérémonies et coutumes religieuses de tous les peuples du monde*, Amsterdam, 1723-1743: Four woodcut illustrations.

For both traveller and conqueror, illustrations were an indispensable complement to the text. After specific cities, we find descriptions of exotic regions recently discovered and providing subjects for pictures. The essential work in this field is Johannes Theodorus de Bry's multivolume collection of voyages and travels, *Collectiones Peregrinationum...*, published from 1590 to 1640 and picturing the New World for the first time, the illustrations being based on field drawings made during the expeditions of the early explorers. Of comparable importance in its scope and outlay was Bernard Picart's *Cérémonies et coutumes religieuses de tous les peuples du monde,* published in the eighteenth century. Such subject inventories called for illustration and acted as a tool for taking over the world. Of such compilations one may say what Roland Barthes said of the plates in the *Encyclopédie*: "Cataloguing means dividing a thing up, the better to take it over." They are at once "a balance-sheet for the mind and a spectacle for the eye."

The pictorial inventory of the world did not stop with exotic places. Men and their ways and their dress, near and far, had to be described. But class barriers were more difficult to cross than frontiers, and it proved a quicker and easier matter to picture the life of savages in America than that of peasants in Europe. Sets of "social types" did not begin to appear till the very end of the sixteenth and the opening of the seventeenth century. They brought an insight into urban life, for it was the social stratification of the city that the illustrator showed. Here again costume was simply a practical way, under cover of picturesqueness and quaintness, of arranging people by categories, like plants and animals. These pictorial records, of which the engraver Abraham Bosse offers one of the most typical examples, show the diversity of society. So do the prints of Jacques Callot, who pictured beggars as well as the nobility of Lorraine. The seventeenth-century illustrator became a chronicler, and a new type of artist appears, typified by Wenzel Hollar, born in Prague and a Protestant, who at the age of twenty, in 1627, settled in London where he enjoyed the patronage of the Earl of Arundel and remained till his death in 1677. The record he engraved of London life extends to 2700 prints (an average of one a week over fifty years!). This was a rich period, one in which, as John Harthan writes, "book illustration reflects the tastes and interests of the monarchy and the upper classes; court life, architecture, military life, horsemanship, fencing and tournaments, horticulture and a certain kind of literature (the emblem books, epic poetry and romances), were the favourite subjects of books." A whole middle-class culture came into existence, in London first of all, prompting artists to turn to plainer themes untouched before. When Hollar represented the Royal Exchange or the execution of Strafford, he was breaking new ground, opening the eyes of the common man to a world hitherto represented only in battle and ceremonial scenes.

Wenzel Hollar: The Royal Exchange of London, 1644, etching.

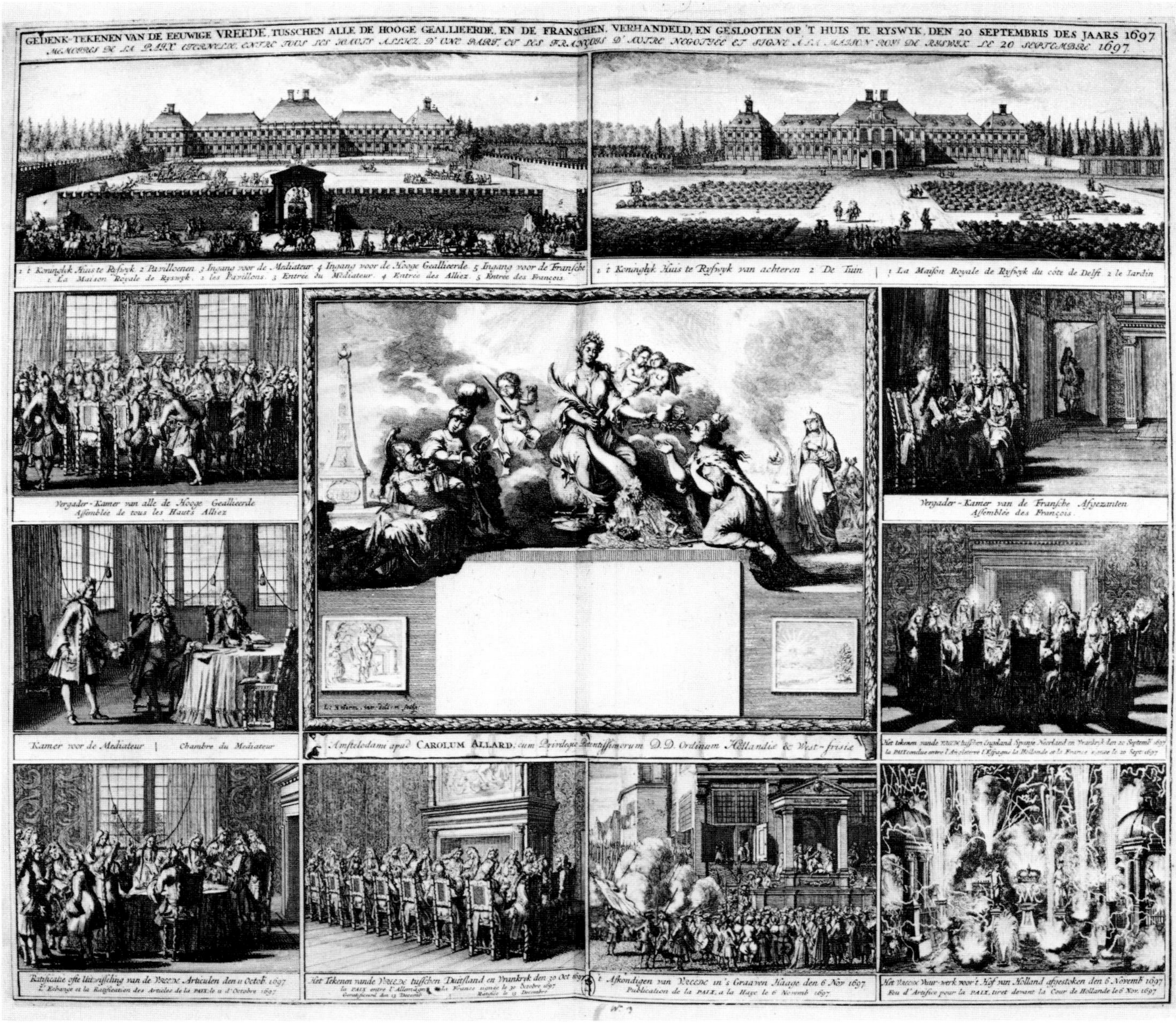

Romeyn de Hooghe: Memorial of the Peace signed at Ryswick between the Grand Alliance and France on 20 September 1697, Amsterdam, 1698, etching.

Romeyn de Hooghe: Funeral of the Princess of Orange at Delft on 21 December 1675, Amsterdam, etching.

At this point a fresh distinction is called for. The notion of illustration now passed beyond the text/image connection, and the term "illustration" began to be applied, as it is today, to any anecdotal scene whose story content seems clear and explicit, and it need not be accompanied by any text. It is in fact reality itself which does duty as the text, and its authority supersedes that of writing. This falling away of the text occurred in the seventeenth century, but it did not occur suddenly; the image is often supported by a long commentary whose dependent and indeed parasitical character becomes increasingly obvious. The book, till then the privileged place for illustrations, turned into an album from which the text was cast out, leaving the image to speak for itself. This trend is clear in technical books, like those on horsemanship or on ceremonies. The description of entertainments and pageantry is reduced to a formal tribute to the dedicatee: what matters is the depiction of the tilting match, the fireworks or the procession (on the occasion of Entries, Marriages and Funerals), which unfold moreover like a page of handwriting set down alternatively, without a break, from left to right and

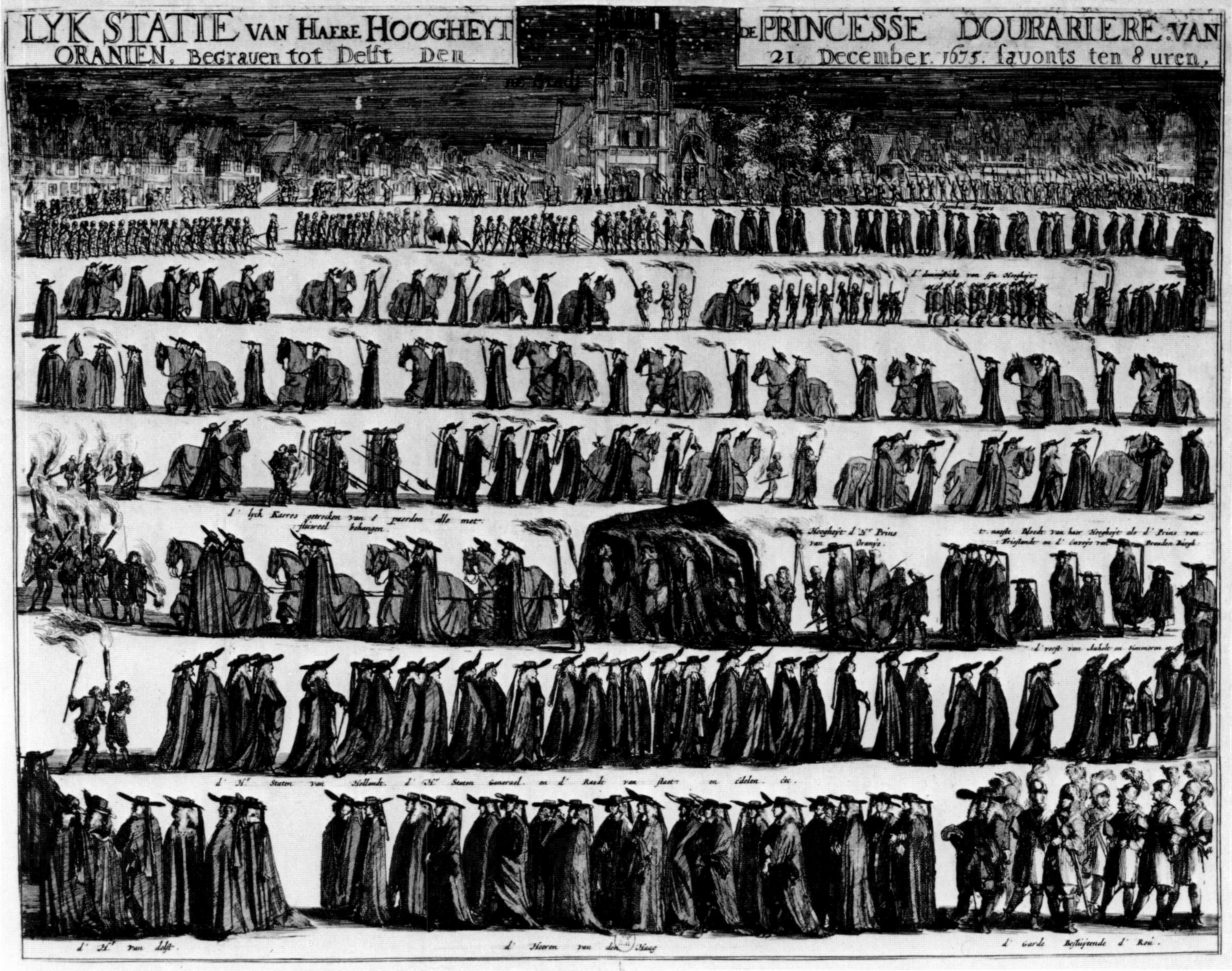

from right to left. One may thus "read" and "contemplate" the sequence of figures both as a narrative and as an image. A striking example of these "reading pictures" is provided by the hundreds of prints of Romeyn de Hooghe, the illustrator-chronicler of Holland in the late seventeenth and early eighteenth century. His large spirited plates of battles and processions are accompanied by printed fly-sheets telling the story behind them or listing the persons and places represented in a series of numbered captions keyed to the tiny numerals dotted over the print itself. Sometimes again, mostly in popular prints, the brief captions are included in the plate and each person in it has his name beside him, as in the phylacteries introducing Scriptural passages into the heart of the medieval miniature. This interlocking of text and image is not confined to emblem books and iconologies, but became a common feature of popular and middle-class prints well into the eighteenth century. These prints were aimed at an uncultivated public, and as such may be seen as the antecedent of comic strips in which the image "brings home" the text; or possibly, in these earlier times, the reverse was true and a public not yet initiated into imagery found the needed prompting in the text. It would seem moreover that the text was meant not only to add specific information but to give the picture a stamp of authenticity that was still necessary to get it accepted.

Finally, illustration proved an apt medium not only for telling a story but for recording history. It testified to events and provided a historical reference to them. In France, at the end of the sixteenth century, the large prints of Perrissin and Tortorel picturing some of the highlights of the Wars of Religion provide historical evidence of some importance.

At the same period the chronicler Pierre de L'Estoile collected pictures and prints of his time, as materials for a history of it, as a picture researcher today might gather illustrations on a given subject. Then came the monumental works of Sandford (*A Genealogical History of the Kings of England*, 1677) and Montfaucon (*Monuments de la monarchie française*, 1729-1733). The dynastic power itself was grateful for the firm basis of pictorial documentation thus provided.

1

The "War of Love"

Jacques Callot, Guerra d'Amore, *etchings, Florence, 1616:*

1. *Floats and costumed figures.*
2. *Plan of the pageant.*
3. *Processions in the Piazza Santa Croce, Florence.*
4. *Sham combats in the Piazza Santa Croce, Florence.*

2

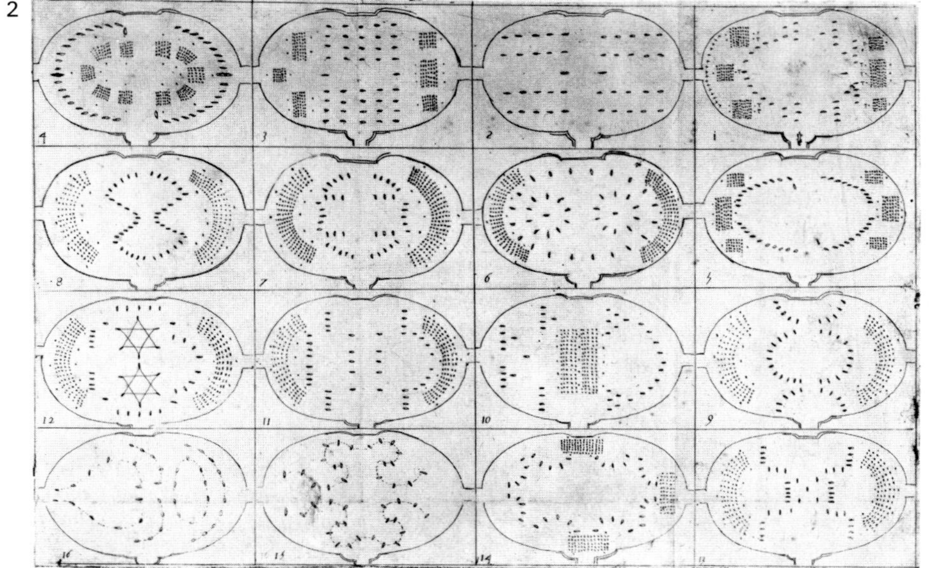

The progress of printmaking and its appeal to a wider public in the latter half of the sixteenth century gave rise to some illustrated books of a new type which may be described as books of ceremony or pageantry. They were at once attractive albums designed to dazzle contemporaries and memorials intended to give a historical dimension to the event. The first ones were devoted to Royal Entries, providing as it were a souvenir book of the temporary architecture erected for the occasion and the pageants that took place. Then came the Famous Funerals, like that of Charles III, Duke of Lorraine, at Nancy in May 1608, which is represented in an etching by the Strasbourg artist Brentel, and which the young Callot may have seen. Later on, in Florence, Callot worked for the Medici court which was particularly fond of such pageantry. There he found a patron, the Grand Duke Cosimo II, and a master, Giulio Parigi, a decorator and organizer of festivities. It was the latter's reputation that had drawn Callot to Florence. Already in 1608 Parigi had commissioned from the etcher Remigio Cantagallina the album recording the regatta on the Arno held for the Grand Duke's marriage. These prints foreshadow those of Callot. The latter began his Florentine career by the publication in 1612 of the album commemorating the funeral of the Queen of Spain, Margaret of Austria; its prints are very close to those in books of pageantry.

In February 1616 Callot collaborated with Parigi on four plates which went to illustrate the album *La Guerra d'Amore* (The War of Love); the text describing this pageant was written by Andrea Salvadori. The "War of Love" was a spectacular "equestrian ballet" with processions, dancing and sham combats. Much the same ingredients entered into the "War of Beauty" held in Florence that same year, as into the *Combat à la Barrière* held in Nancy in 1627. For both, Callot illustrated the albums which served as programme and souvenir offered to the illustrious guests. ■

MOSTRA DELLA GVERRA D'AMORE FESTA DEL SER.MO GRAN DVCA DI TOSCANA FATTA L'ANNO 1615
Iac. Callot. F.
3

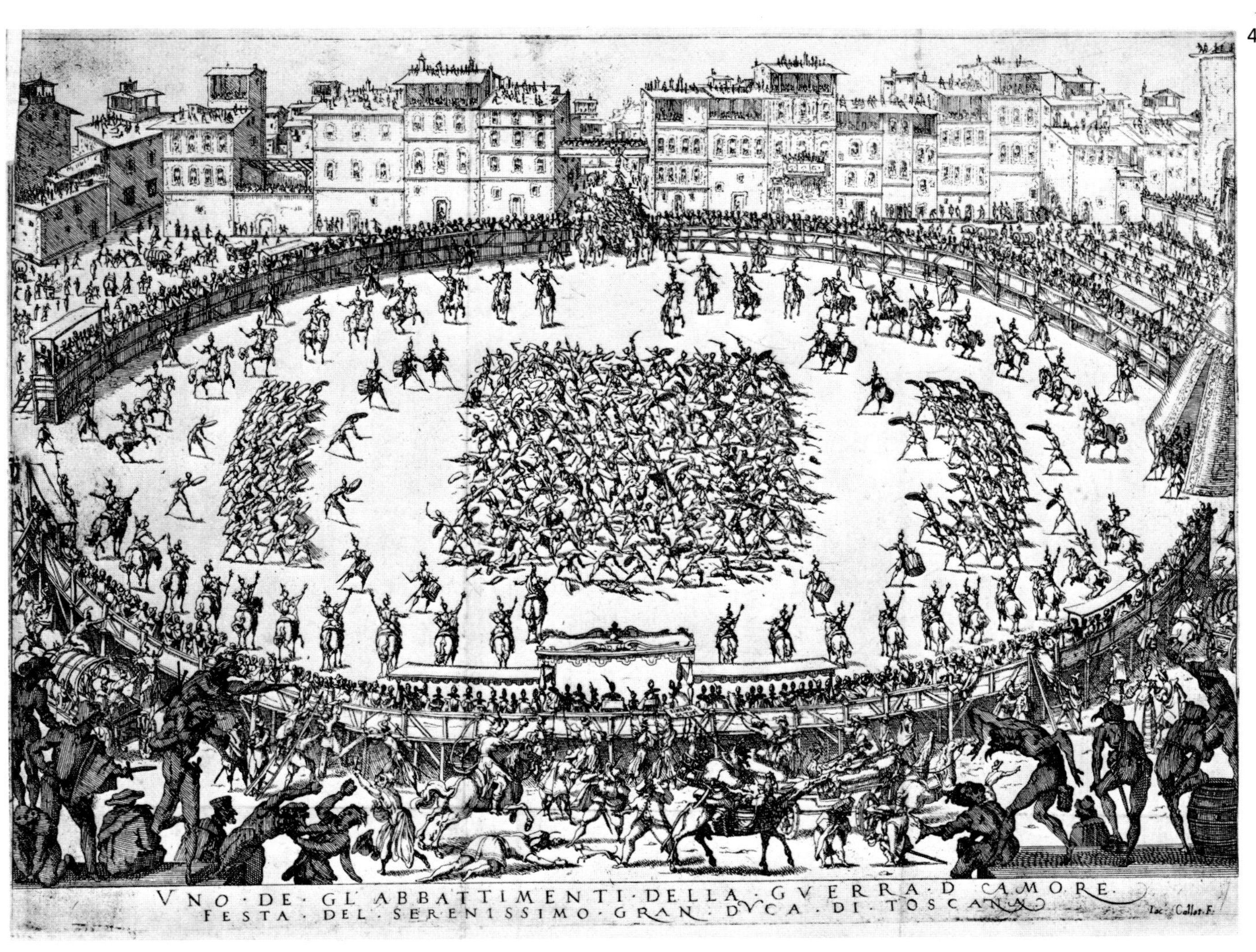
VNO · DE · GL' ABBATTIMENTI · DELLA · GVERRA · D' AMORE.
FESTA · DEL · SERENISSIMO · GRAN · DVCA · DI · TOSCANA
Iac. Callot. F.
4

Street Cries

1. *Itinerant bookseller, from the earliest series of "Street Cries of Paris," hand-coloured woodcut, c. 1500.*
2. *Hawker of religious pictures and rosaries, etching by Giuseppe Maria Mitelli after Annibale Carracci, from* Di Bologna l'Arti, *Bologna, 1660.*

2

1

Street cries provided the subject matter of some of the first sets of prints in which each picture, explained by a caption, prefigures the illustrated book and even the strip cartoon. The theme of street vendors and tradesmen had already been taken up in late medieval miniatures (*Life of St Denis*, fourteenth century). It attracted the first artists with an eye for realism and the picturesque. One of the early printers issued a set of hand-coloured woodcuts on eighteen sheets, now in the Bibliothèque Historique de la Ville de Paris. The full-length walking figures are accompanied by their cry, engraved in black letter in the same wood block as the image. But it was in the classical age that this type of print came into its own, in the urban centres: Paris, Rome, Bologna, then London, Berlin and other cities. The theme naturally appealed to the early realistic artists reacting against Mannerism, chiefly those in the circle around the Carracci, at the very end of the sixteenth century. Giuseppe Maria Mitelli and Ambrosius Brambilla produced something approaching the strip cartoon, sequences of small tradesmen set out as in an atlas of natural history. Annibale Carracci himself made a set of seventy-five drawings, probably before leaving Bologna for Rome in 1595, which was engraved by Simon Guillain and published as a portfolio with a preface by Giovanni Atanasio Mosini. This text is important as giving an early statement of the realistic theory of art and using the newly coined word "caricature." Here, as a matter of fact, the term is still used in the sense of everyday subjects and low life, pictured directly and spontaneously. The elegance of this portfolio of etchings stands in sharp contrast with earlier versions of the theme, aimed at an unlettered public. The poetic survey of *Street Cries*, showing a fresh awareness and highlighting of city life, coincided with the urban diversification of the print-buying public. These *Street Cries* were to reappear in various forms in popular imagery, over a long period of time, down to the *Physiologies* of the ninteenth century and the photographs of Eugène Atget. ■

Hawker of pictures, etching by Simon Guillain after Annibale Carracci, from Le Arti di Bologna, *Rome, 1740.*

MUTUS LIBER, IN QUO TAMEN
tota Philosophia hermetica, figuris hieroglyphicis
depingitur, ter optimo maximo Deo misericordi
consecratus, solisque filiis artis dedicatus,
authore cujus nomen est Altus.
21·11·82·Neg·
93·82·72·Neg·
82·31·33·Jued·
RUPELLÆ
apud PETRUM SAVOURET ⋆ cum Privilegio Regis
M·DC·LXXVII·
T. 617.

SILENT POETRY

Mutus Liber ("Mute Book, in which all hermetic philosophy is yet depicted in hieroglyphic figures"), anonymous work composed entirely of pictures, published at La Rochelle in 1677: Title page and one plate.

The scientific image now drew its force directly from the reality it depicted, and the very fascination of reality gave illustration a growing importance. For the classical mind, the fictional image still owed its force to the writing behind it. Down to the eighteenth century, one may say that every fictional image was in fact a literary illustration, even if at times the text was implied rather than present. And this applies not only to books but to paintings, frescoes, sculpture and any figural decoration which was always the transposition of a story or a thesis whose major mode was speech. The stuff of the image was the Fable, the Story, in the broadest sense, covering the mythological, epic and historical repertory on which the artist drew. In the classical age of Europe, literary illustration was shaped by language: from the latter it borrowed its most obvious structures, it conformed to the latter's rules, and it was through the grid of language that the image had to be decoded.

To give the image and its maker their due, as well as to defend the written word against their encroachments, the mid-seventeenth century laid down the doctrines which regulated their relations, establishing an equivalence between them and even assimilating one to the other according to the precepts "Ut pictura poesis erit; similisque poesi sit pictura" (Ovid) or "Painting is silent poetry, and poetry speaking painting" (Simonides, quoted by Plutarch). The literary rules were set forth throughout Europe after 1600 and imposed after 1640. These rules had their pictorial parallel in the ones formulated a few decades earlier in the theory of emblems, which now were codified on still stricter lines. All this rule-making was meant to consolidate the idealized and abstract side of artistic expression, to prevent it from being contaminated by realism and the concrete content of the image. It was meant to forestall "the tendency of the picture to descend from the general to the specific, from the material to the formal," to halt it "by means of words which shall attach a particular meaning to it" (Père Le Moyne, *De l'art des devises*, 1666).

Here lay the danger for the picture: it was continually being criticized for representing a dog as a dog and the gods as men. In the view of one of the foremost rule-makers: "Art holds up the universal idea of things. It purges them of those defects and peculiar irregularities which history by the severity of its laws must allow to stand"

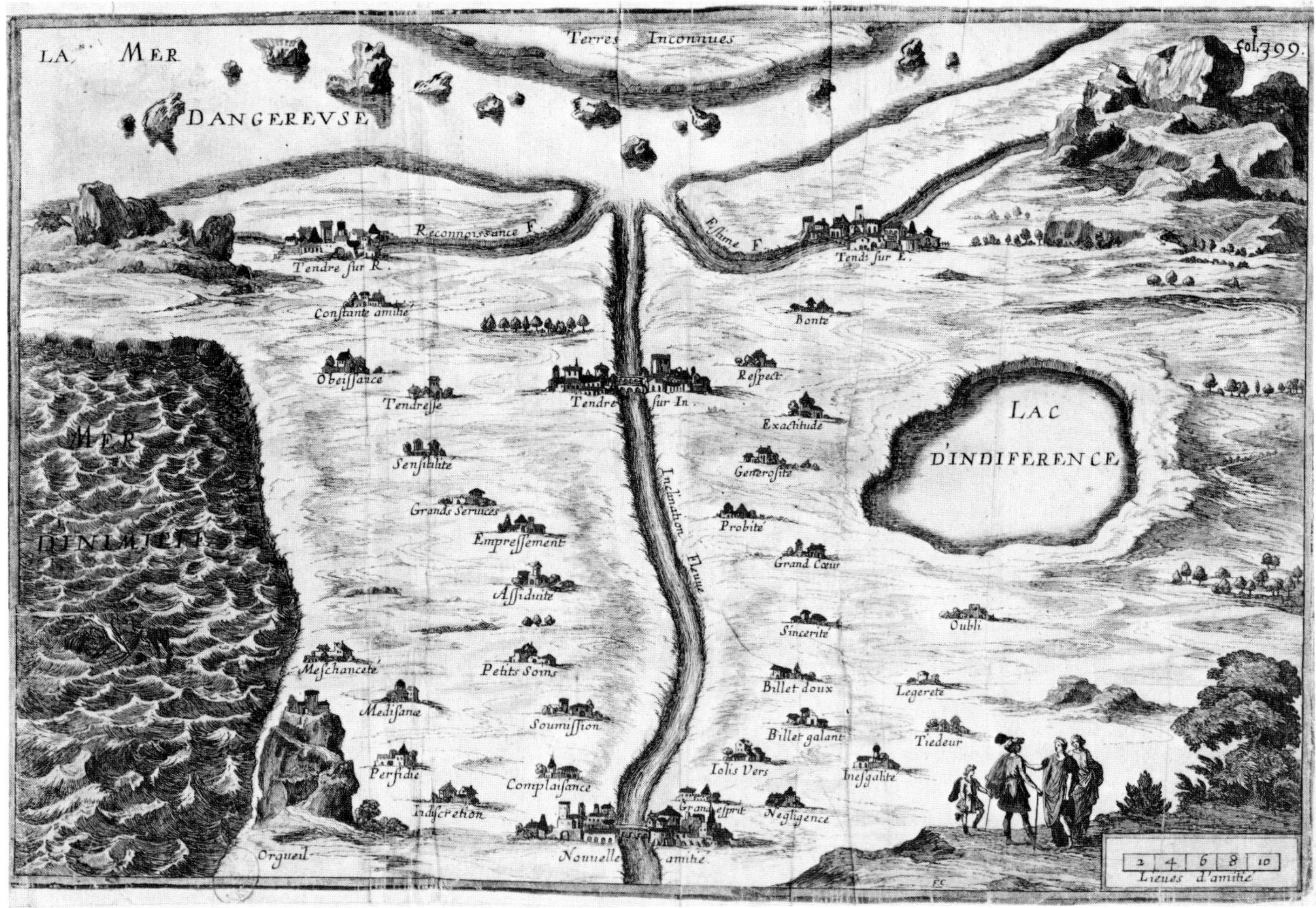

"Carte de Tendre," map of the Realm of Tender Heart in Madeleine de Scudéry's romance *Clélie*, Paris, 1654.

(Jean Chapelain, *Sentiments de l'Académie*, 1637). Illustration let earthly flaws into the ideal, like worms into the fruit. Already in the seventeenth century realism was invading art by way of illustrations, touching off a debate which is still not concluded. Witness this recent comment by J. F. Lyotard, in which, in more polemical terms, we find again the analytical approach of Michel Foucault to the clash between the two main categories of signs: "What is visible is not necessarily legible. Data do not make a text... In them is a thickness or rather a constitutional difference which calls for seeing, not reading. If the world is to be read, this is something quite different. It means that someone on the other side is writing the given data and that with a good angle of sight I could in principle decipher them... That is the imagined goal, having both the wrong side and the right side. That is the sin of pride, having both the text and the illustration. The hesitation between them is that of Christianity itself... This hesitation is recorded not only by the history of Western thought but by the history of painting, which arose from the Scriptures and dared to illustrate them but could not be kept within bounds, continually returning to them and submitting to them and yet breaking away from them" (J. F. Lyotard, *Discours, Figure*). This debate actually covers two contrary ideologies, one in which the signs reflect a higher truth, the other in which man faces a silent world that he can only describe. This debate is transposed literally into the opposition between image and text which has determined the history of illustration. The importance and effectiveness of the image, while finding an outlet in technical books, was at the same time thwarted: the value of the image was downgraded, that of the writing upgraded. Classical literary illustration was still under the spell of the text.

Its field was carefully charted out. If one considers what Meyer Schapiro calls the non-mimetic elements of the image (its frame, position and format), classical illustration is like a new redundant text, isolated from the words. Its place of predilection is the full-page plate where the image is pointedly, strictly and sometimes too emphatically framed and set off: there it is "embedded" in the text and the art work calculated to fix it there is only too conspicuous. The emphasis given to such art work by a specialist of literary illustration like François Chauveau shows how essential a part it played in the book: the art of the scroll became as prominent as that of the vignette it enclosed. The title page was often the only place in the book where a picture was tolerated, the title being enhanced by an architectural design. Then the image made its way into the book, sparingly at first and at set points: the headpiece, the initial letter, the tailpiece, each one embodying a particular design. The timid introduction of vignettes seems to show some misgivings about imagery in this sensitive field, some fear lest it should go too far. Thus in Honoré d'Urfé's *L'Astrée*, though it has been described as a "Baroque museum romance," only a few illustrations were admitted at the beginning of each chapter in the definitive edition of 1633. Likewise with *Don Quixote*: the first, all too insipid illustrations picture the tilting against windmills as an ordinary duel between two knights.

What do we find in the picture then? A sobered down delineation of an ideal moment in the story, standardized more strictly than the text, which itself was cramped by

ALARIC,
OV
ROME VAINCVË.

LIVRE NEVFIESME.

MAIS durant qu'il combat, la Nuit ſombre & paiſible,
Tombant alors du Ciel, rend la Terre inuiſible:
Obligeant le Heros dans ſa Noble chaleur,
A ſuſpendre l'effet de ſa rare valeur.
L'on voit rentrer au Camp, les Enſeignes vollantes;
Retirer loin des Murs, les Machines roullantes;
Et le Grand Roy des Goths, plein d'vn nouueau deſpit,
Seul dans ſon Pauillon, ſe ietter ſur vn Lict:
Mais auec le deſſein de recombatre encore,
Dés que vers l'Orient ſe fera voir l'Aurore.

Types of illustration used in a French heroic poem of the 17th century, Georges de Scudéry's *Alaric ou Rome vaincue*, Paris, 1654: Frontispiece, headpiece and initial letter (left) and title page and tailpiece (below).

rules. Even so, the text and still more the stage admitted effects of the "marvellous" which were taboo in book illustration. The vignettes opening each canto of the *Gerusalemme Liberata* or each book of *Le Grand Cyrus* are a chilling come-down from the warmth and colour of the text. The rule of verisimilitude laid down by the theorists was disregarded, to the reader's delight, by writers like Ariosto and La Fontaine; it was scrupulously respected by their illustrators.

The second rule governing the image was propriety. This meant that all the elements of an illustration had to be in perfect agreement with each other and with the text: the composition well knit and complete, no too prominent detail, no oblique point of view, no side scenes. The setting was expected to be coherent, predictable, justified by the text. The costume must not particularize the figure; facial expression and gesture, the touchstone of history painting, must keep to the conventions and usage of a predetermined vocabulary. Archaeological respect for propriety had to preside over the illustrator's work. It set the limits he must not overstep. It banned the burlesque outright as incompatible with serious work. Even more than the text, the image blushed at anything "unseemly, immodest, barbaric"; and Lessing in the eighteenth century, thought a "liberator" of the image, could still write a whole chapter on the limits of the "repulsive"; and the literary examples he gives went further than the image had ever gone. The uninhibited gusto of Grimmelshausen's *Simplicissimus* (1669) and other picaresque romances breaks out here and there in broadsheets, but the coarseness and "realism" of these images calls for a few remarks. First, they are anterior to 1630, before the movement to purify the arts got underway. Further, they are themselves an offshoot of literature. So true is this that they take their name and genre from categories of speech: the *Street Cries* that appeared in Italy in the late sixteenth century in the form of strip cartoons, or the garrulous *Proverbs* of Jacques Lagniet in France. Most of these low-life illustrations involve punning, farce, riddles; when they are not straightforward illustrations of oral literature or stage comedies, they are plastered with captions, subtitles and numbers keyed to a list of explanatory phrases. The fashion for parodied maps, referring to the human heart or mind, was typical of the seventeenth century; the most famous of them was the Carte de Tendre in Mademoiselle de Scudéry's sentimental romance *Clélie*, the mapping out of an Arcadia where the river of Inclination waters the villages of Billet Doux, Sincerity and so on—with the Lake of Indifference hard by. Any image too indelicate, any invention too fanciful, had to be turned into an allegory: it was watered down and made to conform to the abstractions of literature.

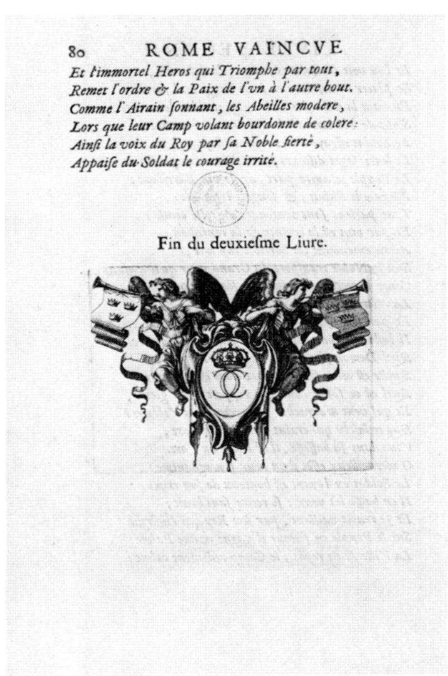
80 ROME VAINCVE
Et l'immortel Heros qui Triomphe par tout,
Remet l'ordre & la Paix de l'vn à l'autre bout.
Comme l'Airain ſonnant, les Abeilles modere,
Lors que leur Camp volant bourdonne de colere:
Ainſi la voix du Roy par ſa Noble fierté,
Appaiſe du Soldat le courage irrité.

Fin du deuxieſme Liure.

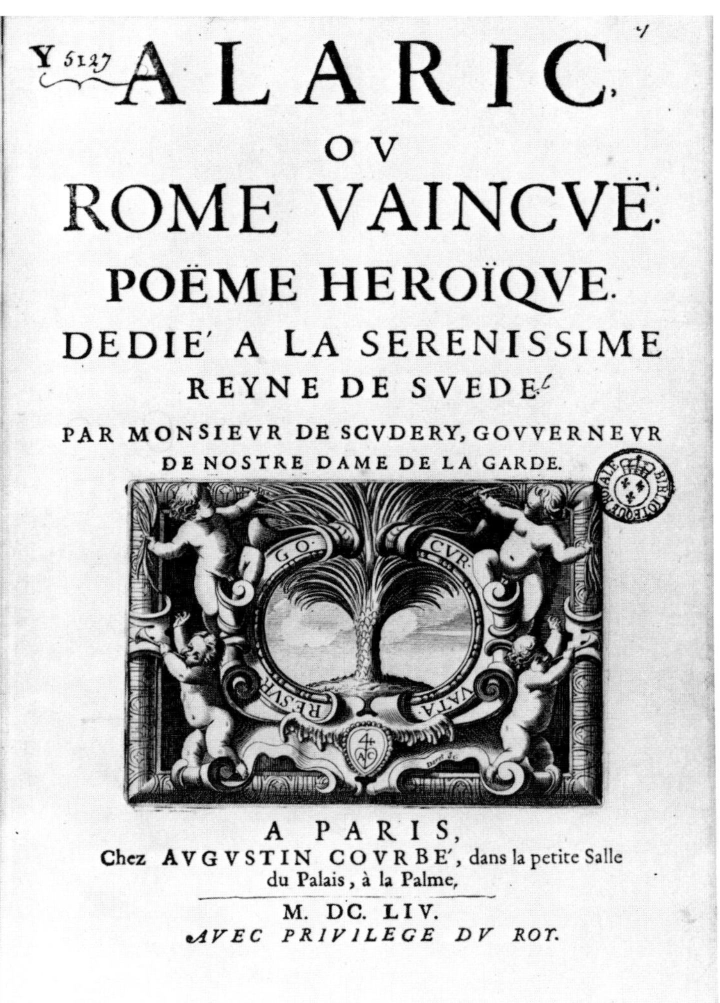
Y 5127
ALARIC,
OV
ROME VAINCVË.
POËME HEROÏQVE.
DEDIE' A LA SERENISSIME
REYNE DE SVEDE.
PAR MONSIEVR DE SCVDERY, GOVVERNEVR
DE NOSTRE DAME DE LA GARDE.

A PARIS,
Chez AVGVSTIN COVRBE', dans la petite Salle
du Palais, à la Palme,
M. DC. LIV.
AVEC PRIVILEGE DV ROY.

The rules of Verisimilitude and Propriety could of course be disregarded—they had to be—under the cloak of a moral or didactic purpose. In France, Chapelain himself justified the use of Aesop's fables for the needs of moral education, with the proviso that their application should remain symbolic and universal. So the comic writer escaped blame if he took care to treat his characters as allegorical types of a given vice rather than individuals, as Molière and La Fontaine had to do. Likewise in imagery, the illustrator could spice his work with a certain amount of realism and a few bold strokes from life if he posed as a man waging a moral contest. The works of Molière failed to profit by these openings, their early illustrations being few and lifeless. But the opportunity of such openings was seized by the romance writers of the eighteenth century and their suite of caricaturists, stimulated as they were by the demand of a public increasingly fond of the concrete details of actual life.

It was now, as fiction gained ground, that pictures based on it came into their own. The illustration achieved a specific value, for it added to the text something that the text could not convey. It seized on a particular point, which it arrested and enlarged on. Its power to suspend the narrative, to single out one moment of the plot, contributed a touch of the marvellous, just as today the still, by

The Box on the Ear, print by Nicolas Le Mire after J.M. Moreau the Younger, illustrating Jean-Jacques Rousseau, *La Nouvelle Héloïse* (Letter LXIII), London, 1774.

Illustrations of the 1761 edition of Rousseau's *La Nouvelle Héloïse* published as a separate volume of prints.

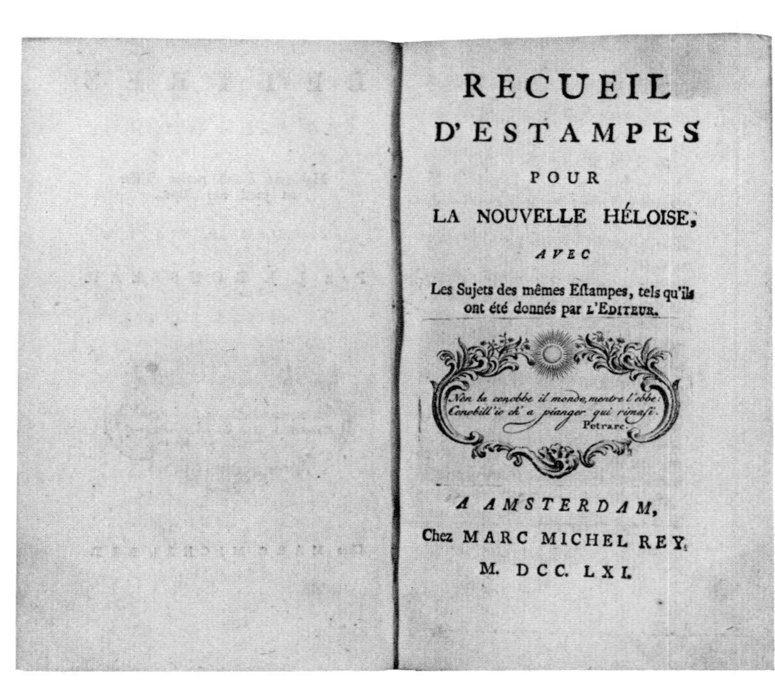

RECUEIL
D'ESTAMPES
POUR
LA NOUVELLE HÉLOISE,
AVEC
Les Sujets des mêmes Estampes, tels qu'ils ont été donnés par L'EDITEUR.

Non la conobbe il mondo, mentre l'ebbe:
Conobbil'io ch'a pianger qui rimasi.
Petrarc.

A AMSTERDAM,
Chez MARC MICHEL REY.
M. DCC. LXI.

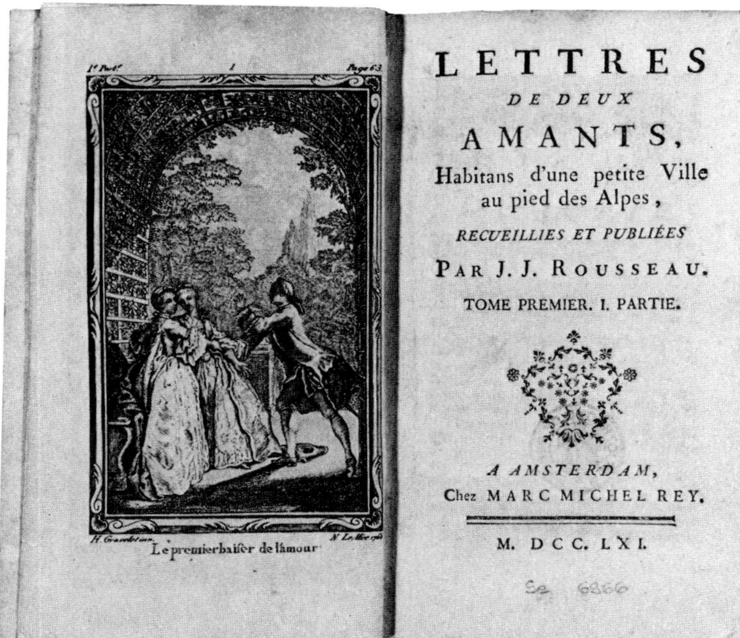

Le premier baiser de l'amour

LETTRES
DE DEUX
AMANTS,
Habitans d'une petite Ville
au pied des Alpes,
RECUEILLIES ET PUBLIÉES
PAR J. J. ROUSSEAU.
TOME PREMIER. I. PARTIE.

A AMSTERDAM,
Chez MARC MICHEL REY.
M. DCC. LXI.

Jean-Jacques Rousseau, *Lettres de deux amants (La Nouvelle Héloïse)*, Amsterdam, 1761, with frontispiece by Gravelot: The First Kiss of Love.

its very immobility, adds a fascination to the cinema. Here lay the illustrator's originality, his specific field of action and responsibility. The illustrator's art, in the classical age of French literature, was the art of choosing the critical moment. Hence the significance of the disagreement between Racine and his illustrator, François Chauveau. The latter, accustomed to illustrating romances of chivalry, saw Racine's tragedies only from the visual point of view as spectacle, while Racine himself expected Chauveau to pick out the critical moments of his characters' inner life. The illustrator's approach thus had to be defined in new terms: the attraction of what was visually distinctive must not be allowed to cloud his insight into the hidden world of emotions. His art at its best had to be an art of discerning observation, of nice distinctions in the rendering of gesture, attitude, facial features. The picturing of costumes and attributes was not enough; he had to respond, and make the reader respond, to a sidelong glance, to the start and flutter of a hand. When in the eighteenth century the illustrator was faced with the new novels and their exploration of the recesses of the human heart, such as Richardson's *Pamela* or Rousseau's *Nouvelle Héloïse*, he had to enter into the world of feelings with as sure a step as he had into that of the natural sciences. A few decades later we find the scene of young Werther's suicide being illustrated by Chodowiecki in the form of an empty room: a figure of rhetoric (litotes or metonymy) turned into a purely visual device. And yet only the caption (what had to be read) gave meaning to the image, which without it was meaningless. It was indeed words, as Père Le Moyne had said, that arrest the image and attach a particular sense to it. But the image in its turn enriched the text with new references, which were no longer of the same order as discourse.

Chalk drawing by J.M. Moreau the Younger illustrating the scene of the Box on the Ear (Letter LXIII) in Rousseau's *La Nouvelle Héloïse*.

Tasso's "Gerusalemme Liberata"

2

1

1. *Sébastien Le Clerc, etching for Tasso's "Jerusalem Delivered," Amsterdam, 1678, Canto III.*
2. *Antonio Tempesta, plate III of a set of etchings illustrating "Jerusalem Delivered," early 17th century.*
3. *Giovanni Battista Piazzetta, etching for "Jerusalem Delivered," Venice, 1745, headpiece for Canto III.*
4. *Bernardo Castello, illustrations for "Jerusalem Delivered," Genoa, 1590, Canto III.*
5. *Charles Nicolas Cochin, illustration for "Jerusalem Delivered," Paris, 1784, Canto III.*

3

ARGOMENTO.

Giunge a Gieruſalemme il campo: e quivi
In fera guiſa è da Clorinda accolto.
Sveglia in Erminia amor Tancredi: e vivi
Fa i propj incendj al diſcoprir d'un volto.
Reſtan gli Avventurier di duce privi:
Ch'un ſol colpo d'Argante a lor l'ha tolto.
Pietoſe eſſequie ſangli. Il pio Buglione,
Ch'antica ſelva ſi recida, impone.

CANTO TERZO.

I.

GIA' L'AURA meſſaggiera eraſi deſta
A nunziar che ſe ne vien l'aurora:
Ella intanto s'adorna, e l'aurea teſta
Di roſe colte in Paradiſo infiora;
Quando il Campo, ch'all'arme omai s'appreſta,
In voce mormorava alta e ſonora,
E prevenia le trombe: e queſte poi
Dier più lieti e canori i ſegni ſuoi.

(27)

Two epic poems of sixteenth-century Italy provided an inexhaustible repertory for painters, decorators and illustrators: Ariosto's *Orlando Furioso* and Tasso's *Gerusalemme Liberata.* The latter even more than the former, since it answered to the aspirations of a wider public. It embodied the Counter-Reformation's ideal of religious reconquest and combined it with the exotic and sensual taste for adventure and love stories. Tasso's poem had the added feature of offering many picturesque or spectacular "points of view" well calculated to stimulate the illustrator's visual imagination; and its division into cantos lent itself to a series of frontispieces. An initial illustrated edition, by the poet's friend Bernardo Castello, was published in Tasso's lifetime, at Genoa in 1590, with prints still in a Mannerist style. Castello illustrated the poem twice again, in 1604 and 1617. But after 1620 Antonio Tempesta renewed the style of this imagery with his usual vigour, in battle scenes and drawings of horses; his two sets of prints were apparently published as separate portfolios without the text. Such was the poem's continued success that through its different illustrators we get something like a history of styles. In Venice, for example, they range from the rather crude woodcuts of the 1599 edition to the refinement of the editions illustrated by Giovanni Battista Piazzetta (1745) or Pier Antonio Novelli (1760), the emphasis here being on love-making rather than fighting. The flavour is definitely exotic and the sentimental reader gets the full benefit of the love intrigues. In France one may compare the five very sober plates of Chauveau (1644) or the vignettes of Sébastien Le Clerc with the gayer scenes of Gravelot (1771) and Charles Nicolas Cochin (1784) who treated the epic poem like a ballet. The *Gerusalemme Liberata* was still being illustrated in the nineteenth century, for example by the neo-classical line engraver Ambroise Tardieu, also by the romantic illustrator Célestin Nanteuil. But it is hardly worth carrying the comparison so far. The fact that it was not illustrated by Gustave Doré was due to the waning popularity of a book which it is by no means easy to find now in a modern edition even without pictures. ■

4

CANTO TERZO.

ARGOMENTO

Giunge à Gierusalemme il campo: e quiui
In fera guisa è da Clorinda accolto.
Sueglia in Erminia amor Tancredi: e viui
Fà i propri incendi al discoprir d'un volto.
Restan gli auuenturier di duce priui:
Ch'un sol colpo d'Argante à lor l'hà tolto.
Pietose essequie fangli. Il pio Buglione,
Ch'antica selua si recida impone.

1

GIA l'aura messaggiera erasi desta
A' nuntiar, che se ne vien l'Aurora:
Ella in tanto s'adorna, e l'aurea testa
Di rose colte in Paradiso infiora;
Quādo il cāpo, ch'à l'arme homai s'appresta,
In voce mormoraua alta, e sonora,
E preuenia le trombe: e queste poi
Dier più lieti, e canori i segni suoi.

2

Il saggio Capitan con dolce morso,
I desiderij lor guida, e seconda:
Che più facil saria suolger il corso
Presso Cariddi à la volubil'onda:
O' tardar Borea all'hor, che scote il dorso
De l'Apennino, e i legni in mare affonda.
Gli ordina, gl'incamina, e'n suon gli regge
Rapido sì, ma rapido con legge.

3

Ali hà ciascuno al core, & ali al piede:
Nè del suo ratto andar però s'accorge.
Ma, quando il sol gli aridi campi fiede
Con raggi assai feruenti, e in alto sorge
Ecco apparir Gierusalem si vede:
Ecco additar Gierusalem si scorge:
Ecco da mille voci vnitamente
Gierusalemme salutar si sente.

Così

5

CANTO III. Ott. 3.

Ecco da mille voci unitamente | 3 | Gerusalemme salutar si sente.

LA GERUSALEMME

LIBERATA.

CANTO TERZO.

ARGOMENTO.

Giunge a Gerusalemme il campo; e quivi
In fera guisa è da Clorinda accolto.
Sveglia in Erminia amor Tancredi; e vivi
Fa i proprj incendj al discoprir d' un volto.
Restan gli Avventurier di duce privi;
Ch' un sol colpo d' Argante a lor l' ha tolto:
Pietose essequie fangli. Il pio Buglione
Ch' antica selva si recida impone.

I.

Già l' aura messaggiera erasi desta
Ad annunziar che se ne vien l' aurora;
Ella intanto s' adorna, e l' aurea testa
Di rose colte in paradiso infiora:
Quando il campo, ch' all' arme omai s' appresta,
In voce mormorava alta e sonora,
E prevenia le trombe; e queste poi
Dier più lieti e canori i segni suoi.

The "Obsidio Bredana" and Rubens' Title Pages

1

OBSIDIO
BREDANA
ARMIS
PHILIPPI IIII.
AVSPICIIS
ISABELLÆ
DVCTV
AMBR. SPINOLÆ
PERFECTA.
SCRIBEBAT
HERMANNVS HVGO
SOCIETATIS IESV.

ANTVERPIÆ EX OFFICINA PLANTINIANA, M.DC.XXVI.

2

Down to the eighteenth century the privileged place for illustration, and often the only place for it, was the title page, opening the book and enhancing its title. For the earlier ornamental designs inspired by architecture (fittingly enough, since the title page was the "entry" of the book), the Baroque age increasingly substituted symbolic and allegorical compositions alluding to the subject of the book. Rubens and his studio assistants were among the most prolific inventors of this genre. On friendly terms with the Antwerp publisher Balthasar Moretus, who had taken over from his father, the son-in-law of Plantin, and directed the most important publishing house in Europe from 1610 to 1641, Rubens designed forty-nine title pages for Moretus from 1612 to 1639; nineteen drawings and four oil studies for them are still extant.

The taste for decorated title pages can be seen from a letter written to Moretus on 1 August 1617 by one of his authors, Bernard Bauhausius: "My dear Moretus, many people would like to find an engraving at the beginning of the book (we see this is being done everywhere...). Such a design interests the reader, attracts the buyer, enhances the book and scarcely increases the price... I am sure that for this page that godlike genius Rubens will find something well suited to my poems." And indeed the inexhaustible imagination of Rubens adapted itself readily to the inexhaustible erudition of Moretus, and together they produced some complex and attractive title pages, whose style was not unrelated to that of the emblem designers.

Antwerp was then under the domination of the Spanish and the Jesuits. It was the spearhead of their "Reconquest" of the North, and it was from there that the Jesuits spread their propaganda and ideology. Typical of their publications is the book of the siege of Breda, *Obsidio Bredana* (1626), written by the Jesuit father Herman Hugo. The title page refers to the contents in terms of allegory: Hercules and Minerva on either side; below, the personified City being strangled by Famine; at the top, the two Winds, suggesting the length of the siege, through winter and spring. For this design we have Rubens' original drawing in a full pictorial style; the flatter, more linear copy in reverse from which the engraver worked; and the final page engraved by Cornelis Galle. ■

3

1. *Title page of Herman Hugo,* Obsidio Bredana, *Antwerp, 1626, designed by Rubens, engraved by Cornelis Galle.*
2. *Reversed interpretation of Rubens' design, by another draughtsman, for the use of the engraver.*
3. *Rubens' original drawing for the title page of the* Obsidio Bredana.

THE WORLD OF THE SENSES

84 LE SPECTACLE

LES RIVIERES. Vous m'obligeriez de me dire ce qu'ils ſont tous en détail.

Saine. *Le Pr.* Commençons par ceux-ci. C'eſt un pere de famille, qui avec ſes enfans jette de deſſus une barque le grand & long filèt qu'on appelle ſaine. Ils en attachent le premier bout au bord de l'eau à un piquèt : & faiſant avec leur barque un circuit qui embraſſe, autant qu'il eſt poſſible, toute la largeur de la rivière, ils étendent & jettent à l'eau les longs replis de leur filèt, & reviennent gagner le bord d'où ils ſont partis. Le haut de la ſaine demeure ſuſpendu à la ſurface de l'eau ſur ſes patenôtres de liege : le bas appéſanti par un long chapelèt de plomb gagne le fond de l'eau, & forme ainſi une muraille ou plûtôt une enceinte circulaire d'où le poiſſon ne peut ſe ſauver que vers le bord de l'eau où l'enceinte n'eſt pas encore entièrement achevée : mais on prend ſoin d'y battre l'eau, & le poiſſon y rencontre les piés des enfans du pêcheur, qui rangés à la file, traînent conjointement le bout du filèt qu'ils rapprochent peu-à peu de celui qui eſt au piquèt. Le poiſſon effrayé par tous ces mouvemens, ſe jette du côté oppoſé, où il eſt de toute part arrêté par le filèt. A force de tirer les deux bouts & de diminuer petit

▲ Fold-out illustration from Abbé Pluche, *Le Spectacle de la Nature, ou entretiens sur les particularités de l'histoire naturelle qui ont paru les plus propres à rendre les jeunes gens curieux et à leur former l'esprit*, Paris, 1739, Vol. III.

◀ Samuel Birmann, View of the Mer de Glace from Montanvert, Savoy, coloured aquatint, early 19th century.

The power of the national language, radiating from the political centre, was not unshared: the image went with it as an ever more necessary complement. Speech, whether spoken or written, owed its effectiveness to its arbitrary, authoritarian and indeed totalitarian character; the image, on the other hand, could be seen as a "natural language." The competition between them was fought out in the ideological war of the eighteenth century, a war against authoritarianism waged by the new middle-class morality, empiric and sentimental, which came to the fore in the English periodicals and the novels of Fielding and Richardson. The moral purposes of these writers were served by imagery, whose documentary realism added a further dimension to the delineation of character. In France, at the close of the reign of Louis XIV, appeared the symptoms of an illustration emancipated from the writing; as when, for example, the picture ventured to vie with the text in humour, in Oudry's illustrations for *Le Roman Comique* or Gillot's for *Le Lutrin*, or with a more unbridled imagination in Charles-Antoine Coypel's designs for *Don Quixote*, which were to act as model for a whole generation of tapestries, paintings and engravings on the theme of Don Quixote. Under the Régence, French illustration came into its own, with the production of deluxe editions which constitute the prototype of the modern collector's edition: here the illustration rises to a new level of eye-flattering refinement, appealing at once to the taste for the picturesque and to the claims of the imagination. Such was the Fermiers Généraux edition of La Fontaine's *Contes*, a book of verse tales both libertine and classical, vividly symbolizing the new fortunes being made in the days of John Law's Mississippi Scheme.

In France, from the early eighteenth century on, the printed book came for the first time to be aesthetically valued for the beauty of its illustrations. This taste was accompanied by the rise of documentary illustrations, appearing now on a more ambitious scale, designed to give a fully rounded picture of a given theme. But illustration was still handicapped by the clumsiness of its reproduction. For these large plates, run off again and again in editions of many thousands of copies, the only techniques available were line engraving and etching. All illustration was as yet still "directed towards the burin," to use the expression of the great collector of eighteenth-century illustrated books, Jean Furstenberg. Pure etching, often

1

LE BÂT.

Un peintre étoit, qui jaloux de ſa femme,
Allant aux champs, lui peignit un baudet
Sur le nombril, en guiſe de cachet.
Un ſien confrere amoureux de la Dame,
La va trouver, & l'âne efface net,
Dieu ſçait comment ; puis un autre en remet,
Au même endroit, ainſi que l'on peut croire.
A celui-ci, par faute de mémoire,
Il mit un Bât ; l'autre n'en avoit point.
L'époux revient, veut s'éclaircir du point.
Voyez, mon fils, dit la bonne commere ;
L'âne eſt témoin de ma fidélité.
Diantre ſoit fait, dit l'époux en colere,
Et du témoin, & de qui l'a bâté.

used for the first states of these prints, was preferred by Furstenberg, for "by the time you get to the eighth printing you have a mere reproduction of the first state, and all the delicacy and nuances are gone." Etching was necessary for rapidity, both of style and execution, but the line engraver's burin was necessary too in order to consolidate the cutting of plates which had to withstand continual reprinting. So it is that all sorts of combinations were tried to reconcile these two imperatives, and French reproductive engravers made a speciality of these mixed media. Let it be remembered moreover that Rembrandt, at the end of his career, only obtained a commission for some illustrations thanks to a stratagem of his son, who vaunted him to the publisher as a great line engraver. Also, in the first half of the eighteenth century, the size of these French prints tended to be reduced, being aimed at a public of slenderer means and designed for cheaper books enlivened with more pictures and motifs. The vignette included in the octavo or the sixteenmo met with a great success in editions of the poetry of J.B. Rousseau, Gessner and Dorat. This vogue culminated about 1750. C.N. Cochin was the engraver most in demand for these vignettes. He turned out so many of them that the chronicler Sébastien Mercier, imagining "The Year 2440" (the title of one of his books), wrote in it that "book vignettes were then called Cochins: such was the word that had been substituted for such miserable words as tailpiece, etc." Illustration followed in the wake of that vogue for gouaches, watercolours, pastels and miniatures on enamel which supplied works of art accessible to the purse and taste of middle-class families of the later eighteenth century. Then illustration went its own way, detached from the book by the vogue for "sets" of prints, sold independently of the book by the printmaker himself. Such were those of Moreau the Younger

2

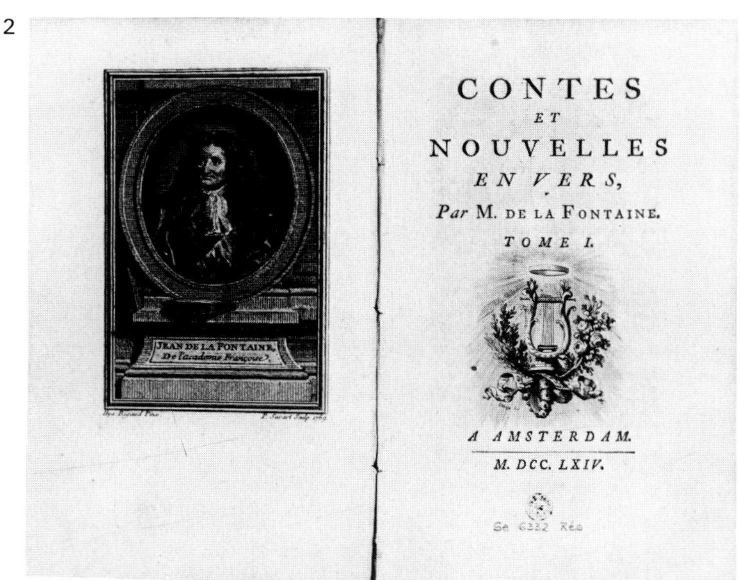

CONTES
ET
NOUVELLES
EN VERS,
Par M. DE LA FONTAINE.
TOME I.

A AMSTERDAM.
M. DCC. LXIV.

Ge 6222 Rés

3

130 FABLES CHOISIES.

FABLE XI.

RIEN DE TROP.

Je ne vois point de créature
Se comporter modérément.
Il eſt certain tempéramment
Que le Maître de la nature
Veut que l'on garde en tout. Le fait-on ? nullement.
Soit en bien, ſoit en mal, cela n'arrive guére.
Le bled, riche préſent de la blonde Cérès,
Trop touffu bien ſouvent épuiſe les guérets :
En ſuperfluités s'épandant d'ordinaire,
Et pouſſant trop abondamment,
Il ôte à ſon fruit l'aliment.
L'arbre n'en fait pas moins, tant le luxe ſçait plaire.
Pour corriger le bled Dieu permit aux moutons
De retrancher l'excès des prodigues moiſſons.
Tout au travers ils ſe jetterent,
Gâterent tout, & tout brouterent ;
Tant que le ciel permit aux loups
D'en croquer quelques-uns : ils les croquerent tous :
S'ils ne le firent pas, du moins ils y tâcherent.
Puis le ciel permit aux humains
De punir ces derniers : les humains abuſerent
A leur tour des ordres divins.

De tous les animaux, l'homme a le plus de pente
A ſe porter dedans l'excès.
Il faudroit faire le procès
Au petits comme aux grands. Il n'eſt ame vivante
Qui ne peche en ceci. *Rien de trop*, eſt un point
Dont on parle ſans ceſſe, & qu'on n'obſerve point.

(*Fable* CLXXX.)

for the complete works of Voltaire. In their initial version, they were issued separately. But, as Jean Furstenberg relates, "Beaumarchais had at the same time been preparing to print, with Baskerville types, his monumental edition of Voltaire in seventy volumes. He could not do without Moreau as the illustrator, and Moreau could not do without him." A fine example, already in the 1780s, of the reputation gained by an illustrator and the pre-eminence gained by illustration.

True, the chief producers of this imagery in the eighteenth century were England and Holland. And some notable French engravers sought their fortunes there, after Nicolas Dorigny emigrated to England in 1711. These émigrés had behind them a fine technical tradition: what they were after were commissions and a public. Among them was Gravelot, called to London to engrave the English edition of Picart's *Religious Ceremonies*, first because he was prolific and his work already formed an anthology of all the "illustratable" literature of his time, but most of

4

1. Jean de La Fontaine, *Contes*, Fermiers Généraux edition, Amsterdam, 1762, with plates by Charles Eisen, tailpiece by Pierre Philippe Choffard.

2. Jean de La Fontaine, *Contes et Nouvelles en vers*, Amsterdam, 1764, frontispiece engraved by Pierre Savart after Hyacinthe Rigaud.

3. La Fontaine's *Fables*, Paris, 1755-1759, with illustrations by Jean-Baptiste Oudry, engraved by P.E. Moitte.

4. Drawing by Jean-Baptiste Oudry, 1732, for La Fontaine's fable "Rien de trop" (Nothing overmuch).

William Hogarth, Sir Hudibras Sallies Forth, etching, 1726, from his first set of illustrations for Samuel Butler's *Hudibras.*

all because as "a draughtsman by taste and engraver by necessity" he stood out as the first great "professional" illustrator, though he was not the only one for long. For these early professionals, engraving was first and foremost a technical language. From its proficiency as such the image drew its authority and force. The maxim "Utile dulci" which had gone to justify all the fancies and fantasies that overstepped the classical rules, was in practice successfully translated into English: "Instruct and amuse." It authorized the multiplication of documentary, moral and satirical images. The idea that illustration is an indispensable tool of knowledge, a necessary complement to the text, not reducible to it, is set forth on the first page of the *Notice historique sur l'art de la gravure* by Pierre Philippe Choffard, one of the virtuoso illustrators of that day: "The service that printing renders to poetry, history and literature is one that it cannot render alone to painting, sculpture, architecture, mechanics, geography and the other sciences: there figures are necessary for the right understanding of the text."

Hogarth was the heir of all these traditions, converging now at a favourable moment. He was the heir of the bourgeois realism of the Italian, Parisian, Lorrainese and Dutch little masters of the seventeenth century, of the English middle-class moralists and philosophers of the eighteenth century, of the caricaturists and technicians of illustration and particularly of the Dutch etcher and lampooner Romeyn de Hooghe. To measure the distance separating the cramped illustration of classical editions from the large plates of eighteenth-century books, one need only compare the two versions Hogarth made of Samuel Butler's mock romance *Hudibras.* From one to the other, the relative proportions change entirely. Hitherto the writing held the image in leash. Now the image prevailed. The title-page design was no longer enough: vignettes, full-page plates and even fold-out plates were added pell-mell, and their weight was so keenly felt that the rivalry between the two modes of expression became a topical issue.

Philosophers were fascinated by the origins of language. This was the subject of Maupertuis' essay *Réflexions philosophiques sur l'origine des langues et la signification des mots* (1752) and of a bravura piece by Rousseau. With them appears a scientific interest in the study of signs which may be said to go back to Athanasius Kircher's studies of the Chinese script and the nature of images (*Ars magnae lucis et umbrae,* 1646). But such work only took on a truly philosophical dimension with William Warburton's essay on hieroglyphs (in *The Divine Legation of Moses,* 1738). It was Warburton, together with Locke, who prompted Condillac to write his *Essai sur l'origine des connaissances humaines* (1746). This book is, as Jacques Derrida has said, "a matter of semiotics through and through." It sets forth the first principles of a lay semiotics: "The use of signs is the principle which develops the germ of all our ideas." This took a materialistic turn in Destutt de Tracy's *Eléments d'Idéologie* (1811-1815): "All our knowledge consists of ideas, and these ideas only appear to us in the form of signs." His enlargement of the notion of a sign, to take in such activities as dancing, costume and music, makes Condillac an essential theorist in this struggle against the absolutism of language and, as an after-effect, in the promotion of imagery. This shift in the relative weight of text and image had its own theorist, the German philosopher Lessing in his *Laokoon* (1766), subtitled "On the limits of painting and poetry." It exerted a strong influence throughout Europe. The point then was to revalorize poetry in the face of the undue prominence given to the plastic arts by Winckelmann and other critics. It was also a reaction against the abuses arising from the confusion between the literary and the pictorial. The literary themes set for competitions and the written notices accompanying pictures at the Salon had assumed an inordinate importance; and the accuracy of archaeological details in them had become the

William Hogarth, Sir Hudibras Sallies Forth, line engraving, 1726, from his second set of illustrations for Samuel Butler's *Hudibras*.

Charles-Antoine Coypel, Don Quixote Taking a Barber's Basin for a Headpiece, from his illustrations for *Don Quichotte*, Paris, 1723.

20 Alpen-Gedicht.

VII.

Glükseliger Verlust von schadenvollen Gütern!
Der Reichthum hat kein Gut, das eurer Armuth gleicht;
Die Eintracht wohnt bey euch in friedlichen Gemüthern,
Weil kein beglänzter Wahn euch Zweytrachtsäpfel reicht:
Die Freude wird hier nicht mit banger Furcht begleitet,
Wo man das Leben liebt, und doch den Tod nicht haßt;
Hier herrschet die Vernunft, von der Natur geleitet,
Die, was ihr nöthig, sucht, und mehrers hält für Last:
Was Epiktet gethan, und Seneka geschrieben,
Sieht man hier ungelehrt und ungezwungen üben.

VIII.

Hier herrscht kein Unterschied, den schlauer Stolz erfunden,
Der Tugend unterthan, und Laster edel macht;
Kein müßiger Verdruß verlängert hier die Stunden,
Die Arbeit füllt den Tag, und Ruh besezt die Nacht.
Hier läßt kein hoher Geist sich von der Ehrsucht blenden,
Des Morgens Sorge frißt des Heutes Freude nie.
Die Freyheit theilt dem Volk, aus milden Mutterhänden,
Mit immer gleichem Maaß, Vergnügen, Ruh und Müh.
Kein unzufriedner Sinn zankt sich mit seinem Glüke,
Man ißt, man schläft, man liebt, und danket dem Geschike.

Albrecht von Haller, *Ode sur les Alpes.../Gedicht von der Schönheit und dem Nutzen der schweizerischen Alpen*, Berne, 1772: Two scenes of the simple life led by the inhabitants of the Swiss Alps.

M.T. Bourrit, *Description des Alpes Pennines et Rhétiennes*, Geneva, 1781: View of the Lake of Kandel Steig.

main standard by which paintings were judged. Pictures could no longer be looked at for their own sake: they had to be justified or explained in writing, at ever greater length. Lessing reacted against this mania for judging painting by the yardstick of literature and vice versa; against Caylus and his *Tableaux tirés de l'Iliade, de l'Odyssée d'Homère et de l'Enéide de Virgile avec des observations générales sur le costume* (1757), in which we are told that "the more images and actions a poem supplies, the higher it is as poetry"; against Spence and his *Polymetis: or, An enquiry concerning the agreement between the works of the Roman poets, and remains of the antient artists. Being an attempt to illustrate them mutually from one another...* (London, 1747). By marking off the domain of the written word and its specific qualities (linearity, sequence, narration) from that of the image as characterized by wholeness, simultaneity, concreteness and delineation, Lessing rendered a signal service to illustration, which with him came of age, recognized as being endowed with an intrinsic value as a medium of expression in its own right, irreducible to language. These views were not put forward by chance at this time. Lessing cited as an example Albrecht von Haller's poem *Die Alpen* (1729). The growth of geographical and historical literature had made this aesthetic conflict inevitable. The preface to the lavishly illustrated French edition of Haller's poem begins as follows: "Painting and Poetry have between them a natural affinity... If the painter, unlike the poet, cannot give movement to his images or continuity and a dramatic turn to the actions he represents, he makes up for this impotence by some advantages which the poet will never have. The painter's strokes are a surer means, prompter and more general, of depicting to the imagination..." At a time when man was being seen as the docile pupil of Nature, it was the image which showed the way. It was through pictures that Europe discovered the Alpine glaciers, the Swiss lakes, the Rhine falls. An eight-volume work on the "Spectacle of Nature" by Abbé Pluche became popular with the French public on its publication in 1732. It opened with this profession of faith: "Nature is the most learned and perfect of all the books fit to cultivate our mind, since it contains the objects of all the sciences at once and intelligence can there range freely, unrestricted to any one language or any one person." Thus the world was set up as Spectacle and knowledge of it necessarily called for illustration.

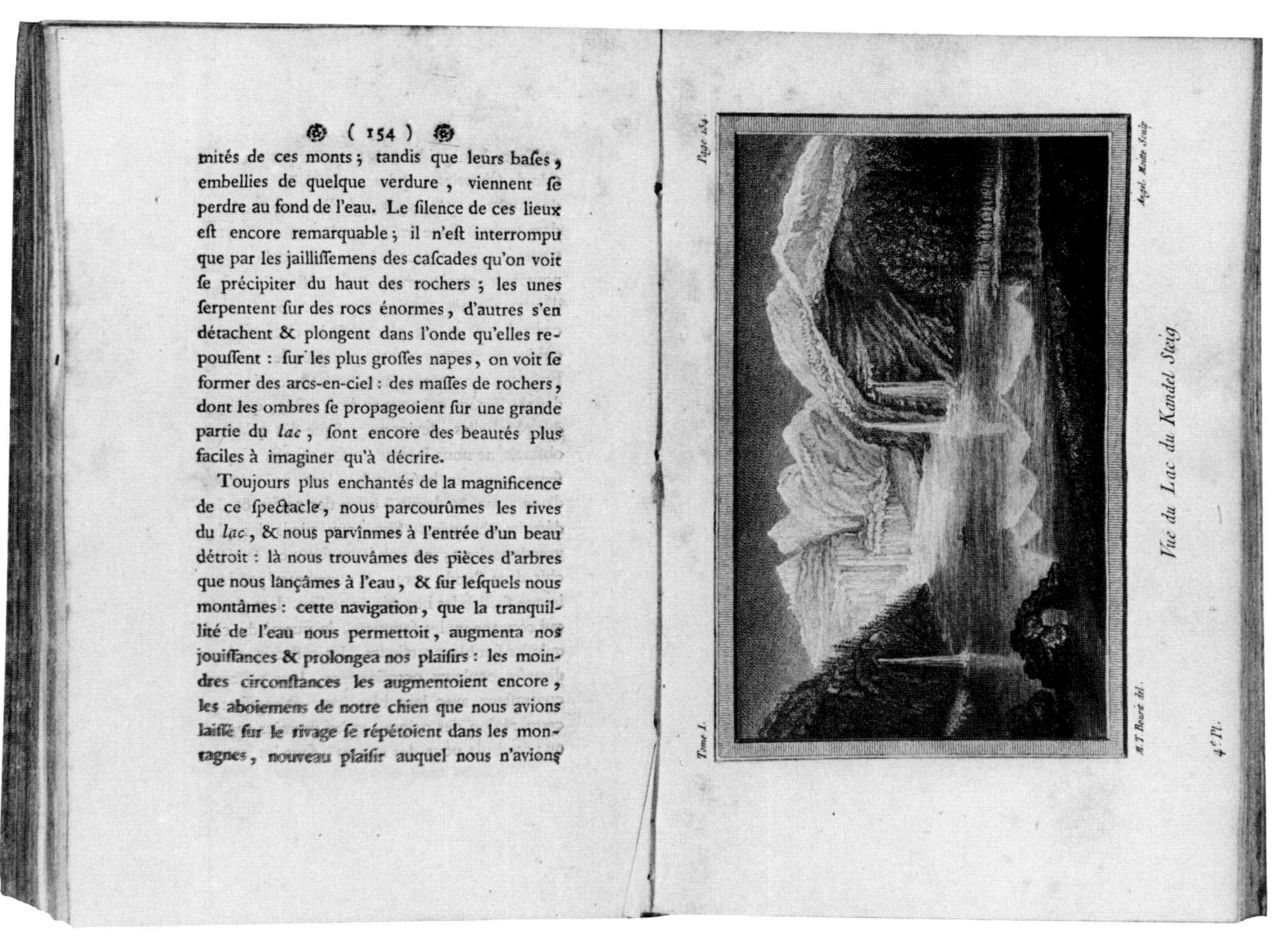

(154)

mités de ces monts ; tandis que leurs baſes, embellies de quelque verdure, viennent ſe perdre au fond de l'eau. Le ſilence de ces lieux eſt encore remarquable ; il n'eſt interrompu que par les jailliſſemens des caſcades qu'on voit ſe précipiter du haut des rochers ; les unes ſerpentent ſur des rocs énormes, d'autres s'en détachent & plongent dans l'onde qu'elles repouſſent : ſur les plus groſſes napes, on voit ſe former des arcs-en-ciel : des maſſes de rochers, dont les ombres ſe propageoient ſur une grande partie du *lac*, ſont encore des beautés plus faciles à imaginer qu'à décrire.

Toujours plus enchantés de la magnificence de ce ſpectacle, nous parcourûmes les rives du *lac*, & nous parvînmes à l'entrée d'un beau détroit : là nous trouvâmes des pièces d'arbres que nous lançâmes à l'eau, & ſur leſquels nous montâmes : cette navigation, que la tranquillité de l'eau nous permettoit, augmenta nos jouiſſances & prolongea nos plaiſirs : les moindres circonſtances les augmentoient encore, les aboiemens de notre chien que nous avions laiſſé ſur le rivage ſe répétoient dans les montagnes, nouveau plaiſir auquel nous n'avions

Tableaux de la Suisse ou Voyage pittoresque fait dans les XIII Cantons du Corps Helvétique, Paris, 1784: View of the Rhine Falls.

The Almanac of Göttingen

1

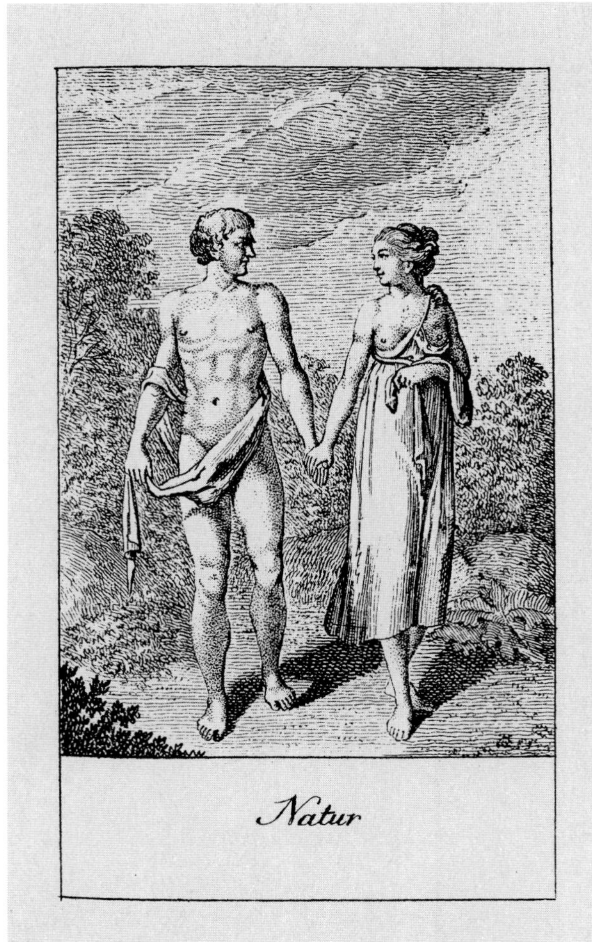

2

3

Published in their hundreds of thousands in the late eighteenth century, the almanacs were small books full of practical information, also of chit-chat and small pictures, being designed for a wide public newly awakened to the pleasures of reading for whom the vignette was an indispensable element of attraction. France set the tone in 1765 with the *Almanach des Muses,* imitated at Göttingen in 1770 by the *Musenalmanach* and then by the *Göttinger Taschenkalendar.* They owed their reputation to the illustrations contributed by Daniel Chodowiecki, from 1778 to 1794, and to the intelligent editorship of the writer Georg Christoph Lichtenberg. Chodowiecki had begun his career as a graphic artist in 1769, with the almanac of the Berlin Academy. Working at first in the Rococo manner, with its theatrical affectation, its allegorical and mythological fancies, he soon developed a style and vein better suited to his readers, picturing scenes of everyday middle-class life and becoming the favourite artist of the almanac public. The mainstay of such publications as the *Almanach et portefeuille des joies domestiques et sociales* (1796) and the *Almanach dédié à l'amour et à l'amitié* (1800), Chodowiecki produced a body of graphic work amounting to 2075 plates; only 170 of them are independent prints; 1905 of them are book illustrations, and of these 1275 were published in almanacs. No less able and active was Lichtenberg. A professor of physics at Göttingen University, he became sole editor in 1778 of the *Göttinger Taschenkalendar,* filling it singlehandedly with scientific, humorous and satirical articles. In its pages he engaged in a witty controversy with Lavater, whose "science" of physiognomy he ridiculed. This was followed by his amusing series of "Marriage Proposals" (1781), the "follies" of the *Centifolium Scultorum* (1783) and his interpretation of Hogarth's engravings (1784). The success of these almanacs continued throughout the Romantic period, gradually changing their nature with the vogue for the English Keepsake and the German Taschenbuch. ■

4

5

6

7

From the "Almanac of Göttingen,"
line engravings by Chodowiecki, captions by Lichtenberg:

1.2.3. Nature and Affectation, second series, 1781.

4.5.6.7. Marriage Proposals, first series, 1781
(the Sick Man, the Officer, the Windbag, the Runaway Match).

The Plates of the "Encyclopédie"

1

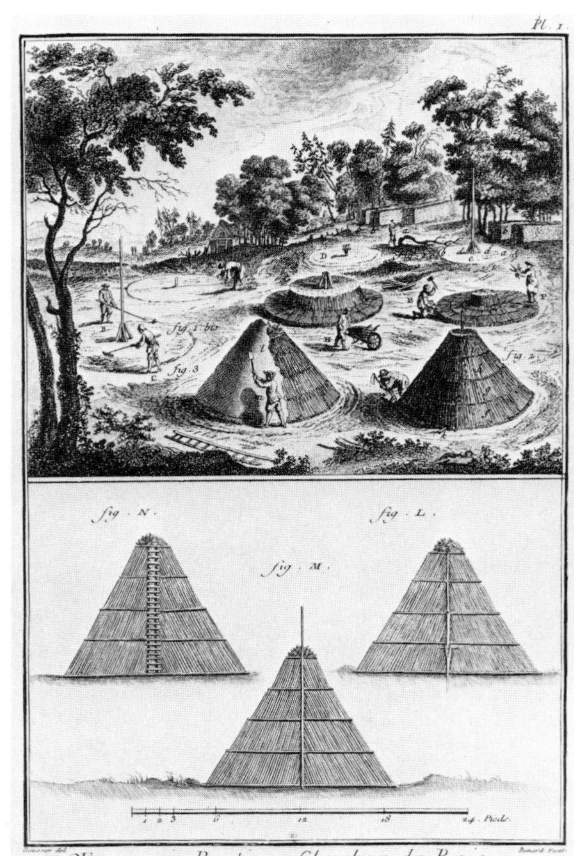

3

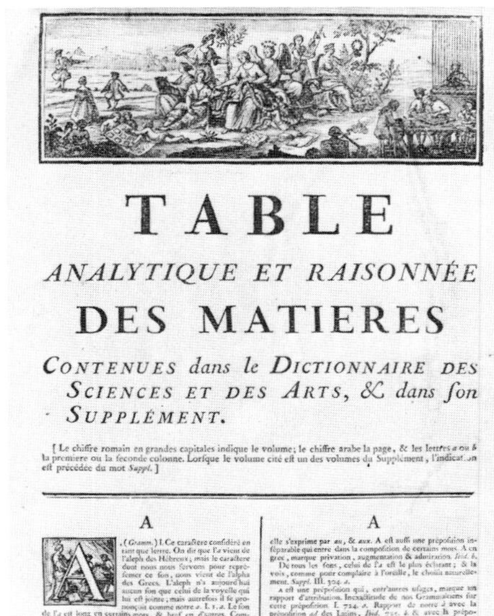
TABLE

ANALYTIQUE ET RAISONNÉE

DES MATIERES

CONTENUES dans le DICTIONNAIRE DES SCIENCES ET DES ARTS, & dans son SUPPLÉMENT.

A A

2

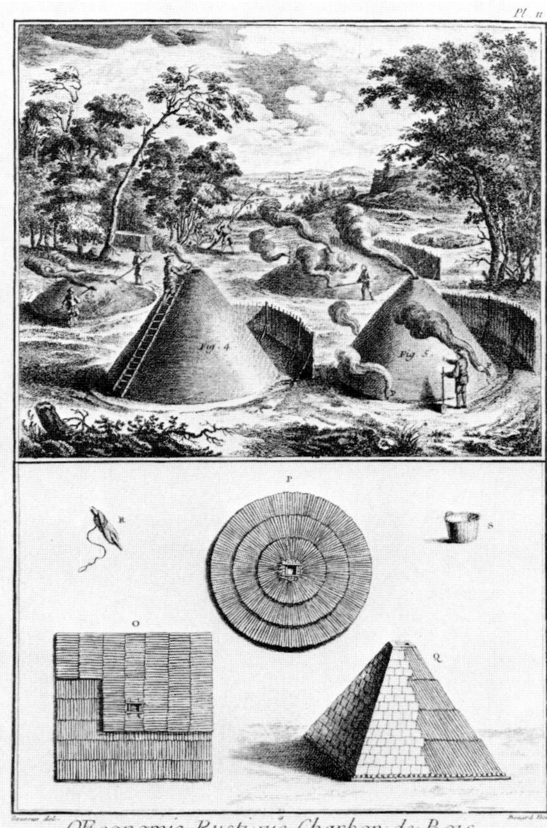

The publication of the *Encyclopédie* (1751-1772), edited by Diderot and d'Alembert, was an epoch-making event, both for its illustrations and its text. The number and quality of the plates, which have been continually reused since then, accurately reflect the conception which the French *philosophes* had of human knowledge. Diderot clearly stated his point of view in the prospectus of 1750, which already provided for two extra volumes with a complement of 600 plates: "But we are unaccustomed both to writing about the Arts and to reading about them. This makes it difficult to explain things in an intelligible way. Hence the need for pictures." Hence, too, the precision and clarity of these plates, designed to bring out the very points that are apt to remain obscure in a written text. This means that the editors had thought about the content and organization of their pictures, in which each element had to be selected and arranged to show, within a single plate, the sequence of a mechanical operation. "It would be an endless business," wrote Diderot, "if one set out to picture all the stages through which a piece of iron passes before being transformed into a needle. It is all very well to describe the procedure in writing down to the last detail. For the pictures, we have restricted them to the important movements of the workman's hand and to those moments alone of the operation which can easily be pictured but not readily explained." This reflection on the capacities and limits of the image refers back to the problematics of illustration as envisaged at the same period, in the domain of literature, by Lessing. Illustration here was being called upon to serve the purposes of a manufacturing economy, as indeed it had been already in the similar plates of Alvaro Alonso Barba's *Arte de los metales* (1640) and as it was about to do again in the official French survey of the arts and crafts (*Description des Arts et Métiers*). The complete set of the *Encyclopédie* plates was finally published in twelve volumes between 1762-1772. ■

4

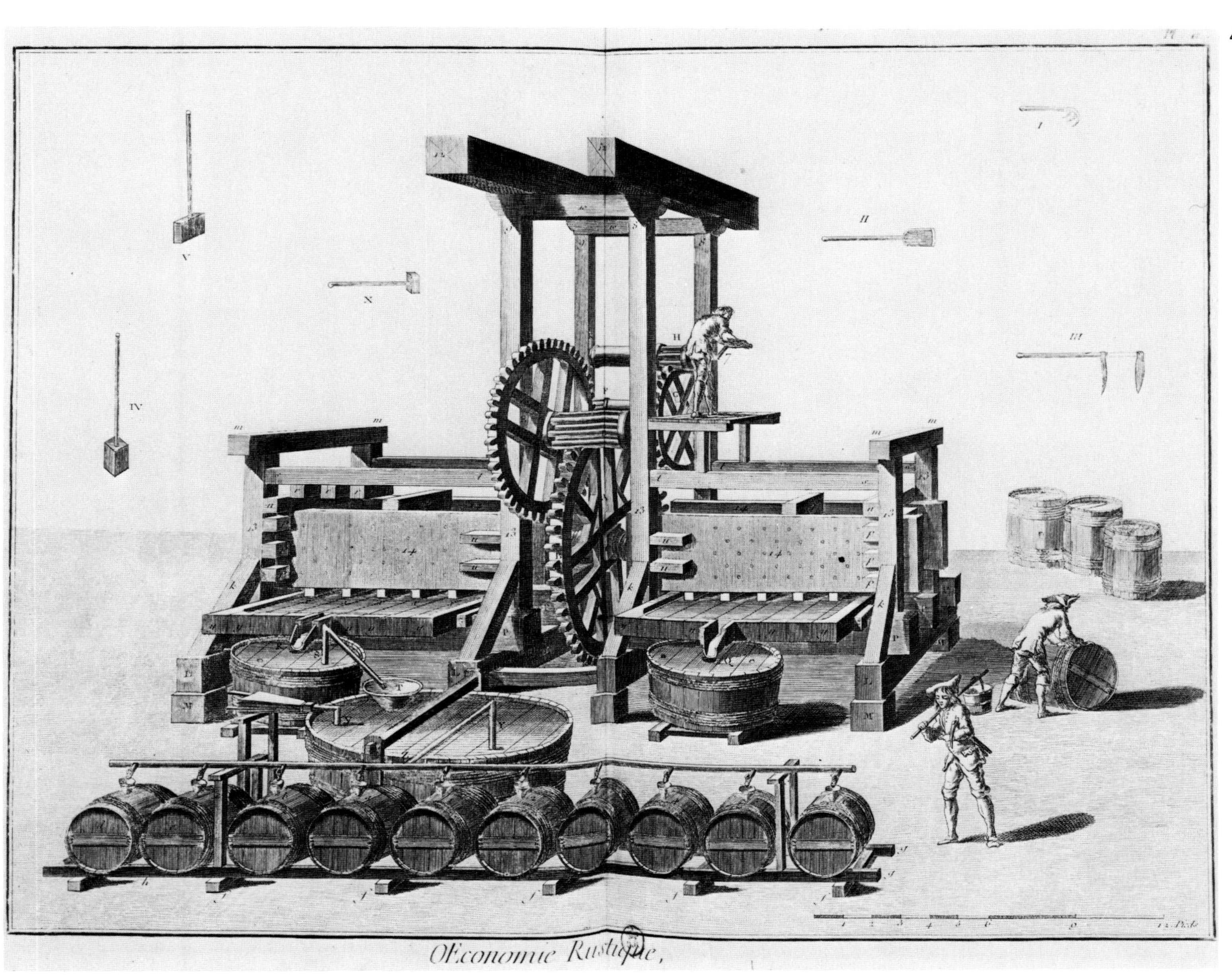

From the Encyclopédie, *Paris, 1762-1772:*

1.2. The making of charcoal, from the chapter on "Rural Economy."

3. Frontispiece and headpiece of the Table of Contents.

4. Wine-press, from the chapter on "Rural Economy."

MODERN ATHENS,

DISPLAYED IN A SERIES OF VIEWS;

OR

EDINBURGH.

IN THE

NINETEENTH CENTURY;

EXHIBITING THE WHOLE OF THE

NEW BUILDINGS, MODERN IMPROVEMENTS,

Antiquities & Picturesque Scenery,

OF THE

SCOTTISH METROPOLIS & ITS ENVIRONS,

FROM ORIGINAL DRAWINGS,

BY

M^r. THO^s. H. SHEPHERD.

WITH HISTORICAL TOPOGRAPHICAL & CRITICAL ILLUSTRATIONS.

Drawn by Tho. H. Shepherd

Engraved by W. Wallis

EDINBURGH CASTLE.

LONDON,

Published by Jones & Co. Temple of the Muses, Finsbury Square, Jany. 1, 1829.

ROMANTIC ILLUSTRATION

▲ Achille Devéria, Rothsay Kissing Louise, from *The Fair Maid of Perth*, one of a set of lithographs illustrating subjects from Sir Walter Scott's novels, c. 1850.

◄ Thomas H. Shepherd, title page design of *Modern Athens, Displayed in a Series of Views, or Edinburgh in the Nineteenth Century*, London, 1829.

When they began appearing in England and France about 1825, "romantic books" were a novelty, both in their make-up and in the system of manufacture and distribution behind them. In England first of all book production advanced with industrialization. Modern printing techniques meant longer printings and cheaper books. This came with the Stanhope press, permitting a new precision in the reproduction of vignettes, and stereotyping which combined text and pictures in the same mould. In London the eighteenth-century bookseller was superseded by publishers (Ackermann, Virtue, Fisher), in the sense in which we use that word today, who took over the investment which a book represents, paying author, printer and binder, and organizing its manufacture and sale. A product of the market economy, the book sought out and revealed a new public. And this new public, ranging over all classes of society, called for illustrations. Such were the peasant-soldier in France, coming home on half pay from the Napoleonic wars, unlettered but politically conscious, who liked to look at books picturing his own story; the bourgeois of London or Paris, no great reader but eager for knowledge and enjoyment, who discovered with pleasure the pictures of a world he was helping to build; the provincial notable, taking over from the aristocracy, feeling the need for a modern education, intent on facts, on taking in all that his eyes and ears could teach him about what lay beyond the horizon. To such people, pictures were often more important than words, offering a realistic and picturesque nourishment beyond the scope of the latter. These values, embodied in illustration, were the new counterweight to the accepted truths of the past embodied in texts of hitherto unquestioned authority. The image, more appealing and credible, developed into a system of its own, supported by new reproductive techniques and the demand of a widening readership. The image, the illustration, projected beyond the text and for simpler people overshadowed it.

Little by little the scientific, bourgeois and popular demands for illustrated information and teaching found their technical solution. When Thomas Bewick perfected his technique of wood engraving, using the end grain as distinct from the plank, he was conscious, as a good craftsman, of working for the glory of God and popular education. By working with the graver or burin instead of a knife and gouge, he gained an ease and rapidity of cutting

HISTORY OF QUADRUPEDS. 145

THE TWO-HORNED RHINOCEROS.

We have given the figure of this animal from Mr Sparrman, whoſe authenticity there is every reaſon to depend upon, and who has given a moſt exact anatomical deſcription of this hitherto undeſcribed animal. Of two that were ſhot, he only mentions the ſize of the ſmaller of them, which was eleven feet and a half long, ſeven feet high, and twelve in circumference. It was without any folds on the ſkin, which was of an aſh colour; excepting about the groin, where it was of a fleſh-colour. The ſurface of the ſkin was ſcabrous and knotty, of a cloſe texture, and when dry extremely hard. There were no hairs on any part of the body, except the edges of the ears and the tip of the tail, which were furniſhed with a few dark briſtly hairs, about an inch long.

The horns of this animal are placed one behind the other, in a line with the noſe: The foremoſt of them meaſures about eighteen inches in length, and is always

K the

Thomas Bewick, wood engraving from his *General History of Quadrupeds*, Newcastle and London, 1790.

which made the wood engraving qualitatively competitive with the copperplate engraving, and had this formidable advantage over it: that it could be printed typographically together with the letterpress. Cheap pictures became in Bewick's hands something more than coarse drawings. They became art. And so he carried out the illustrations of the first book conceived with this new technique, *A General History of Quadrupeds*, begun in 1785, published in 1790 in 1500 copies with 200 vignettes and 103 tailpieces. It was followed by the two volumes of *A History of British Birds* (1797 and 1804). Each page offers a picture and a simple text, of no scientific pretensions, but apposite. Neither the imagery in itself nor the page layout was really new. But the conception of the book as a source of general knowledge and above all the public at which he aimed—this was indeed something new in the history of illustration. Bewick's *General History of Quadrupeds* was so successful that it was reprinted in 1791 and 1792, reaching its eighth edition in 1824.

Casting techniques (like the *polytypage* already used in Paris under the Empire), and above all the electrotype after 1830, enabled pictures and letterpress to be brought together in the same relief mould; so that the disadvantages of copperplate engraving for illustration were reduced. It was a long time yet before these processes were adapted to lithography which, till the mid-nineteenth century, remained a non-relief process reserved for large full-page plates, and for this reason it was less used by publishers, despite the ease with which it could be drawn and printed. Steel engraving, perfected by Charles Warren in 1818, was also well adapted to the industrial advances of printing and answered the growing demand of the middle classes for illustrated books. Like etching on copper, it permitted the fine detail called for by realism and the taste for the picturesque. Thanks to the toughness of the steel plate, several thousand prints could be pulled without blurring the fine detail. This was a cost-reducing advantage for the new publishers, who depended for their profit on large editions of cheap books. But, like copperplate engravings, the steel cut could not be printed with the letterpress; it required a separate pull in another press. This drawback made it more expensive than wood engraving, and so it was largely confined to illustrating medium-priced books. The heyday of steel-cut illustrations was in the two decades from 1825 to 1845. It was used mostly for travel books: descriptions of Great Britain, of the beauties of Europe or distant lands. It served too for the lavishly illustrated editions, choice but accessible to the middle-class, of leading British authors like Sir Walter Scott and Lord Byron. Turner took a keen interest in steel engraving, a medium considered too popular and even vulgar by aesthetes. He provided some five hundred drawings for the steel engravers, supervising and occasionally retouching the reproductions, intended for the albums of his collectors, like his *Liber Studiorum*. Many of his English and French landscapes were reproduced in this medium, and he contributed regularly to *The Keepsake* and *The Amulet*, the small album books so much in vogue in English drawing-rooms.

J.M.W. Turner, Blois on the Loire,
watercolour and body-colour, c. 1830.

Blois, engraved by Robert Brandard after Turner's watercolour,
for *Turner's Annual Tour - The Loire*, London, 1833.

In France the booksellers' guild was dissolved in 1791 and the Direction de la Librairie was set up in 1810 to direct the book trade. Some 46 million pages were printed in 1814, 145 million in 1826. Cheap journalism began in Paris in 1836 when Emile de Girardin launched the first popular daily paper; the subscription cost 40 francs a year. In 1838 the publisher Charpentier brought out his pocket-size paperbacks, bringing the price of a book down from 7.50 francs (the weekly wage of a French worker) to 3.50. By 1860 Charpentier's series of small classics cost only one franc per volume. The neo-classical masterpieces of a great publisher like Didot, with their fine, few, stately illustrations, had had their day. "We want vignettes," wrote Edouard Thierry in the preface to his "evening tales," *Sous les rideaux*. "The bookseller wants vignettes and the public want them too." The success of a book, especially in the provinces, often depended on them. "A book and a ballad are bought today not for the text but for the pictures" (Régnier-Destourbet, *Un bal chez Louis-Philippe*). Some illustrators became household names: Achille Devéria was hailed by one critic as "the superlative of Delacroix"; Tony Johannot made a fortune. So did his publishers—before going bankrupt, when they misjudged a market still uncertain and fickle and overreached themselves in costly illustrated editions like Curmer's *Paul et Virginie* or Paulin's *Gil Blas*, its 974 pages illustrated with 580 vignettes by Jean Gigoux. Eye-pleasing books were carried far. Witness the fashion in England for "keepsakes," the annual gift-books whose very name has become synonymous with the sumptuously inane, a medley of occasional texts and illustrations. The original *Keepsake* was published from 1827 to 1856. They were curios rather than books.

George Cruikshank, illustration for Dickens' *Oliver Twist*, c. 1838.

Tony Johannot, illustration for *The Last of the Mohicans* in *Œuvres Complètes de Fenimore Cooper*, Paris, 1827-1830.

This wave, carried forward by the economic expansion of the 1820s, subsided in England with the slump of 1841. But the great English illustrator George Cruikshank had by 1870 produced over five thousand plates; and the catalogue of Gustave Doré, who died in 1883 at the age of fifty-one, runs to ten thousand items.

Wood engraving by Gustave Doré for
Louis Enault, *Londres*, Paris, 1876:
"Travellers will go and sit on
the ruins beside the Thames."

1

dra que vous rentriez avec quelqu'un ou que

sa loge soit remplie par les bonnes de la maison : ainsi, du moins, tous les étages vont savoir que vous ne payez pas vos billets, que vous êtes dans de mauvaises affaires, que vos meubles vont être saisis, que vous allez être conduit à la prison pour dettes... Heureux si toutes ces bonnes langues ne vous conduisent pas jusqu'aux galères.

Et si votre domestique a oublié de descendre

votre bougie, elle vous laissera monter l'escalier sans lumière, dans la douce espérance que vous vous y casserez le cou. « Que je suis donc fâchée, vous dira-t-elle ; mais je n'ai pas le plus petit bout de chandelle, et je viens de prêter mon rat à madame Patureau. »

Et si vous rentrez passé minuit et qu'il pleuve à torrents ! oh ! alors, la portière nage dans la joie. Vous frappez précipitamment, pan,

2

L'ÉPICIER.

'AUTRES, des ingrats, passent insouciamment devant la sacro-sainte boutique d'un épicier. Dieu vous en garde ! Quelque rebutant, crasseux, mal en casquette que soit le garçon, quelque frais et réjoui que soit le maître, je les regarde avec sollicitude, et leur parle avec la déférence qu'a pour eux *le Constitutionnel*. Je laisse aller un mort, un évêque, un roi, sans y faire attention ; mais je ne vois jamais avec indifférence un épicier. A mes yeux, l'épicier, dont l'omnipotence ne date que d'un siècle, est une des plus belles expressions de la société moderne. N'est-il donc pas un être aussi sublime de résignation que remarquable par son utilité ; une source constante de douceur, de lumière, de denrées bienfaisantes ? Enfin, n'est-il plus le ministre de l'Afrique, le chargé d'affaires des Indes et de l'Amérique ? Certes, l'épicier est tout cela ; mais, ce qui met le comble à sa perfection, il est tout cela sans s'en douter. L'obélisque sait-il qu'il est un monument ?

Ricaneurs infâmes, chez quel épicier êtes-vous entrés qui ne vous ait gracieusement souri, sa casquette à la main, tandis que vous gardiez votre chapeau sur la tête ? Le boucher est rude, le boulanger est pâle et grognon ; mais l'épicier, toujours prêt à obliger, montre dans tous les quartiers de Paris un visage aimable. Aussi, à quelque classe qu'appartienne le piéton dans l'embarras, ne s'adresse-t-il ni à la science rébarbative de l'horloger, ni au comptoir bastionné de viandes saignantes où trône la fraîche bouchère, ni à la grille défiante du boulanger : entre toutes les boutiques ouvertes, il attend, il choisit celle de l'épicier pour changer une pièce de cent sous, ou pour demander son chemin ; il est sûr que cet homme, le plus chrétien de tous les commerçants, est à tous, bien que le plus occupé ; car le temps qu'il donne aux pas-

1

3

1. The Doorkeeper, wood engravings after Daumier for James Rousseau, *La Physiologie de la portière*, Paris, 1841.

2. The Grocer, wood engravings after Gavarni for Curmer's *Les Français peints par eux-mêmes*, Paris, 1840-1842.

3. The Temple Market, etching by C.F. Daubigny for Eugène Sue, *Les Mystères de Paris*, Paris, 1843-1844.

Alongside these literary illustrations in which the romantic imagination was given free rein, the imagery of the period includes a solid body of documentary plates characteristic of the generation of positivists and empiricists. Science, as a growth industry, needed pictures. The wood engraving, cheap and accurate, answered various practical and scientific purposes, in handbooks, monographs and even official reports and documents, like the parliamentary Blue Books on the living conditions of British workers and other issues. These early "statistical" pictures, meant to be coolly objective and almost schematic, gave a quasi-official endorsement to the authority of the image and its demonstrational value, even in the human sciences. Social investigation, probing into the workings of the class society, rose in its illustrated matter to an almost mythological level. As in Balzac's "Human Comedy" or Eugène Sue's "Mysteries of Paris," human "types" went to replace the gods and classified society was visualized as a schematic sampling–highly successful in albums like *Les Français peints par eux-mêmes* (Curmer, 1840-1842), which sold 18,000 copies, or the *Physiologies*, part-publications full of vignettes and journalistic gossip with a sensational appeal. Alongside fiction and reporting came a large production of travel books whose main interest lay in their lavish illustrations. Among these, modelled on the great compilations of the eighteenth century, were multivolume publications spanning decades, like the series of *Voyages pittoresques et romantiques dans l'ancienne France* edited by Taylor and Nodier. At the opposite end of the scale were the new railway guidebooks illustrated with small woodcuts: seeing them at the Great Exhibition of 1851 in London, the publisher Hachette took up the idea in France and secured a state monopoly for their sale at station bookstalls. More and more illustrated books were devoted to exotic countries. These were the fruit not only of tourism, steadily on the rise, but of colonization, then at its peak. The pictures were a sugared-over version of reality: they had, and were meant to have, the charm of a dream. "Our century," wrote Baudelaire, "has the cult of pictures."

"Les Voyages pittoresques et romantiques dans l'ancienne France"

1

ROUEN. 69

cienne splendeur qu'une partie des peintures de sa voûte. Là brilloient encore quand nous avons visité cette église pour la dernière fois, des caissons chargés de monogrammes et entourés de cartouches, dont l'ordonnance ne manquoit ni d'élégance ni de richesse. Cette opulence bizarre contraste d'une manière étrange avec le triste délâbrement des murailles poudreuses, et l'œil ne redescend pas sans surprise le long des auges qui embrassent la nef, et sur la litière immonde qui cache les pavés du chœur.

2

Rue du gros Horloge
Rouen.

These "Picturesque and Romantic Travels in Old France" represent one of the nineteenth century's biggest ventures in illustrated publishing: twenty volumes, containing upwards of three thousand lithographs, issued from 1820 to 1878. This venture was also one of the most significant. It stands out from a mass of illustrated books designed for the growing body of tourists and travellers interested in archaeology, history and sightseeing, also for that provincial public which in France, as already in England, was waking up to "local culture."

Indicative also of the strong influence exerted by England on French art after 1815, this new type of literature combining pictures and letterpress had arisen in England–where there was already a long-standing tradition of landscape art–but reached its full flowering in France around 1830. Of the 150 artists who contributed to the *Voyages pittoresques et romantiques*, fifteen were English, and the printing of the plates was shared out between two French printers, Engelmann and Lemercier, and an English one, Hullmandel. Two artists in particular stood out from the rest, the Englishman Richard Parkes Bonington and the Frenchman Jean-Baptiste Isabey: these two here created the peculiar style of Romantic lithography. But among the others were some of the great names of French Romantic art: Géricault, Vernet, Charlet, Devéria, Nanteuil, Huet and even Daguerre and Viollet-le-Duc. The letterpress was written by Charles Nodier, and continued after his death in 1844 by Alphonse de Cailleux. The publisher was one of the great patrons of French romanticism, Baron Isidore Taylor. Stretching as it did over a time-span of nearly half a century, this publication offers a remarkable survey of the history of lithography, with the appearance of tinting in 1835 (Vol. X, Picardy), the introduction of zinc plates about 1840, and finally the use of photographs as designs with the volume on Burgundy in 1863. This publication could not in fact have long withstood the inexorable rise of photography, and it came to an end in the 1870s just as photolithographic techniques were taking over. ■

3

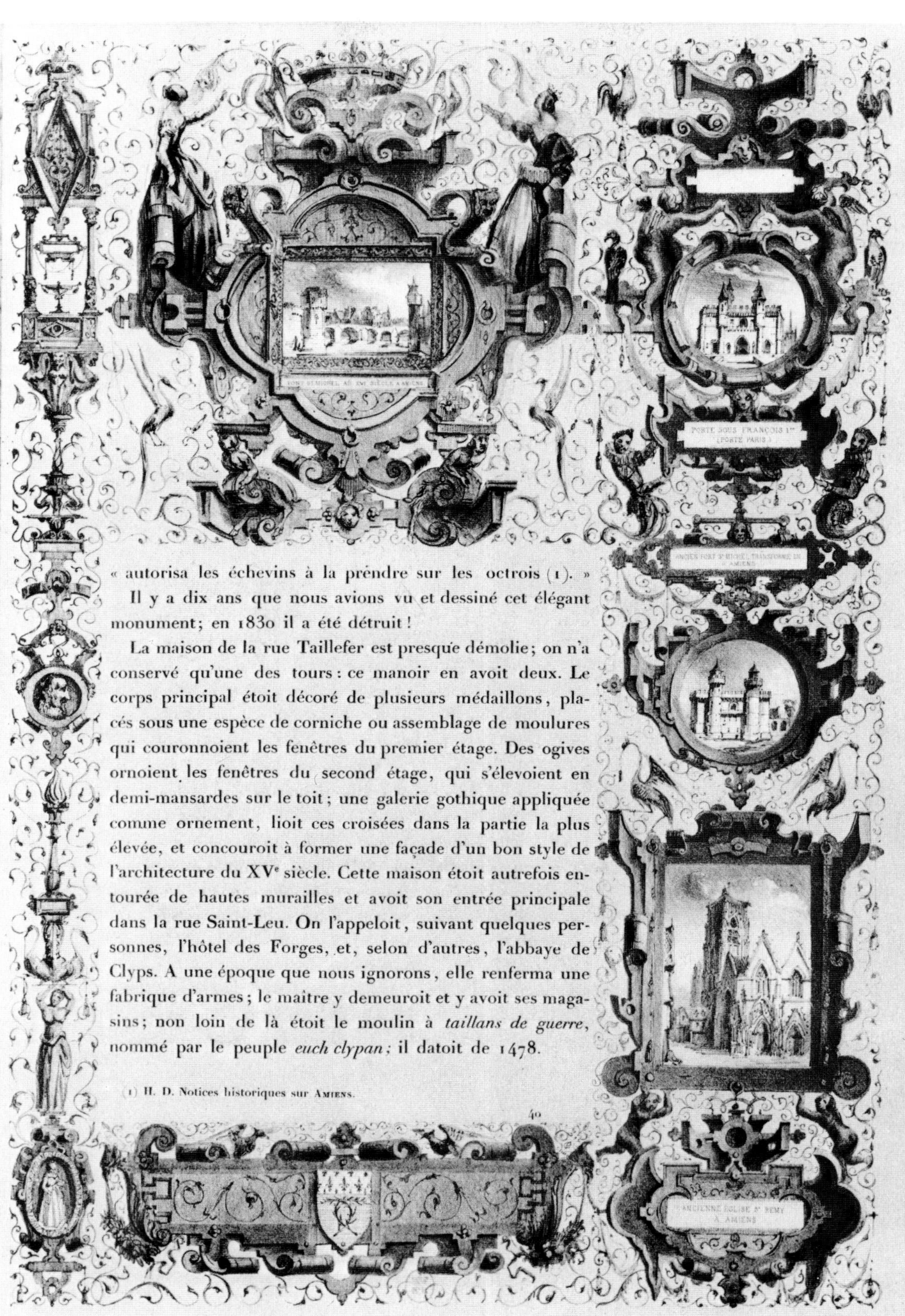

« autorisa les échevins à la prendre sur les octrois (1). »

Il y a dix ans que nous avions vu et dessiné cet élégant monument; en 1830 il a été détruit!

La maison de la rue Taillefer est presque démolie; on n'a conservé qu'une des tours: ce manoir en avoit deux. Le corps principal étoit décoré de plusieurs médaillons, placés sous une espèce de corniche ou assemblage de moulures qui couronnoient les fenêtres du premier étage. Des ogives ornoient les fenêtres du second étage, qui s'élevoient en demi-mansardes sur le toit; une galerie gothique appliquée comme ornement, lioit ces croisées dans la partie la plus élevée, et concouroit à former une façade d'un bon style de l'architecture du XVe siècle. Cette maison étoit autrefois entourée de hautes murailles et avoit son entrée principale dans la rue Saint-Leu. On l'appeloit, suivant quelques personnes, l'hôtel des Forges, et, selon d'autres, l'abbaye de Clyps. A une époque que nous ignorons, elle renferma une fabrique d'armes; le maître y demeuroit et y avoit ses magasins; non loin de là étoit le moulin à *taillans de guerre*, nommé par le peuple *euch clypan*; il datoit de 1478.

(1) H. D. Notices historiques sur Amiens.

40

Charles Nodier, Voyages pittoresques et romantiques dans l'ancienne France, *published by Baron Isidore Taylor:*

1. *Rouen Cathedral, lithograph in Vol. II,* Ancienne Normandie, *Paris, 1825.*
2. *Rue du Gros Horloge, Rouen, lithograph by Richard Parkes Bonington in Vol. II,* Ancienne Normandie, *Paris, 1825.*
3. *Monuments of Amiens, lithograph in Vol. X,* La Picardie, *Paris, 1835.*

1

Curmer's Edition of "Paul et Virginie"

Among the leading French publishers of the Romantic period (such as Paulin, Renduel, Dubochet, Hetzel and so on), Curmer stands out for the bold ventures he embarked on: *Les Français peints par eux-mêmes, Le Jardin des Plantes,* the periodical *Les Beaux-Arts,* the reproduction of Fouquet's miniatures. His most ambitious venture was the illustrated edition of Bernardin de Saint-Pierre's novel *Paul et Virginie* by a team of young artists, including Johannot, Français and Meissonier, who worked on it from 1835 to 1838. Curmer invested 233,000 francs in it, an enormous outlay for a book at that time, printing 30,000 copies priced at 45 francs (only 6000 copies were sold). English engravers were hired at record fees; for their wood and steel cuts, embellishing each page, they were better paid than the artists who designed them. This Romantic edition was a deliberate departure from the first illustrated edition of this famous novel, by Moreau the Younger in 1789, and from the fine classical edition by Didot of 1806. For the first time the pictures were inserted in the text. The vignettes begin with the opening line, as if to put the reader in the mood for more. Curmer reverted to the initial letter, as a pretext for graphic fantasies, and to the illustrated margin, as in manuscripts, while also including full-page illustrations and chapter frontispieces. The great novelty of the Curmer illustrations, with respect to previous periods, is the absence of frames: the pictures run free, even spreading into the text. The great device was to slip them into the heart of the sentence they illustrated and obtain a harmonious page design. The image then acted as mediator between the reader and his text, enhancing both the story and the pleasure of reading. ■

2

Mme DE LA TOUR.

3

BERNARDIN
DE SAINT-PIERRE

Le sentiment qu'on a de la nature physique extérieure et de tout le spectacle de la création appartient sans doute à une certaine organisation particulière et à une sensibilité individuelle; mais il dépend aussi beaucoup de la manière générale d'envisager la nature et la création elle-même, de l'envisager comme création ou comme forme variable d'un fond éternel; d'apprécier sa condition par rapport au bien et au mal; si elle est pleine de piéges pour l'homme, ou si elle n'est animée

b

4

Jacques Henri Bernardin de Saint-Pierre, Paul et Virginie, *published by L. Curmer, Paris, 1838:*

1. *Title page designed by François-Louis Français.*
2. *Madame de La Tour, illustration by Tony Johannot.*
3. *Ornamental initial letter and headpiece.*
4. *"Each of us had two children," illustration by Henry Corbould.*

THE

COMPLAINT.

OR,

Night-Thoughts

ON

LIFE, DEATH, *and* IMMORTALITY.

NIGHT *the* EIGHTH.

VIRTUE's APOLOGY:

OR,

The MAN *of the* WORLD *Answer'd.*

In which are Considered,

The LOVE *of* THIS LIFE;

The AMBITION *and* PLEASURE, *with the* WIT *and* WISDOM *of the* WORLD.

LONDON:

Printed for G. HAWKINS, at *Milton's* Head, between the *Two Temple-Gates, Fleet-street*, near *Temple-Bar*.

And Sold by M. COOPER, at the *Globe*, in *Pater-noster Row*.

MDCCXLV.

THE WAY OF THE WRITERS

▲ William Blake, "The Blossom" from *Songs of Innocence*, relief etching tinted with watercolour, 1789: poem and design engraved on the same plate.

◄ William Blake, watercolour title page design for Edward Young's *Night Thoughts*, c. 1795-1797.

The image having reached an equal footing with literature, thanks to the French *philosophes* in the latter half of the eighteenth century, the communion of the two was practised by certain writers whose temperament and gifts led them to both media. Goethe drew prolifically; so did Hoffmann; so did Thackeray. And the Geneva cartoonist and draughtsman Rodolphe Toepffer was a writer. But the most wonderful example of all was William Blake, poet, philosopher, draughtsman and engraver. The meaning he wished to impart to his writings is indissociable from the material form in which he presented them. He engraved his poems himself (as Restif de La Bretonne had also engraved his writings, expressing himself through the very choice of the typeface). Not only that, but he engraved his handwritten text and his illustration together to form a decorative unit. In the whole history of printing till then, the illustrated plate had had to be adapted to the letterpress. Blake, on the contrary, treated the text as a drawing. The handwritten text was an integral part of the decorative page and could nevertheless be printed. This formula gave his books an original, somewhat mysterious appearance which enhanced the lyrical, prophetic tone of his poems. Thus the idea with which the reader came away from his reading was imbued with the very look of the text, its halo of imagery. Here was a double flow of poetry. This "total writing" (for such it was in the artist's view) launched no school; it was too individual a creation, unsuited to diffusion. But it reappeared a century later in France with the *livre d'artiste*.

If writing became picturesque in its style and referents, so did handwriting, in the very shaping of the letters. For it was now, with the help of the new techniques of reproduction, that the letter broke free from the strict frame and form so long imposed upon it by typography. By 1800 stereotype plates were being used (by Firmin Didot, for example), with text and image cast in the same type mould. Lithography permitted the drawing of letters. The return to handwriting in the reproduction itself—an old dream of typographers—now became possible and answered the urge to individual creation. These new letters with their often fancy shapes and stems appeared in books but chiefly in other products of the printer's trade which are of by no means negligible interest: song titles, booksellers' posters, illustrated covers. Songs and ballads were then published in large numbers and their covers designed by all the leading Romantic illustrators. Those of Célestin Nanteuil and Tony Johannot are like a museum of fanciful letter design, revealing the exotic taste of the day (neo-Gothic, Moorish, etc.). Here perhaps for the first time the form of the printed letter took on an evident and particularized semantic value. The poster, a key element now in the new system of market distribution, began by being essentially literary and offered a new field of expression in which the design of the letter and that of the image interacted. Théophile Gautier himself designed a promotional poster for his novel *Capitaine Fracasse*. About 1835, in France, appeared the first illustrated book covers: on their design, then as now, often depended the success of a book. In all these fields the text assumed an image value from its layout and presentation; and like modern pictograms of undefined meaning the words wound their way over the sheet, clashing or flying off at an angle, the letters cracking or wobbling or jostling against each other. Writing did not merely describe the picturesque; it had itself become picturesque.

As the image came to vie with the text within the book itself, in the titles with their fanciful swirls and shapes, in the vignettes that adorned and deformed initial letters, it also came to modify the use and readership of books. The proud position of the author could not hold out against this assault. Whether he liked it or not, the author had to reckon with the illustrations. It was in answer to a publish-

1

2

1. Title page by Célestin Nanteuil for the first number of *L'Artiste, Journal de la Littérature et des Beaux-Arts*, Paris, 1831.

2. Poster by Tony Johannot for Alfred de Musset and P.J. Stahl, *Voyage où il vous plaira*, Paris, c. 1843.

3. Illustration by Phiz (Hablôt Knight Browne) for Dickens' *Posthumous Papers of the Pickwick Club*, London, 1836-1837.

4. Lithograph cover by Célestin Nanteuil for a song, "Madrid," by Alfred de Musset and Hippolyte Monpou, Paris, 1832.

3

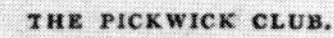

THE PICKWICK CLUB. 95

"My eldest brother was troubled with that complaint," said Sam, "it may be catching—I used to sleep with him."

"This is a curious old house of yours," said the little man, looking round him.

"If you'd sent word you was a coming, we'd ha' had it repaired;" replied the imperturbable Sam.

The little man seemed rather baffled by these several repulses, and a short consultation took place between him and the two plump gentlemen. At its conclusion, the little man took a pinch of snuff from an oblong silver box, and was apparently on the point of renewing the conversation, when one of the plump gentlemen, who in addition to a benevolent countenance, possessed a pair of spectacles, and a pair of black gaiters, interfered—

"The fact of the matter is," said the benevolent gentleman, "that my friend here (pointing to the other plump gentleman,) will give you half a guinea, if you'll answer one or two—"

"Now, my dear Sir—my dear Sir," said the little man, "pray allow me—my dear Sir, the very first principle to be observed in these cases, is this; if you place a matter in the hands of a professional man, you must in no way interfere in the progress of the business; you must repose implicit confidence in him. Really, Mr. (he turned to the other plump gentleman, and said)—I forget your friend's name."

"Pickwick," said Mr. Wardle, for it was no other than that jolly personage.

"Ah, Pickwick—really Mr. Pickwick, my dear Sir, excuse me—I shall be happy to receive any private suggestions of yours, as *amicus curiæ*, but you must see the impropriety of your interfering with my conduct in this case, with such an *ad captandum* argument, as the offer of half a guinea. Really, my dear Sir, really," and the little man took an argumentative pinch of snuff, and looked very profound.

"My only wish, Sir," said Mr. Pickwick, "was to bring this very unpleasant matter to as speedy a close as possible."

"Quite right—quite right," said the little man.

"With which view," continued Mr. Pickwick, "I made use of the argument which my experience of men has taught me is the most likely to succeed in any case,"

"Ay, ay," said the little man, "very good, very good, indeed; but you should have suggested it to *me*. My dear Sir, I'm quite certain you cannot be ignorant of the extent of confidence which must be placed in professional men. If any authority can be necessary on such a point, my dear Sir, let me refer you to the well-known case in Barnwell and—"

"Never mind George Barnvell," interrupted Sam, who had remained a wondering listener during this short colloquy; "every body knows vhat sort of a case his was, tho' it's always been my opinion, mind you, that the young 'ooman deserved scragging a precious sight more than he did. Hows'ever, that's neither here nor there. You want me to except of half a guinea. Werry well, I'm agreeable: I can't say no fairer than that, can I, Sir? (Mr. Pickwick smiled.) Then the next

er's request that he pen some sketches of contemporary life to accompany a series of comic illustrations by Robert Seymour that Dickens was led to write *The Pickwick Papers*. Dickens constantly wrote with pictures in mind. Even if it had not been natural with him, publishing conditions would have compelled him to. Serial novels were published in monthly parts, and the publisher required scenes that prompted illustration, and they had to come at strategic points of climax or suspense. Indeed the publisher expected the author to specify the scenes calling for illustration. These requirements meant that the writer had to visualize his characters and set them in picturesque situations. Further, the pace of publication in monthly serial parts meant that author and illustrator had to work hand in hand; sometimes the latter preceded the former, picturing scenes which the author then wrote up. Dickens' regular illustrator, Hablot K. Browne ("Phiz"), who illustrated ten of his fifteen novels, freely suggested scenes and sketched out the physical features of this or that character, from which Dickens took his cue. It was George Cruikshank who illustrated *Oliver Twist*; indeed the famous old illustrator claimed credit for inventing not only the figure of the hero but the plot of the novel–suggested, according to him, during a talk with Dickens. Few successful authors were prepared to do without pictures, even though they may have frowned on them at first, like Scott who in his bankruptcy welcomed the additional profits brought in by illustration, or Musset who had dismissed them as "fancy trifles for luxury books."

4

1

1. The Cat (St Goarshausen), pen and sepia drawing by Victor Hugo, 1840.

2. City in the Plain, with the artist's name in the foreground, pen, sepia and gouache drawing by Victor Hugo.

3. Battle of Romans and Carthaginians, pen drawing made by Victor Hugo in an exercise book at the age of fifteen, 1817.

Most writers adapted themselves to them. Thackeray was his own best illustrator and initiated himself into etching. Writers of the Romantic period welcomed this departure from the old "author" status. This new conception of the artist, as demiurge as much at home with his pen as with his graving needle, chimed in with their view of writing, as individual creation unamenable to rules. Writing was affected at all levels of style and meaning. The image was no longer the rival of the text, nor its foil, it was neither an aid to understanding nor a concession to the eye: it was an alternative form of writing. On its side, the text in its drive towards realism and picturesqueness often became a verbal delineation, rich in figural details.

Balzac described Auvergne on the basis of the popular guidebooks of the day or of Taylor's *Voyages pittoresques et romantiques*, as pointed out by Mademoiselle Mespoulet: "He describes the sites pictured in the principal plates of Taylor, sites, he says, whose 'wild and rugged features are beginning to tempt the brush of our artists': the *Monts d'Or*, the *Pic de Sancy*, the *Capucin* (which he underlines like the caption of a plate) and its *Aiguilles*. He describes them in sentences whose movement and colour suggest the approach to the Monts d'Or. At the Capucin he sees 'at the bottom of *that bowl* perhaps the old *crater* of a volcano'; and the writer in Taylor sees in it 'some *craters* inclined like an empty *bowl*'. Balzac wonders at 'the *rocks gashed* or splitting open, in *ravines* from which *overhang* chunks of lava whose *spill* had been prepared by the rainwaters'; Taylor's author describes them as 'basalt debris tumbling into the *ravines*... and *loosened rocks* about to cascade down over terrain already stripped clear by the *spill* of this great boulder wreckage'." Balzac obviously owed something, even much, to Taylor's *Voyages*

2

pittoresques. Flaubert too, when he describes Bouvard and Pécuchet in their country cottage ("Already they saw themselves in their shirtsleeves by a flower bed, pruning rose-bushes, digging and turning the soil, and unpotting tulips"), ridicules them in the same spirit and style, almost "in the same terms," as Daumier does when he pictures his *Bons Bourgeois* in the country. Literature, and the historical novel in particular, not only lent itself to illustration, it called for it to the point of merging with it. No need to speak of influence here, for the two media pointedly signified the same thing, at the same time, to the same public.

3

Without being entirely new, this phenomenon became systematic when artists, poets and philosophers developed the theory of the "correspondence between the arts."

Victor Hugo's love of drawing, and his amazing gift for it, exemplifies the temperament of the Romantic writer, whose writing was rooted in gesture. Through his personalized writing and his sensual fascination with drawing, Hugo achieved the full revelation of his powers. He produced a body of some three thousand drawings, whose graphic sweep and intensity (physically inscribed in the ink strokes and washes) already made a strong impression on his contemporaries. The proud sense of individual creation, the hybrid character of the writing and drawing, the sensuality of the line and pattern—these features are all summed up in Hugo's taste for oversized signatures, panoramic outsweeps of his own name, evoking in their far-flung perspectives the landscape of a genius bold enough to vie with God. His signature was an inscription in which the poet condensed his mighty personality. With his keen eye for imagery, inward and outward, Hugo conjures up pictures again and again in his descriptions and recollections. He advocated an aesthetic in which word and picture are two inseparable media of expression. His manifesto was the preface to *Cromwell* (1827), where in support of his views he cites both Callot and Shakespeare, both Michelangelo and Dante, coupling them together in equations that would never have occurred to the theorists of classical art.

Just as text and image no longer had any distinct frontier between them, so writers and illustrators often merged into each other. Literary history throughout shows how well they got on together. All the literary groups in France included artists: the Johannot brothers at Nodier's, Louis Boulanger and Célestin Nanteuil at Hugo's, the fancy-dress balls of Alexandre Dumas and Gérard de Nerval, the Hôtel de Pimodan where Daumier and Baudelaire were often together. It became customary for the writer to publish art criticism. His reputation had to pass the test of Salon reviews published with reproductions in specialized papers, like *L'Artiste* in France and the *Art Journal* in England, in which literature and the fine arts were intimately mingled. These are well-known facts. What is worth noting about this new link is the interest writers now took in looking at pictures, which they analysed like other facts of experience. Jean Adhémar has made an impressive listing of quotations from realist and naturalist writers bearing on the popular imagery of nineteenth-century France; nothing like it existed in the eighteenth century. This love of the pictorial is evidenced in the attention writers paid to their own handwriting: Goethe and Victor Hugo are the prototypes. Writers seem intent on drawing their text, or else drawing in the margin of it, and spontaneously became their own illustrators. With some, like Flaubert, the manuscript became a significant object in itself, worthy of display.

Entwined initials of Juliette Drouet and Victor Hugo, with view of Marine Terrace, Jersey. Pen wash and gouache drawing by Victor Hugo, 1855.

4

Goethe and Delacroix

1. *Eugène Delacroix, pen and wash drawing for the first plate of his Faust illustrations.*
2. *Eugène Delacroix, Mephistopheles above the City, lithograph illustration for Goethe's* Faust, *1828.*
3. *Goethe's* Faust, *French translation by Albert Stapfer, with seventeen lithographs by Eugène Delacroix, Paris, 1828: Frontispiece and title page design by Achille Devéria.*
4. *Eugène Delacroix, Gretchen's Image Appearing to Faust, lithograph for Goethe's* Faust, *first state with remarks, before letters.*
5. *Eugène Delacroix, Gretchen's Image Appearing to Faust, lithograph for Goethe's* Faust, *third and last state (as published), with letters.*

1

2

3

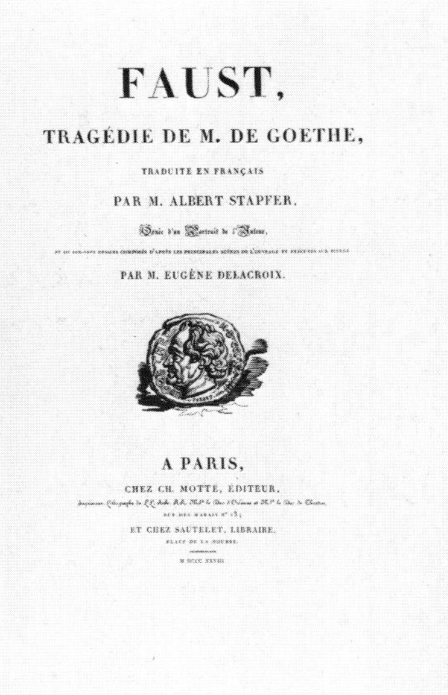

FAUST,

TRAGÉDIE DE M. DE GOETHE,

TRADUITE EN FRANÇAIS

PAR M. ALBERT STAPFER.

Ornée d'un Portrait de l'Auteur,

PAR M. EUGÈNE DELACROIX.

A PARIS,

CHEZ CH. MOTTE, EDITEUR,

RUE DES MARAIS N° 13;

ET CHEZ SAUTELET, LIBRAIRE,

PLACE DE LA BOURSE.

M DCCC XXVIII

Here is the classic example of the meeting of minds between a great writer and a great artist. So true is this that Victor Hugo could write of the *Faust* illustrations: "*Faust* is the work of two great poets: Goethe and Delacroix." The story began in 1821 when Delacroix, then twenty-three years old, saw Retzsch's neo-classical illustrations. In London in 1825 he saw a stage adaptation of Goethe's verse tragedy: "I've seen a Faust play which is the most diabolical thing you can imagine... They have made it into an opera combining comedy with all that is darkest in tragedy... The effect could not be carried further on the stage." Already, regretting that Goethe's illustrators had "forgotten the Hell in it, and the terrific mixed with the comic," he was thinking of some lithographs on this by now popular theme. In 1828 he was approached by the printer Charles Motte: "If you can spare me a few moments, perhaps one evening we could arrange a diabolical affair with Faust. I have a few ideas for you about the exploitation of this wizard." Delacroix responded, Motte issued the lithographs, critics made light of them, and they went largely unsold. Unexpectedly, it was the old poet himself, in spite of his known taste for neo-classical design at its purest, who showed the liveliest understanding of this French interpretation of his work: "Monsieur Delacroix is a great talent who in Faust has found the right fare. The French reproach him for being wild, but here that wildness is called for... It is curious indeed that an artist's mind should have found so much pleasure in this obscure work and should have absorbed so much of its darker side in his initial conception that he was able to trace out the main scenes with a pencil as stormy as the hero's fate... Delacroix is a painter of unquestionable talent; but he has received a poor welcome, as the young so often do from us old men. Connoisseurs and art lovers hardly know what to say of him in Paris, for it is impossible not to recognize his abilities and yet people cannot commend his disorderly manner" (Goethe's conversations with Eckermann, 1836-1848). ■

4

5

Meph. Laisse cet objet, on ne se trouve jamais bien de le regarder tu as bien entendu raconter l'histoire de meduse? Faust. Assurément ce sont là les yeux d'un mort, qu'une
main amie n'a point fermés, c'est là le sein que Marguerite m'a livré, c'est le corps charmant que j'ai possédé

Lewis Carroll, Lear, and Grandville

1

2

3

"Why, there the are!" said the Kin triumphantly, pointin to the tarts on th table. "Nothing can b clearer than *that* The again—'*before she ha this fit*—' you neve had fits, my dear, think?" he said to th Queen.

"Never!" said th Queen furiously throw ing an inkstand at the Lizard as she spoke

When *Alice's Adventures in Wonderland* was published in 1865, the book was seen to be as much an album as a text, and Sir John Tenniel's illustrations were an integral part of the whimsical charm of this literary masterpiece by the Rev. Charles L. Dodgson, better known as Lewis Carroll. The text came first, and stays first, but the book was nevertheless the fruit of a collaboration, master-minded by Dodgson. For this was the heyday of that period when the writer, with illustrations in mind, could choose his illustrator, team up with him, and prompt him and inspire him. So it was between Tenniel, a humorous and satirical artist and *Punch* cartoonist, and Dodgson, whose interest in pictures carried him through an astonishing hobby-career as a photographer of little girls. First published by Macmillan in 1865, *Alice* was steadily reprinted, its success never flagging, nor were Tenniel's original illustrations ever superseded by the many other pictured versions of *Alice*, including modern films and cartoons. Neither alone nor with any other writer did Tenniel ever repeat this success, except with Lewis Carroll again in *Through the Looking-Glass* (1871). So here the stimulus of the writer seems to have been decisive. It has been pointed out by Mario Praz that this new "visual" dimension of the fantastic, going beyond the classical conception of the "marvellous," was not an isolated case, but part rather of the Romantic discovery of an "absurd" vein of illustration, which Praz explains as a kind of catharsis of the bourgeois world. This graphic delirium reached its height in Grandville's *Un Autre Monde* (1844) and Edward Lear's *Book of Nonsense* (1846). With Lewis Carroll, the writer dictates his will to the illustrator, thanks to a text fertile in images. With Lear, the hilarious illustrations and the limericks are by the same man and run inseparably. Grandville's book is even more novel, for the author of it, the journalist Taxile Delord, deliberately kept his text in a low key, leaving the centre of the stage to the illustrations and the resourceful imagination of Grandville. So true is this that it has even been wondered whether Taxile Delord really existed; it has been wondered too just how much Grandville's whimsical subjects may have influenced Lewis Carroll. ■

4

1. *Grandville,* Un Autre Monde, *Paris, 1844: The Battle of Cards.*

2. *Edward Lear,* A Book of Nonsense, *London, n.d. (first edition, 1846).*

3.4. *Lewis Carroll,* Alice's Adventures in Wonderland, *illustrations by John Tenniel, London, 1865.*

Erster Band.

Erscheinen monatlich dreimal. — Man abonnirt bei allen Buch- und Kunsthandlungen, allen Postämtern und Zeitungsexpeditionen. **Nro. 1.** Preis für einen Band von 24 Nummern 3 fl. rhein., oder 1 Rthlr. 21 Sgr. Einzelne Nummern kosten 9 kr. rhein., oder 3 Sgr.

Der Küster und sein Ziegenbock.

Eine Dorfgeschichte.

War wieder Sonntagnachmittag,
Das Kirchlein auf dem Kirchhof lag
Im hellen Sommersonnenschein
Und hielt umschlossen Groß und Klein.
Des Liedes Hall schon ist verweht,
Der Pfarrer auf der Kanzel steht
Und die Gemeinde rings herum
Vernimmt die Predigt still und stumm;

Des Friedens Geist hat sich ergossen,
Die Kirchenthür' ist nicht verschlossen,
Und draußen am Hollunderstock
Da nagt des Küsters Ziegenbock.
Lustwandelnd auf der Gräber Flur,
Entdeckt er leicht der Menschen Spur
Und tritt zu seines Herren Graus
Bedächtig ein in's Gotteshaus.

1

written. It will have much to say about this silent complicity between text and picture, a complicity arising behind the back of both writer and artist and creating a new type of expression whose meaning was determined by the editor who put the two elements together.

Like Paul Valéry's Faust who found out "what a wonder it is to be able to see anything at all," the readers of illustrated papers soon learned, with no less naïveté, that illustration could show "anything at all." Taken up as a direct and artless substitute for reality, the image then possessed a power whose authority was no more questioned than the Scriptures had once been. True, this power stimulated the growing appetite for illustrations and burst out in a seemingly unlimited extension of the themes treated: topical events, discoveries, travels, shows, street scenes, home life and so on. But each of these themes was nevertheless the result of a deliberate choice and reflected a particular point of view. With the commercial marketing of picture-printing techniques, it becomes much more difficult to classify or categorize this output, and with the invention of photography and its rapid spread after 1840 this "picture world" overleapt all previous bounds. But even in the face of this profusion, one soon comes to realize that, though a "closed" vocabulary had given place to an "open" one, the number of terms in it was no less finite and their choice most of the time was conventional. Most important of all was the fact that this new, unquestioned tool became a formidable opinion-shaper in the hands of the editor wielding it.

Le Cabinet des Modes, Amsterdam, 4th issue of 1789, fold-out illustration, hand-tinted etching.

14 LES MODES PARISIENNES.

Un second chapeau, en velours *pensée*, est orné d'une touffe de *roses de haie* en même couleur et d'une plume blanche sortant de la touffe.

Une délicieuse capote de satin blanc piquée a un bavolet en velours *noir;* l'ornement se compose d'une barbe de blonde, avec plissé vers la droite et petite aigrette noire dans une touffe d'herbes mortes. En dessous, double tuyauté noir et boutons de roses.

Nous avons remarqué chez la même modiste un chapeau de taffetas noir piqué, dont voici le détail : flots de tulle noir brodé garnissant la calotte; bande de plumes noires et boucles de velours *rouge*, avec bouts retombant sur le bavolet. Au milieu de la passe, gros chou en velours *rouge* et intérieur en rapport.

Nous avons admiré à la *Couronne royale* plusieurs manteaux destinés à de très-grandes dames. L'un est en velours *violet*, forme paletot; manches à coude, demi-larges; poches et col; engrêlure à boules gaufrées pour garniture.

Une autre confection aussi élégante est en velours noir; ce modèle, demi-ajusté, a des manches à coude, des poches et un col, garnis d'un petit tuyauté; des boutons *olives* complètent l'ornement.

C'est encore dans cette maison, si justement renommée, que nous avons vu un camail noir en soie côtelée et contours dentelés; une frange chenille à boules et un haut volant de quarante centimètres au moins composent la garniture.

En lingerie, nous avons à la *Couronne royale* les plus jolies choses du monde. C'est un plaisir d'admirer les magnifiques trousseaux qui s'exécutent chaque semaine.

Les manches de dessous deviennent de plus en plus compliquées. Il y en a en mousseline faisant coude, avec entre-deux à la place des coutures. Ces entre-deux, en valenciennes, s'entourent d'une petite dentelle. Les poignets, faits pour passer la main, ont une garniture tombante. Des manches de ce genre se portent avec des cols droits et des cravates assorties.

Une autre jolie parure, composée d'un col-plastron et de manches-ballons, est ornée de médaillons en valenciennes entourés d'une petite dentelle. Les médaillons ont à peu près quatre centimètres de largeur sur cinq et demi de longueur; ils sont séparés et posés sur transparent *mauve*. La cravate est pareille.

Les bonnets du matin sont d'une coquetterie extrême, et nous en avons vu de ravissants ces jours-ci. Les formes fanchons, toujours très-goûtées par les femmes du grand monde, sont ornées de jolis nœuds et de brides posées en dessous. Ces brides passent sous les coques de cheveux en laissant tomber des pans.

Des bonnets ronds, avec encadrement de belle dentelle, ont des fonds sillonnés de valenciennes brodées. D'autres, des passes à jour et de nombreux petits plis faisant *mát* à travers mille sinuosités. Des pompomnettes, des nœuds faits à ravir, des boucles et des flots tombants, se posent sur ces fonds ouvragés; ainsi le goût de la lingère se révèle de mille façons.

La passementerie s'impose en produisant des merveilles. Les garnitures de la *Ville de Lyon* sont adaptées sur les belles étoffes, et toute femme qui sait se mettre leur accorde une préférence marquée. Le comptoir qui contient ces garnitures offre aussi des franges admirables, des galons, des boutons, des imitations de guipure au crochet, des points de Venise et une foule d'autres articles du même genre. Les corsages *hongrois* plaisent toujours, et les ceintures suissesses sont encore bien portées.

Les gants du même magasin sont recherchés par les femmes d'ordre et d'économie; leur souplesse est parfaite, et la coupe des gants *Joséphine* irréprochable.

CÉLESTINE DE B....

Détails du dessin.

Première toilette. — Robe de tulle blanc bouillonné ornée de deux bouillonnés de tulle *rose* remontant du côté droit. Tunique de tulle suivant la même disposition; un courant de verdure orne le contour de la tunique, fixée par une touffe de *roses* et une écharpe de dentelle. Le vide qui se trouve entre les bouillonnés est rempli par une touffe de *roses*. Corsage à pointe garni d'une berthe *rose* bouillonnée, avec le tour du cou *blanc;* petites manches bouillonnées en tulle blanc. Coiffure de *liserons roses* et *blancs*, traîne derrière. Gants blancs.

Seconde toilette. — Robe de tulle blanc entièrement bouillonnée. Pardessus de gros de *Thèbes bleu* clair orné d'une fourrure blanche. Ornements d'épaules en passementerie. Le devant du pardessus fait châle. Capuchon de dentelle blanche. Gants blancs.

Nous avons parlé la semaine dernière de l'ouvrage de M. L. Figuier, LA TERRE AVANT LE DÉLUGE, illustré par E. Riou. Nous donnons encore à nos abonnées trois vignettes tirées de ce livre intéressant publié par la maison L. Hachette et Cie, 77, boulevard Saint-Germain.

LA FÊTE DU PRINCE DE SCHWARZENBERG.

I.

L'empereur et l'impératrice ayant accepté l'invitation, la fête, après plusieurs ajournements, resta enfin fixée irrévocablement au 1er juillet.

A cette époque, l'ambassadeur habitait l'ancien

Les Modes Parisiennes, 10 January 1863, page 14 and full-page plate engraved by A. Carrache after Compte-Calix.

In 1832, just as Charles Philipon in Paris was founding *Le Charivari*, Charles Knight in London founded *The Penny Magazine* for the Society for the Diffusion of Useful Knowledge. It contained only a few wood engravings, but it was followed in 1833 by *The Penny Cyclopaedia*, also started by Knight, and in France by Edouard Charton's weekly *Magasin Pittoresque*. This latter, thanks to several teams of wood engravers working in shifts day and night, and to two steam presses, could cover eight entire pages with illustrations and print 1800 pages an hour, selling 100,000 copies each week at two *sous*. It was completed by the monthly *Musée des Familles*, which sold for half a franc and was subtitled "Evening Readings." The popular illustration of news events really came to the fore, however, with the weekly *Illustrated London News* (1842). It was soon followed by many imitators: *Harper's Weekly* in New York, *L'Illustration* in Paris and the *Illustrirte Zeitung* in Leipzig. Their mainstay was the wood engraving, as it was also of such travel and adventure journals as *Le Tour du Monde*, *Le Monde Illustré* and *Le Journal des Voyages*, in Paris, and of *The Graphic* in London after 1869.

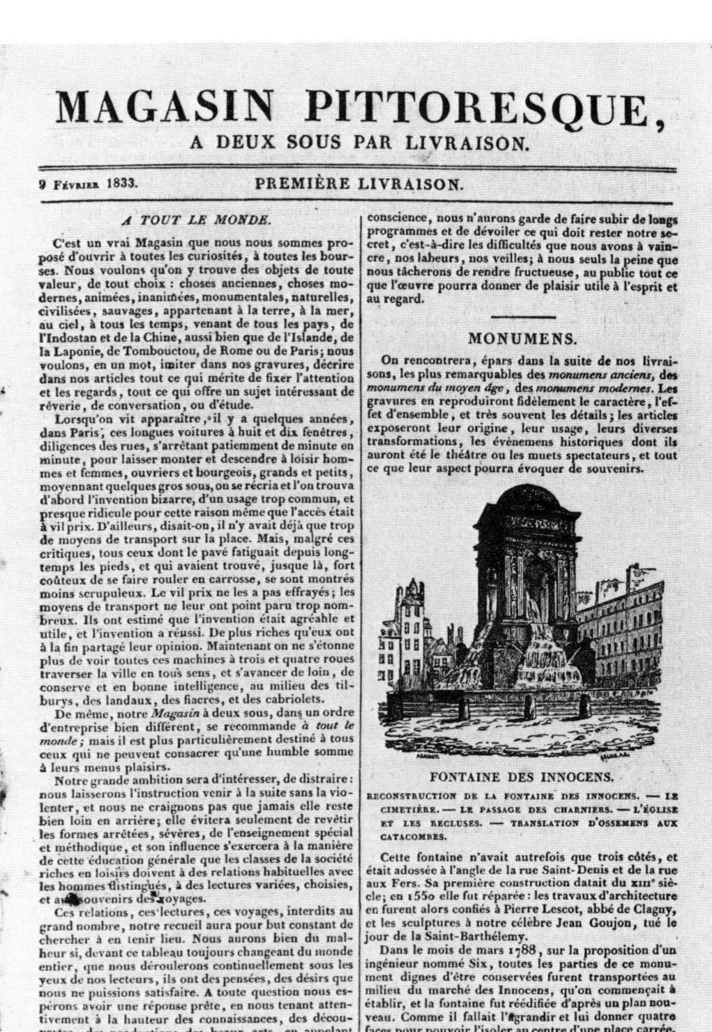

MAGASIN PITTORESQUE,

A DEUX SOUS PAR LIVRAISON.

9 Février 1833. PREMIÈRE LIVRAISON.

A TOUT LE MONDE.

C'est un vrai Magasin que nous nous sommes proposé d'ouvrir à toutes les curiosités, à toutes les bourses. Nous voulons qu'on y trouve des objets de toute valeur, de tout choix : choses anciennes, choses modernes, animées, inanimées, monumentales, naturelles, civilisées, sauvages, appartenant à la terre, à la mer, au ciel, à tous les temps, venant de tous les pays, de l'Indostan et de la Chine, aussi bien que de l'Islande, de la Laponie, de Tombouctou, de Rome ou de Paris; nous voulons, en un mot, imiter dans nos gravures, décrire dans nos articles tout ce qui mérite de fixer l'attention et les regards, tout ce qui offre un sujet intéressant de rêverie, de conversation, ou d'étude.

Lorsqu'on vit apparaître, il y a quelques années, dans Paris, ces longues voitures à huit et dix fenêtres, diligences des rues, s'arrêtant patiemment de minute en minute, pour laisser monter et descendre à loisir hommes et femmes, ouvriers et bourgeois, grands et petits, moyennant quelques gros sous, on se récria et l'on trouva d'abord l'invention bizarre, d'un usage trop commun, et presque ridicule pour cette raison même que l'accès était à vil prix. D'ailleurs, disait-on, il n'y avait déjà que trop de moyens de transport sur la place. Mais, malgré ces critiques, tous ceux dont le pavé fatiguait depuis longtemps les pieds, et qui avaient trouvé, jusque là, fort coûteux de se faire rouler en carrosse, se sont montrés moins scrupuleux. Le vil prix ne les a pas effrayés; les moyens de transport ne leur ont point paru trop nombreux. Ils ont estimé que l'invention était agréable et utile, et l'invention a réussi. De plus riches qu'eux ont à la fin partagé leur opinion. Maintenant on ne s'étonne plus de voir toutes ces machines à trois et quatre roues traverser la ville en tous sens, et s'avancer de loin, de conserve et en bonne intelligence, au milieu des tilburys, des landaux, des fiacres, et des cabriolets.

De même, notre *Magasin* à deux sous, dans un ordre d'entreprise bien différent, se recommande *à tout le monde;* mais il est plus particulièrement destiné à tous ceux qui ne peuvent consacrer qu'une humble somme à leurs menus plaisirs.

Notre grande ambition sera d'intéresser, de distraire : nous laisserons l'instruction venir à la suite sans la violenter, et nous ne craignons pas que jamais elle reste bien loin en arrière; elle évitera seulement de revêtir les formes arrêtées, sévères, de l'enseignement spécial et méthodique, et son influence s'exercera à la manière de cette éducation générale que les classes de la société riches en loisirs doivent à des relations habituelles avec les hommes distingués, à des lectures variées, choisies, et aux souvenirs des voyages.

Ces relations, ces lectures, ces voyages, interdits au grand nombre, notre recueil aura pour but constant de chercher à en tenir lieu. Nous aurons bien du malheur si, devant ce tableau toujours changeant du monde entier, que nous déroulerons continuellement sous les yeux de nos lecteurs, ils ont des pensées, des désirs que nous ne puissions satisfaire. A toute question nous espérons avoir une réponse prête, en nous tenant attentivement à la hauteur des connaissances, des découvertes, des productions des beaux arts, en appelant tour à tour nos artistes, nos écrivains, à représenter, à dire ce qui est vrai, ce qui est beau, ce qui est utile, sans mélange d'exagération ou d'imaginations mensongères. Ces promesses faites, résolus à les tenir avec conscience, nous n'aurons garde de faire subir de longs programmes et de dévoiler ce qui doit rester notre secret, c'est-à-dire les difficultés que nous avons à vaincre, nos labeurs, nos veilles; à nous seuls la peine que nous tâcherons de rendre fructueuse, au public tout ce que l'œuvre pourra donner de plaisir utile à l'esprit et au regard.

Tome I.

MONUMENS.

On rencontrera, épars dans la suite de nos livraisons, les plus remarquables des *monumens anciens*, des *monumens du moyen âge*, des *monumens modernes*. Les gravures en reproduiront fidèlement le caractère, l'effet d'ensemble, et très souvent les détails; les articles exposeront leur origine, leur usage, leurs diverses transformations, les évènemens historiques dont ils auront été le théâtre ou les muets spectateurs, et tout ce que leur aspect pourra évoquer de souvenirs.

FONTAINE DES INNOCENS.

RECONSTRUCTION DE LA FONTAINE DES INNOCENS. — LE CIMETIÈRE. — LE PASSAGE DES CHARNIERS. — L'ÉGLISE ET LES RECLUSES. — TRANSLATION D'OSSEMENS AUX CATACOMBES.

Cette fontaine n'avait autrefois que trois côtés, et était adossée à l'angle de la rue Saint-Denis et de la rue aux Fers. Sa première construction datait du XIIIe siècle; en 1550 elle fut réparée : les travaux d'architecture en furent alors confiés à Pierre Lescot, abbé de Clagny, et les sculptures à notre célèbre Jean Goujon, tué le jour de la Saint-Barthélemy.

Dans le mois de mars 1788, sur la proposition d'un ingénieur nommé Six, toutes les parties de ce monument dignes d'être conservées furent transportées au milieu du marché des Innocens, qu'on commençait à établir, et la fontaine fut réédifiée d'après un plan nouveau. Comme il fallait l'agrandir et lui donner quatre faces pour pouvoir l'isoler au centre d'une place carrée, on fut obligé de compléter l'architecture. Jean Goujon avait sculpté cinq naïades, on eut soin de les laisser entre les pilastres des arcades, où les artistes admirent encore ces figures d'un caractère si naïf et si gracieux;

1

8 MAGASIN PITTORESQUE.

On en a vu un qui traversait ainsi un arbre formant un pont sur un torrent, et qui tenait un jeune cheval mort entre ses bras.

L'ours dans sa manière de combattre a quelques rapports avec la nôtre. Il se dresse sur ses pieds de derrière et assène des coups de poing, des gourmades d'importance, ne se servant presque jamais de ses dents; il paraît même certain que lorsqu'il est poussé à bout, il s'accule contre un rocher, et tient le chasseur en respect à l'aide de pierres qu'il lui lance avec raideur.

L'ours, quand il est pris jeune, est susceptible de recevoir une éducation assez brillante. Qui n'a pas vu la danse de l'ours? En Lithuanie, à Smorgonié, il y a même une sorte d'académie où ce docile quadrupède, enlevé tout mal léché à ses montagnes, reçoit les leçons des meilleurs instituteurs. On doit lui savoir d'autant meilleur gré de cette complaisance, qu'il se plaît dans la solitude, et apprécie les lieux farouches. Le spleen paraît être son état habituel; car, pendant une partie de l'hiver, il se blottit sans provisions dans une caverne, où il partage son temps entre le plaisir de dormir et celui de lécher ses pieds, surtout la plante de ceux de devant, ce qui est assez original. On voit qu'il fait carême; mais il ne résisterait pas à un jeûne rigoureux, s'il n'avait pris la précaution de s'engraisser solidement dans l'arrière-saison; cette graisse lui suffit dans les temps de froidure et de repos. Après le carnaval vient la pénitence, voilà qui est fort juste.

L'homme qui est tout entier à son métier, s'il a du génie, devient un prodige; s'il n'en a point, une application opiniâtre l'élève au-dessus de la médiocrité.

Diderot, *Mélanges.*

Savoir et sentir, voilà toute l'éducation.

Corinne. Madame de Stael.

Que ta vie soit douce, simple, et que ton esprit soit dans les cieux! Imite l'alouette, qui pose humblement son nid près de la terre, sur quelques tiges de froment, et de cette modeste demeure s'élève en chantant vers le séjour de la lumière.

Auguste Lafontaine.

MOSQUÉE D'ACHMET A CONSTANTINOPLE.

Les *Mosquées* sont les temples des musulmans; les tourelles élancées qui s'élèvent à côté des dômes de ces édifices religieux se nomment *minarets* (en arabe *signal* ou *fanal*), et c'est du haut des galeries qui forment comme les anneaux de ces doigts qui montrent le ciel, suivant une expression de Wordsworth, que, cinq fois par jour, la voix grave et mélancolique du *muezzin* fait entendre au loin l'*ezann*, chant solennel qui appelle à prier Dieu, non seulement les fidèles croyans, mais toutes les nations de la terre.

Sainte-Sophie, à Constantinople, est la mosquée la plus célèbre, parce quelle a servi de type à toutes les autres : c'était dans l'origine une église chrétienne. Mais la mosquée du sultan Achmet Ier dont nous donnons le plan, pris à vue d'oiseau, est beaucoup plus remarquable. Ce monument, d'une magnificence merveilleuse, a été construit en 1610. Achmet était si impatient de la voir terminer, que, tous les vendredis, il travaillait lui-même avec les ouvriers. La mosquée est accompagnée de six minarets d'une extrême hauteur et d'une grande beauté; ils sont entourés de trois galeries dans le style maure, et terminés par des aiguilles. La grande cour d'entrée est environnée d'une colonnade en marbre et en porphyre. Au milieu de la cour est une fontaine de marbre; les portes en sont de cuivre travaillé. Intérieurement les murs sont peints à fresque; on y voit suspendues des tables dorées où sont des inscriptions arabes. Le dôme est supporté par quatre grands pilastres cannelés et partagés dans leur milieu par une astragale; quatre grands demi-dômes sont liés avec le dôme central, et dans les quatre coins de l'édifice il y a autant de petites coupoles; enfin les fenêtres sont faites de verres colorés en petits compartimens très riches, qui ne laissent pénétrer dans le temple qu'une transparence mystérieuse.

Les Bureaux d'abonnement et de vente sont rue du Colombier, n° 30, près de la rue des Petits-Augustins.

Imprimerie de Lachevardière, rue du Colombier, n° 30.

Magasin Pittoresque, cover and page 8 of the first number, Paris, 1833.

The success of these illustrated papers, from the 1840s on, opened new careers to artists with any inclination for topical illustration. On condition of adapting themselves to the discipline, pace and constraints of journalism, such artists could become highly successful. Such was the case with the first great *Punch* cartoonist, John Leech, who was succeeded in 1864 by George Du Maurier. *Punch* attracted some outstanding talents: Charles Keene, whose delicate and smiling caricatures were focused on City men and common people, leaving upper-class life and the satire of "aesthetes" to George Du Maurier; and above all the painter John Tenniel, whose opinions as well as the distinction of his design helped to set the trend of the paper towards conservatism.

A greater responsibility lay with the draughtsmen working for the topical papers, who came before the public as unpolitical artists enlisting the image in the service of Truth and Progress. More than illustrative draughtsmen, they were reporters and opinion-shapers. The most famous illustrative draughtsman in London was Hubert Herkomer, a virtuoso of the free sketch. Van Gogh, who was attracted by the same career, admired Herkomer and collected his illustrations. "Each week I went and looked at the window of the printer of the *Graphic* and the *London News*. The impressions they made on me there on the spot were so strong that I have kept a clear and accurate memory of those drawings." Van Gogh also admired the popular French illustrator Paul Renouard, of *L'Illustration*, who made vivid sketches from the life of the silk-weavers' strikes in Lyons, official visits and famous trials, before being gradually replaced after 1904 by the photographic reporter.

Most of these papers followed a similar trend, flaunting progressive or even radical views, like *Le Charivari*, whose forceful and satirical drawings appeared like a shaft of light and truth; but their radical views were apt to be softened down as their readership moved upward into the moderate bourgeoisie. The revolutions of 1848, by liberalizing the rule of censorship, brought Germany and Italy closer to France and England; and Turin first, with *Il Fischietto*, then Rome, Milan, Florence and Bologna, and Berlin too with *Kladderadatsch*, and also Frankfurt, had their illustrated political journals. But in France under the Second Empire (1852-1870) *Le Charivari* lost its political edge and disappeared in 1893, while in London *Punch* grew increasingly conservative, becoming after 1880, under the editorship of F. C. Burnand, a magazine of anaemic humour, always a respected institution, but a vehicle of no great meaning.

The Penny Magazine, cover of the first number, London, 1832.

THE PENNY MAGAZINE

OF THE

Society for the Diffusion of Useful Knowledge.

No. I.] PUBLISHED EVERY SATURDAY. [March 31, 1832.

READING FOR ALL.

In a book upon the Poor, published in 1673, called 'The Grand Concern of England explained,' we find the following singular proposal:—"that the multitude of stage-coaches and caravans, now travelling upon the roads, may all, or most of them, be suppressed, especially those within forty, fifty, or sixty miles of London." The evil of the stage-coaches is somewhat difficult to be perceived at the present day; but this ingenious author had no doubt whatever on the matter, "for," says he, "will any man keep a horse for himself, and another for his man, all the year, for to ride one or two journies, that at pleasure, when he hath occasion, can step to any place where his business lies, for two, three, or four shillings, if within twenty miles of London, and so proportionably into any part of England?"

We laugh at the lamentation over the evil of stage-coaches, because we daily see or experience the benefits of the thousands of public conveyances carrying forward the personal intercourse of a busy population, and equally useful whether they run from Paddington to the Bank, or from the General Post-Office to Edinburgh. Some, however, who acknowledge the fallacy of putting down long and short stages, that horses may be kept all the year, "for to ride one or two journies," may fall into the very same mistake with regard to knowledge that was thus applied to communication. They may desire to retain a monopoly of literature for those who can buy expensive books; they may think a five-guinea quarto (like the horse for one or two journies) a public benefit, and look upon a shilling duodecimo to be used by every one "at pleasure, when he hath occasion," (like the stage-coach) as a public evil.

What the stage-coach has become to the middle classes, we hope our Penny Magazine will be to *all* classes—an universal convenience and enjoyment. The Society for the Diffusion of Useful Knowledge have considered it proper to commence this publication, from the belief that many persons, whose time and whose means are equally limited, may be induced to purchase and to read it. The various works already published by the Society are principally adapted to diligent readers,—to those who are anxiously desirous to obtain knowledge in a condensed, and, in most cases, systematic form. But there are a very great number of persons who can spare half an hour for the reading of a newspaper who are sometimes disinclined to open a book. For these we shall endeavour to prepare an useful and entertaining Weekly Magazine, that may be taken up and laid down without requiring any considerable effort; and that may tend to fix the mind upon calmer, and, it may be, purer subjects of thought than the violence of party discussion, or the stimulating details of crime and suffering. We have, however, no expectation of superseding the newspaper, and no desire to supersede it. We hope only to share some portion of the attention which is now almost exclusively bestowed upon "the folio of four pages," by those who read little and seldom. We consider it the duty of every man to make himself acquainted with the events that are passing in the world,—with the progress of legislation, and the administration of the laws; for every man is deeply interested in all the great questions of government. Every man, however, may not be qualified to understand them; but the more he knows, the less hasty and the less violent will be his opinions. The false judgments which are sometimes formed by the people upon public events, can only be corrected by the diffusion of sound knowledge. Whatever tends to enlarge the range of observation, to add to the store of facts, to awaken the reason, and to lead the imagination into agreeable and innocent trains of thought, may assist in the establishment of a sincere and ardent desire for information: and in this point of view our little Miscellany may prepare the way for the reception of more elaborate and precise knowledge, and be as the small optic-glass called "the finder," which is placed by the side of a large telescope, to enable the observer to discover the star which is afterwards to be carefully examined by the more perfect instrument.

Vol. I.

CHARING CROSS.

This place has been recently greatly improved by clearing away decaying houses, and enlarging the space for the public convenience, and for the display of newly-erected handsome buildings. It derives its name from having been anciently a village, detached from London, called *Charing*, and from a stately *Cross*, erected there by order of Edward I., to commemorate his affection for Eleanor, his deceased queen. The cross occupied the last spot on which her body rested in its progress to sepulture in Westminster Abbey. The other resting-places of her sumptuous funeral were dignified by similar edifices.

Two centuries and a half ago, Charing-Cross was within bow-shot of the open country, all the way to Hampstead and Highgate. North of the Cross there were only a few houses in front of the Mews, where the King's falcons were kept. The Hay-market was a country road, with hedges on each side, running between pastures. St. Martin's lane was bounded on the west side by the high walls of the Mews, and on the other side by a few houses and by old St. Martin's church, where the present church stands. From these buildings it was a quiet country lane, leading to St. Giles's, then a pleasant village, situated among fine trees. Holborn was a mere road between open meadow land, with a green hedge on the north side. In the Strand, opposite to St. Martin's lane, stood the hospital and gardens of St. Mary Rouncival, a religious establishment founded and endowed by William, Earl of Pembroke, in the reign of Henry III. In the middle of the road leading to the Abbey, and opposite to Charing-Cross, stood a hermitage and chapel dedicated to St. Catherine.

Charing-Cross is represented in the above engraving. It was of an octagonal form and built of stone, and in an upper stage contained eight figures. In 1643 it was pulled down and destroyed by the populace, in their zeal against superstitious edifices. Upon the ground of similar zeal, Henry VIII. suppressed the religious houses of the kingdom, and seized their estates and revenues to his own use: the hospital of St. Mary of Rouncival was included in this fate. On its ancient site stands the palace of the Duke of Northumberland. It was built in the reign of

B

MUSÉE

DES FAMILLES.

LES MAGASINS ANGLAIS.

De omni re et quibusdam aliis.
On parlera de tout et de plusieurs choses encore.

Déjà nous pouvons réaliser pour la France un cours d'instruction familière, amusante, variée, à la portée de tous, presque gratuite tant elle est à bon marché, tel que le font en Angleterre les meilleurs esprits dans tous les genres, unis aux artistes les plus habiles. Chez nous aussi, il est temps que le peuple ait un livre de

Musée des Familles, page from the first number, Paris, 1833.

While the first generation of illustrated papers was losing its wind, outdistanced by a more demanding public and improved techniques, the press was widening its appeal, not yet to all social classes, but to all shades of middle-class opinion. And in France, in the latter half of the nineteenth century, this bourgeoisie comprised a wide range of opinion, from the social monarchists on the right to the anarchists on the left. In 1863 the French cartoonist Marcelin started an illustrated weekly of a new kind, frivolous and fashionable, reflecting the life style of the *parvenus* of the Second Empire: *La Vie Parisienne*. As the Empire came to an end, the opposition papers were giving new life to the political cartoon, taken over from *Le Charivari*; and once the Third Republic was firmly established the Royalists, in 1878, founded *their* opposition paper, *Triboulet*, using in it the same weapons that the anarchists were taking up in their hard-hitting sheets. The flood was unleashed with the law on the liberty of expression, passed in France on 29 July 1881: by the end of the century there were six thousand papers in Paris alone, and full-page illustrations appeared regularly in art magazines and political journals. This vogue for the "big cut," large-sized colour cartoons, humorous or satirical, intellectual and modern-styled, reached its height in *Simplicissimus*, founded in Munich in 1896, *L'Asino*, founded in Rome in 1892, and *L'Assiette au Beurre*, founded in Paris in 1901. From the conservatives to the revolutionaries, the European middle classes were united in this at least, that their rise had brought illustration to power.

"Le Charivari"

1

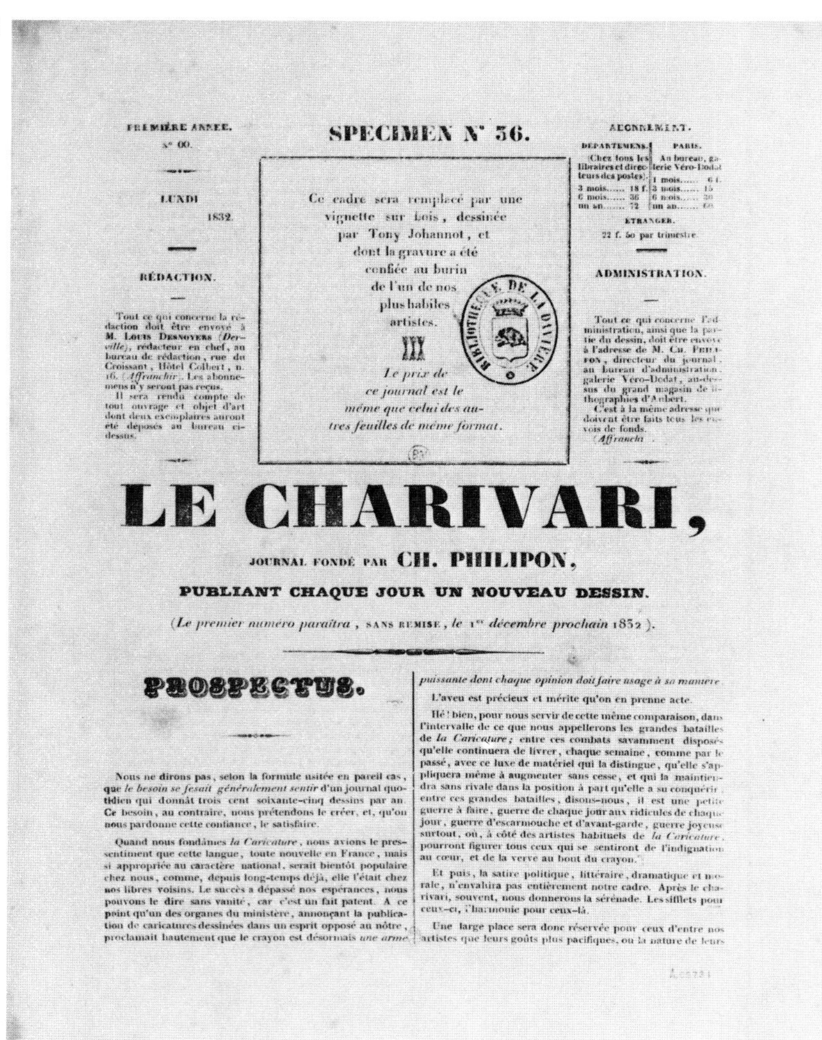

PREMIÈRE ANNÉE.
N° 00.

LUNDI
1832.

RÉDACTION.

Tout ce qui concerne la rédaction doit être envoyé à M. LOUIS DESNOYERS (*Derville*), rédacteur en chef, au bureau de rédaction, rue du Croissant, Hôtel Colbert, n. 16. (*Affranchir*). Les abonnemens n'y seront pas reçus.

Il sera rendu compte de tout ouvrage et objet d'art dont deux exemplaires auront été déposés au bureau ci-dessus.

SPECIMEN N° 36.

Ce cadre sera remplacé par une vignette sur bois, dessinée par Tony Johannot, et dont la gravure a été confiée au burin de l'un de nos plus habiles artistes.

Le prix de ce journal est le même que celui des autres feuilles de même format.

BIBLIOTHÈQUE DE LA DAVIÈRE

ABONNEMENT.

DÉPARTEMENS.	PARIS.
(Chez tous les libraires et directeurs des postes).	Au bureau, galerie Véro-Dodat
	1 mois...... 6 f.
3 mois...... 18 f.	3 mois...... 15
6 mois...... 36	6 mois...... 30
un an...... 72	un an...... 60

ÉTRANGER.
22 f. 50 par trimestre.

ADMINISTRATION.

Tout ce qui concerne l'administration, ainsi que la partie du dessin, doit être envoyé à l'adresse de M. CH. PHILIPON, directeur du journal, au bureau d'administration, galerie Véro-Dodat, au-dessus du grand magasin de lithographies d'Aubert.

C'est à la même adresse que doivent être faits tous les envois de fonds.
(*Affranchir*.)

LE CHARIVARI,

JOURNAL FONDÉ PAR CH. PHILIPON,

PUBLIANT CHAQUE JOUR UN NOUVEAU DESSIN.

(*Le premier numéro paraîtra*, SANS REMISE, *le 1er décembre prochain* 1832).

PROSPECTUS.

Nous ne dirons pas, selon la formule usitée en pareil cas, que *le besoin se fesait généralement sentir* d'un journal quotidien qui donnât trois cent soixante-cinq dessins par an. Ce besoin, au contraire, nous prétendons le créer, et, qu'on nous pardonne cette confiance, le satisfaire.

Quand nous fondâmes *la Caricature*, nous avions le pressentiment que cette langue, toute nouvelle en France, mais si appropriée au caractère national, serait bientôt populaire chez nous, comme, depuis long-temps déjà, elle l'était chez nos libres voisins. Le succès a dépassé nos espérances, nous pouvons le dire sans vanité, car c'est un fait patent. A ce point qu'un des organes du ministère, annonçant la publication de caricatures dessinées dans un esprit opposé au nôtre, proclamait hautement que le crayon est désormais *une arme puissante dont chaque opinion doit faire usage à sa manière*.

L'aveu est précieux et mérite qu'on en prenne acte.

Hé! bien, pour nous servir de cette même comparaison, dans l'intervalle de ce que nous appellerons les grandes batailles de *la Caricature*; entre ces combats savamment disposés qu'elle continuera de livrer, chaque semaine, comme par le passé, avec ce luxe de matériel qui la distingue, qu'elle s'appliquera même à augmenter sans cesse, et qui la maintiendra sans rivale dans la position à part qu'elle a su conquérir, entre ces grandes batailles, disons-nous, il est une petite guerre à faire, guerre de chaque jour aux ridicules de chaque jour, guerre d'escarmouche et d'avant-garde, guerre joyeuse surtout, où, à côté des artistes habituels de *la Caricature*, pourront figurer tous ceux qui se sentiront de l'indignation au cœur, et de la verve au bout du crayon.

Et puis, la satire politique, littéraire, dramatique et morale, n'envahira pas entièrement notre cadre. Après le charivari, souvent, nous donnerons la sérénade. Les sifflets pour ceux-ci, l'harmonie pour ceux-là.

Une large place sera donc réservée pour ceux d'entre nos artistes que leurs goûts plus pacifiques, ou la nature de leurs

2

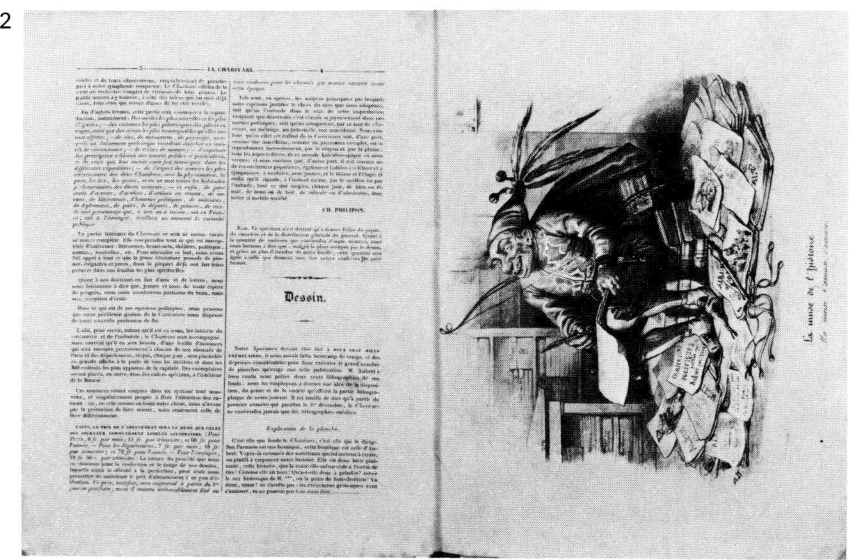

LE CHARIVARI.

CH. PHILIPON.

Besoin.

5

PUNCH

OR THE

LONDON CHARIVARI

VOLUME THE FIRST.

LONDON:
PUBLISHED AT THE OFFICE, 85, FLEET STREET.

Founded by Charles Philipon and the businessman Aubert with a team of young, republican-minded lithographers, Traviès, Pigal, Raffet, Grandville and above all Daumier (who alone, till his death in 1879, supplied the paper with four thousand prints), *Le Charivari* took over on 1 December 1832 from *La Silhouette* (1829) and *La Caricature* (1830). The latter had collapsed under an avalanche of libel suits, despite the publication of some superb plates in its monthly issue, their sale being intended to pay the fines. In theory the press was free under Louis-Philippe; yet he sent both Philipon and Daumier to prison. *Le Charivari* was at first an extreme left-wing paper, out to convince the lower middle class that the 1830 revolution had been "confiscated" by the ruling class. It was the first daily whose stated aim was to "publish a new drawing every day"—to which was added, after 1835, "... censorship permitting." Consisting of four pages, the third occupied by a lithograph, it printed three thousand copies, price 20 centimes or 6 francs a month. Its illustration policy was announced in its prospectus: "Reproduction of the latest and smartest fashions; of picturesque costumes; of hit plays and the most noteworthy scenes in them; of places, monuments and landscapes on which some event of the day may focus attention; of scenes of daily life; sketches of major pictures in public museums or privately owned, and others attracting notice in the different exhibitions; views of the most interesting sittings of the two Chambers with the features, pose, mannerisms, gestures and in a word all the parliamentary ways of the different speakers; and finally portraits of actors, actresses, artists of renown, scientists, men of letters, politicians, ministers, diplomats, peers, deputies, princes, kings and any personality who rightly or wrongly, in France or abroad, may for a moment arouse the public curiosity." Here, from the start, was the programme laid down for illustrated journalism everywhere, for a long time to come. ■

3

3 — LE CHARIVARI. — 4

C'est la cuisinière de M. Evariste Dumoulin, qui, le 16 *novembre* dernier, a entendu deux individus qu'elle ne reconnait pas en la personne des accusés, et qui se disaient : « Il » faut que le roi tombe ; il faut que ce soit pour le *premier* » *de l'an!* »

C'est le sieur Fromont, épicier, comme c'est facile à voir, dont l'épouse lui a dit, dit-il, qu'un monsieur bien couvert, qu'il ne reconnaît pas, était venu acheter chez lui une bouteille d'eau-de-vie, ce qui lui a paru extraordinaire. Déposition *grave*, en effet, d'où, si l'on ne peut tout à fait conclure pour l'attentat horrible, il faut du moins supposer que l'eau-de-vie de M. Fromont ne jouit pas d'une grande réputation dans son quartier. M. Fromont ne paraît guère bien fourni d'esprit.

C'est le sieur Genaille, balayeur, qui répond obstinément à tout : « Pas chez le perruquier. C'est pas le perruquier, pas » chez le perruquier ! »

C'est M. Marville, petit clerc de M. Devauriex, avoué, qui raconte comme quoi il a causé théâtre et littérature avec un jeune homme se disant carliste, et qu'il ne reconnaît pas.

C'est M. Pajol qui certifie quil n'a pas entendu siffler la balle, et qu'il n'a aucune espèce de notions sur l'homme qui a fait le coup. C'est M. Bernard, *idem*. C'est M. Gallois, *idem*. Ce sont dix autres témoins, *idem*; ce qui doit singulièrement éclairer MM. les jurés. Mais vraiment les jurés non plus n'ont point entendu siffler de balles, et n'ont aucune notion sur l'homme qui a fait le coup. Nous en sommes tous là.

C'est ensuite le sieur Petit Didier qui *s'est précipité ;* le sieur Bourdel qui *s'est élancé ;* le sieur Scherer qui *s'est jeté*, etc., etc. Il est inutile de dire que les témoins de cette dernière espèce sont sergens de ville, gendarmes ou gardes municipaux. Ces messieurs se *jettent*, *s'élancent* et se *précipitent* toujours.

Du reste, une déposition fort remarquable, c'est celle de M. Rafé, colonel d'état-major, déposition corroborée par celle de M. Gallois, capitaine d'état-major, et laquelle est ainsi conçue : « Nous étions d'ailleurs instruits d'avance aux Tuile- » ries qu'on devait à son passage tirer sur le roi. — D. Le roi » avait-il été prévenu de cela? — R. Mais, monsieur.... je » l'ignore. » (*Chuchottemens dans l'auditoire.*)

Ainsi, on était instruit d'avance aux Tuileries ! Il paraît qu'on en savait davantage avant l'événement, que MM. les jurés après. Le témoin, toutefois, n'a pas su dire si sa majesté était instruite aussi, et si l'eau de Cologne était déjà prête pour les évanouissemens de Mlle Boury ; mais ce n'est pas probable.

Enfin, ce qui prouve bien toute l'ardeur qui anime M. Dubois (dont on fait les flûtes) à rechercher la vérité, c'est la question adressée par lui à plusieurs témoins, et qui consiste à savoir bien précisément contre qui était dirigé l'attentat horrible. — « Comment, a-t-il demandé à M. Rafé notamment, avez-vous pensé que le coup de pistolet était dirigé sur le roi? » Question qui prouve d'autant mieux son amour du vrai, qu'un instant auparavant M. Gabriel Delessert avait cru pouvoir prendre sur lui de penser qu'il était évident que le coup était dirigé sur la personne du roi.

Cette circonstance, du reste, semble maintenant tout à fait hors de doute. La première séance a déjà amené ce résultat satisfaisant. Espérons que, grâce à l'habileté de M. le président et à son ingénieux système d'interrogatoire, la seconde prouvera qu'il y a un Pont-Royal ; la troisième, une rivière dessous ; la quatrième, un pistolet; la cinquième, un roi ; la sixième un 19 novembre ; la septième, un président nommé Dubois (dont on fait les flûtes), etc.

Après quoi, il ne restera plus à prouver que la culpabilité des deux accusés. C'est ce que, je le répète, nous laissons à MM. les jurés le soin de décider : à eux, le fond; mais à nous la forme.

QUI PAIERA? — LA FRANCE. — PARBLEU !

Réponse lumineuse de M. Imbroglio.

L'éloquence négative dont nous avons signalé, ces jours derniers, l'intronisation dans la rhétorique parlementaire, poursuit décidément ses rapides progrès. Elle a définitivement pris son rang au milieu des figures à l'usage de la meilleure des républiques. Ces figures sont au nombre de trois.

S'agit-il d'une demande de fonds secrets à faire accueillir sans trop de résistance, ou d'un vote délicat qu'il faille enlever à la course ? le ministère évoque le spectre sanglant de la république, le fantôme hideux de la terreur ; lesdits fantôme et spectre secouant d'une main la torche de l'anarchie, et de l'autre la hache révolutionnaire. — C'est la prosopopée.

S'agit-il de budget? tout le monde a déjà compris que ces deux monstruosités sont du ressort de l'hyperbole.

S'agit-il enfin d'une demande d'explication formulée par un député de l'opposition? — c'est alors que le ministère appelle à son aide l'éloquence négative.

La police fit la prosopopée, les finances enfantèrent l'hyperbole, et la diplomatie créa l'éloquence négative.

Avec ces trois choses-là, je gouvernerais, moi qui vous parle, ce qu'il y a de plus ingouvernable au monde, un troupeau de rois-citoyens.

Et, de fait, remarquez l'influence que ces trois figures constitutionnelles exercent aujourd'hui sur les destinées de la France. — L'hyperbole? elle vous coûte assez cher ! — La prosopopée? elle vous environne de ses lueurs fantastiques, et vous étreint de ses bras de spectre. Chaque jour, dans la bouche de M. Barthe, elle fait dresser les cheveux sur les perruques du centre. Hier encore, M. Persil évoquait par elle l'ombre du 6 juin, à l'effet de prouver : 1° que lui, Persil, avait eu deux fois raison de poursuivre d'urgence le livre de M. Cabet, lequel n'a paru qu'en juillet ; 2° que lui, susdit Persil, avait quatre fois raison d'attendre maintenant les kalendes grecques ou le désarmement universel pour faire juger le même ouvrage.

Quant à l'éloquence négative, je vous ai fait connaître l'autre jour quel précieux secours avait tiré d'elle M. Soult, pour établir que le gouvernement était tout à fait décidé à garder Alger, à moins qu'il ne se décidât à l'abandonner.— Là ne devaient point se borner ses services : du département de la guerre, l'éloquence négative vient de passer aux relations extérieures, son véritable berceau.

M. Mauguin avait prié M. de Broglie, ou plutôt M. Imbroglio, de déclarer qui, de la France, ou de la Belgique, ou de la Hollande, paierait les frais des deux campagnes.

A quoi M. Imbroglio a répondu : « Le gouvernement belge ne prétend pas que ces frais doivent être mis à la charge du gouvernement français ; mais il prétend qu'ils ne doivent pas tomber à la charge du gouvernement belge. Quant à la Hollande, nous ne sommes pas positivement en paix avec elle ; mais nous ne sommes pas non plus positivement en guerre. Ainsi, nous devons attendre pour savoir à qui nous devons réclamer le paiement ; car le gouvernement belge et le gouvernement hollandais se refusant à payer, je ne puis pas dire que le gouvernement belge ait raison, ni que le gouvernement hollandais ait tort. »

M. Mauguin n'a-t-il pas judicieusement remarqué que cette simple argumentation prouve, bien mieux que les plus magnifiques discours, que les diplomates sont une race à part, des hommes d'une nature particulière? A coup sûr, sur cent noms triés, même par M. de Bondy, dans la collection la plus propre aux exercices de ce genre, même dans l'*Almanach de la cour*, je défierais qu'on trouvât un seul individu capable de produire à jeun la phrase ci-dessus. — Evidemment on naît diplomate, comme on naît Viennet, ou Mahul, ou crétin, ou porc-épic, ou Vérollot, ou rhinocéros.

Obélisque élevé à la gloire d'une révolution, et découvert en 1830, au juste milieu de l'arabie heureuse par une caravane d'épiciers

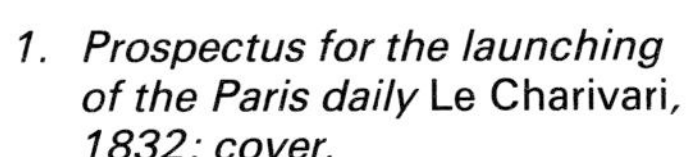

1. *Prospectus for the launching of the Paris daily* Le Charivari, *1832: cover.*
2. *Prospectus for* Le Charivari *: inner pages showing the layout of the paper, with text on the second page and a lithograph on the third.*
3. *Two inner pages of* Le Charivari, *No. 103, 13 March 1833. (The pear was the caricaturist's symbol of King Louis-Philippe, from the shape of his head and face.)*
4. *Text of the sentence for libel passed on the managing editor, as printed on the front page of* Le Charivari, *No. 58, 27 February 1834.*
5. *Cover of the first number of* Punch, *or* The London Charivari, *London, 1841.*

4

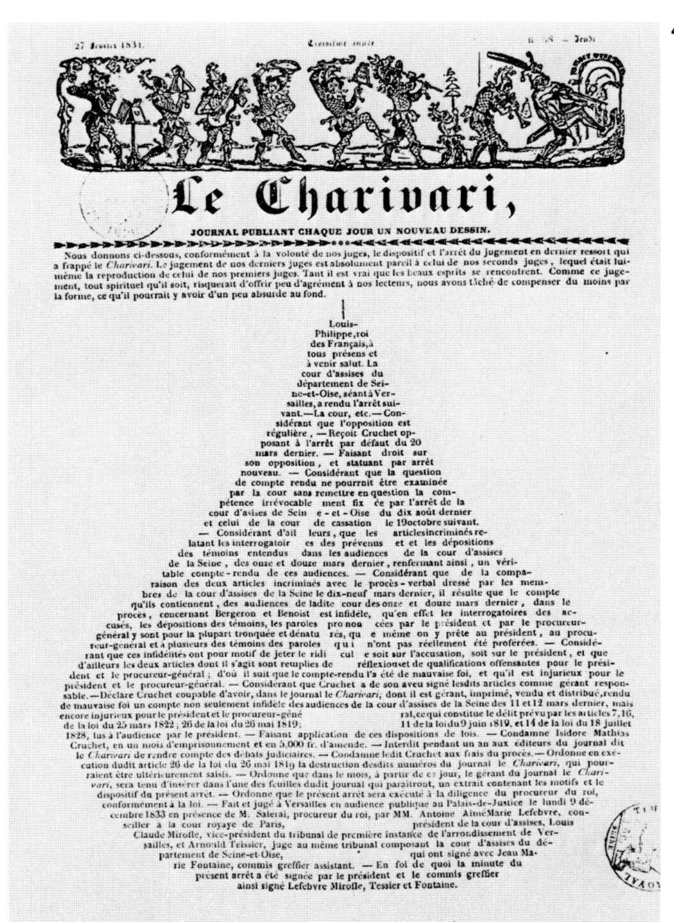

Le Charivari,

JOURNAL PUBLIANT CHAQUE JOUR UN NOUVEAU DESSIN.

Nous donnons ci-dessous, conformément à la volonté de nos juges, le dispositif et l'arrêt du jugement en dernier ressort qui a frappé le *Charivari*. Le jugement de nos derniers juges est absolument pareil à celui de nos seconds juges, lequel était lui-même la reproduction de celui de nos premiers juges. Tant il est vrai que les beaux esprits se rencontrent. Comme ce jugement, tout spirituel qu'il soit, risquerait d'offrir peu d'agrément à nos lecteurs, nous avons tâché de compenser du moins par la forme, ce qu'il pourrait y avoir d'un peu absurde au fond.

Louis-Philippe, roi des Français, à tous présens et à venir salut. La cour d'assises du département de Seine-et-Oise, séant à Versailles, a rendu l'arrêt suivant.—La cour, etc.—Considérant que l'opposition est régulière, —Reçoit Cruchet opposant à l'arrêt par défaut du 20 mars dernier. — Faisant droit sur son opposition, et statuant par arrêt nouveau. — Considérant que la question de compte rendu ne pourrait être examinée par la cour sans remettre en question la compétence irrévocablement fixée par l'arrêt de la cour d'assises de Seine-et-Oise du dix août dernier et celui de la cour de cassation le 19 octobre suivant. — Considérant d'ailleurs, que les articles incriminés relatant les interrogatoires des prévenus et et les dépositions des témoins entendus dans les audiences de la cour d'assises de la Seine, des onze et douze mars dernier, renfermant ainsi, un véritable compte-rendu de ces audiences. — Considérant que de la comparaison des deux articles incriminés avec le procès-verbal dressé par les membres de la cour d'assises de la Seine le dix-neuf mars dernier, il résulte que le compte qu'ils contiennent, des audiences de ladite cour des onze et douze mars dernier, dans le procès, concernant Bergeron et Benoist est infidèle, qu'en effet les interrogatoires des accusés, les dépositions des témoins, les paroles prononcées par le président et par le procureur-général y sont pour la plupart tronquée et dénaturés, que même on y prête au président, au procureur-général et à plusieurs des témoins des paroles qui n'ont pas réellement été proférées. — Considérant que ces infidélités ont pour motif de jeter le ridicule soit sur l'accusation, soit sur le président, et que d'ailleurs les deux articles dont il s'agit sont remplies de réflexions et de qualifications offensantes pour le président et le procureur-général ; d'où il suit que le compte-rendu l'a été de mauvaise foi, et qu'il est injurieux pour le président et le procureur-général. — Considerant que Cruchet a de son aveu signé lesdits articles comme gérant responsable.—Déclare Cruchet coupable d'avoir, dans le journal le *Charivari*, dont il est gérant, imprimé, vendu et distribué, rendu de mauvaise foi un compte non seulement infidèle des audiences de la cour d'assises de la Seine des 11 et 12 mars dernier, mais encore injurieux pour le président et le procureur-général, ce qui constitue le délit prévu par les articles 7, 16, de la loi du 25 mars 1822 ; 26 de la loi du 26 mai 1819; 11 de la loi du 9 juin 1819, et 14 de la loi du 18 juillet 1828, lus à l'audience par le président. — Faisant application de ces dispositions de lois. — Condamne Isidore Mathias Cruchet, en un mois d'emprisonnement et en 5,000 fr. d'amende. — Interdit pendant un an aux éditeurs du journal dit le *Charivari* de rendre compte des débats judiciaires. — Condamne ledit Cruchet aux frais du procès.— Ordonne en exécution dudit article 26 de la loi du 26 mai 1819 la destruction desdits numéros du journal le *Charivari*, qui pourraient être ultérieurement saisis. — Ordonne que dans le mois, à partir de ce jour, le gérant du journal le *Charivari*, sera tenu d'insérer dans l'une des feuilles dudit journal qui paraîtront, un extrait contenant les motifs et le dispositif du présent arrêt. — Ordonne que le présent arrêt sera exécuté à la diligence du procureur du roi, conformément à la loi. — Fait et jugé à Versailles en audience publique au Palais-de-Justice le lundi 9 décembre 1833 en présence de M. Salerai, procureur du roi, par MM. Antoine Aimé Marie Lefebvre, conseiller à la cour royaye de Paris, président de la cour d'assises, Louis Claude Miroffe, vice-président du tribunal de première instance de l'arrondissement de Versailles, et Arnould Teissier, juge au même tribunal composant la cour d'assises du département de Seine-et-Oise, qui ont signé avec Jean Marie Fontaine, commis greffier assistant. — En foi de quoi la minute du présent arrêt a été signée par le président et le commis greffier ainsi signé Lefebvre Miroffe, Tessier et Fontaine.

"The Illustrated London News"

1

After the fashion magazines of the late eighteenth century and the satirical papers of the 1820s, the third generation of illustrated journalism, the one most pregnant with consequences, appeared on Saturday 14 May 1842 with the first issue of *The Illustrated London News*, a weekly of large format (sixteen pages), low price (sixpence) and large circulation (26,000 copies), containing thirty wood engravings, some of them panoramic views. Illustrated in the first issue were the state ball of two days before, at which the queen and the prince consort appeared, and the fire that swept Hamburg on 5 May. News of the fire had reached London on the 10th; to picture it, a draughtsman borrowed a view of Hamburg from the British Museum and added flames and smoke.

From now on, this paper presented the news of each week in pictorial form: ceremonies and demonstrations, travels and explorations, catastrophes and the wonders of industry (beginning with the huge steam press which printed the paper). But its first and most immediate interest was "with the highest region of newspaper literature—the Political," to which the paper pledged itself to add "a whole battery of vigorous illustration." The founder of *The Illustrated London News* was Herbert Ingram, a self-made man who had begun as a printer's apprentice in Hull and, from the occasional pictures published in the *Weekly Chronicle* (1837) and the *Observer* (1838), realized the latent power of illustrated journalism. Ingram's venture was an enormous success. He saw the possibilities of photography at once and by 1843 was using large plates made from daguerreotypes. By 1851, with the Scott Archer process, the photograph could be transferred directly to the woodblock, doing away with the draughtsman; but it was not till the late 1880s that the hand-cut wood engraving was superseded by photolithography. *The Illustrated London News* was soon being imitated in Paris (*L'Illustration*, 1843, and *Le Monde Illustré*), in Leipzig (*Die Illustrirte Zeitung*, 1848), in Holland (*Hollandsche Illustratie*) and in New York (*Harper's Weekly*). In England it swallowed up its competitors (*Pictorial Times*, 1843, and *Illustrated Times*, 1855). The ancestor of the great illustrated magazines, it still continues its career today. ■

2

3

No. 1.] FOR THE WEEK ENDING SATURDAY, MAY 14, 1842. SIXPENCE

OUR ADDRESS.

In presenting the first number of the ILLUSTRATED LONDON NEWS to the British Public, we would fain make a graceful entrée into the wide and grand arena, which will henceforth contain so many actors for our benefit and so many spectators of our career. In plain language, we do not produce this illustrated newspaper without some vanity, much ambition, and a fond belief that we shall be pardoned the presumption of the first quality by realizing the aspirations of the last. For the past ten years we have watched with admiration and enthusiasm the progress of illustrative art, and the vast revolution which it has wrought in the world of publication through all the length and breadth of this mighty empire. To the wonderful march of periodical literature it has given an impetus and a rapidity almost coequal with the gigantic power of steam. It has converted blocks into wisdom, and given wings and spirit to ponderous and senseless wood. It has in its turn adorned, gilded, reflected, and interpreted, nearly every form of thought. It has given to fancy a new dwelling-place, to imagination a more permanent throne. It has set up fresh land-marks of poetry, given sterner pungency to satire, and mapped out the geography of mind with clearer boundaries and more distinct and familiar intelligence than it ever bore alone. Art—as now fostered, and redundant in the peculiar and facile department of wood engraving—has, in fact, become the bride of literature; genius has taken her as its handmaid, and popularity has crowned her with laurels that only seem to grow the greener the longer they are worn.

And there is now no staying the advance of this art into all the departments of our social system. It began in a few isolated volumes—stretched itself next over fields of natural history and science—penetrated the arcanæ of our own general literature—and made companionship with our household books. At one plunge it was in the depth of the stream of poetry—working with its every current—partaking of the glow, and adding to the sparkles of the glorious waters—and so refreshing the very soul of genius, that even Shakspeare came to us clothed with a new beauty, while other kindred poets of our language seemed as it were to have put on festive garments to crown the marriage of their muses to the arts. Then it walked abroad among the people, went into the poorer cottages, and visited the humblest homes in cheap guises, and, perhaps, in roughish forms; but still with the illustrative and the instructive principle strongly worked upon, and admirably developed for the general improvement of the human race. Lastly, it took the merry aspect of fun, frolic, satire, and *badinage*; and the school of *Charivari* began to blend itself with the graver pabulum of Penny Cyclopœdias and Saturday Magazines.

And now, when we find the art accepted in all its elements, and welcomed by every branch of reading into which it has diverged; now, when we see the spirit of the times everywhere associating with it, and heralding or recording its success; we do hold it as of somewhat triumphant omen that WE are, by the publication of this very newspaper, launching the giant vessel of illustration into a channel the broadest and the widest that it has ever dared to stem. We bound at once over the billows of a new ocean—we sail into the very heart and focus of public life—we take the world of newspapers by storm, and flaunt a banner on which the words "ILLUSTRATED NEWS" become symbols of a fresher purpose, and a more enlarged design, than was ever measured in that hemisphere till now.

The public will have henceforth under their glance, and within their grasp, the very form and presence of events as they transpire, in all their substantial reality, and with evidence visible as well as circumstantial. And whatever the broad and palpable delineations of wood engraving can be taught to achieve, will now be brought to bear upon every subject which attracts the attention of mankind, with a spirit in unison with the character of such subject, whether it be serious or satirical, trivial or of purpose grave.

And, reader, let us open something of the detail of this great intention to your view. Begin, *par exemple*, with the highest region of newspaper literature—the Political. Why, what a field! If we are strong in the creed that we adopt—if we are honest, as we pledge ourselves to be, in the purpose that we maintain—how may we lend muscle, bone, and sinew to the tone taken and the cause espoused, by bringing to bear upon our opinions, a whole battery of vigorous illustration. What "H. B." does amid the vacillations of parties, without any prominent opinions of his own, *we* can do with double regularity and consistency, and therefore with more valuable effect. Moreover, regard the homely illustration which nearly every public measure will afford:—your Poor-laws—your Corn-laws—your Factory bills—your Income taxes! Look at the field of public portraiture presented in your Houses of Legislature alone, and interesting to every constituency in the land. Open your police-offices, your courts of law, your criminal tribunals—all the pith and marrow of the administration of justice—you can have it broadly before you, with points of force, of ridicule, of character, or of crime; and if the pen be ever led into fallacious argument, the pencil must at least be oracular with the spirit of truth.

In the world of diplomacy, in the architecture of foreign policy, we can give you every trick of the great Babel that other empires are seeking to level or to raise. Is there peace? then shall its arts, implements, and manufactures be spread upon our page. The literature—the customs—the dress—nay, the institutions and localities of other lands, shall be brought home to you with spirit, with fidelity, and, we hope, with discretion and taste. Is there war? then shall its seat and actions be laid naked before the eye. No estafette—no telegraph—no steam-winged vessel—no overland mail, shall bring intelligence to our shores that shall not be sifted with industry, and illustrated with skill in the columns of this journal; and whether the cowardice of China or the treachery of Affghanistan be the theme of your abhorrence or resentment, you shall at least have as much historical detail of both as, while it gratifies general curiosity, shall minister to the natural anxieties at home of those who have friends and relations amid the scenes delineated and the events described.

Take another fruitful branch of illustration, the pleasures of the people!—their theatres, their concerts, their galas, their races, and their fairs! Again, the pleasures of the aristocracy—their court festivals, their *bals masqués*, their levees, their drawing rooms—the complexion of their grandeur, and the circumstance of all their pomp!

In literature, a truly beautiful arena will be entered upon; for we shall not only, in most instances, have the opportunity of illustrating our own reviews, but of borrowing selections from the illustrations of the numerous works which the press is daily pouring forth, so elaborately embellished with woodcuts in the highest style of art.

In the field of fine arts——but let the future speak, and let us clip promise in the wing. We have perhaps said enough, without condescending to the littleness of too much detail to mark the general outline of our design; and we trust to the kindness and intelligence of our readers to imagine for us a great deal more than we have been able to crowd into the compass of an introductory leader. Moreover, we would strongly premise an expression of gratitude for all suggestions that may hereafter reach us, and assure our volunteers of these, that wherever there seems a possibility of acting upon them creditably, that course shall be taken with promptitude, vigour, and effect.

Here we make our bow, determined to pursue our great experiment with boldness; to associate its principle with a purity of tone that may secure and hold fast for our journal the fearless patronage of families; to seek in all things to uphold the great cause of public morality, to keep continually before the eye of the world a living and moving panorama of all its actions and influences; and to withhold from society no point that its literature can furnish or its art adorn, so long as the genius of that literature, and the spirit of that art, can be brought within the reach and compass of the Editors of the ILLUSTRATED LONDON NEWS!

DESTRUCTION OF THE CITY OF HAMBURGH BY FIRE.

By the arrival of the General Steam Navigation Company's boat Caledonia, off the Tower, on Tuesday evening, news has been brought of an immense conflagration which took place on Thursday morning, the 5th instant, at one o'clock, in that city. The district in which the fire broke out consists entirely of wood tenements, chiefly of five and six stories high, and covering an area of ground of about thirty to forty acres. The whole of the buildings on this large space have been totally consumed to the number of more than 1000. The fire was by some thought to have originated in the street known by the name of the Stein Twite, in the warehouse of a Jew, named Cohen, a cigar manufacturer, and who, upon good grounds, has been taken up on suspicion as the incendiary. The wind at the time blew a stout north-west, which caused the flames rapidly to spread; and proceeding in the direction of Rodings-market, and from thence to Deich-street, entirely consuming the whole of the following streets, among which is the Hoppen-market, and St. Nicholas Church, a fine stone fabric, and the handsomest in Hamburgh. Grutz Twite, Cressnon (back and end), Grosser Burstah, Muhlen Brucke, Alte Borse, Bohnen Strasse, Monkedam Twite, Altewalle Strasse, Grosse and Rlaire, Joannes Strasse, Nassewall (partially), Alter and Neuer Jungferstieg Berg, New Berg Strasse, St. Petrie Trichie, Kunigs Strasse, Greenhoff a Grasskiller (partially), Rathaus, Borsenhalle, Zuichhaus, Spinnhaus, and Detenwinshaus, Schmidt Wassenkunst (Nue Bose), Zuchstrausse Strasse, Kunst, Caulstrausse, Kobdam, Dullhaus, Sperort, and Steinstrausses.

View of the Conflagration of Hamburgh, from the Alster.

1.2. The Illustrated London News, *7 January 1843: London in 1842, views from the south and the north.*

3. The Illustrated London News, *cover of the first number, London, 1842.*

III

The Work of the Image

h. Le Secq.
Chartres.

PHOTOGRAPHIC ILLUSTRATION

▲ Photogravure by Charles Nègre, before 1857: Column statues of the Kings and Queens of Judea, royal porch of Chartres Cathedral.

◄ Photolithograph by Henri Le Secq, 1875-1880: Column statues, north porch of Chartres Cathedral.

Photography, invented after long experimentation by Niepce, Daguerre, Fox Talbot and Bayard, came as the long-sought answer to the need for accuracy which the modern ideology required of pictures. The daguerreotype, commercialized in 1839, had the disadvantage of being a unique image, only one print being possible; and economics required serial reproduction if any profits were to be realized. At this very time book production was being industrialized, on the principle of longer printings and lower costs per copy. The calotype process, patented by Fox Talbot in 1841, was tried out at first, but the difficulties of printing on paper were not solved till 1851, by Blanquart-Evrard. So initially photographic illustrations had to be pasted into books whose text had already been printed, a laborious operation. What Niepce had been after was photogravure, permitting photographic plates to be inked and printed directly. But it took a long time to work this process out. H. L. Fizeau's successful experiment with it, in printing his *Excursions Daguerriennes* (1842), was not followed up, and till about 1860 it was accepted that books could not be illustrated with photographs except by pasting them in or redrawing them by hand on wood blocks or stone and reverting to traditional procedures. But researchers kept on experimenting and in Paris, in 1856, the Duc de Luynes offered a prize to encourage them. It could not be awarded till 1867, to Alphonse Poitevin, who won out over some serious rivals like Charles Nègre and Paul Pretsch. As late as 1863, in an essay on the history of wood engraving, Firmin-Didot considered that "insurmountable obstacles, economic if not technical," stood in the way of the photographic illustration of books by direct printing.

Its printed text pages alternating with hand-pasted photographs, the book illustrated with photographs still seemed like a backward step with respect to the fine prints of Romantic books. Moreover, the use of actual photographs still had some major drawbacks. In the first place, they tended to fade, and who would buy a book illustrated with faded pictures? Only printing ink could overcome this drawback. Secondly, they were not cheap. Blanquart-Evrard sold them for 5 or 6 francs apiece, while the large lithographs from Taylor and Nodier's *Voyages pittoresques* were sold separately for 3.35 francs and the current price of an ordinary print in Paris was 1 or 2 francs. Thirdly, the long delicate manipulation involved in developing, pasting and pressing permitted only a small printing of books illustrated with photographs, a few hundred at most, whereas books were normally printed in their thousands. This meant that the manual processes still had a future. It also favoured a hybrid production of books designed, in spite of its drawbacks, to capitalize on the prestige of the photograph as the most modern and accurate form of reproduction. And so it was that many composite albums were issued as being "photographic," but in fact contained only a single plate actually photo-engraved or photolithographed; or else contained plates which were only engravings made from daguerreotypes. Thus appeared as early as 11 January 1840 the *Album du daguerréotype* of Bruneau, followed that same year by *Paris et ses environs reproduits par le daguerréotype* edited by Charles Philipon. Only the calotype process as yet permitted actual photographic prints on paper, like those in Fox Talbot's *Pencil of Nature* (1844) and his *Sun Pictures in Scotland* (1845). These were followed by William Stirling's *Talbotype Illustrations to the Annals of the Artists of Spain* (London, 1847) and Eugène Piot's *L'Italie monumentale* (Paris, 1851).

From *Paris et ses environs reproduits par le daguerréotype*, edited by Charles Philipon, Paris, 1840: The Bourse. (Actually a lithograph reproduction.)

Text page and hypostyle hall at Thebes, aquatint by Hector Horeau, from his *Panorama d'Egypte et de Nubie*, Paris, 1841.

THÈBES.

PETITS TEMPLES PRÈS DE MÉDINET-ABOU, COLOSSES DITS DE MEMNON, RHAMESSEION.

Au Sud, près de Médinet-Abou, est un petit temple dédié à Thoth; cet édifice contient un pronaos et trois salles décorées de mauvaises sculptures du temps de Ptolémée Évergète II et de sa sœur, la reine Cléopâtre. Près de ce temple, sont les traces du vaste camp retranché dont j'ai déjà parlé, à l'extrémité Sud duquel existe un petit temple à propylon, qui fut élevé à Isis par l'empereur Adrien et que les Arabes appellent Deir Schelvait.

Au Nord-Ouest de Médinet-Abou, vers la chaîne libyque, on voit, au milieu d'une enceinte de briques crues, un petit temple qui s'annonce par un propylon en avant d'une cour représentée ci-contre; dans le fond de cette cour à galerie, on aperçoit les entrées de trois sanctuaires décorés de sculptures des Ptolémées Épiphane, Évergète et de leurs femmes Cléopâtre; à gauche, près d'une croisée à colonnettes évidées dans le mur, un escalier conduit sur le dessus du temple, qui est en terrasse. Si de ce temple on se dirige vers le Nil, on trouve, presque au niveau du sol, des fragments de monuments et des restes de colossales figures monolithes qui, par une étrange destinée, ont leurs membres épars çà et là dans les différents musées du monde.

C'est au Nord de ce champ de monuments ravagés que s'élèvent les colossales figures d'Amenoph III, de la 18ᵉ dynastie, qui ont si vivement éveillé l'attention des voyageurs grecs et romains, à cause des sons que rendait celle qui est le plus au Nord et occupe le deuxième plan dans la gravure ci-dessous; cette merveilleuse statue rendait, en effet, presque tous les jours, au lever du soleil, un son pareil à celui que peut rendre une corde de harpe, c'est tout au moins ce qu'attestent les soixante-douze inscriptions grecques et latines que de hauts personnages ont fait graver sur les jambes et sur le socle de ce colosse. (Voyez l'ouvrage de M. Letronne.)

Mais, avant d'entretenir le lecteur des sons merveilleux, je dois d'abord considérer ces statues en elles-mêmes, dire qu'elles sont en brèche siliceuse agatifère de la première cataracte; qu'elles ont 20 mètres de hauteur; que la mère et la sœur d'Amenoph sont représentées à droite et à gauche, dans la hauteur des siéges; que, sur les faces latérales, des figures symboliques de haute et basse Égypte relient le trône du roi avec des tiges de lotus; que des inscriptions ornent les dossiers des siéges et le sommet des socles; que ces prodigieux colosses, qui furent élevés environ 1680 ans av. J. C., précédaient un temple élevé par Amenoph qui est aujourd'hui entièrement détruit; qu'enfin ces statues, malgré les nombreuses dégradations qui les défigurent, commandent encore le respect par leur grandeur, par leur imposante immobilité et par la régularité de leurs proportions.

Revenant maintenant aux mystérieux sons rendus par la statue vocale, à cette merveille des temps passés qu'on a voulu expliquer par tant de systèmes différents, je dirai que l'on explique généralement cet effet physique par la vibration qui pouvait rapprocher, sinon grandir une fissure existant dans le granit sonore qui compose la statue; cette vibration peut effectivement se concevoir lorsque la statue, échauffée à son sommet par les premiers rayons du soleil, était dans des conditions froides à sa base, non seulement par la terre rafraîchie pendant la nuit, mais encore par le limon du Nil, qui la recouvre en partie depuis l'époque même de sa sonorité qui n'a été remarquée que peu de temps avant J. C.

L'examen approfondi du colosse brisé de bas en haut semble justifier cette opinion, fondée d'ailleurs sur la tradition venue jusqu'à nous que le prodige n'avait pas lieu tous les jours; en effet, le soleil pouvait être plus ou moins radieux, et rester, ainsi que la terre, plus ou moins enveloppé de vapeurs contraires à la vibration. Un si étrange phénomène fit sanctifier ce merveilleux colosse parlant : il devint l'objet d'un culte religieux. Ce fut à l'époque du tremblement de terre de l'an 27 av. J. C. que la partie supérieure de cette figure se détacha; le monolithe ne rendit plus de sons. Septime Sévère, pensant que la voix deviendrait plus belle s'il rétablissait le colosse, et espérant faire de ce miracle une objection contre le christianisme qui s'introduisait en Égypte, fit compléter le colosse avec les treize assises que l'on voit aujourd'hui, et qui, loin d'atteindre le but proposé, mettaient plutôt le monolithe dans des conditions moins probables de sonorité. En effet, cette célèbre figure ne dit plus rien aujourd'hui; cependant les Arabes l'appellent encore Salamalek (salut).

19

The Great Temple of Denderah, Egypt, from Maxime Du Camp, *Egypte, Nubie, Palestine, Syrie*, Paris, 1852 (photographs taken in 1849-1851).

From the 1870s on, by photogravure or collotype, it was possible to illustrate books directly with photographs, and so appeared the five instalments of the *Voyage d'exploration à la Mer Morte* (1871-1874) by the Duc de Luynes illustrated by Charles Nègre. But these processes remained costly and untrustworthy, besides being unsuited to industrial production. The results, at their best, were very fine, but the delicacy of the shadings required intaglio engraving, which could not be combined with letterpress. The old problem of printing pictures arose again with fresh acuteness: how to reduce the image to blacks and whites. Line-block processes, carried out from lithographs, zincographs or autographic paper (and so calling for a draughtsman) left only the blacks and whites in reserve. They were widely used in industrial printing (Tissier from 1840, Gillot from 1850, etc.), but how could they be used to reproduce photographs? These techniques, developed from electrotyping, were good enough for cheap, third-rate illustration work in certain magazines and also, for example, the illustrated albums of the Paris Salon (*L'Autographe au Salon*, 1863). Various procedures were tried for bringing up the metal surface in an electrolytic bath and transforming the photographic negative into a relief plate, but it was only with the invention of the half-tone screen by Berchtold, patented in 1856, that the rapid and reliable mechanical printing of photographs became possible. Here again progress took time, the process being perfected by Barret in 1868 and, in the United States, by Ives in 1885. In France the first book illustrated with half-tone photo-engravings appears to have been that of Dr Le Bon, *La Civilisation des Arabes* (Firmin-Didot, Paris, 1884). Here, with a considerable sacrifice in the delicacy of the shading and the quality of the cliché, the problem of photographic illustration was solved, and progress has been continuous from then to now.

With these technical innovations, illustration began to flourish as never before and its role in the media was ensured. But what about their impact on the content and aspect of the illustrated book? It is noteworthy that the first books illustrated with photographs were mostly travel

1

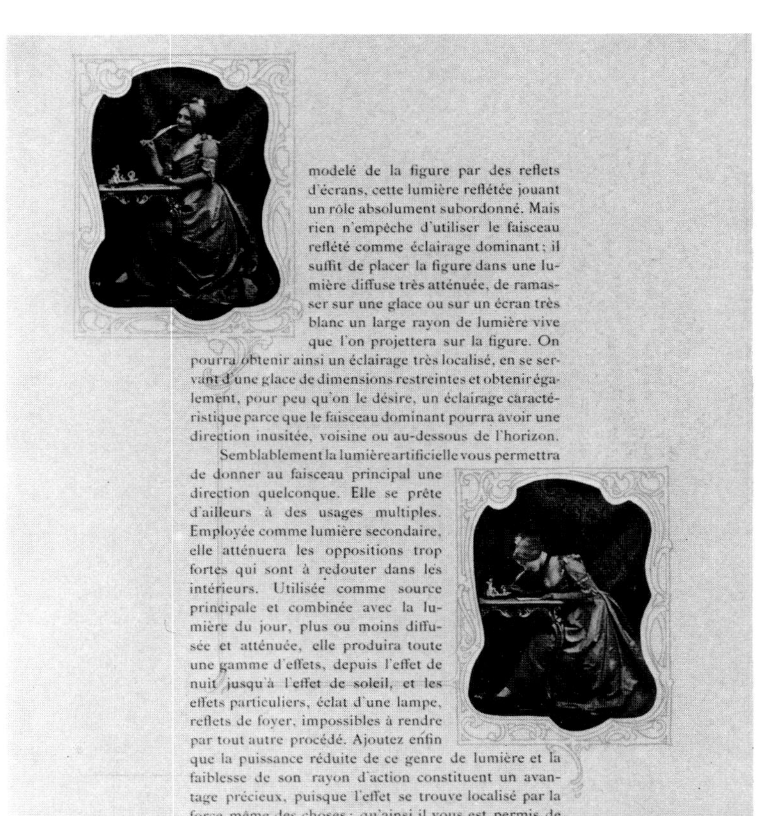

modelé de la figure par des reflets d'écrans, cette lumière reflétée jouant un rôle absolument subordonné. Mais rien n'empêche d'utiliser le faisceau reflété comme éclairage dominant; il suffit de placer la figure dans une lumière diffuse très atténuée, de ramasser sur une glace ou sur un écran très blanc un large rayon de lumière vive que l'on projettera sur la figure. On pourra obtenir ainsi un éclairage très localisé, en se servant d'une glace de dimensions restreintes et obtenir également, pour peu qu'on le désire, un éclairage caractéristique parce que le faisceau dominant pourra avoir une direction inusitée, voisine ou au-dessous de l'horizon.

Semblablement la lumière artificielle vous permettra de donner au faisceau principal une direction quelconque. Elle se prête d'ailleurs à des usages multiples. Employée comme lumière secondaire, elle atténuera les oppositions trop fortes qui sont à redouter dans les intérieurs. Utilisée comme source principale et combinée avec la lumière du jour, plus ou moins diffusée et atténuée, elle produira toute une gamme d'effets, depuis l'effet de nuit jusqu'à l'effet de soleil, et les effets particuliers, éclat d'une lampe, reflets de foyer, impossibles à rendre par tout autre procédé. Ajoutez enfin que la puissance réduite de ce genre de lumière et la faiblesse de son rayon d'action constituent un avantage précieux, puisque l'effet se trouve localisé par la force même des choses; qu'ainsi il vous est permis de placer dans un motif les grands blancs où il vous plait, comme le ferait la main du peintre.

43

plaque l'ensemble du tableau que nous avons devant les yeux. Si les premiers plans sont à une distance suffisante, l'appareil placé à la hauteur de l'œil reproduira le sujet dans des conditions normales et dans ce cas une simple lentille biconvexe nous suffira, mais il peut se produire telle circonstance de rapprochement de l'objet principal qui nous interdise cette position sous peine de nous obliger à plonger. Nous aurions alors des déformations d'un effet désastreux que nous éviterons en armant notre appareil d'un second viseur nous permettant de le placer à la hauteur de la ceinture.

Quelle doit être la dimension de l'image fournie par ces viseurs? Y a-t-il intérêt à ce qu'elle soit égale à celle donnée par la plaque elle-même?

Pour répondre à ces deux questions force nous est, au préalable, d'indiquer une fois de plus le rôle que doit jouer le viseur. Il n'est qu'un guide, nous le répéterons encore. Il faut donc, à notre avis, que les viseurs soient nets et clairs, et qu'ils fournissent une réduction exacte de l'image. Il faut qu'ils soient nets et clairs parce que, dans certains cas, nous avons intérêt à suivre un objet en mouvement pour nous rendre compte qu'il se trouve exactement à la place qu'il doit occuper pour animer heureusement un paysage, et cela au moment où notre obturateur se déclanche. Et si nous ne demandons au viseur qu'une réduction de l'image, c'est que, dans la plupart des cas, sa trop grande dimension serait une gène. Si nous avions la tentation de nous en servir comme d'un verre dépoli, nous risquerions de perdre un temps précieux et, qui plus est, nous enlèverions peut-être à l'image obtenue ce que nous

65

1. Two pages from *Esthétique de la Photographie*, Paris, 1900.

2. Page from Robert de La Sizeranne, *La Photographie est-elle un art?*, Paris, 1899.

3. Double page from Paul Laurence Dunbar, *Candle-Lightin' Time*, New York, 1901.

books; a genre, that is, firmly anchored in an eighteenth-century tradition. Unable to record movement, the photograph served initially to reproduce monuments and places, before venturing into the field of ethnography, first at home (peasants, mountaineers, sailors), then in exotic countries. The repertory of this early photographic illustration was very different from that of the daguerreotype which, yielding only one print, was usually confined to portraiture. In contradistinction to this exclusive devotion to the individual, the early books illustrated with photographs represent rather a collective survey of the world, focused on its natural and artistic riches, and there soon came into existence a wealth of documentary material reputedly objective and authentic. One field of illustration was necessarily sacrificed: that of fiction and literature in general, which till now had had pride of place. On the other hand, the possibilities opened up by photographic illustration may account for the rise, still unflagging today, of a new literary genre: the documentary essay, the reportage, the study in human sciences, which vitally widened the scope and popularity of such disciplines as geography, ethnology and archaeology.

The form taken by the photographic book, quite apart from layout requirements, also imposed a new conception of the text—not always well coped with by publishers—in order to avoid repetition and paraphrasing of the image. It is certain that, from the outset, the fascination of the camera image lessened the interest accorded to the text, to word descriptions in particular. The image now was accepted as conclusive proof, and the text suspected of inaccuracy. Such is the case, for example, in one of the earliest books illustrated with photographs, Auguste Salzmann's *Jérusalem* (1856), where the author takes his own photographs to witness against the views of previous archaeologists, because "photographs are not stories but hard and conclusive facts." The picture, being unchallengeable, thus overrode the text and made description superfluous: "It is easier to refer the reader to the photograph of this bas-relief than to write a description of it... To describe it is impossible, and so I am compelled to refer to

2

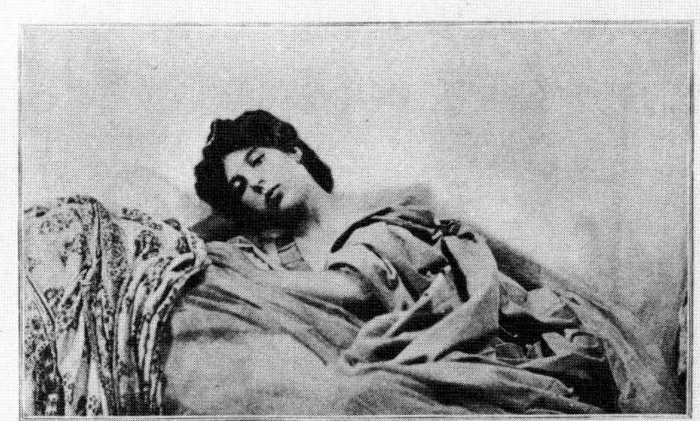

R. DEMACHY. — RÊVERIE.

AVANT-PROPOS

R. LEBÈGUE. — L'ADIEU.
Gravure de Bertin et Cie.

Quelque chose change ou va changer dans l'esthétique du noir et du blanc. Un mouvement nouveau entraîne les photographes hors et à rebours des voies où ils avaient accoutumé de cheminer jusqu'ici. Ce mouvement est international. Tant à Vienne qu'à Bruxelles et à Londres qu'à Paris, aussi bien sur les terrasses de Taormine en Sicile qu'en Nouvelle-Zélande sur la côte d'or de Coromandel, partout où il y a des photographes, ils semblent agités d'inquiétudes que leurs devanciers n'avaient pas connues. Ils flânent plus volontiers en plein air, par les bois, les plaines et les grèves, même dans les lieux sans monuments et à des heures sans soleil. Que cherchent-ils? Si un vieux professionnel de la chambre noire les suit et les observe, il s'étonne et se scandalise. Il les voit s'arrêter devant un espace vide de « site », un néant. Là, il aperçoit avec horreur que ces jeunes confrères se placent à contre-jour, en face du soleil. Il ne mettent

my photographs in order to give a correct idea of it" (Salzmann). The text therefore assumed another role, that of a commentary, relegated to an appendix, as the reader was informed in a publisher's note to one of the three volumes of Salzmann's book: "This volume contains the explanatory text to the photographic views, which are issued simultaneously in two editions of different format." So the text was turned into an accompaniment, added to the pictures and all too often scarcely needed, acting merely as a kind of meta-language or parallel discourse, as shown by Michel Wiedemann in his analysis of Fox Talbot's *Pencil of Nature*.

One final consequence may be noted. Set apart in a specific place of its own, the photograph occupied in the book a space radically cut off from the text: this was a trend diametrically opposed to that of book illustration in the Romantic period. But in this return to a "classical" page layout where picture and text faced each other, the balance of forces had shifted: the picture dwarfed the text. Not till the twentieth century will we find a more equal combination of the two, with a more flexible, more responsive technique in the placing of text illustrations. The first signs of it appear in the early attempts to illustrate popular novels with photographs—the ancestors of our photo-novels. These began appearing in the last years of the nineteenth century (the books of Georges Montorgueil in 1897 or Hugues Rebell's *La Brocanteuse d'Amours* in 1901). A further sign of it comes in the massive use of photography in journalism. The photographic image had become an object of fascination with an undisputed authority of its own.

3

I have seen full many a sight
Born of day or drawn by night:
Sunlight on a silver stream,
Golden lilies all a-dream,
Lofty mountains, bold and proud,
Veiled beneath the lacelike cloud;
But no lovely sight I know
Equals Dinah kneading dough.

15

1

The First Book illustrated with Photographs: "The Pencil of Nature"

This first book to be photographically illustrated was the work of William Henry Fox Talbot, who developed the negative-positive process and vied with Daguerre. At first, however, the necessity of using a negative to obtain paper prints was felt as a useless complication; it also presented technical difficulties, seeming unreliable and offering no guarantee of permanence. To substantiate his claims, Talbot published *The Pencil of Nature,* a sampling of his photographs mounted on folio pages with a descriptive text by himself. Most of them represent still lifes and places, like Paris, Oxford and Lacock Abbey, his own home. Containing twenty-four photographs (instead of the fifty originally planned), the book was published in six parts over two years (1844-1846). Realizing the commercial and industrial potential of Talbot's serial production of paper prints and foreseeing their use in books, the French chemist Blanquart-Evrard of Lille perfected it and set up a printing works where thousands of photographic prints were daily exposed to sunlight and mounted in books by women workers. In 1851 he published his first *Album photographique à l'usage de l'artiste et de l'amateur,* which he followed up with a further twenty titles. But his process was only a provisional stage in the development of photography, and the subsequent success of photogravure put him out of business. ■

2

3

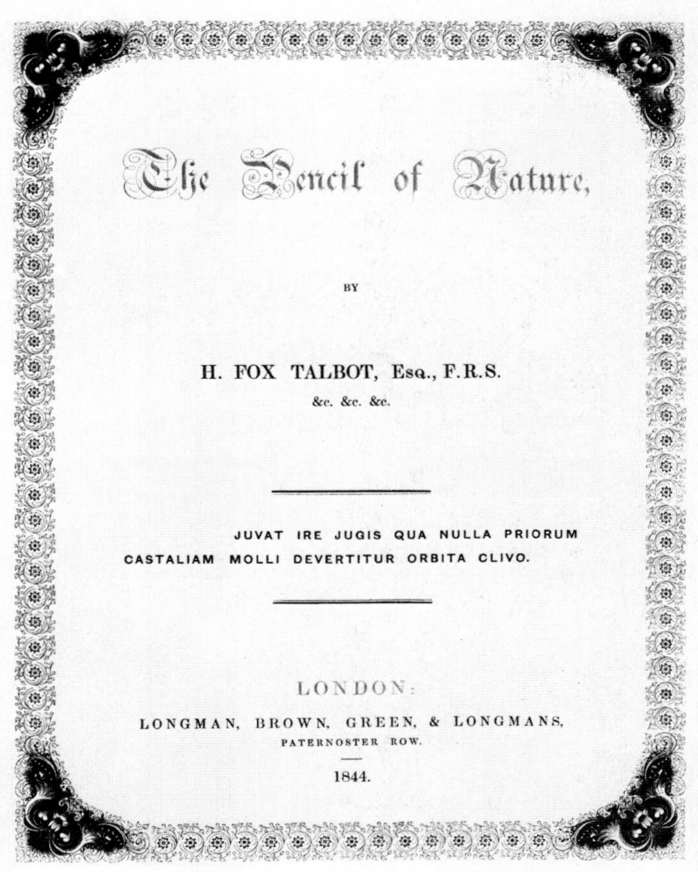

The Pencil of Nature,

BY

H. FOX TALBOT, Esq., F.R.S.

&c. &c. &c.

JUVAT IRE JUGIS QUA NULLA PRIORUM
CASTALIAM MOLLI DEVERTITUR ORBITA CLIVO.

LONDON:

LONGMAN, BROWN, GREEN, & LONGMANS,
PATERNOSTER ROW.

1844.

Calotypes from The Pencil of Nature, *1844:*

1. *View of the Boulevard at Paris, plate II.*
2. *The Open Door, plate VI.*
3. *Title page.*
4. *A Scene in the Library, plate VIII.*

4

The "Excursions Daguerriennes" and the First Printed Photographs

1

2

3

Published in Paris in 1842, the *Excursions Daguerriennes* contained a series of views which photographers had been commissioned to take in Europe, Africa and the United States. Actually they were aquatints on steel made from photographs collected and printed in the gallery of the publisher, N.P.M. Lerebours: "Once the drypoint tracing of the photograph is transferred onto the steel plate, the artist's special share in the work is to complete, with the addition of colour, the expression of the sites, monuments and objects represented." The first volume contained 60 plates. Among the 52 plates in the second volume (January 1843) was an initial daguerreotype transformed into an engraved plate "by purely chemical means and without any retouching by the artist," thanks to the Fizeau process. To obtain this first printed photogravure (representing a bas-relief in Notre-Dame of Paris), Fizeau had engraved the silver plate coated with an acid which did not bite into the whites (protected by mercury). Unable to cut the plate deeply enough to permit intaglio inking, he greased the sunk areas to protect them and, by electrotyping, heightened the relief areas with gold, left unbitten by the acid, which was then used again to deepen the hollows. This process yielded a faithful reproduction, but required a delicacy of handling which precluded any immediate development of it. Despite some successful innovations (Charles Nègre's heliogravures in 1854 and Poitevin's photolithographs in 1856), it was another thirty years before photography entered into the making of printed books. ■

4

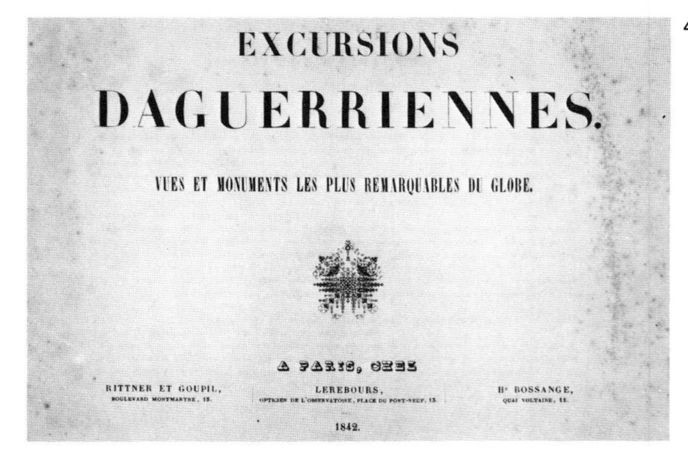

EXCURSIONS

DAGUERRIENNES.

VUES ET MONUMENTS LES PLUS REMARQUABLES DU GLOBE.

A PARIS, CHEZ

RITTNER ET GOUPIL, | LEREBOURS, | Hr BOSSANGE,

1842.

5

From the Excursions Daguerriennes, *"The most Remarkable Views and Monuments of the Globe," Paris, 1842:*

1. *Binding.*
2. *View at Bas-Meudon near Paris, aquatint by C. F. Daubigny from a daguerreotype.*
3. *Niagara Falls, aquatint from a daguerreotype.*
4. *Title page.*
5. *The Town Hall in Paris, one of the first two photo-engravings by the Fizeau process, from a daguerreotype.*

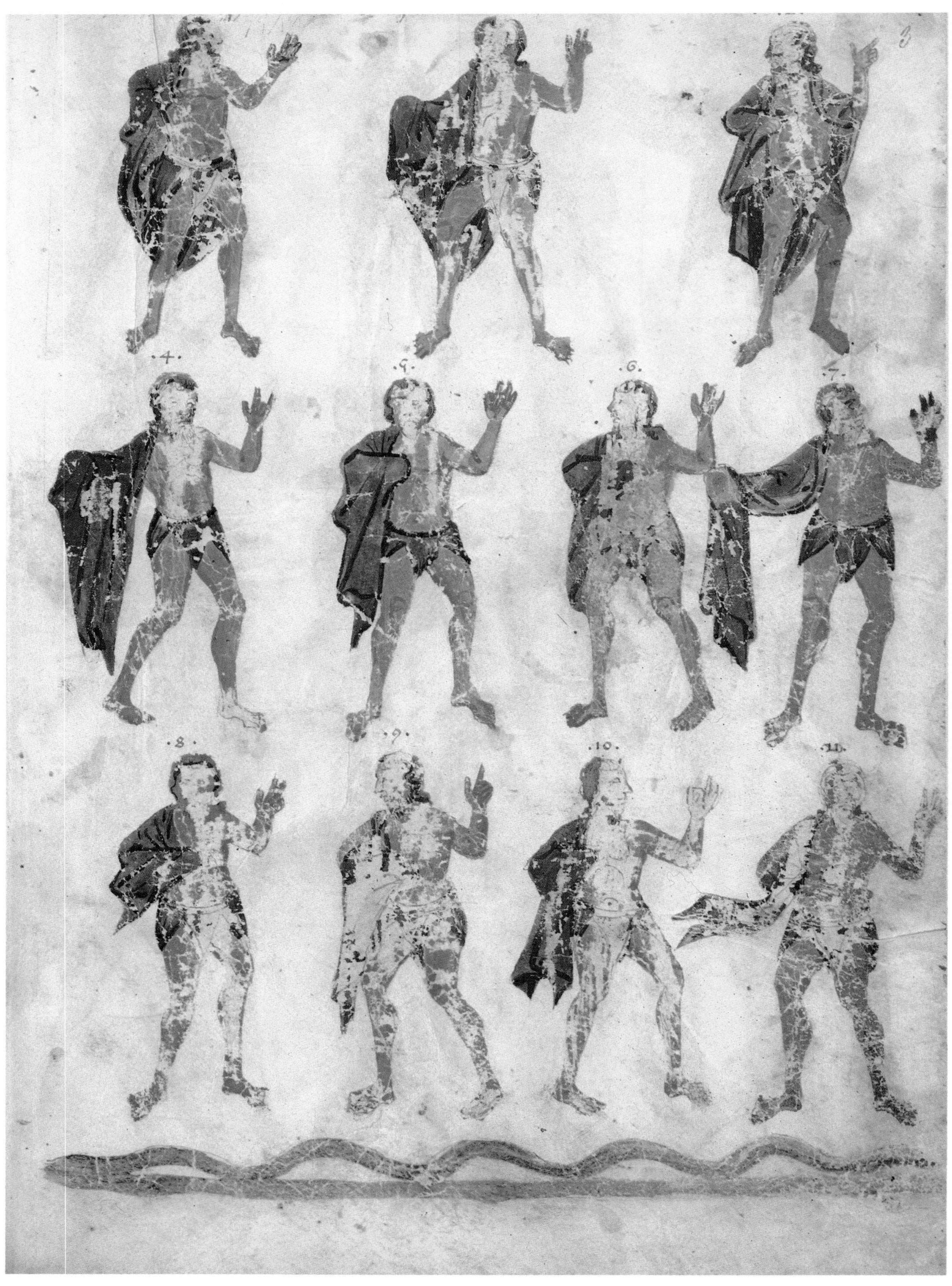

ILLUSTRATING DAILY LIFE

▲ Table of Bleeding, early 15th century. Painting on vellum.

◀ Coloured drawing of the 14th century, showing how to count on one's fingers. Illumination on vellum from the Venerable Bede's *De temporum ratione.*

While scholars and men of letters were apt to be suspicious or scornful of illustration, they admitted its usefulness for the working classes; they recognized it, even in the seventeenth century, as a medium of communication well suited to empirical knowledge (calendars and almanacs) and to manual work. It is clear that, for the working classes, this conception of "practical" illustration contained the seeds of progress and also seeds of danger. Progress, because pictures did offer the readiest access to necessary knowledge, the one way around the handicap of illiteracy; danger, because in the hands of the educated, of those with the techniques and knowledge needed to use them, pictures were a formidable instrument for the bracketing and conditioning of the masses. This danger is still with us today. It lay then, it lies now, in the profitable ambiguity of these pictures which are manipulated, and manipulate us, in cheap handbooks, in encyclopaedias and guidebooks, in magazines and games, in posters and cards of all kinds, in covers and packaging and advertising, and finally in television. In earlier centuries the bulk of a man's working knowledge was acquired through illustrated primers, calendars and flysheets, through divinatory signs, through diagrams and sketches. Histories of illustration are apt to pay little attention to these ephemera, which at one time nevertheless accounted for the bulk of it and which, from the fifteenth century, when books began reaching the middle classes, went to determine in part their design and content and distinctive refinements.

The enumeration of these ephemera could begin with illustrated schoolbooks, but these are of recent origin. What we find even before the invention of printing are, for example, medical textbooks (*Table of Bleeding,* early fifteenth century), taken over from the Arabs; also an illustrated manuscript vaunting the healing powers of the *Baths of Pozzuoli* (late fourteenth century). The first cookery books, dating from the early fourteenth century, are anterior to the famous recipe book known as the *Viandier Taillevent,* drawn up by Guillaume Tirel or Taillevent, and they are not illustrated. But several of the fourteen extant manuscripts of *Le Rustican,* the most popular gardening manual under King Charles V of France, are illustrated. So are the two incunabula of the *Liber ruralium commodorum* of the Italian Pietro de Crescenzi. Through pictures, too, children (and grown-ups) were taught to count on their fingers in the curious Italian manuscript of

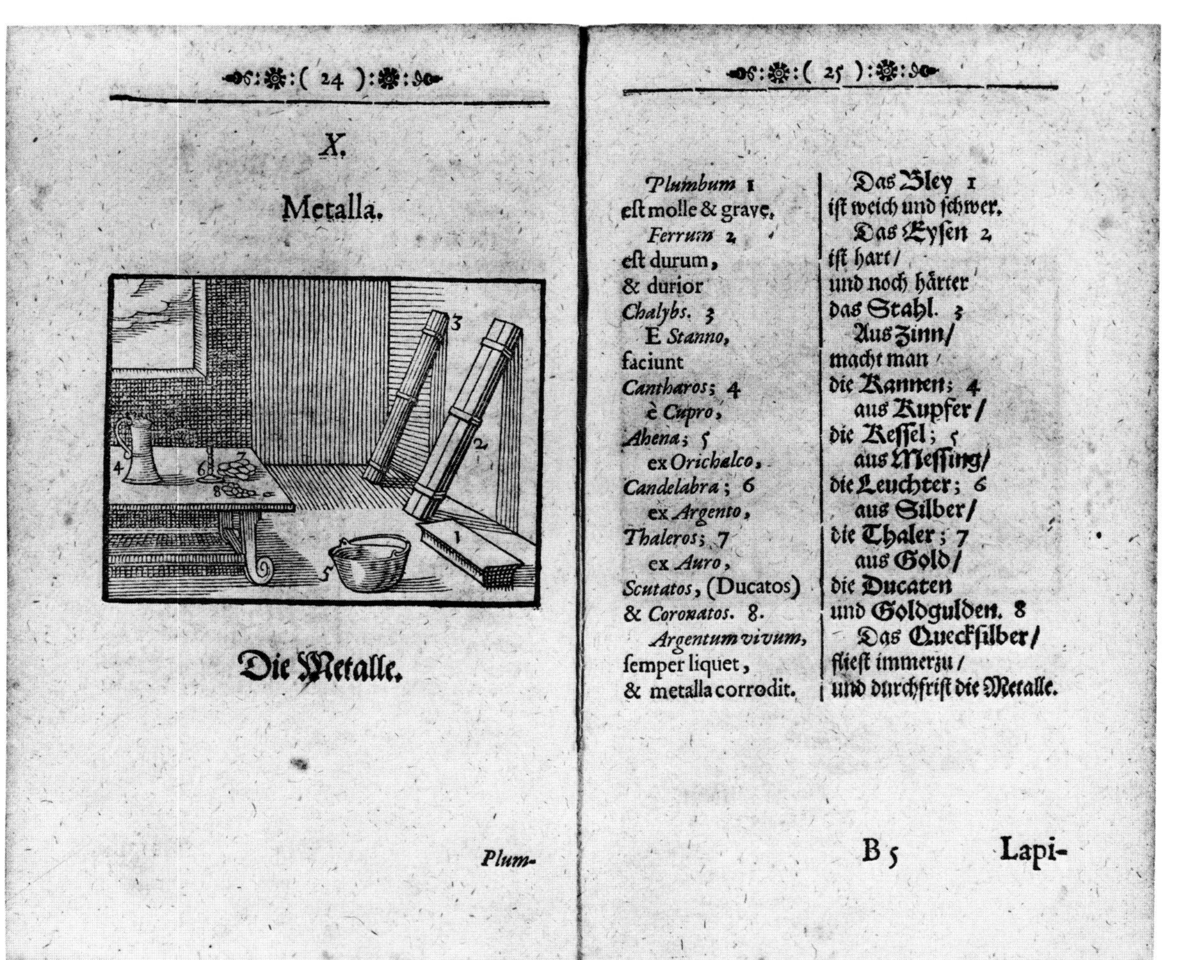

(24)

X.

Metalla.

Die Metalle.

Plum-

(25)

Plumbum 1	Das Bley 1
est molle & grave,	ist weich und schwer.
Ferrum 2	Das Eysen 2
est durum,	ist hart /
& durior	und noch härter
Chalybs. 3	das Stahl. 3
E *Stanno,*	Aus Zinn /
faciunt	macht man
Cantharos; 4	die Kannen; 4
è *Cupro,*	aus Kupfer /
Ahena; 5	die Kessel; 5
ex *Orichalco,*	aus Messing /
Candelabra; 6	die Leuchter; 6
ex *Argento,*	aus Silber /
Thaleros; 7	die Thaler; 7
ex *Auro,*	aus Gold /
Scutatos, (Ducatos)	die Ducaten
& *Coronatos.* 8.	und Goldgulden. 8
Argentum vivum,	Das Quecksilber /
semper liquet,	fliest immerzu /
& metalla corrodit.	und durchfrist die Metalle.

B 5 Lapi-

Three pages from Comenius, *Orbis sensualium pictus,* Nuremberg, 1658.

the early fourteenth century illustrating the first chapter of the *De temporum ratione*, written by the Venerable Bede in the eighth century. As time passed, such popularization of practical knowledge came, by its very nature, more and more into line with the empirical knowledge of modern scientists. So it is that the rise of this popular illustration is directly linked with that of the human sciences. Not far removed from them is the growing number of travel books, followed in our day by tourist guidebooks, where illustration goes to counterpoint the text and owes its relevance to the development of sciences like geography, ethnology and archaeology. It would be interesting to follow the rise and spread of the first pictorial surveys on sociological or ethnological themes, such as the sets of costume prints issued during the French Revolution by Grasset de Saint-Sauveur or the first guidebooks for travellers in Europe, a genre inaugurated by Heinrich Reichard at Weimar in 1793 (before the great series launched by Baedeker in Germany and Joanne in France). Thereafter, illustrations became more detailed and more numerous both in scientific works and in the popular guidebooks, thanks to the development of railways after 1830 (the Joanne Guidebooks were taken over by Hachette in 1856 and went to form part of their "French Railway Library"); and thanks, later on, to the automobile (the first Michelin Guide appeared in 1900 and still carries on today the tradition of line drawings which illustrated the first "picturesque itineraries"). For in the field of what is illustratable, popularization follows and accompanies discovery. Scientific pictures of a biological or astronomical discovery can be published immediately in a widely read magazine. Here there is no need for two levels of comprehension, as there so often is in the written commentary. It is not a "lower" level of knowledge that the picture offers, but simply a

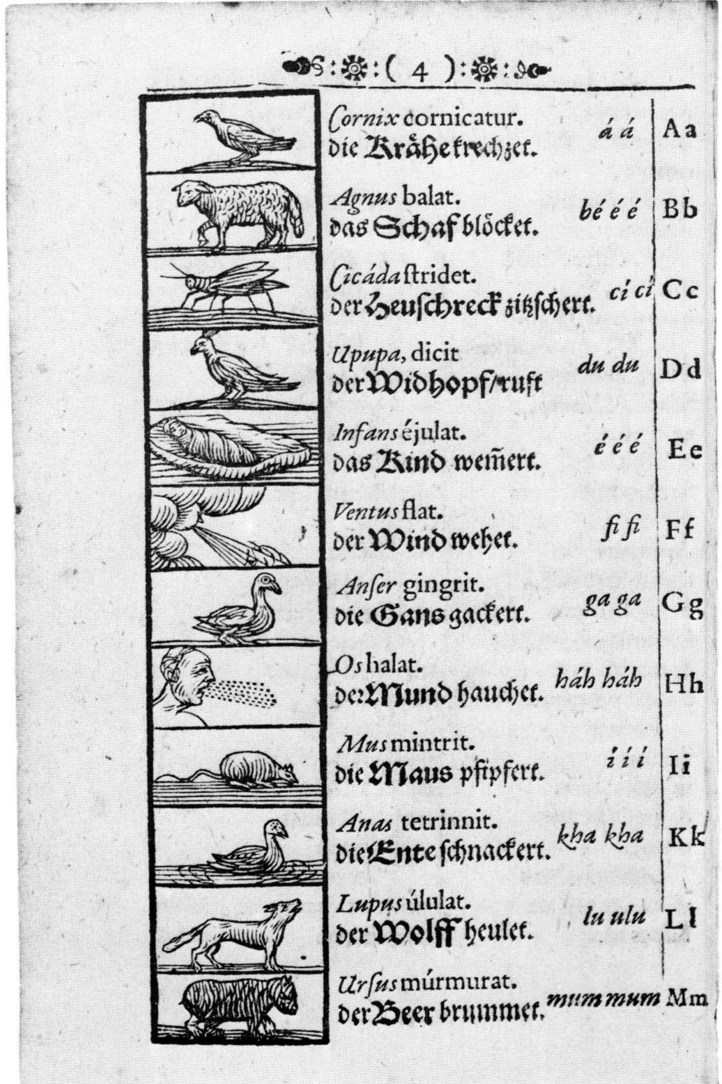

(4)

Cornix cornicatur. die Krähe krechzet.	*á á*	Aa
Agnus balat. das Schaf blöcket.	*bé é é*	Bb
Cicáda stridet. der Heuschreck zitzschert.	*ci ci*	Cc
Upupa, dicit der Widhopf/ruft	*du du*	Dd
Infans éjulat. das Kind weinert.	*é é é*	Ee
Ventus flat. der Wind wehet.	*fi fi*	Ff
Anser gingrit. die Gans gackert.	*ga ga*	Gg
Os halat. der Mund hauchet.	*háh háh*	Hh
Mus mintrit. die Maus pfipfert.	*i i i*	Ii
Anas tetrinnit. die Ente schnackert.	*kha kha*	Kk
Lupus úlulat. der Wolff heulet.	*lu ulu*	Ll
Ursus múrmurat. der Beer brummet.	*mum mum*	Mm

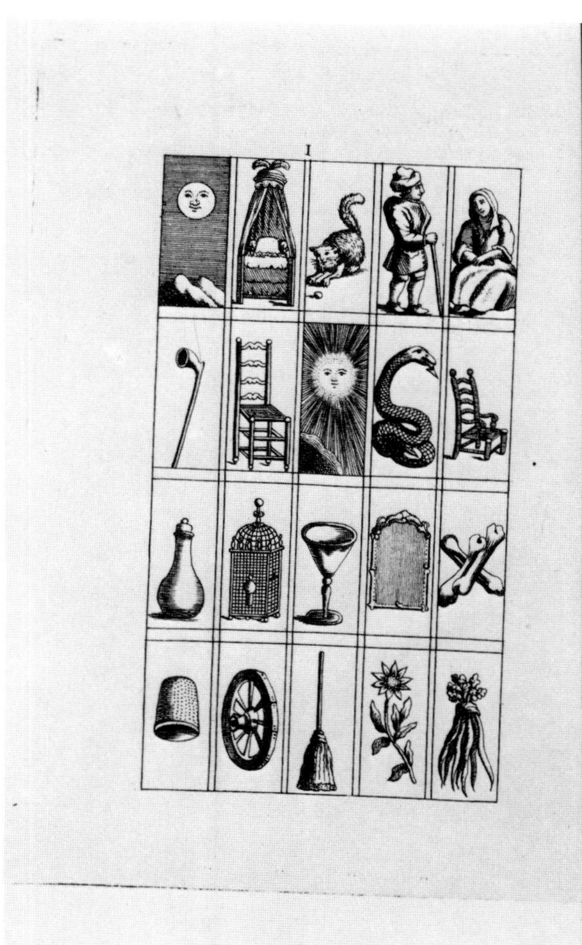

Sons finals qui répondent aux figures de la Iere Planche. 17

PREMIERE LEÇON.

Voyez les n°. 1, 2 & 3 de l'Inſtruction.

EXPLICATION DES FIGURES

DE LA PREMIERE PLANCHE.

la lune.... une	une pipe....ip	une carafe...af	un dez.....é
un lit..... i	une chaiſe..aiſe	une cage...age	une roue.....e
un chat.... a	le Soleil....eil	un verre.....er	un balai.....ai
un bouſſu..u	un ſerpent..en	une glace...ace	une fleur...eur
une femm. emme	un fauteuil. euil	des os......o	des raves... av

Sons finals qui répondent aux figures de la Iere Planche.

une	i	a	u	emme
ip	aiſe	eil	en	euil
af	age	er	ace	o
é	e	ai	eur	av

Premiere répétition des ſons précédents.

i	u	ip	eil	euil
age	ace	é	ai	av
une	a	emme	aiſe	en
af	er	o	e	eur

Two pages from Abbé Berthaud, *Le Quadrille des enfans*, "wherein, by means of 84 pictures, and without spelling, children can be taught to read at the age of four or five, and below," fifth edition, Paris, 1783.

different one, accessible to all. The culture of illustration is by no means a culture of illiterates. First, because it appears in books, always accompanying a text; second, because figure and caption go together inseparably, being arranged in connected pictures (zodiac, labours of the months) and developing in the same proportion as the text. But it is a culture which, unlike the culture remodelled by writing, can claim to make a direct appeal to experience and squares with it. This is the kind of knowledge that the school authorities stand out against, being suspicious of pictures, even today, and putting emphasis always on the learning of figures and letters. Anatole France remembered the barbarous way his schoolmaster tore out the illustrated frontispiece of his Greek textbook, considered a frivolous embellishment, before handing the book over to the pupil. This way of "teaching in the dark" (Anatole France) became less and less acceptable as education spread, and was even unacceptable to the Jesuits in the seventeenth century, as shown by the attractiveness of their *Janua linguarum* published at Salamanca in 1611, a pictorial textbook which inspired Comenius. The most important book in the whole history of illustration may well be the latter's *Orbis sensualium pictus* of 1658, in which the Czech pedagogue used pictures as the primary stepping-stone to knowledge. Language was by-passed. Comenius' idea was that "things should be put with words and words with things." As against the dogmatic and scholastic teaching then all too common and uninspiring, he worked out direct, attractive, empirical methods. Then, in 1658, he took the decisive step, and in the *Orbis sensualium pictus*, which has been described as the first children's picture-book, he relied on pictures, teaching directly and simultaneously object lessons and grammar. The appeal to visual experience thus entered

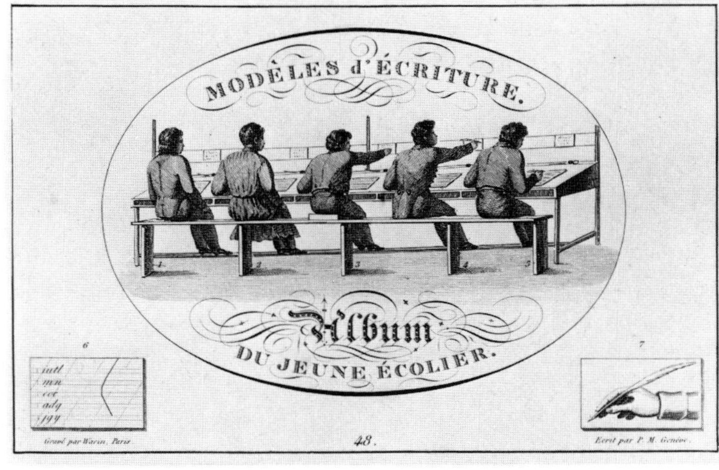

"Models of Penmanship. Album of the Young Schoolboy," Paris, n.d., with two examples of writing: "work" and "pleasure."

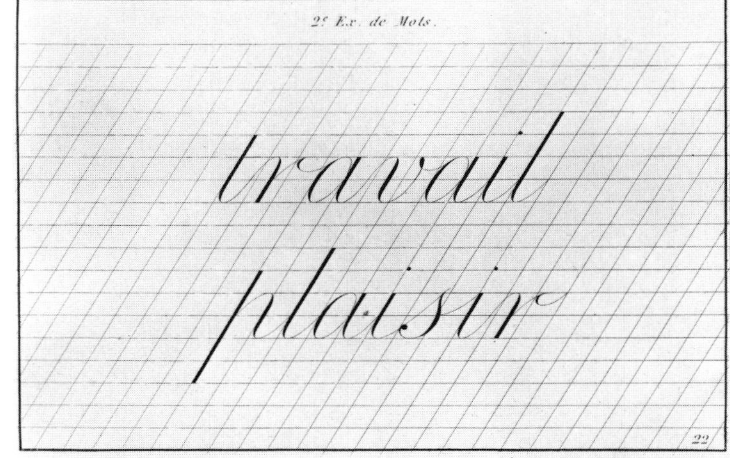

EFFROYABLE CATACLYSME
DE LA MARTINIQUE
UNE VILLE TOUT ENTIÈRE DÉTRUITE
Dernières dépêches. — Les éruptions continuent dans toutes les Antilles. — Un deuil national. — Les secours. — Récits des survivants. — Les navires perdus. — L'Emotion en Europe. — Historique de la Martinique. — Explications scientifiques du cataclysme.
FORT-DE-FRANCE MENACÉ

"Dreadful cataclysm at Martinique, an entire town destroyed," broadsheet published in Paris, May, 1902.

HORRIBLE CATASTROPHE

Qui a répandu l'alarme dans le village de Mont-Souris, près la barrière Saint-Jacques, par un cheval enragé qui s'est jeté subitement sur son maître, l'a terrassé, et traîné dans la plaine en le tenant suspendu par le bras droit, que ce terrible animal tenait entre ses mâchoires et qu'il lui a cassé à deux endroits.

Lundi vers 7 heures du matin, le nommé HEBERT, âgé de 30 ans, homme d'une taille gigantesque et doué d'une force peu commune, cultivateur et propriétaire de la ferme de Mont-Souris, près la barrière St. Jacques, a été victime d'une affreuse mutilation qui a répandu la consternation parmi les habitans de la commune de Mont-Souris, dont il est généralement estimé.

Il était sorti le matin et avait emmené un de ses plus forts chevaux, pour labourer un champ lui appartenant et situé non loin de sa demeure, près d'un Moulin, dit le Moulin-Noir.

Il s'arrêta un instant chez un de ses voisins qui l'appela en passant, et laissa son cheval à la porte sans même l'attacher, comme font d'ordinaire les habitans des campagnes; aucune démonstration jusqu'alors, n'avait fait soupçonner la férocité dont cet animal n'avait donné aucune marque, puisqu'il y avait dix ans qu'il faisait le service de la ferme.

Après avoir échangé quelques paroles avec son voisin le fermier, accompagné de son cheval, se dirige vers son ouvrage, étant arrivé il s'apprêtait à ateler l'animal à la charrue, lorsqu'une rage s'empare du cheval, qui se câbre et s'abattant sur son maitre, lui porte un coup de pied de devant qui lui à abimé l'œil droit et lui a fait à la figure une large cicatrice, il terrasse son maitre et le saisissant des dents par le bras droit, il le secoue horriblement : les cris du malheureux fermier se font entendre, des personnes qui étaient heureusement dans le Moulin accourent à son secours, mais le féroce animal, les voyant accourir et craignant de se voir ravir sa proie, s'enfuit au grand galop à travers les terres, entraînant avec lui sa victime toujours suspendue par le bras à ses mâchoires.

Enfin épuisé et cerné de toutes parts par les habitans accourus sur le lieu de cette terrible scène, on cherche à se saisir du cheval; un des plus hardis veut l'arrêter en le prenant par la bride, mais le féroce animal lui lance un coup de pied qui lui enlève le gras de l'épaule, et qui heureusement n'a pas fracturé l'os, on parvient cependant à s'en rendre maitre et on lui arrache le malheureux HEBERT, dans un effroyable état de mutilation; transporté chez lui, trois médecins arrivèrent spontanément, et rivalisèrent de zèle pour lui prodiguer les premiers soins : on espère cependant sauver les jours de cet infortuné jeune homme, qui aurait inévitablement été tué sur la place par son terrible adversaire, sans les prompts secours de ses voisins. Il y avait long-tems qu'un pareil accès de rage n'avait atteint les animaux.

IMPRIMERIE D'HIPPOLYTE TILLIARD,
Rue Saint-Hyacinthe, n° 30.

A Paris, chez GARSON, éditeur, rue des Boucheries-Saint-Germain, n° 57.

"Horrible catastrophe... in the village of Mont-Souris... a wild horse attacked its master," broadsheet, Paris, c. 1834.

European education and became a major concern of modern pedagogues. Echoing Comenius, and before Jean-Jacques Rousseau, John Locke wrote in *Some Thoughts Concerning Education* (1693): "If his [i.e. the child's] Aesop has Pictures in it, it will entertain him much the better, and encourage him to read, when it carries the increase of Knowledge with it. For such visible Objects Children hear talked of in vain, and without any satisfaction, whilst they have no Idea's of them; those Idea's being not to be had from Sounds; but from the Things themselves, or their Pictures. And therefore I think, as soon as he begins to spell, as many Pictures of Animals should be got him, as can be found, with the printed names to them, which at the same time will invite him to read, and afford him Matter of Enquiry and knowledge" (section 156). Then, after Rousseau, came Pestalozzi, the Swiss educational reformer. With him, observation and the apprenticeship of pictures preceded the apprenticeship of writing: "It became clear to me that it is unreasonable to put a child to spelling before having given him a considerable sum of knowledge about the real world and speech... So art had to be resorted to, and I was inevitably led to feel the need of picture books, even before primers. Such books, thanks to well-chosen and attractive drawings, would elucidate in advance the ideas which would have to be communicated to the child by means of language" (*How Gertrude teaches her Children*, 1801). J.F. Oberlin, in the schools which he founded in Alsace, made systematic use of pictures for the teaching of geography and botany. Primers and spelling books came to depend heavily on pictures and illustrated anecdotes; and the toybook, introduced in England about 1850, went beyond them, being simply an album of pictures without text for the stimulus of infants. Today the audiovisual media have revived the controversy over teaching through pictures, and yet, for all the use made of illustration in schoolbooks, there exists no critical apparatus of the image comparable to the highly ramified methodology of language worked out over the centuries. Thus the daily manipulation of images goes forward without any control over its users. Indeed, "popular" illustration seems to have resisted the assaults of the "well educated" by the very fact of its being so effective as propaganda and mystification. Witness the topical imagery already widespread a century ago and more successful than ever today in the sensational press, its twofold staple being violence on the one hand and triviality on the other. Witness the devotional imagery designed to diffuse doctrines whose true import wholly escapes the public it is aimed at. Witness the so-called popular imagery which triumphed when, in 1866, Victor Duruy commissioned pictures for schoolroom use from the Epinal printer Pellerin; or when Gallieni in 1895 commissioned pictures with captions in Malagasy to help on the colonization of Madagascar. Such pictures have no more to do with the art of Madagascar than the *images d'Epinal* have to do with folk art.

There were however types of illustration that did reflect the common people's view of life: votive pictures and illustrated cards for anniversaries, betrothals, christenings, etc. Here unfortunately the picture, even more than the text, called for a technicalness of execution fatally overcentralized by industrialization. Take the example of the postcard, the very type of personalized illustration. In France the first picture postcard to be deposited in the Bibliothèque Nationale (and this may be taken as proving that it was actually published) dates from 1882 and represents Le Havre as seen from Sainte-Adresse, the Mecca of the Parisian tourist of that day. There followed a highly diversified output of such cards by local photographers everywhere, picturing every place and street of any interest. The explosive demand for them meant ever larger print-runs and wider networks of distribution, so that the picture illustrating the text on the other side became vulgarized and impoverished—until new techniques and a broader appeal permitted a redeployment of postcard publishing and a more distinctive style of picture corresponding to the text. If every sender of a picture postcard, besides being a writer, had also been an illustrator, then perhaps one could have spoken of popular illustration. But the ordinary run of illustration continues to swamp us and condition us with readymade pictures without our ever calling to account their makers or their content. And so we are carried away by this "logic of the image" (Marshall McLuhan), which in itself has nothing negative about it and only arouses our anxiety in so far as, in this field, we all of us voluntarily remain illiterate.

"Tragedy in a butcher's shop," coloured wood engraving on the cover of the illustrated supplement of *Le Petit Journal*, Paris, 2 July 1892.

"History of France," coloured lithograph imagery in the style of the *images d'Epinal*, printed at Pont-à-Mousson, c. 1900.

An Early Illustrated Schoolbook

6

LE RECTEUR.

Mon fils, juſqu'au Cercueil, faut aprendre,
Et tenir pour perdu le jour qui s'eſt paſſé,
Si tu n'y a de quelque choſe profité,
Pour plus ſage & ſçavant te rendre.

Commence à faire attention ſur ce qui eſt ici Repreſenté par les NOMS & FIGURES de Fleurs, d'un Chien, de la Femme, d'un Homme, d'une Maiſon, d'un Chapeau, du Pain & d'un Coûteau : & continuë d'obſerver, peu à peu, ce qui ſuit.

7

Dulcia non meruit, qui non guſtavit amara.
Pour le bon tems trouver, faut la Mer paſſer.

PAYS DE COCAGNE

Déſiré par les Pareſſeux & Fainéants.

Ce Païs ainſi repreſenté, avec ſes Aloüettes Roties, Montagnes de Beurre, Ruiſſeaux & Riviéres de Miel, Vin, Lait, &c. ne ſe découvre qu'aux Gens d'eſprit, leſquels par leurs ſciences, ſont bien élevés, venu & reçûs par tout.

Pages from Roti-Cochon, *Dijon, late 17th century.*

8 *Parva leves animos capiunt.*
L'Enfant eſt apaiſé de peu de choſes.

Les Pommes ſont bonnes à l'Eau Roſe & force Sucre.

Poſt Pira ſuma potunt.
Aprés la Poire faut boire.

LesPoiresdefil d'or ou de bon chrétien ſont meilleures que les Pommes Turc.

Uva

Uva ſemper fuit ſacrata Deo. 9
Le Raiſin a toûjours été conſacré à Dieu.

RAISINS blancs & noir, ſert à faire le bon Vin, qui eſt néceſſaire ſur les Autels; il réjouït le cœur de l'Homme, ſert de Lait aux Viellards, de Nectar aux Repas & fait le bon Sang, lorſqu'il eſt pris à propos: mais il gâte tout quand on en prend trop.

Conſervat induſtria fruges.
Les fruits ſe gardent par artifices.

Les PRUNES de Damas ſont bonnes à manger pour ceux qui les aiment.

B

A curious booklet of 36 pages, entitled *Roti-Cochon* ("Roast Pig"), was published at Dijon in the late seventeenth century, with no indication of author or date. It might almost be taken for a parody of an emblem book, for on each page is a Latin tag, with a free (and sometimes quite wrong) translation into French, a rudimentary vignette (apparently an old woodcut taken from the printer's stock and re-used more or less at random) and finally a naive commentary usually evoking some appetizing dish or delicacy in the form of a truism. This presentation of the matter is typical of the emblem book, but here with none of the latter's refinement; on the contrary, the text is comic in its banality and the pictures are insignificant. It is not an emblem book, however, but an illustrated schoolbook, perhaps the first of its kind in France, its full title being: "Roast Pig, or very easy method of teaching children to read in Latin and in French, by written phrases morally explained through pictures of different things known to them; very useful, and even necessary, both for life and salvation and for the glory of God. At Dijon, from Claude Michard printer and bookseller at the sign of St John the Evangelist." The only thing definitely known about this Claude Michard is that he practised his trade from 1689 to 1704. Only one copy of this astonishing publication is extant (Bibliothèque de l'Arsenal, Paris). Looking at it, one is struck by the blithe incoherence of the type-faces employed, haphazardly, it would seem, but to charming effect; by the engaging uncouthness of the woodcuts, whose connection with the text, if any, is never very close; and by the vapidness of the "moral" maxims which were expected to initiate provincial youngsters into the art of reading. One of them says: "Rabbits, ducks and parts of mutton, well cooked, are good to eat, by anyone who can get them." Another: "Preserved cherries and plums taste better to those who like sweets than to those who don't." The foreword to the book solemnly lays down some guidelines for the schoolmaster, from which we learn that "it is often a waste of time trying to teach lazy and feckless boys." ■

14 *Pascit ægros & sanos.*
Il nourrrit les sains & les Malades.

CUISINE GARNIE.

BOUILLI
pour abattre la
grosse faim ;
avec le ROTI
pour les Festins.

Convivas familiares convoca. 15
Invite les plus familiers à Banqueter.

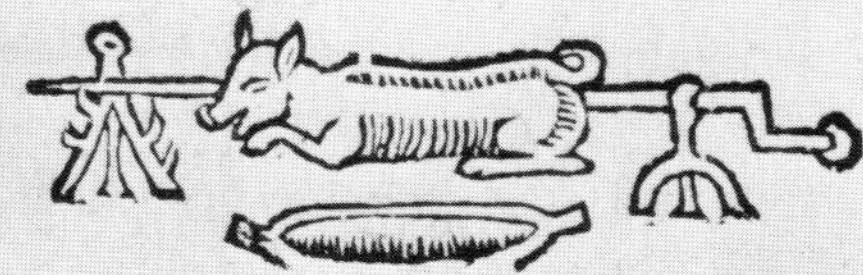

Du Cochon Roti,
vive la Peau,
étant chaud.

Principibus servire & Populo.
Il sert aux Princes & au Peuple.

LE JAMBON
de Pourceau
bien Mayencé, est bon à Manger,
non pas sans boire.

C ij

16

VILLE FORTIFIE'E.

Les Villes ont
leurs agrémens
d'Abondances &
de Peuples, que la
Campagne n'a pas.

Sic transit gloria mundi. 17
Ainsi passe la gloire du monde.

L'E'POUSE'E
est conduite par ses Parens en honneur & joye ; c'est pour Elle le plus beau jour de tous les autres.

Trois Menetriers
vont devant & autant derriére.

1

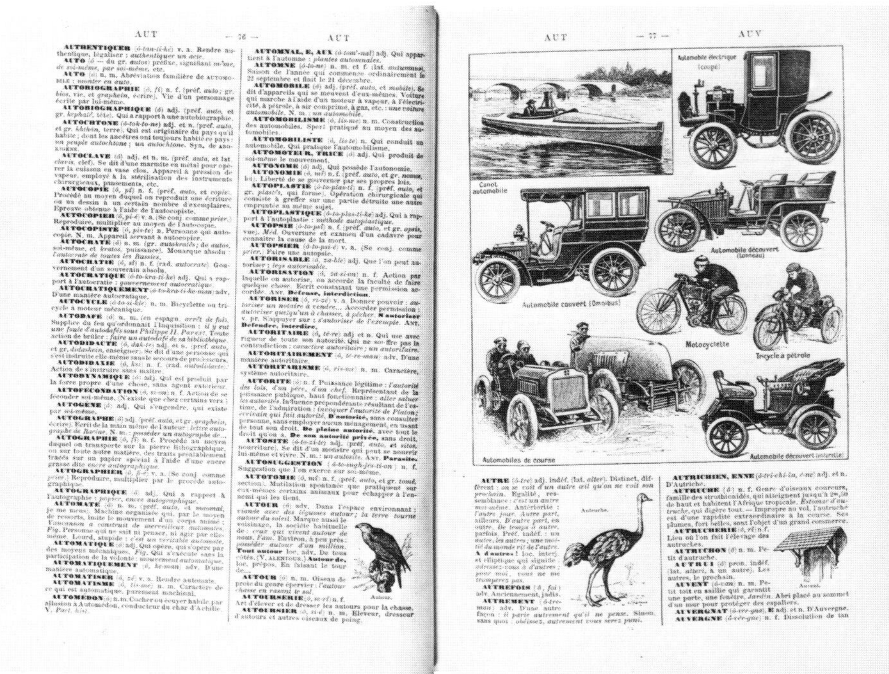

The Illustrated Larousse Dictionary

A copy of the illustrated *Petit Larousse* is to be found in most French homes. Pierre Larousse founded his publishing house in 1849 and issued in 1856 his *Dictionnaire de la langue française,* which was not illustrated. The success of his dictionaries followed the development of public education in France under the Third Republic (1871-1940), and pictures came to figure ever more prominently in these small family dictionaries, of encyclopaedic scope, designed to appeal to a wide public. The first illustrated edition came in 1879 with the *Dictionnaire complet de la langue française,* containing 1500 small woodcuts. The first edition of the *Petit Larousse illustré* dates from 1905 (published 1906) and contains 5800 line engravings, 130 pictures and 120 maps, the engravings being in black and white. Halftone engravings, permitting the reproduction of photographs, appeared in the 1935 edition, serving to reproduce works of art and portraits of contemporary celebrities. In 1959 offset printing brought about a more flexible layout, and plate pages were introduced combining drawings and photographs. Colour, hitherto reserved for full-page illustrations of flags and uniforms, invaded the whole dictionary in 1968. The latest edition of the *Petit Larousse* (1984) is still a bestseller in France: its daily presence in the home is taken for granted. Its illustrations are more abundant than ever, full-page plates more numerous, the vignettes larger. But the traditional line or wash drawing is still preferred to photographs for all the technical plates, including zoological and botanical illustrations, for it permits a clearer exposé of mechanical devices, a neater regrouping of different types within the same image, a pictorial synthesis closer to the written, abstract word, than photography does.
Nowhere better than in these illustrated dictionaries can one observe the contending interaction between the general and the particular that is so characteristic of the text/image pairing. ■

2

Pages on the Automobile from the Petit Larousse Illustré, *Paris:*

1. *Edition of 1906.*
2. *Edition of 1936.*
3. *Edition of 1959.*
4. *Edition of 1968.*

3

AUT

84

autobus

autocar

autochenille

automitrailleuse

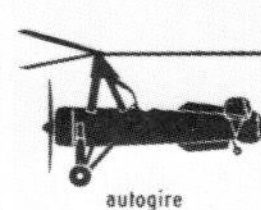

autogire

AUTO-ALARME n. m. *Mar.* Appareil récepteur de T. S. F. qui enregistre automatiquement les signaux de détresse.
AUTO-ALLUMAGE n. m. Allumage spontané du mélange détonant dans le cylindre d'un moteur à explosion, souvent provoqué par la calamine.
AUTO-AMORÇAGE n. m. Amorçage spontané d'une machine ou d'une réaction, qui s'opère sans recourir à l'action d'un agent extérieur.
AUTOBIOGRAPHIE n. f. Vie d'un personnage écrite par lui-même.
AUTOBIOGRAPHIQUE adj. Qui a rapport à la vie même d'un auteur.
AUTOBUS n. m. (de *auto,* abrév. de *automobile,* et *bus,* abrév. de *omnibus*). Grand véhicule automobile de transport en commun urbain.
AUTOCANON n. m. Canon antiaérien monté sur automobile (employé en 1914-1918).
AUTOCAR n. m. Grand véhicule automobile de transport collectif, routier ou touristique.
AUTOCHENILLE n. f. Automobile montée sur chenilles.
AUTOCHROME [*krom'*] adj. Se dit de certaines plaques photographiques enregistrant les couleurs.
AUTOCHTONE [*tok*] adj. et n. (préf. *auto,* et gr. *khthôn,* terre). Qui est originaire du pays qu'il habite et dont les ancêtres ont toujours habité le pays : *les Berbères sont les populations autochtones de l'Afrique du Nord.* ‖ — SYN. : *aborigène.*
AUTOCLAVE n. m. et adj. (préf. *auto,* et lat. *clavis,* clé). Récipient métallique à parois épaisses et à fermeture hermétique, pour opérer la cuisson ou la stérilisation par la vapeur sous pression. ‖ *Industr.* Appareil où se réalisent des réactions sous fortes pressions.
AUTOCOPIE n. f. Procédé de reproduction de l'écriture ou d'un dessin à un certain nombre d'exemplaires.
AUTOCRATE n. m. (gr. *autokratês,* qui gouverne lui-même). Monarque absolu. ‖ Titre officiel des anciens empereurs de Russie.
AUTOCRATIE n. f. Système politique dans lequel le souverain tire ses pouvoirs de lui-même et de lui seul; despotisme.
AUTOCRATIQUE adj. Qui a rapport à l'autocratie : *gouvernement autocratique.*
AUTOCRATIQUEMENT adv. De façon autocratique.
AUTOCRATOR n. m. (gr. *autokratôr,* qui a les pleins pouvoirs). A Byzance, titre de l'empereur.
AUTOCRITIQUE n. f. Jugement qu'une personne porte sur sa propre conduite, particulièrement dans le domaine politique.
AUTOCUISEUR n. m. Appareil pour cuire les aliments sous pression.
AUTODAFÉ n. m. (portug. *auto da fe,* acte de foi). Supplice du feu qu'ordonnait l'Inquisition. ‖ *Par ext.* Toute action qui a pour objet de détruire par le feu. ‖ Pl. des *autodafés.*
AUTODESTRUCTION n. f. Destruction par soi-même.
AUTODÉTERMINATION n. f. Action de décider par soi-même : *le droit d'autodétermination.*
AUTODIDACTE adj. et n. (préf. *auto,* et gr. *didaskein,* enseigner). Se dit d'une personne qui s'est instruite elle-même, sans professeur.
AUTODROME n. m. (*auto,* abrév. de *automobile,* et gr. *dromos,* course). Piste pour courses et essais d'automobiles.
AUTO-ÉCOLE n. f. Ecole où des moniteurs enseignent la conduite automobile à des candidats aux permis de conduire. ‖ Pl. des AUTO-ÉCOLES.
AUTOFÉCONDATION n. f. *Bot.* Union de deux éléments de sexe différent, portés par la même plante.
AUTOFINANCEMENT n. m. Financement d'une entreprise par l'affectation aux investissements d'une fraction des profits.
AUTOGAMIE n. f. (préf. *auto,* et gr. *gamos,* mariage). Fécondation directe des ovules d'une fleur par le pollen de la même fleur.
AUTOGÈNE adj. (préf. *auto,* et gr. *gennân,* engendrer). *Soudure autogène,* soudure de deux fragments d'un même métal par fusion partielle obtenue à l'aide d'un chalumeau.
AUTOGIRE n. m. (préf. *auto,* et gr. *guros,* cercle). Type d'avion dont les ailes ont été remplacées par une hélice horizontale tournant librement.
AUTOGRAPHE adj. et n. m. (préf. *auto,* et gr. *graphein,* écrire). Ecrit de la main même de l'auteur : *lettre autographe de Napoléon.*
AUTOGRAPHIE n. f. Reproduction, au moyen de l'impression, d'une écriture ou de dessins tracés avec une encre et sur un papier préparés à cet effet.
AUTOGRAPHIQUE adj. Qui a rapport à l'autographie.
AUTOGUIDAGE n. m. Procédé permettant à un mobile de diriger lui-même son mouvement vers le but qui lui a été assigné.
AUTOGUIDÉ, E adj. Se dit d'un mobile dirigé par autoguidage.
AUTO-IMPOSITION n. m. Assujettissement à l'impôt des services et établissements publics.
AUTO-INTOXICATION n. f. Ensemble des troubles produits par les déchets, non ou mal éliminés, de l'organisme : *l'urémie est le type des auto-intoxications.*
AUTOLYSE n. f. *Biol.* Destruction des tissus par les enzymes qu'ils contiennent en eux-mêmes : *la viande faisandée a subi un début d'autolyse.*
AUTOMATE n. m. (gr. *automatos,* qui se meut par lui-même). Machine imitant le mouvement d'un corps animé : *l'automate de Vaucanson.* ‖ *Philos.* Personne qui se meut de soi-même, spontanément. ‖ *Fig.* Personne qui ne pense ni n'agit par elle-même.
AUTOMATICITÉ n. f. Caractère de ce qui est automatique.
AUTOMATION ou **AUTOMATIQUE** n. f. Coordination automatique de tous les travaux d'usinage, de manutention des pièces d'un poste de travail à un autre et de leur présentation en position convenable devant les machines-outils, ces travaux étant eux-mêmes réalisés automatiquement.
AUTOMATIQUE adj. Qui s'exécute sans la participation de la volonté : *mouvement automatique.* ‖ *Philos.* Qui provient de l'être lui-même, et non d'une cause extérieure. ‖ Immédiat : *si l'on excite un nerf sensitif, la réponse motrice est automatique.* ‖ Qui opère par des moyens mécaniques : *téléphone automatique.* ‖ *Arme automatique,* arme à feu dans laquelle la pression due au gaz de combustion de la poudre effectue, à la place du tireur, la plupart des opérations nécessaires au fonctionnement.
AUTOMATIQUEMENT adv. D'une manière automatique.
AUTOMATISATION n. f. Action et effet d'automatiser.
AUTOMATISER v. t. Rendre automatique : *automatiser une usine.*
AUTOMATISME n. m. Caractère de ce qui est automatique, de ce qui échappe à la volonté.
AUTOMÉDON n. m. (gr. *Automedôn,* nom propre). Ecuyer ou cocher habile. (S'emploie par ironie.)
AUTOMITRAILLEUSE n. f. Automobile blindée, rapide et tout terrain, armée d'un canon et de mitrailleuses.
AUTOMNAL [*tom'-nal*], **E, AUX** adj. (lat. *autumnalis*). Qui appartient à l'automne : *plantes automnales.*
AUTOMNE [*ton'*] n. m. (lat. *autumnus*). Saison de l'année qui, dans notre hémisphère, s'étend du 22 ou du 23 septembre au 21 décembre. ‖ *Fig.* Déclin : *l'automne de la vie.*
AUTOMOBILE adj. Se dit d'appareils qui se meuvent par eux-mêmes. ‖ — N. f. Véhicule progressant de lui-même par l'effet d'un moteur à essence, à vapeur, électrique, à air comprimé, à gaz, etc. (V. CARROSSERIE et MOTEUR.)
AUTOMOBILISME n. m. Sport, tourisme pratiqué en automobile.
AUTOMOBILISTE n. Personne qui conduit une automobile.
AUTOMOTEUR, TRICE adj. Qui produit de lui-même son mouvement : *affût automoteur.* ‖ — N. f. Syn. d'AUTORAIL. ‖ — N. m. Grande péniche de transport fluvial, à moteur, et se déplaçant par ses propres moyens.
AUTONOME adj. Qui est régi par ses propres lois : *gouvernement autonome.* ‖ Libre, indépendant : *individu autonome.* ‖ *Gestion autonome,* système d'organisation interne des entreprises dans lequel chaque atelier est considéré comme autonome.

AUTOMOBILE

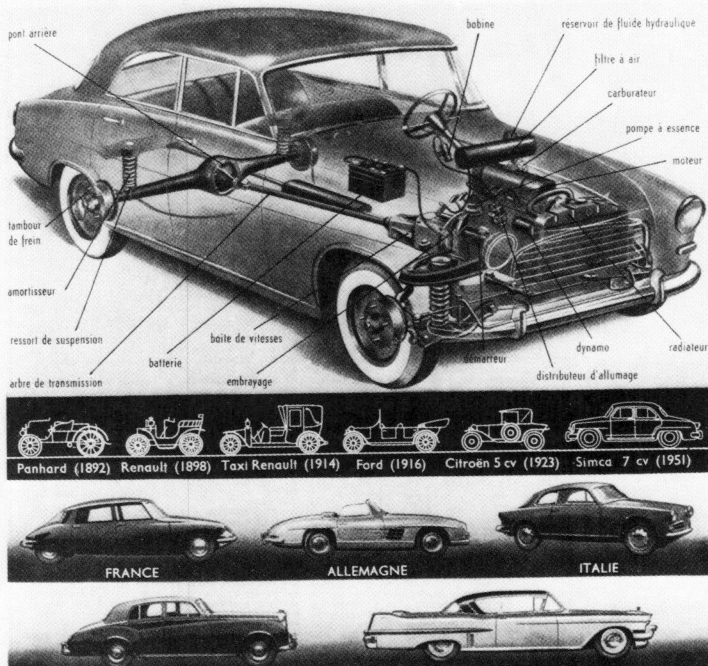

Panhard (1892) Renault (1898) Taxi Renault (1914) Ford (1916) Citroën 5 cv (1923) Simca 7 cv (1951)

FRANCE ALLEMAGNE ITALIE

GRANDE-BRETAGNE U. S. A.

AUTONOMIE n. f. (préf. *auto,* et gr. *nomos,* loi). Liberté de se gouverner par ses propres lois. ‖ Pour un véhicule à moteur (navire, avion, char, etc.), distance franchissable correspondant à la consommation totale du combustible embarqué. ‖ *Autonomie financière,* situation d'un service dont la gestion financière est indépendante de celle de la collectivité publique qui l'a créé et le contrôle. ‖ — CONTR. : *assujettissement, dépendance, subordination, tutelle, vassalité.*
AUTONOMISTE n. Partisan de l'autonomie.
AUTOPLASTIE n. f. (préf. *auto,* et gr. *plassein,* former). Opération chirurgicale qui consiste à greffer sur une région détruite des tissus de même nature, empruntés au sujet lui-même.
AUTOPOMPE n. f. Camion automobile équipé d'une pompe à incendie actionnée par le moteur.
AUTOPORTRAIT n. m. Portrait d'un artiste par lui-même.
AUTOPROPULSÉ, E adj. Qui assure sa propulsion par ses propres moyens : *projectile autopropulsé.*
AUTOPROPULSEUR adj. et n. m. Se dit d'un dispositif assurant l'autopropulsion.
AUTOPROPULSION n. f. Propriété de certains engins de se propulser par leurs propres moyens.
AUTOPSIE n. f. (gr. *autopsia,* action de voir de ses propres yeux). *Méd. légale.* Examen et dissection plus ou moins étendue d'un cadavre, en vue de déterminer les causes de la mort.
AUTOPSIER v. t. Faire l'autopsie.
AUTOPTIQUE adj. *Psychol.* Introspectif.
AUTOPUNITION n. f. (préf. *auto,* et *punition*). *Psychol.* Conduite née d'un sentiment de culpabilité et d'un désir de se punir soi-même.
AUTORADIOGRAPHIE n. f. Empreinte laissée sur une plaque ou sur du papier photographique par un objet contenant un produit radio-actif, dont les émissions ont impressionné la couche sensible.
AUTORAIL n. m. Voiture automotrice sur rails, pour le transport des voyageurs.
AUTORISATION n. f. Action par laquelle on accorde la faculté de faire quelque chose. ‖ Ecrit constatant une permission donnée : *nul ne peut construire sans l'autorisation des pouvoirs publics.*
AUTORISÉ, E adj. *Personne autorisée,* celle qui a l'autorité pour déclarer, exécuter une chose.

4

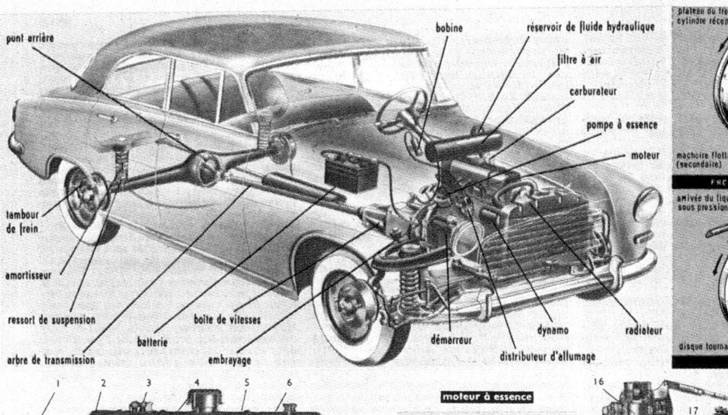

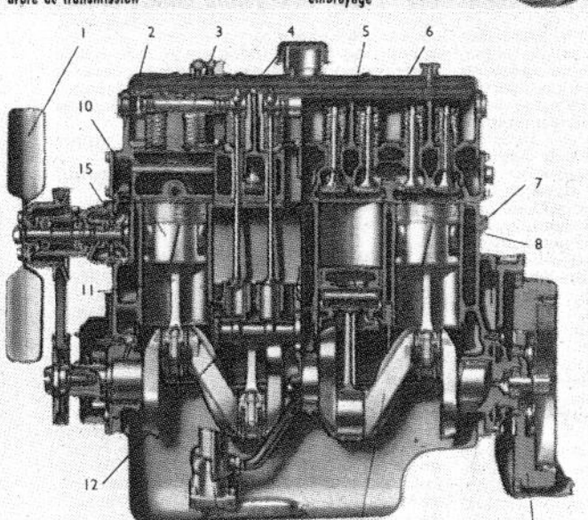

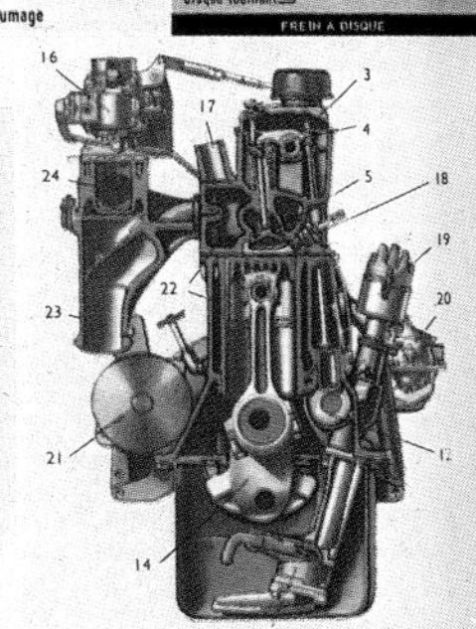

moteur à essence

Moteur à 4 cylindres pour voiture automobile : 1. Ventilateur ; 2. Culasse ; 3. Axe des culbuteurs ; 4. Culbuteurs ; 5. Soupape ; 6. Ressort de soupape ; 7. Carter-cylindres ; 8. Segments ; 9. Volant ; 10. Piston ; 11. Bielle ; 12. Arbre à cames ; 13. Pompe à huile ; 14. Vilebrequin ; 15. Pompe à eau ; 16. Carburateur ; 17. Pipe de sortie d'eau ; 18. Bougie ; 19. Distributeur d'allumage ; 20. Pompe à essence ; 21. Démarreur ; 22. Chambre d'eau ; 23. Collecteur d'échappement ; 24. Tubulure d'admission.

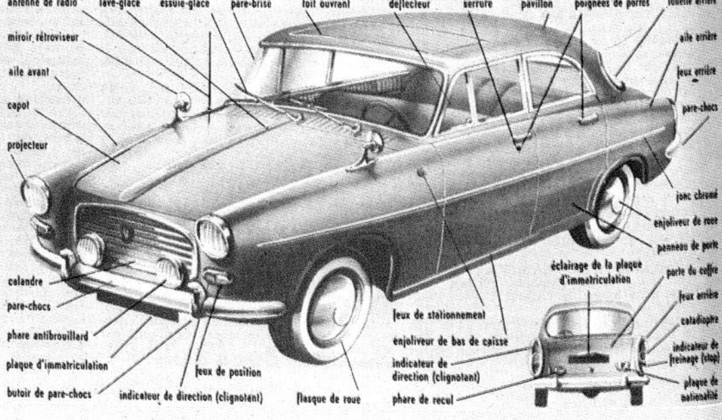

AVA

autorité [ɔ *ou* o-tɔrite] n. f. (lat. *auctoritas*). Puissance légitime, droit de commander : *l'autorité des lois, d'un père, d'un chef.* ‖ Administration, gouvernement : *décision de l'autorité compétente.* ‖ Ascendant, influence résultant de l'estime, d'une pression morale, etc. : *avoir de l'autorité sur quelqu'un.* ‖ Opinion sur laquelle on s'appuie : *l'autorité de Platon.* ● *Autorité de la chose jugée,* effet attribué par la loi aux décisions de justice, et qui interdit de remettre en discussion ce qui a fait l'objet d'un jugement définitif. ‖ *D'autorité,* sans consulter personne; d'une façon impérative. ‖ *De pleine autorité,* avec tout le droit qu'on a. ‖ *De sa propre autorité,* sans l'autorisation de personne. ‖ *Faire autorité,* faire loi, servir de règle. ‖ — Pl. Représentants de la puissance publique, hauts fonctionnaires : *les autorités civiles et militaires.*
autoroute n. f. Route à deux chaussées séparées, dont les accès sont spécialement aménagés, et qui, uniquement conçue pour la circulation à grande vitesse des automobiles et des motocyclettes, ne croise à niveau aucune autre voie.
auto sacramental [autosakramɛntal] n. m. (mots esp. signif. *drame du saint sacrement*). Représentation dramatique qui avait lieu en Espagne le jour de la Fête-Dieu, après les cérémonies religieuses, sur des théâtres dressés dans les rues. (Le genre s'est développé surtout aux XVIe et XVIIe s.) ‖ Pl. des *autos sacramentales.*
auto-stop n. m. Pratique consistant à arrêter un automobiliste sur la route pour lui demander de prendre place gratuitement dans sa voiture.
auto-stoppeur, euse n. Personne qui pratique l'auto-stop.
autostrade n. f. (ital. *autostrada*). Syn. de AUTOROUTE.
autosuggestion n. f. Influence d'une idée persistante sur notre conduite : *la haine peut mener au crime par autosuggestion.*
autotomie n. f. (préf. *auto,* et gr. *tomê,* coupure). Mutilation réflexe d'une partie du corps, observée chez certains animaux (appendices des crustacés, queue des lézards), et leur permettant d'échapper au danger : *l'autotomie est souvent suivie d'une régénération.*
autotransformateur n. m. Transformateur électrique dont les enroulements primaire et secondaire possèdent des parties communes.
autotrophe [otɔtrɔf] adj. (préf. *auto,* et gr. *trophê,* nourriture). Se dit des organismes végétaux (plantes vertes et certains végétaux inférieurs) qui sont capables d'élaborer leurs aliments organiques à partir d'éléments minéraux. (Contr. HÉTÉROTROPHE.)
autour [otur] n. m. (lat. *accipiter,* épervier). Oiseau de proie, rapace diurne, attaquant le gibier et les oiseaux de basse-cour, mais très apprécié en fauconnerie. (Long. 60 cm.)
autour de loc. prép. (de *tour*). Dans l'espace environnant : *la Terre tourne autour du Soleil.* ‖ Marque aussi le voisinage, la société habituelle : *ceux qui vivent autour de nous.* ‖ *Fam.* Environ, à peu près : *posséder autour d'un million.* ‖ — **Autour** adv. Alentour : *de la viande avec des légumes autour.* ‖ — **Tout autour** loc. adv. De tous côtés.
autovaccin n. m. Vaccin obtenu à partir de germes prélevés sur le malade lui-même.
autre [otr] adj. indéf. (lat. *alter*). Distinct, différent : *on se voit d'un autre œil qu'on ne voit son prochain.* ‖ Second (pour exprimer la ressemblance, l'égalité) : *c'est un autre Alexandre.* ● *L'autre jour,* un de ces jours derniers. ‖ — Pr. indéf. Une autre personne en général : *un autre; les autres.* ‖ — Loc. adv. **Autre part,** ailleurs. ‖ **D'autre part,** en outre. ‖ **De temps à autre,** parfois. ‖ — Contr. : IDENTIQUE, MÊME, PAREIL, SEMBLABLE.
autrefois [otrəfwa] adv. Anciennement, jadis : *on croyait autrefois que...*

Phot. Atlas-Photo.

autruche

autrement [otrəmɑ̃] adv. D'une façon différente : *il parle autrement qu'il ne pense.* ‖ Dans le cas contraire; sinon, sans quoi : *obéissez, autrement je vous punis.* ● *Autrement plus* (Fam.), beaucoup plus.
autrichien [otriʃjɛ̃], **enne** [-ɛn] adj. et n. D'Autriche.
autruche [otryʃ] n. f. (lat. *avis,* oiseau, et *struthio,* autruche). Oiseau vivant en bandes dans les steppes et les déserts africains, aux ailes réduites, inaptes au vol, mais capable, grâce à ses pattes longues et fortes, de courir à une vitesse de 40 km à l'heure. (On chasse et on élève l'autruche pour les longues plumes blanches de ses ailes, dont on fait des parures.) [Haut. 2,60 m; poids 100 kg; longévité 50 ans; sous-classe des ratites.] ● *Estomac d'autruche,* estomac qui digère tout. ‖ *Pratiquer la politique de l'autruche,* se refuser à envisager le danger.
autrui [otrɥi] pr. indéf. (de *autre*). Les autres, le prochain : *il ne faut pas convoiter le bien d'autrui.* ‖ Toute personne humaine considérée sur le plan moral : *le respect d'autrui.*
autunite [otynit] n. f. (de *Autun*). Phosphate naturel d'uranium et de calcium, le plus connu des minerais uranifères exploités en France.
auvent [ovɑ̃] n. m. (orig. celtique). Petit toit en saillie au-dessus d'une porte, d'une fenêtre, pour garantir de la pluie. ‖ Abri placé au sommet d'un mur pour protéger des espaliers.
auvergnat [ovɛrɲa], **e** [-at] adj. et n. D'Auvergne. ‖ — N. m. Dialecte parlé en Auvergne.
auxiliaire [ɔ *ou* o-ksiljɛr] adj. et n. (lat. *auxiliaris;* de *auxilium,* secours). Qui aide, prête son concours : *commis auxiliaire.* ‖ Employé recruté à titre provisoire par l'Administration, et qui ne bénéficie pas, de ce fait, du statut des fonctionnaires. ● *Auxiliaire de justice,* dénomination commune des personnes qui concourent à l'administration de la justice (avocats, avoués, experts, syndics, commissaires de police, etc.). ‖ *Auxiliaires médicaux,* appellation générale des infirmiers, sages-femmes, masseurs, kinésithérapeutes, pédicures, professeurs de gymnastique médicale. ‖ *Verbes auxiliaires,* les verbes *avoir* et *être,* qui, perdant leur signification propre, servent à former les temps composés des verbes actifs et pronominaux, et les temps simples et composés des verbes passifs. ‖ — N. m. pl. *Mar.* Machines d'un navire, autres que ses machines motrices.
auxiliairement adv. De façon auxiliaire.
auxiliateur, trice adj. et n. Qui donne du secours.
auxine [oksin] n. f. Hormone végétale qui gouverne la croissance des plantes.
— Découvertes dans le sommet du coléoptile d'avoine, les *auxines* se trouvent dans tous les tissus végétaux embryonnaires. Provenant des végétaux consommés, elles sont abondantes dans l'urine de l'homme et des animaux.
avachi [avaʃi], **e** adj. Déformé, usé : *des souliers avachis.* ‖ *Fam.* Fatigué, sans énergie : *il se sent tout avachi.*
avachir (s') v. pr. (du francique *waikjan,* rendre mou). Devenir mou, se déformer : *costume qui s'avachit.* ‖ *Fam.* Perdre son énergie, son entrain.
avachissement n. m. Déformation, usure. ‖ *Fig.* et *fam.* Perte totale d'énergie.
aval [aval] n. m. (de *à* et *val*). Partie d'un cours d'eau vers laquelle descend le courant. (Contr. AMONT.) ‖ — **En aval de** loc. prép. En descendant vers l'embouchure; au-dessous de : *Nantes est en aval de Tours, sur la Loire.*
aval n. m. (ital. *avallo*). Garantie donnée sur un effet de commerce par un tiers, qui s'engage à en payer le montant s'il n'est pas acquitté par le signataire : *bon pour aval; donner son aval.* ‖ Pl. des *avals.*
avalanche [avalɑ̃ʃ] n. f. (mot de la Suisse romande; de *avaler,* descendre). Masse de neige qui se détache des flancs d'une montagne et qui dévale avec une grande vitesse en entraînant des boues et des pierres. ‖ Masse d'objets qui tombent : *une avalanche de dossiers.* ‖ *Fig.* Multitude de choses qui vous accablent : *une avalanche d'ennuis.* ● *Avalanche de fond,* avalanche de neige compacte, lourde et très humide. ‖ *Avalanche de poudre* ou *poudreuse,* avalanche de neige fraîche tombant en nuage de poussière blanche. ‖ *Cône d'avalanche,* zone de débris au débouché du couloir d'avalanche. ‖ *Couloir d'avalanche,* passage emprunté par une avalanche.
avaler [avale] v. t. (de *aval*). Faire descendre par le gosier : *avaler une gorgée d'eau.* ‖ *Fig.* Accepter, supporter quelque chose : *avaler un affront.* ‖ *Fam.* Croire sottement : *on lui fait tout avaler.* ● *Avaler des yeux* (Fam.), regarder avidement.
avaleur, euse n. Personne qui avale : *un avaleur de sabres.*
avaliser [avalize] v. t. Revêtir d'un aval : *avaliser un effet de commerce.* ‖ *Fig.* Appuyer en donnant sa caution : *avaliser une politique.*
avaliseur adj. et n. m. Qui donne son aval.
à-valoir n. m. inv. Somme à imputer sur une créance.
avaloire [avalwar] n. f. Pièce de harnais fixée au brancard et descendant derrière les cuisses des chevaux de timon, pour retenir ou faire reculer le véhicule. (On dit aussi AVALOIR n. m.)
avance [avɑ̃s] n. f. Espace parcouru avant quelqu'un : *prendre une certaine avance.* ‖ Espace de temps qui anticipe sur le moment prévu : *arriver avec une heure d'avance.* ‖ Action de marcher en avant : *l'avance d'une armée.* ‖ *Mécan.* Déplacement de l'outil d'une machine, après chaque course, pour l'amener devant une nouvelle partie de la pièce à usiner. ‖ Paiement anticipé : *verser des avances à un employé.* ‖ Prêt remboursable dans un délai et selon des conditions bien déterminés : *les avances du Trésor.* ‖ — Pl. *Fig.* Premières démarches faites en vue d'une réconciliation, d'une liaison d'amitié : *faire des avances à un voisin.* ‖ — **En avance, d'avance, par avance** loc. adv. Avant l'heure; par anticipation.
avancé, e adj. Presque terminé : *travail avancé.* ‖ D'une grande perfection : *civilisation avancée.* ‖ Qui est d'avant-garde : *idées, opinions avancées.* ‖ Près de se gâter, de se corrompre : *gibier avancé; fruits avancés.* ● *Ouvrage, poste avancé* (Mil.), celui qui est en avant des autres vers l'ennemi.

75

Rouchon, Imp.,
Rue de la Verrerie, 87.
Salle
BONNE-NOUVELLE
OUVERTURE DES
Spectacles-Concerts
PRIX D'ENTRÉE
1 franc
par personne

connotations, while the text, often reduced to conveying the briefest information, accordingly became more telling and memorable. The first great poster designer was Jules Chéret, duly rewarded with fame and fortune. To attract the eye, he relied on vaporous forms and soft colours: these went to vaunt luxury products and shows intended to appeal to a public of some refinement. The great designers who followed him around 1900, like Mucha or de Feure, conveyed in their work the notion of an opulent sweetness. Ten years later a truculent illustrator like Jossot aimed on the contrary at an aggressive design, ruffling and browbeating the spectator. What he puffed were ordinary consumer products, like tinned foods, and so he worked with a wider public in mind. The "cubist" school of poster designers, men like Cassandre and Loupot, tried to keep a balance between these two conceptions. Here, in fact, all styles could co-exist: it would be an illusion to suppose that the history of the poster follows the history of modern art. Every poster is commissioned for a purpose, and its style, as publicity men know, is determined by the taste of the public which is expected to consume the product advertised. On the effectiveness of the poster will also depend the relation observed between the text and the picture. In the nineteenth century the text was usually limited to the brand name or the title of the show. The picture was expected to be self-sufficing, self-explanatory; so it was largely descriptive. But the influence of magazines and broadcasting has begotten the slogan: this is now the common denominator of the publicity campaign, the concentrated product of speech, writing and design.

4

Charles Loupot, St Raphaël Quinquina, poster, 1945.

Vladimir and Georgii Stenberg, Camera Man, poster, 1929.

The sway of the image can be carried to the point of making do with no more than a word or two, as in the "Exactitude" poster (meaning punctuality) of the French State Railways, designed by Fix-Masseau, much in the manner of an emblematic figure of the sixteenth century. The designer may even set out to dissolve the letter in the image, as Loupot tried to do with the black, white and red forms of "St Raphaël Quinquina," first taken from the figural image, then transposed into letter forms, and finally used in an abstract way, rather like the colours of a flag. But these were unusual experiments. The important thing to note is that the presence of a text, however discreet, seems necessary to the poster: the effectiveness of its message depends on the redoubled meaning conveyed by the pairing of picture and text, each enhancing and setting off the other, and casting a joint spell over the spectator.

The publicity poster then is a matter of both pictures and writing, a fusion of the seen and the spoken distilled into the gist of the poster: the brand name. In the resulting image we find all the elementary effects of the pictogram of long ago, which had to show and denote simultaneously. This trend towards a primary mode of meaning is further emphasized with the trade-mark, which refers back to the seal, or rather to the blazon or the cross. So it would be a mistake to assume that illustration has followed a line of progress from primitive forms to the more complex forms of today. The fact is rather that all types of relationship between text and image now exist at the same time. The straightforward view of Fifth Avenue in New York or the Avenue de l'Opéra in Paris sums up all the figured imagery of the past: the heraldic type of emblem, the signal and the pictogram (road signs), the text designed for seeing (neons), the diagram (traffic schemes), the illustration (posters, photograms), the shopsign, the mark, the symptom, the figure, the seal and so on. A big city can only function thanks to a multitude of illustrational effects which make it a kind of "sign world." Before the Industrial Age, nature represented this "sign world," and its maker was God. While the signs now have changed their master, they have not changed their victims, for the power and complexity of the messages around us, impinging upon us, is such as to disarm criticism. And the face behind them is anonymous. The sender of the sign makes a point of keeping in the background, so that his message shall appear absolute. Whether that sender is religious or commercial, our only hope is to trace it back to its origin and so find out who profits from the sign.

Pierre Fix-Masseau, poster for the French State Railways, 1932.

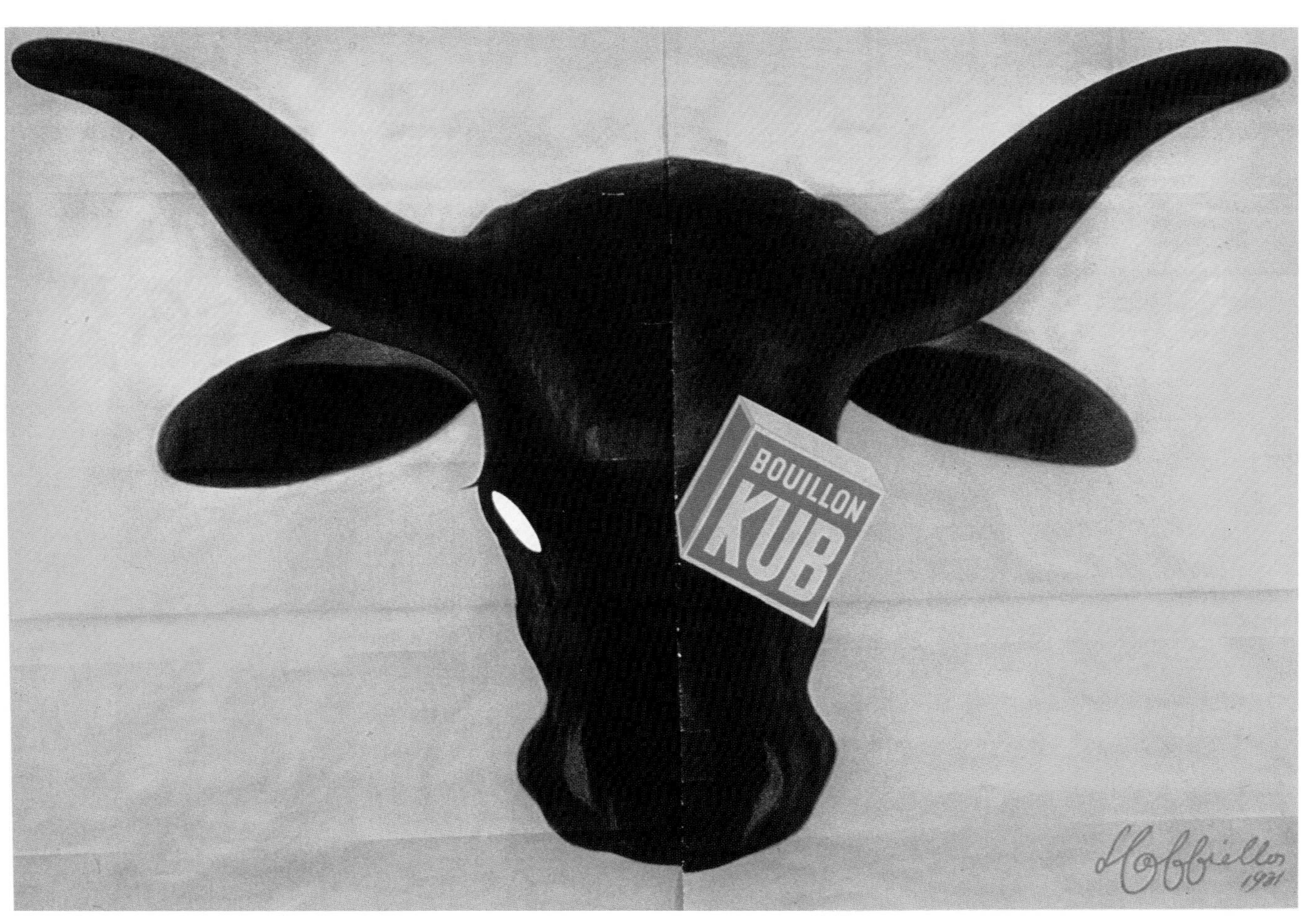

Leonetto Cappiello, poster for Bouillon Kub, 1931.

It is in the perspective of this strategy that the intrusion of the poster into art must be seen. It entered art at the very time when, on the strength of the image, it asserted itself as lyrical rather than merely informative. The values it relied on in its form and substance being no longer controllable, it now had to appeal to an aesthetic ideology in order to credit them. One is surprised to find that in France, almost from the start, the rise of the commercial and advertising poster aroused the interest of collectors and brought into existence a parallel market, with its historians (Ernest Maindron), its critics (André Mellerio), its magazines (*L'Estampe et L'Affiche*), its exhibitions (the Salon des Cents), its dealers (Clovis Sagot). In this marginal but essential sector, the poster was an image and an object of art. So true is this that the real purpose of the poster was a matter of indifference; attention was focused on the artist who designed it, and his work was assimilated to a picture or anyhow a print. Aesthetic interest in them was so keen in France that they were singled out before letters and instead of being posted were kept in portfolios, or folded in albums and bound up like books. Artists accordingly turned to the poster as a new medium of expression. They designed them unprompted, waiting for no orders, seeing here a way of escape from isolation, a way of descending into the street and speaking to all comers. From the early 1900s, they used the poster to voice their political commitments or for their own propaganda, for this was the heyday of provocative manifestoes and secessions. So in France there arose an *affiche d'artiste* which detached itself from the poster, just as the *livre d'artiste* detached itself from the book. This aesthetic deviation took several forms, affecting in different ways the relation of the text to the image. Often, indeed generally, the lettering of the poster stood in the artist's way. So, as in the *livre d'artiste*, the written words were sometimes kept outside the image, set in flawless typography alongside Picasso's dove, for

1

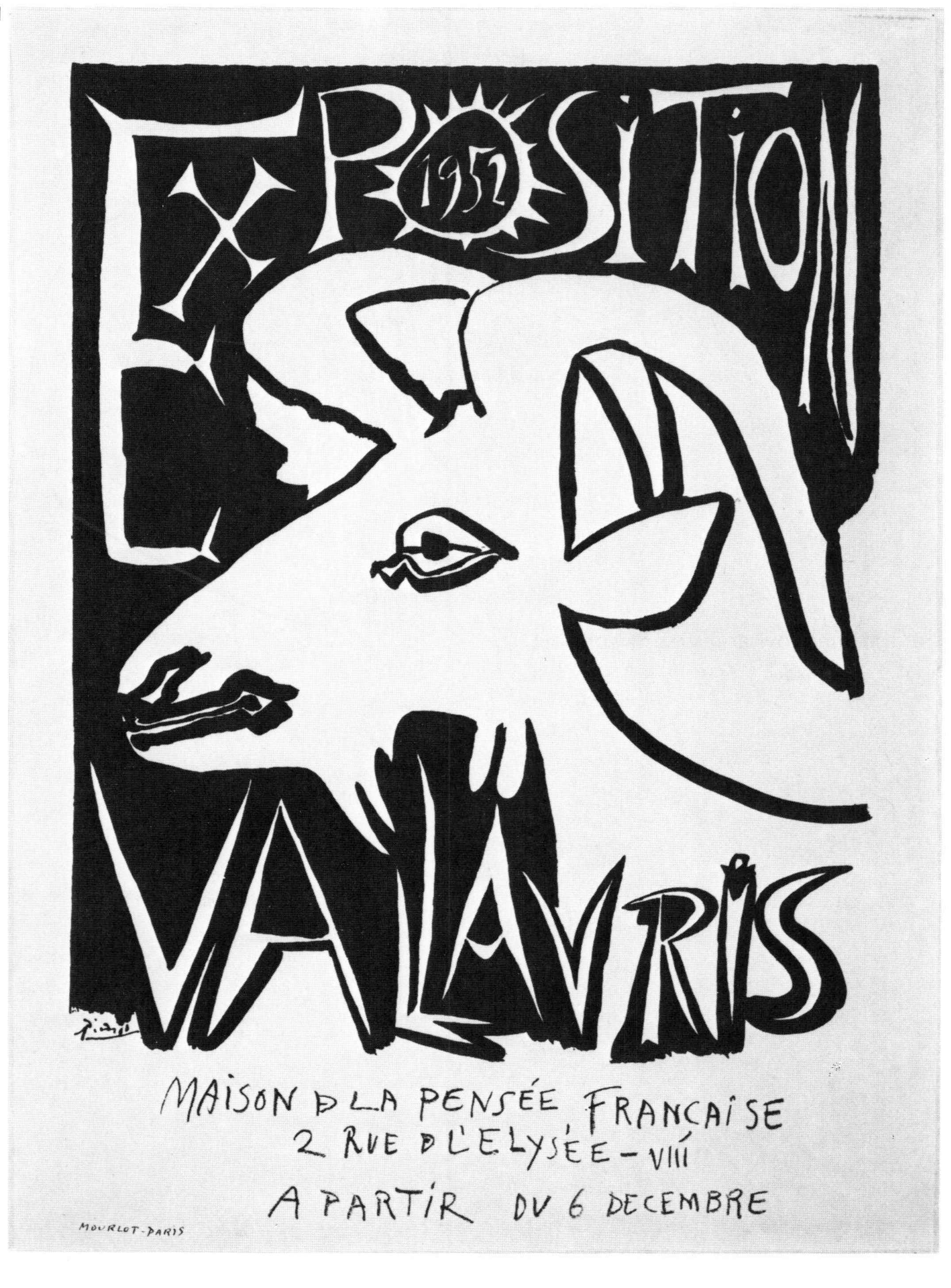

2

3

1. Pablo Picasso, poster for his Vallauris Exhibition at the Maison de la Pensée Française, Paris, 1952.

2.3. American posters against the war in Vietnam by the Student Workshop Berkeley, 1970.

example, and in many exhibition posters; and sometimes so wholly integrated into the image as to merge with it, as in the poster designs of the Glasgow and Vienna schools, of the Futurists, of the Constructivists. Finally, there was the militant poster, where the artist committed himself and his art, espousing the political line laid down from above: it was here that the mutual respect of text and image, each playing its part in a formal unity, had the best chance of prevailing, and such was the case with the posters of the Russian Revolution and the silkscreen prints of the May 1968 student uprising in Paris.

As one looks back over the history of illustration and notes the massive forward thrust of the image in the course of the Industrial Age, the rise of the illustrated poster is seen to stand out as a particularly significant phenomenon. Although it does not touch the heart of the matter (i.e. the book), the poster represents the most extreme manifestation of this powerful trend and points to its underlying economic motivations. One might say today that the image precedes the text, as one could say that "existence precedes essence." As an apt and telling medium for the representation of things, even on purely symbolic lines, the poster appears directly connected with the necessity of producing them.

Secession Posters

1

2

3

1. *Alfred Roller, Ninth Exhibition of the Secession, Vienna, 1901.*
2. *Gustav Klimt, First Exhibition of the Secession, Vienna, 1898.*
3. *Egon Schiele, Forty-ninth Exhibition of the Secession, Vienna, 1918.*

On 3 April 1897, revolting from the official association of Viennese artists (Genossenschaft bildender Künstler Wiens), where they were unable to exhibit freely, a number of Viennese painters headed by Gustav Klimt founded a "secession" group (Vereinigung bildender Künstler Österreichs). Their options were akin to those of the German Jugendstil movement, to the whole trend of Art Nouveau whose forms and patterns were meant to harmonize with architecture and launch a new style of interior decoration. In these experiments, aiming at the integration of art with life, the poster provided a fruitful field of endeavour for the Secession painters. Their output here is well known from the pages of *Ver Sacrum*, the Secession magazine where they were published, and from the 3,000 showbills and publicity and exhibition posters which were printed. From 1898 to 1914 the Vienna Secession organized forty exhibitions. In Austria posters could not be sold separately to collectors, as they were in France, and the whole of the printing was expected to be posted. A few art lovers, however, like Ottokar Mascha and Julius Paul, succeeded in collecting them, and thanks to them they are now preserved in the Albertina. Among them are some designs remarkable for their flawless alliance of text and picture, and they number among the finest graphic works of the Secession artists–Gustav Klimt, Oskar Kokoschka, Frank Karl Delavilla, Rudolf Kalvach, Alfred Roller, Emil Pirchan and Josef Hoffmann. ■

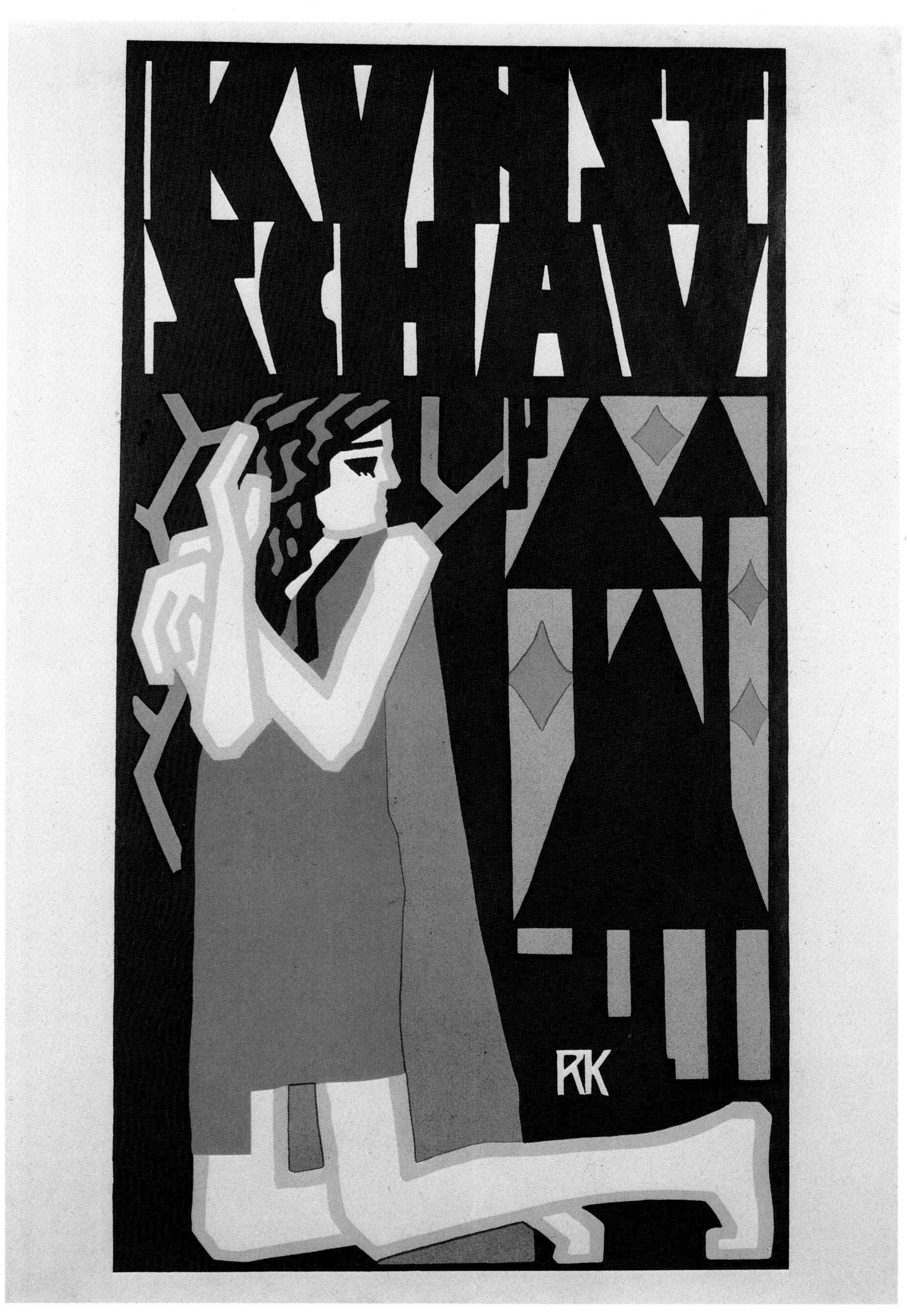

Rudolf Kalvach, Kunstschau, Vienna, 1908: exhibition poster for the Klimt group which in 1905 had broken away from the Secession.

Mayakovsky's "Rosta Windows"

"To the Polish front. RKP (Russian Communist Party)." Picture by Ivan Malyutin, text by Vladimir Mayakovsky, 1920.

"RKP (Russian Communist Party), To the Polish front." Picture by Ivan Malyutin, text by Vladimir Mayakovsky, 1920.

"Ukrainians and Russians have only one cry—the Pan (Polish overlord) shall not be the workers' master!" Picture and text by Vladimir Mayakovsky, 1920.

Posters played a part of some importance in the Russian Revolution. Throwing themselves into it heart and soul, avant-garde artists seized on the poster both as a medium of mass communication and as a vehicle of constructivist experiments with form, combining pictures with typography. In this battle of militant aesthetics, the poet Vladimir Mayakovsky stood in the forefront and wrote with reference to posters: "A handful of painters spoke out for a 150 million people." Mayakovsky himself composed propaganda texts and pictures for the Rosta Agency which, around 1920, printed and diffused 1,300 of those satirical posters skilfully designed in a direct, naively appealing style and known as "Rosta Windows." Rodchenko tells how he brought the poet to do this work: looking together at a propaganda poster inscribed "No citizen of the Soviet Union is the man who is not a shareholder of Aeroflot," he convinced Mayakovsky that "if poets did no more than laugh at bad publicity texts, there would never be any good ones." So Mayakovsky turned his hand to slogans in the form of poems whose very wording fitted neatly into the dynamic graphic design of the poster. The vivid colours answered to the urgency of the statement; the simplicity of the forms answered to the pointedness of the slogan. These posters met with enormous success, and their militant diffusion went hand in hand with revolutionary cultural ventures like the agit-prop railway carriages, the photographic surveys and the constructivist posters of El Lissitzky. Paper was short, but one poster brought the message to many. In *I Ask Leave to Speak,* Mayakovsky wrote: "The demand for the poster was such that the printer could not satisfy it. When it did arrive, it was desperately late, so that by then its power of agitation was waning... The agitation poster effective for a day has been taken over entirely by 'craftsmen' working by hand. These posters had immense qualities." ■

THE ILLUSTRATED BOOK

▲ Woodcut by Will H. Bradley for *Bradley His Book*, Wayside Press, Springfield, Mass., 1896.

◄ Illustration by Aubrey Beardsley for Sir Thomas Malory, *Le Morte Darthur*, Dent, London, 1893-1894: How Queen Guenever made her a nun in Almesbury, Book XXI, chapter VII.

There have always been book lovers and collectors, and a day came when books began to be specially designed and published with this select public in mind, illustrated books in particular. This period is comparatively recent: it may be said to begin with the first large illustrated books of the eighteenth century and the appearance in France of book-lovers' clubs known as Sociétés de Bibliophiles. These stately illustrated volumes were quite distinct in purpose and presentation from ordinary commercial books. They were not meant to be read and were generally modern or Renaissance classics (La Fontaine, Cervantes, Ariosto) whose prestige set a standard of value for the book and its owner. Illustration was as essential to them as illumination had been to the fine devotional manuscripts of the Middle Ages. But in addition to its ornamental and indeed sacralizing purpose, illustration here also had to enliven the text and make it more attractive to a public of aesthetes and amateurs, and of well-to-do parvenus, rather than scholars and intellectuals. From the outset, even if this does not always appear clearly, it was really a matter, not of books, but of an *objet d'art* in book form—a book considered and treated as a precious object. From the eighteenth century to the present, the meaning of this trend has become increasingly clear, today blindingly clear: the *livre d'artiste* is first and foremost a work of art into which a text has been integrated.

This trend was accentuated by the industrialization of book production in the nineteenth century. The reaction against that begot the fine private press book, reserved for connoisseurs. It is a significant fact, pointed out by J.P. Bouillon, that at the end of the nineteenth century collectors of fine books began focusing their attention on the incunabula of the genre: the large illustrated books of the eighteenth century, the first which had been specially designed to appeal to a clientele of collectors. The fine books of the Romantic period were conceived in a wholly different spirit, being lavishly illustrated and intended for a wide public, for at that time the alliance of art and industry was still believed in. The period 1860-1880 saw book lovers turning against the products of industrial art, and it was then that eighteenth-century books became the object of a speculative market, soon to be followed by the rise of a modern production of fine books aimed at satisfying the demand of this new clientele. One can of course point out, in the "prehistory" of this peculiar genre, such works as Delacroix's *Faust* and Goya's great sets of prints (which, on the strength of their captions, may indeed rank as genuine literary works). But the history of modern fine printing only really begins with William Morris in England and, in France, with the large books of colour lithographs.

Like that of the print, the history of the *livre d'art*, as distinct from the ordinary commercial book, takes its rise as a progressive reaction against the vulgarization of industrial printing. Such books were "art" only to the extent that they stood apart from mass-production techniques, as being craft-made for private buyers. It may therefore be said that the large books of Gustave Doré are the last representatives of the Romantic style (employing modern industrial techniques for the making of deluxe books), and that between these *fine books* intended for the public at large and the *livre d'art* or private press book, as conceived over the past century, there is a real divide and it was made by William Morris.

Morris's work was carried out in a spirit of militant socialism and anti-commercialism. He saw the alienation that industry was bringing with it and he wanted to save people from it. Paradoxically, through his attachment to an inaccessible artistic ideal, he was led straight to elitism and aestheticism. Longing for the simplicities of pre-industrial times, he decided to make his own books on the model of the early printers, designed and cut his own type-faces, and learned to make handmade paper himself, reviving the formula of a Bolognese paper-maker of 1473. The illustrations were engraved in the old way, by side-grain woodcutting, by the Pre-Raphaelite painter Burne-Jones. Likewise, Morris wove his own tapestries, illuminated books by hand on a special vellum with gold ground, and even prepared his own inks. His initial idea in founding the Kelmscott Press (1891) was to print a mere twenty copies for friends of its first book (unillustrated), his own *Story of the Glittering Plain*. Its success changed all this, and in the next seven years 52 titles were issued in 64 volumes; they were much sought after and still are. There existed in England a solid tradition of private presses, going back to Horace Walpole's at Strawberry Hill. Morris revived and renewed it, preparing himself by working in the 1880s at the Chiswick Press and other printers. It was in England too that the industrial deluxe book, illustrated in colour by chromolithography or the Baxter process, had reached the utmost limit of low-priced refinement. Morris gave a fresh stimulus to the

HEREBEGINNETH THE TALES OF CANTER-
BURY AND FIRST THE PROLOGUE THEREOF

Whan That Aprille with hise shoures soote
The droghte of March hath perced to the roote,
And bathed every veyne in swich licour
Of which vertu engendred is the flour;
Whan Zephirus eek with his swete breeth
Inspired hath in every holt and heeth
The tendre croppes, and the yong sonne
Hath in the Ram his halfe cours yronne,
And smale foweles maken melodye
That slepen al the night with open eye,
So priketh hem Nature in hir corages,
Thanne longen folk to goon on pilgrimages,
And palmeres for to seken straunge strondes,
To ferne halwes, kowthe in sondry londes;
And specially, from every shires ende
Of Engelond, to Caunterbury they wende
The hooly blisful martir for to seke
That hem hath holpen whan that they were
seeke.
BIFIL that in that seson on a day,
In Southwerk at the Tabard as I
lay,
Redy to wenden on my pilgrym-
age
To Caunterbury with ful devout
corage,
At nyght were come in-to that hostelrye
Wel nyne-and-twenty in a compaignye,
Of sondry folk, by aventure y-falle

Opening page of the Prologue to "The Canterbury Tales" in *The Works of Geoffrey Chaucer*, Kelmscott Press, London, 1896. Woodcut illustration by Burne-Jones, border decorations and initials by William Morris.

Book illustration was largely the work of established painters, its progress paralleling that of the original print and often merging with it. With Gustave Doré, his reputation as a popular illustrator overshadowed that of the painter he would have liked to be. With other great names of French book illustration, the reverse is true: they were painters before being illustrators. Manet's position is an equivocal one, since he employed lithographic transfer paper (in effect an industrial technique) to illustrate Poe's *The Raven* (1875); but this marks the appearance in France of the great *livre d'artiste*. Likewise, the publication of *Sonnets et Eaux-fortes* (1869), edited by Philippe Burty, with etchings by Corot, Millet, Manet and Jongkind, marked the beginning of the *livre de peintres*, published in a limited edition (350 copies) with original prints. After that, the way was open and there was a public ready to purchase and appreciate the large colour lithographs by painters, accompanying rather than illustrating reprints of literary classics or modern texts. Some notable landmarks are the *Yvette Guilbert* album (1894) and Jules Renard's *Histoires Naturelles* (1899), by Toulouse-Lautrec; Vollard's editions of Verlaine's *Parallèlement* (1900) and Longus' *Daphnis et Chloé* (1902), by Bonnard; and Kahnweiler's editions of Apollinaire's *L'Enchanteur Pourrissant* (1909), with woodcuts by Derain, and Max Jacob's *Saint Matorel* (1911) with etchings by Picasso. The feature role, in all these books, was obviously that of the illustrator, the text being the setting necessary to show him off to advantage. So true is this that we speak of "Derain's Pantagruel" or "Dufy's Tartarin de Tarascon." *Daphnis et Chloé* served not only for Bonnard but also for Maillol and Chagall. Here it was a question of fine art rather than literature. Literature entered into the *objet d'art* and became an object itself, concretely magnified by the flawless typography of Marthe Fequet and Pierre Baudier, on fine old sheets of handmade Arches and

1

2

3. Handwritten text and cut and pasted design by Henri Matisse, from his *Jazz*, Tériade, Paris, 1947.

4. Cover by Salvador Dalí for *Minotaure*, No. 8, Albert Skira, Paris, 1936.

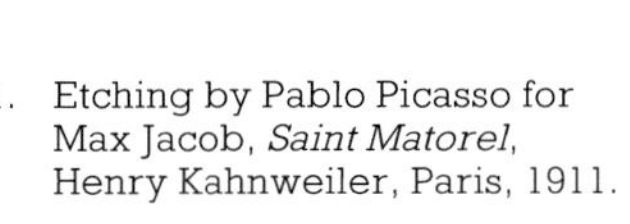

1. Etching by Pablo Picasso for Max Jacob, *Saint Matorel*, Henry Kahnweiler, Paris, 1911.

2. Etching by Pablo Picasso for *Les Métamorphoses d'Ovide*, Albert Skira, Lausanne, 1931.

Auvergne paper, encased in fine bindings by Paul Bonet or Henri Creuzevault.

Thanks to the printers of graphic work, Roger Lacourière, Jacques Frélaut and Georges Leblanc for intaglio work, Auguste Clot and Ancourt for lithography, Arcay and Caza for silkscreen—it is thanks to them and the long tradition of fine craftsmanship and book-making behind them that this school can be called French, for apart from them it was an international movement promoted by publishers who were not French: Tériade, a Greek; Iliazd, a Ukrainian; Skira, a Swiss. In 1928, as Europe and America were sinking into the Depression, Albert Skira boldly commissioned from Picasso some illustrations for Ovid's *Metamorphoses* (1931); and in 1930, from Matisse, those for *Poésies de Stéphane Mallarmé* (1932). These ventures, like Picasso's *Vollard Suite* later on, saved the fine illustrated book, for the collectors who had stopped buying pictures responded to these books, attracted precisely by the literary and craft tradition behind them. The perfectionism of Albert Skira's book design answered to the then revival of the classical style, and the choice of texts and style of the plates confirmed this tendency, which met with the favour of book lovers. Classicism by no means excluded innovation: it is found abundantly, most of all in the art magazines like Skira's *Minotaure* and Tériade's *Verve*. Tériade also published Matisse's *Jazz* (1947) and Léger's *Cirque* (1950). After 1950 this delicate balance between classicism and invention became more precarious. Vieira da Silva's illustrations for the publisher Berès and Braque's for Maeght came as the last embodiments of this harmony, which now broke down, either in favour of an uninspired conservatism, with a commissioned text simply placed at the head of a set of original prints; or in favour of *objets d'art* of a new type deriving their form, or something of their form, from the illustrated book.

un moment
si libres.
Ne devrait-on
pas faire ac-
complir un
grand voyage
en avion aux
jeunes gens
ayant terminé
leurs études.

54

3

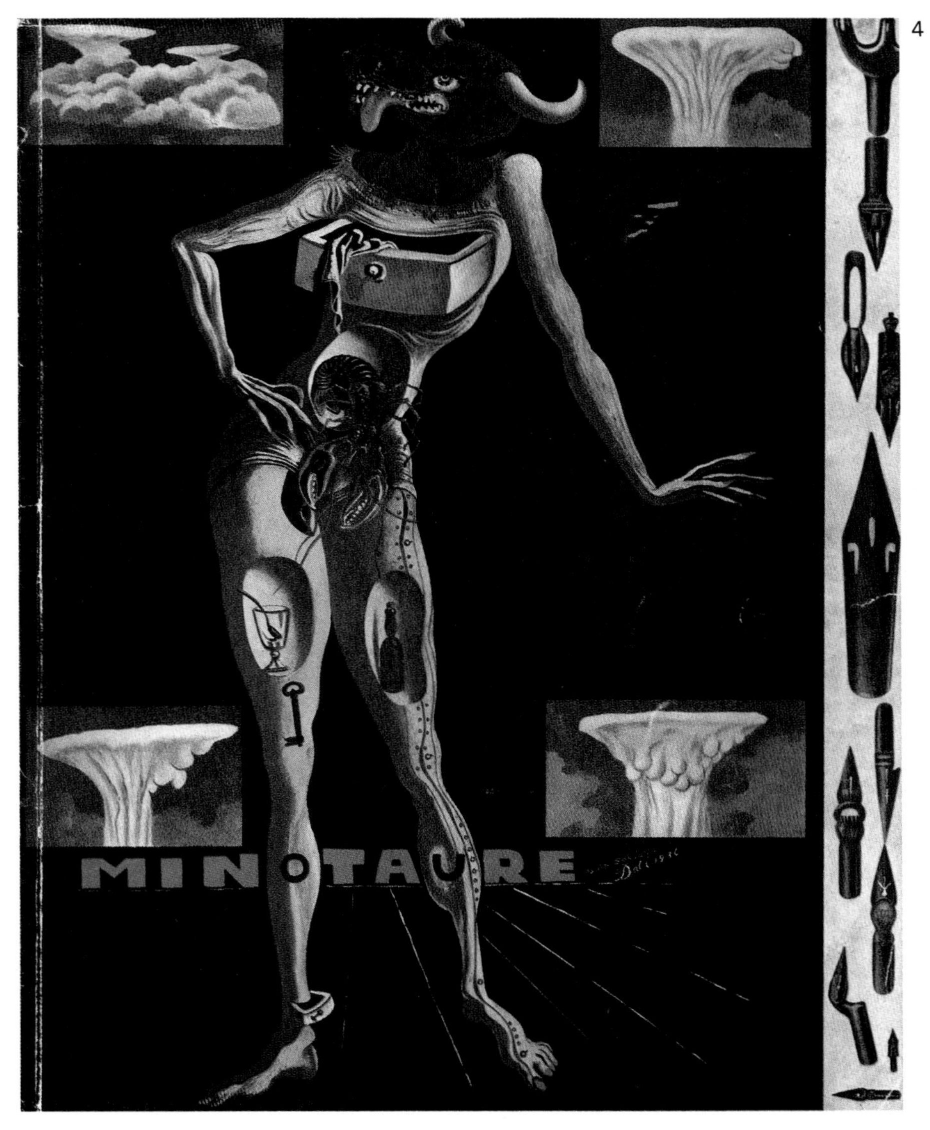

4

Odilon Redon's "Temptation of St Anthony"

1. *Odilon Redon,* Tentation de Saint-Antoine, *first set of lithographs, 1888, cover.*
2. *Second set, 1889, cover.*
3. *Third set, 1896, cover.*
4. *"St Anthony: Help me, O Lord," drawing on stone from the third set, 1896.*

4

1

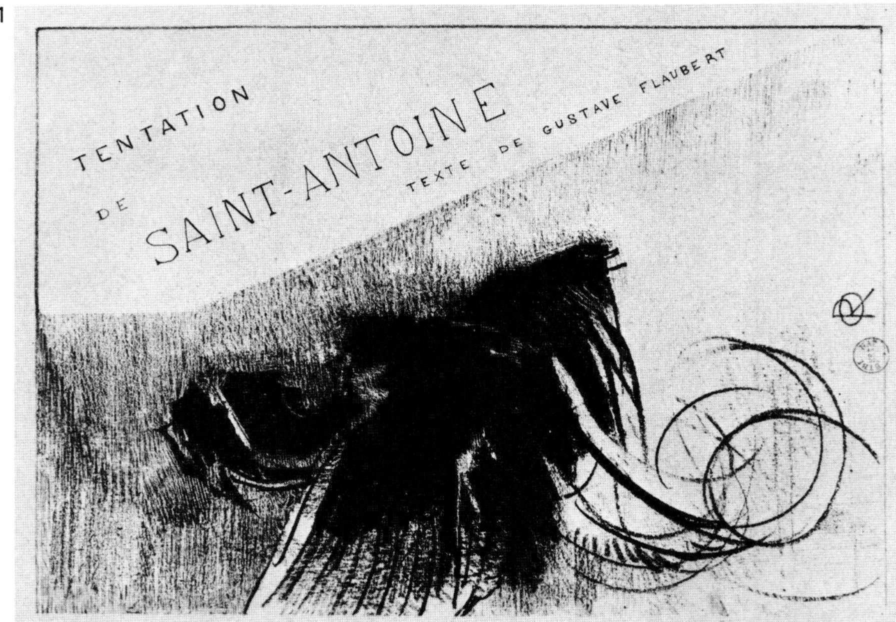

2

3

Nothing better indicates the pre-eminence acquired by the illustrator than Odilon Redon's sets of lithographs for Flaubert's prose poem *La Tentation de Saint Antoine.* First because in the rise of the *livre d'artiste* in the late nineteenth century they come early (1888, 1889 and 1896); secondly because they take the liberty of doing without the parallel publication of the text and stand alone as albums of prints. Yet the literary reference is clearly stated in the title, and indeed literature is minimally present in them in the captions—brief quotations from the book which, thus out of context, are more reminiscent of Goya than Flaubert.

Redon had got into the habit of issuing his lithographs in sets, with *Dans le Rêve* (1879), *A Edgar Poe* (1882) and so on. In 1888 he brought out an initial "Temptation of St Anthony" set, inspired by Flaubert's book: ten lithographs and a title page design, published by Deman in Brussels, nominally in 60 copies (actually 58), printed by Becquet in Paris. Among the other albums he issued up to *L'Apocalypse de Saint Jean* (1899), he reverted twice to Flaubert's "St Anthony": in 1889, with six lithographs and a title design, published by Dumont in Paris; and in 1896, with twenty-four "drawings on stone," printed by Clot and Blanchard. By then the idea of deluxe editions of major writers with illustrations by major artists was gaining ground, and Vollard had these sets reprinted in view of an illustrated edition of Flaubert. But Redon's lithographs without the text remain in their own right a fine tribute to Flaubert, whose spirit was akin to that of Redon. In both pictures and text we find, as André Mellerio has written, "a jumbled and bewildering amalgam, a strange and taking attractiveness in which an inexhaustible and wholly Oriental superabundance of evocation arises from a groundwork of accurate scholarship." Flaubert's theme appealed to Redon, who worked over it and lived with it for years, so that he was able to do more than illustrate it: he made it his own, reinvented it in his own terms and medium, and gave it an "interpretation unlimitedly free"—an ideal followed by most of the painter-illustrators who came after him. ■

"First a puddle of water," lithograph from the first set, 1888.

"To the Glory of the Hand"

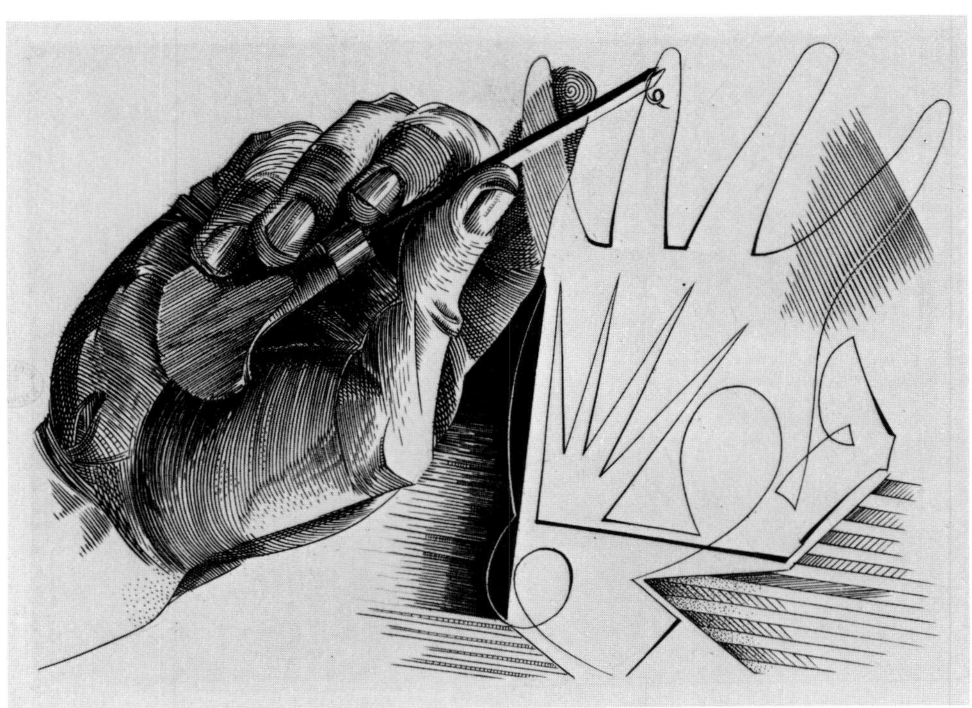

Six prints from A La Gloire De La Main, Paris, 1949:

My Hand, line engraving by Albert Flocon, plate 7.

Woman Messenger, etching by Roger Chastel, plate 2.

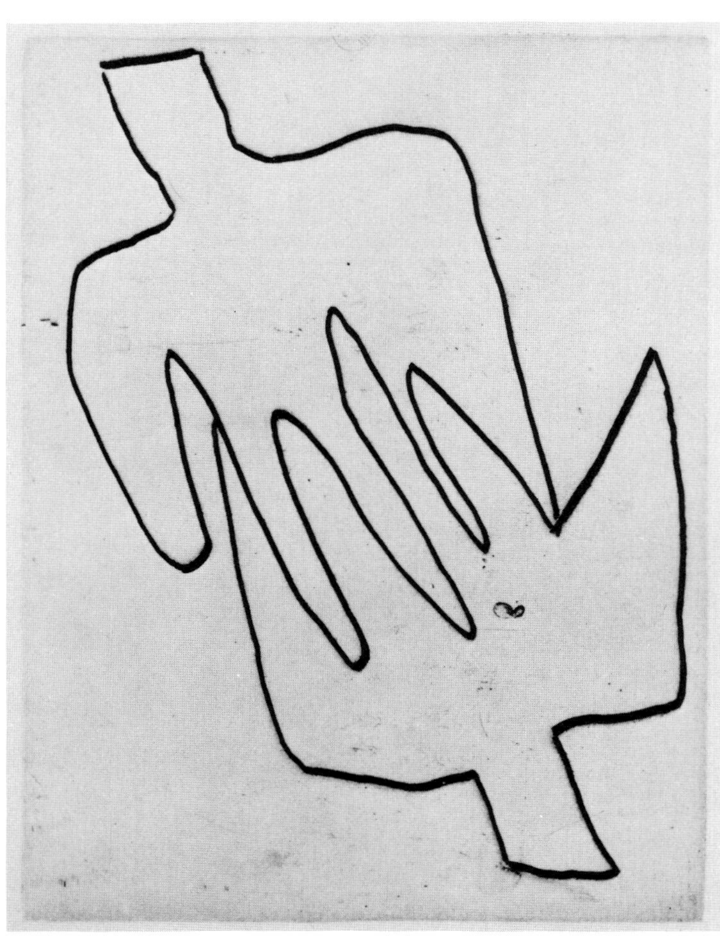

The illustration of fine books by major painters remains essentially an art of the first half of the twentieth century. After the Second World War the public of bibliophiles was no longer numerous enough to carry publishers into new ventures. But the painters themselves were still keenly interested in the illustration of literary texts, even when there was no prospect of publishing. From 1948 on, René Char undertook to have some of his manuscript poems illuminated by his painter friends, so that in time an extraordinary collection of these poem-paintings came into existence through the collaboration of Miró, Léger, Brauner, Hélion, Lam, Arp, de Staël, Vieira da Silva, Villon, Ernst, Sima, Giacometti, Braque, Picasso, Matisse and others. At the same period, some other painters and engravers experimented with works which would normally have been published, but remained rare or unique, by the practice of what might be called "sublimation." The "Graphies" group of painter-engravers thus held an exhibition in 1949 at La Hune in Paris, displaying a variety of creative work on the borderline between print, drawing, painting and even sculpture (Ubac's engraved slates). The same group proceeded to publish "at the expense of an art lover" (who in fact was one of them, Albert Flocon) an album of original prints on a common theme: the hand. It consisted of a series of engraved or lithographed variations by G. Vulliamy, A.E. Yersin, Jean Signovert, Raoul Ubac, Roger Vieillard, Henri Goetz, Léon Prébandier, Christine Boumeester, Sylvain Durand, Marcel Fiorini, Albert Flocon, Jacques Villon, Roger Chastel, Pierre Courtin, Jean Fautrier and Germaine Richier–to which answered symmetrically a series of short texts on the same theme by Gaston Bachelard, Paul Valéry, René de Solier, Francis Ponge, Henri Mondor, Jean Lescure, Paul Eluard and Tristan Tzara. The contributing painters, engravers and sculptors confronted the same theme as the writers, but handled it with freedom and imagination. This fresh conjunction of design and writing was aptly expressed both by the name of the group, *Graphies* ("Patternings"), and by the theme and title of the book, *A La Gloire De La Main.* ■

12 May 1949, line engraving by Pierre Courtin, plate 3.

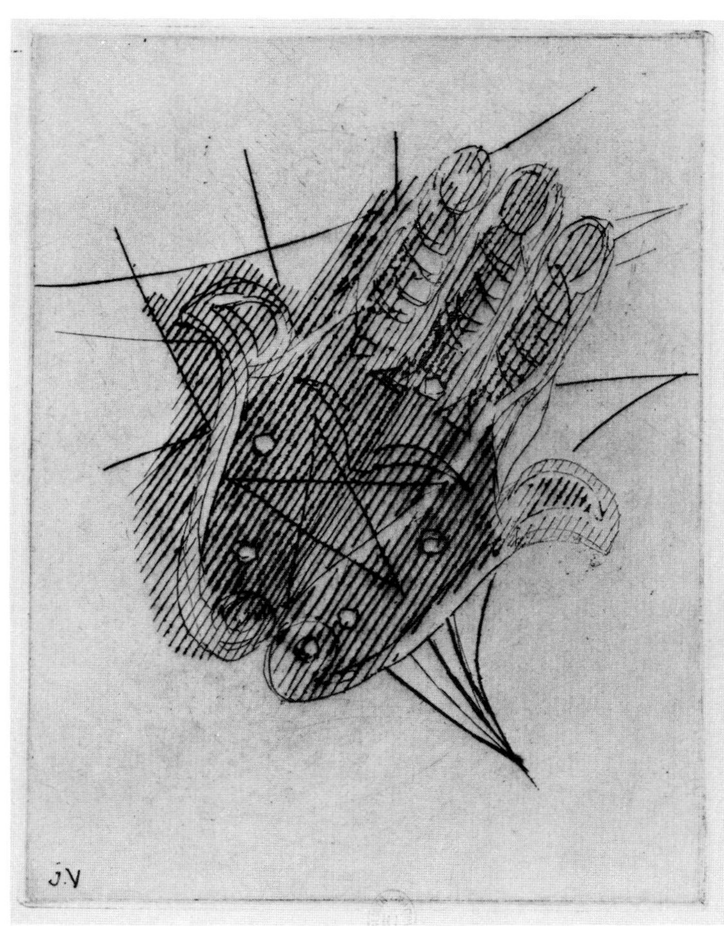

At a Venture, etching by Jacques Villon, plate 14.

Committed Woman, etching by Jean Fautrier, plate 5.

Line of Head, etching by Germaine Richier, plate 10.

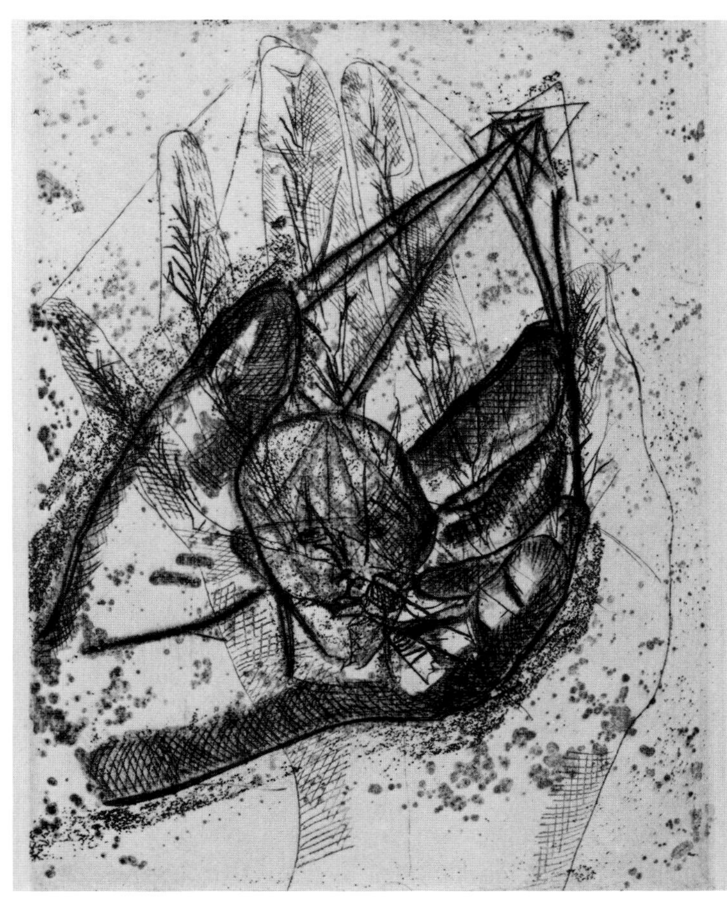

THE "LIVRE D'ARTISTE" IN FRANCE

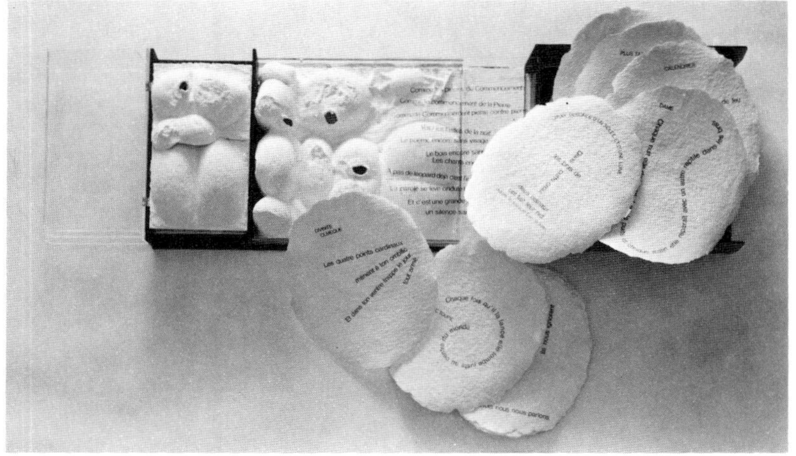

▲ Rodolfo Krasno, sound bookobject for *Pierres éparses* after twenty-two poems by Octavio Paz, 1970.

◄ Marcel Duchamp, The Valise, 1936-1941. Edition of 1956.

Something has just been said about the *livre d'art*, conceived by the publisher and carried out by the printer with the artist or artists. It may be distinguished from the *livre d'artiste*, whose history runs parallel to it, with no very sharp dividing line, but whose making has gained ground only since the early twentieth century and today thrives increasingly, compared to the recession of the *livre d'art*. Both give precedence to illustration and both treat the book as a fine art object. But while the *livre d'art* aims at harmonizing text and pictures in a balance of mutual respect, the *livre d'artiste* breaks down the barriers and aims at a new language conceived at once as object, poem and spectacle fused into the overall form of a book—and a surprising form it often is. This notion can be seen taking shape in Mallarmé's *Un Coup de dé jamais n'abolira le hasard* (1897), Cendrars' *Prose du Transsibérien* (1913), Apollinaire's *Calligrammes* (1918), Duchamp's *Bride Stripped Bare* and many Dadaist works; and it is from this notion that now proceed the latest and most fruitful experiments in the field of illustration. Unlike the *livre d'art* which came to look more and more like a fine album of prints, with the text often serving as no more than a set-off, the *livre d'artiste* is often a literary work of high standing in its own right. In the *livre d'art*, it was the artist who came to the fore, refusing a mere paraphrase of the text and venturing on a transposition, or even a transfiguration, in his own graphic terms. In the *livre d'artiste*, this distinction between different means of expression cannot be admitted, the object being conceived as an indivisible whole. But here, inasmuch as the main idea is to produce an organic work of art, the text in the end is inevitably governed by the status of the image; the text here is first of all something visible, only secondly something intelligible; as with the poster, the text is meant to be seen rather than read.

Apollinaire was the first theorist of this new language, which aimed at overcoming the contradiction in kind between text and picture, at bridging the gap between speculation and contemplation. Taking up the idea of reading as immediate, intuitive apprehension and living experience, an idea already in vogue in French philosophy and literature of the early 1900s, he reinvented the calligram, the poem as a visual design—far removed, with him, from the scholarly preoccupations of medieval philosophers who in the order of words sought for an order of the

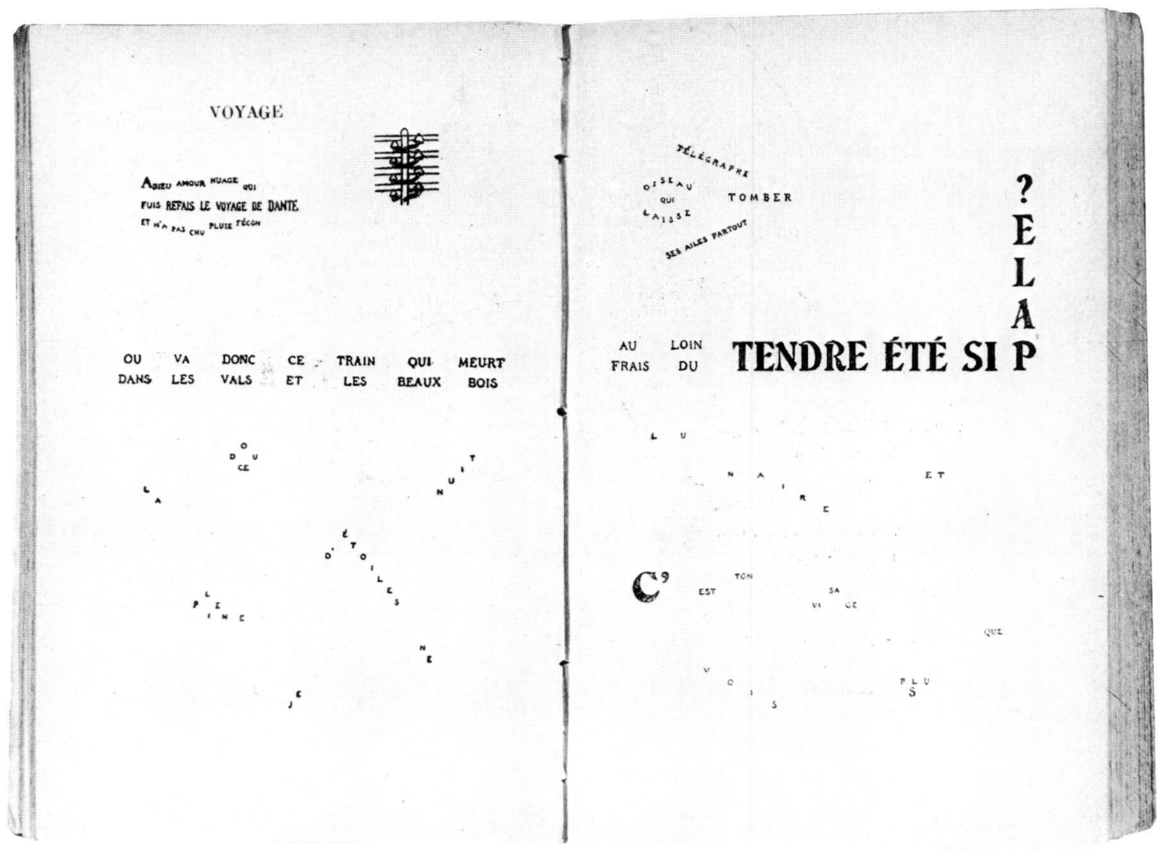

Two pages from Guillaume Apollinaire, *Calligrammes, poèmes de la paix et de la guerre, 1913-1916*, Paris, 1918.

F. T. Marinetti, *Les mots en liberté futuristes*, Paris, 1919: "Après la Marne, Joffre visita le front en auto" (After the Marne, Joffre visited the front by car).

Le Cœur à Barbe, Journal Transparent (The Bearded Heart, Transparent Journal), sole number of a Dada review edited by Eluard, Ribemont-Dessaignes and Tzara, Paris, April 1922.

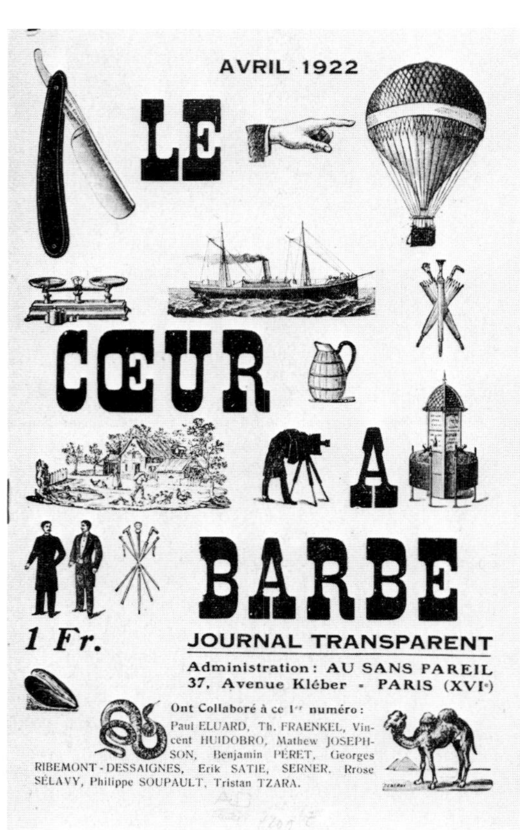

world. With Apollinaire, it was a revolutionary act, a violation of language by the image. The suppression of punctuation in his *Alcools* had tended already to impart to writing a sort of material solidity. After Mallarmé and Apollinaire, it was the visual, typographical articulation of words which replaced the conventional syntactical articulation. Once again the word became image by assuming the form of its referent, or simply by evoking it by way of allusions. It was not the play of fancy, but the appearance of a mode of intelligence intent on merging with language, for the deliberate purpose of interacting with the reader. Thanks to the image, the reader singled out the meaning of what he read, singled out a meaning for himself. Seizing on the word, the image imposed its own status upon it, imposed upon it its own simultaneity, to use a word much in vogue at the time. It was the poster and its slogan which had become poems: the calligram is deeply rooted in the culture of the twentieth century, "at the dawn of the new means of production represented by the cinema and the phonograph," as Apollinaire wrote himself.

At that same period the Futurists and the Dadaists dreamed of breaking literature down and tackling the stuff it was made of: typography. In 1915 Marinetti wrote his *Parole in libertà*; in 1914 Giovanni Papini had published his typographic essays in the Florentine review *Lacerba*. The letter was under attack from all sides: by the Italian and Russian Futurists who made pictures out of it; by the Dadaists who disrupted both its shapes and sounds; by the Surrealists who radically contested it when Man Ray in 1924 published his *Lautgedicht Poeme* in which the text had disappeared, replaced by lines. Literature reduced to its real image, this was the end result aimed at in many lettering, spacing and graphic experiments and by the concrete poets and the visual poets. When André Breton introduced photographs into his novel *Nadja*, they were not of course meant as illustrations in the traditional sense; they were part of the text, just as the text or its parody was part of the pictures of Magritte or Max Ernst. The Dadaist and Surrealist output of ephemeral tracts, handbills, pamphlets and magazines really put an end to the totalitarian sway of the classic typography which had monopolized the manifestation of meaning. The origin of this movement lay in the necessity of using the image both in knowledge systems and production systems. Herbert Bayer's design workshop at the Dessau Bauhaus in 1925 was significantly called "Publicity Typography and Morphology." The surprising thing is the resistance or indifference of traditional typography: in industrial book production, hand in hand with well-disciplined illustrations, it went its way along this road booby-trapped by artists, as if nothing had changed.

The work of an artist like Iliazd shows clearly both the force of this revolution and its lack of impact on mass-produced books. A boisterous and resourceful Futurist in St Petersburg from 1911 to 1917, he invented an unintelligible language called *zaoum*, pronounced with one's tongue in one's cheek. In Paris in 1921 he was a Dadaist and in 1923 organized the "Bearded Heart" show at the Théâtre Michel. As poet-artist-publisher after 1940, his books were the outcome of a lifetime's experiments, from the letter patterning of *Poésies de mots inconnus* to the variably spaced typography and pictographic writing of

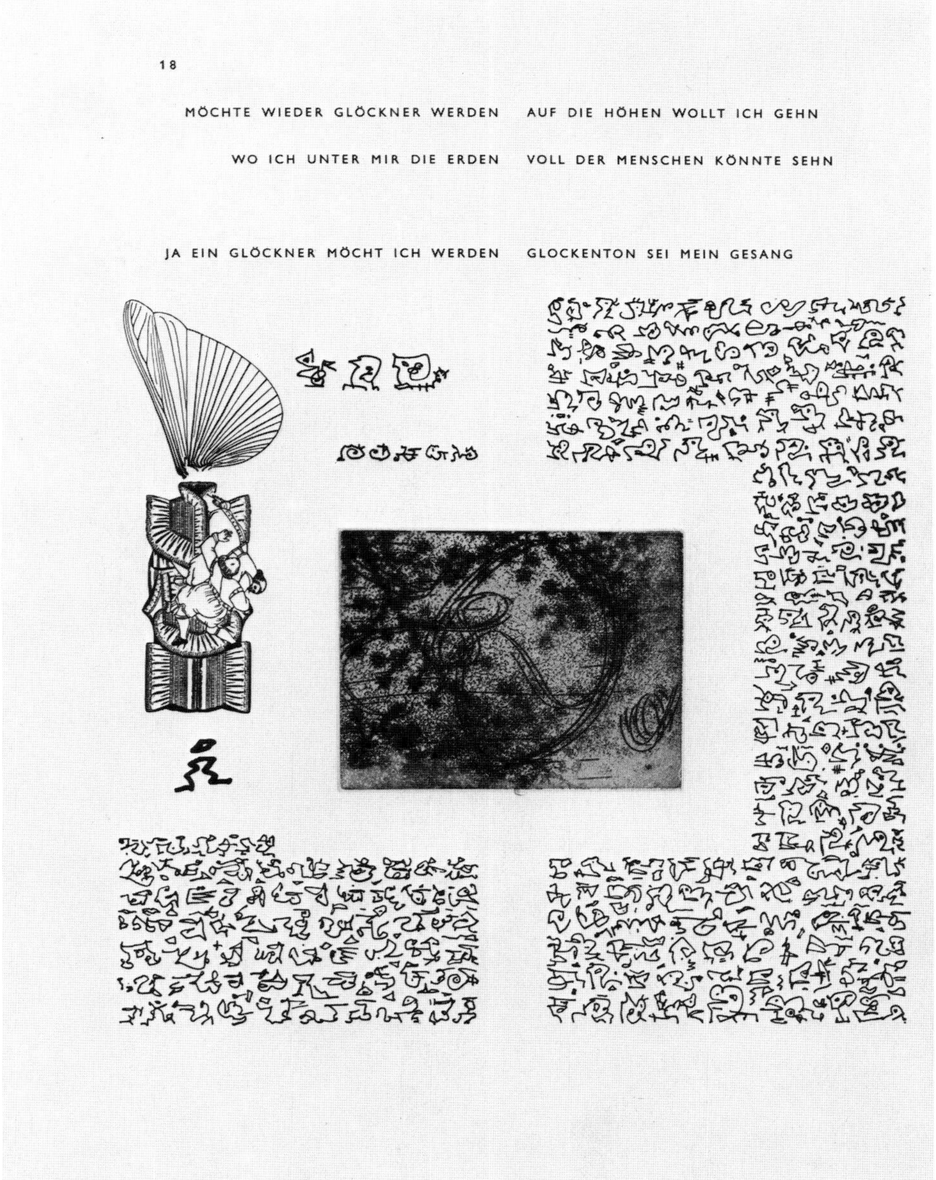
18

MÖCHTE WIEDER GLÖCKNER WERDEN AUF DIE HÖHEN WOLLT ICH GEHN

WO ICH UNTER MIR DIE ERDEN VOLL DER MENSCHEN KÖNNTE SEHN

JA EIN GLÖCKNER MÖCHT ICH WERDEN GLOCKENTON SEI MEIN GESANG

Page with illustrations and secret script from Max Ernst, *Maximiliana ou l'Exercice illégal de l'Astronomie*, Iliazd, Paris, 1964.

1

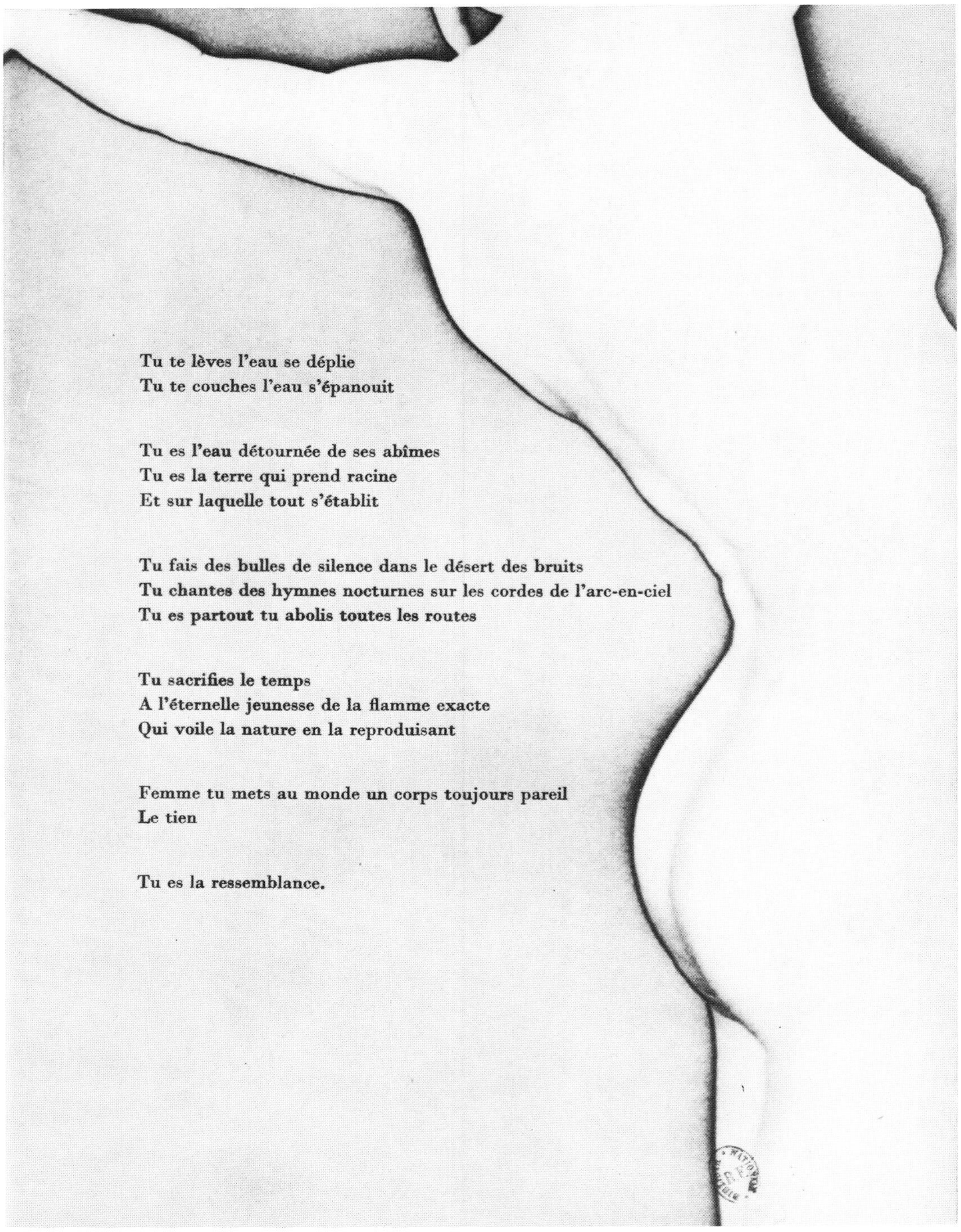

Tu te lèves l'eau se déplie
Tu te couches l'eau s'épanouit

Tu es l'eau détournée de ses abîmes
Tu es la terre qui prend racine
Et sur laquelle tout s'établit

Tu fais des bulles de silence dans le désert des bruits
Tu chantes des hymnes nocturnes sur les cordes de l'arc-en-ciel
Tu es partout tu abolis toutes les routes

Tu sacrifies le temps
A l'éternelle jeunesse de la flamme exacte
Qui voile la nature en la reproduisant

Femme tu mets au monde un corps toujours pareil
Le tien

Tu es la ressemblance.

2

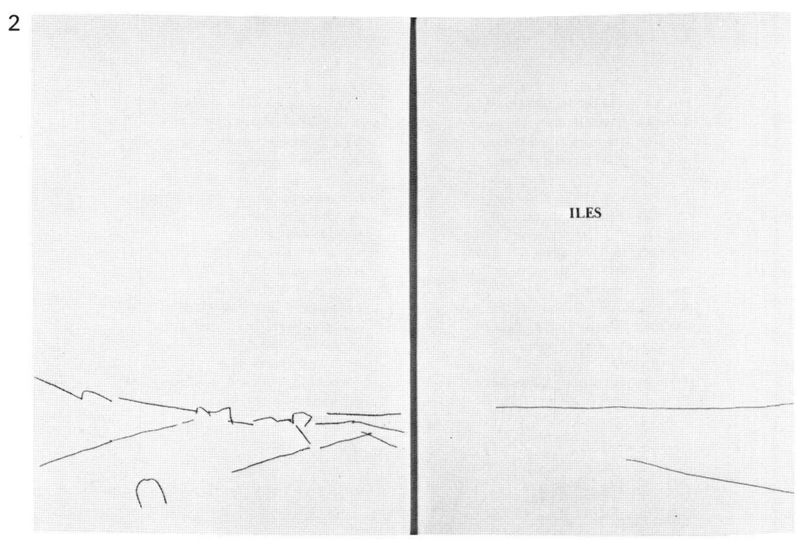

Max Ernst's *Maximiliana*. His books nevertheless owe something to the French tradition of impeccably produced art books, but Iliazd published his own poems in them, for example the seventy-six sonnets illustrated by Picasso in *Afat* (1940), his first book. Another poet who came from the Surrealist movement is Guy Lévis Mano, whose work is made up of books entirely put together by himself. Illustration for him was not a prestige domain intended to raise the book to the status of a deluxe object. For the most part, his illustrations are line or half-tone reproductions of drawings by his painter friends, harmonizing perfectly with his books whose elegance is in their very simplicity, with never a hint of showiness about them. Here again it is the book as a whole, over and above any text/image opposition, that is envisaged. Another fusion between the poet's and the bibliophile's book is achieved in the work of Pierre Lecuire. He himself is author, designer, maker and publisher, all in one. So that for Lecuire the text is not a separate entity contributed by an outside author; it is inseparable from the book's material

3

These two people resting on a five-bar gate. Such a simple easy thing to do and yet there is a little more to the story. Observe for instance the similarity of their poses or look to the differences, one dark, one light. See the walking stick. One single-breasted suit and one double-breasted suit. Think of all that diagonal relaxation, for only the picture behind is symmetrical. This really is a very charming picture.

27

REST

28

3. Double page from *Side by Side* by Gilbert and George, London, 1971.

4. Double page from Jochen Gerz, *Die Beschreibung des Papiers*, Darmstadt, 1973.

4

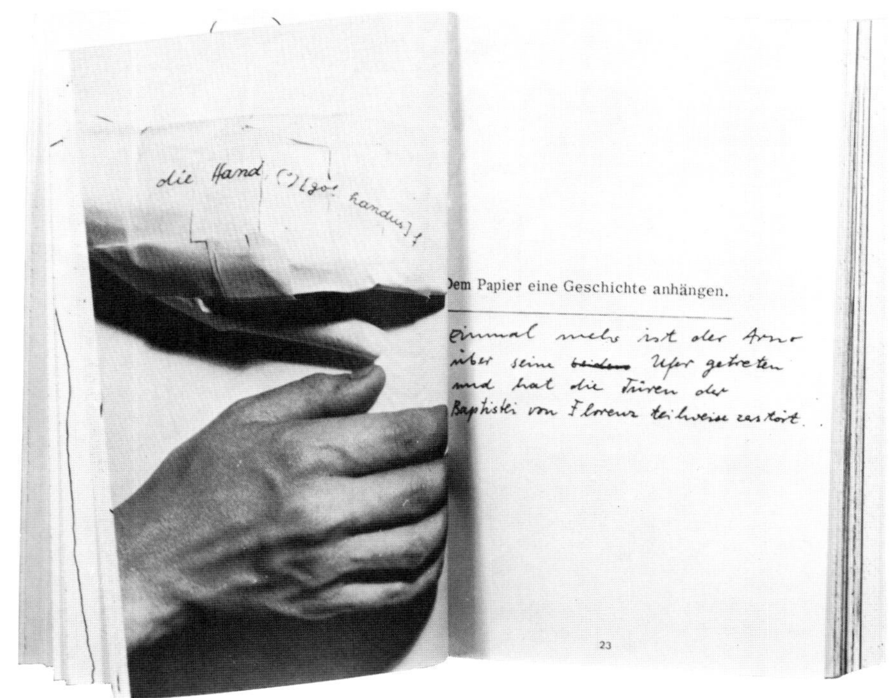

1. Page from a publication by Guy Lévis Mano, with poem by Paul Eluard and photographic illustration by Man Ray, Paris, 1935.

2. Double page from Pierre Lecuire, *Les Ballets-Minute*, Paris, 1954, with etchings by Nicolas de Staël.

form, and might almost be called its embodiment. Like William Morris a century ago, he sees it as a fine object put together from carefully chosen parts; he devises the signatures and the form and layout of each leaf, letter and picture. His books sometimes consist of letterpress alone, and yet Lecuire says: "I don't want my books to be read, but to be seen." Their meaning stems not only from the printed signs they contain, but also from the page material, from the layout, spacing and relationships. As if taking upon himself the project outlined by Mallarmé, Lecuire pursues his great venture in which different artists are invited to remake the image of the "Books" of Hercules Seghers, which Lecuire entitles "The Book of Books."

So here again, as in the Romantic period, are writers seized on by the image and by the image of their writing. They are drawn into it ever more deeply, to the point of no longer being able to distinguish the wheat of their literature from the chaff of typography. It is impossible to see Alain Robbe-Grillet and Marguerite Duras otherwise than as writer-plasticians. Michel Butor has written and theorized about this ambiguous position of the poet and novelist as prisoners of the image structures: "Painters teach me to see, to read, to compose, and therefore to write, to set out signs over a page. In the Far East calligraphy has always been considered as the necessary communication between painting and poetry. Today we have the arrangement of the book... I am not interested in having a mere juxtaposition or what is usually called an illustration. It has got to be more than that, there has got to be something which passes over from the text into the print and vice versa. The two of them have got to act upon each other." Butor regrets that, for reasons of productivity and economy, modern printing techniques should have yielded a growing standardization of forms, when they might have facilitated this break-up of genres and a diversification of writing and layout. In fact the two phenomena are at once opposed and proportional. It is true that the book trade looks to technical progress only for longer print-runs and lower costs and continues to produce more and more books with compartmentalized illustrations; but

1

2

3

1. A book object by Pierre Alechinsky, *Le Bleu des fonds*, by Joyce Mansour, Paris, 1968.

2. Christian Dotremont, Cry Out Harmony and Sing Out Chaos, pen and ink drawing, 1970.

3. Double page from Jean Dubuffet, *La Botte à nique*, Skira, Geneva, 1973.

at the same time advertising and journalism, as also the *livre d'artiste*, contrive to "break up" these new technologies and make them yield a maximum of significant effects. One might say that the more the illustrated book is vulgarized and becomes a symbol of our culture, the more it is exploited as such by artists who make it the subject of their work.

For some years now there has been a rising output in this field. The recent trend of the *livre d'artiste* came before the public about 1974, chiefly in Germany and Italy, at the Venice Biennale and the Kassel Dokumenta. There had been some direct precedents, most clearly in the work of Jean Dubuffet. The latter, at once artist, designer, writer and theorist, taking inspiration from the breakdown of barriers between writing and picturing spontaneously achieved in Art Brut (the art of madmen, children, misfits, outsiders, naives, etc.), has often given his graphic work a form subversive of the book: scrolls, folders, handwritten texts in naive language, marks taken from walls and used as images (*Phenomena Suite*) and so on. One thinks too of the vogue of the object-book in which the reified text (cassette-recorded, plastified, etc.) was given with an object or a set of symbolic objects, as in Marcel Duchamp's *Valise*.

The *livre d'artiste* shows an undiminished vitality today, reflecting the preoccupation of conceptual art. It is a sculpture, wood, metal and other materials going into its make-up. It is a testimony of performances, a sheaf of affidavits and photographs. It is a symbol of the book, left quite blank or wrapped up in adhesive tape. It is an artist's notebook containing jottings, sketches, diary notes. It is a symbol of the text, made up of dottings, traces, marks, holes. It may be a unique copy, handwritten, illuminated, carved; or it may be printed off profusely on newsprint or photocopied. If the *livre d'artiste* is so rich today, it is because the name in fact covers a multiplicity of very different works. Yet this diversity has one thing in common: its expressive power as a place of convergence of inspirations amounting to an absolute, virtually obsessional symbol of the book as transfigured by the artist's hand.

Sonia Delaunay's "Prose du Transsibérien"

1

PROSE DU TRANSSIBÉRIEN ET DE LA PETITE Jeanne DE FRANCE
REPRESENTATION Synchrome
PEINTURE Simultané TEXTE
Mme Delaunay-Terk BLAISE CENDRARS

Apart from a few historical precedents like the work of William Blake, *La Prose du Transsibérien* stands out as one of the very first attempts by an artist to treat the book in itself as an object of reflection and creation, taken in its totality as support, text and image. The text was a poem by Blaise Cendrars. What Sonia Delaunay set out to do was, not to illustrate it, but (to use the neat expression of Cendrars himself) to "soak it in light," to materialize it in a graphic object which in the end was not a book but a fold-out some seven feet long, made up of four pasted sheets. Typographically, it was a highly original composition, with a dozen different type-faces set out like a picture. It amounted to a "simultaneous" vision of large colour areas bathing the text and so executed as to be reproducible by stencils. This astonishing book was meant to be issued in an edition of 8 copies on vellum, 28 on Japan paper and 114 on imitation Japan. In the end, only 60 copies were illuminated by stencilling. Blaise Cendrars had met Sonia and Robert Delaunay in late 1912 and begun working on this project in 1913, when he sent Sonia an initial version of the poem. Sonia Delaunay then made some studies and designs, the key idea behind them being a simultaneous conjunction of painting and text; and a prospectus was issued in September 1913. Though not published till November, the book was reviewed by André Salmon on 11 October in the Paris daily *Gil Blas*: "Presumably it was the peculiarities of the text that called for so original a commentary from the illustrator." To this, Cendrars and Sonia Delaunay wrote an answer, explaining the originality of their approach, in relation to the calligrams and other typographical compositions of Apollinaire and the Futurists: "The simultaneism of this book lies in its simultaneous and non-illustrative presentation. The simultaneous contrasts of colours and texts open up depths and movements which are the new inspiration." ■

2

Max Ernst, The Hundred Headless Woman Opens Her August Sleeve, 1929. Collage for La Femme 100 Têtes.

Melolonthae hae vulgares
Nobis sunt familiares.

Mense Maio milia
Susurrant per folia.

Max et Moritz quassaverunt.
Melolonthae ceciderunt.

melolontha vulgaris = zoolg. Name des Maikäfers

34

Nunc curiose colliguntur,
Tum papyro involvuntur,

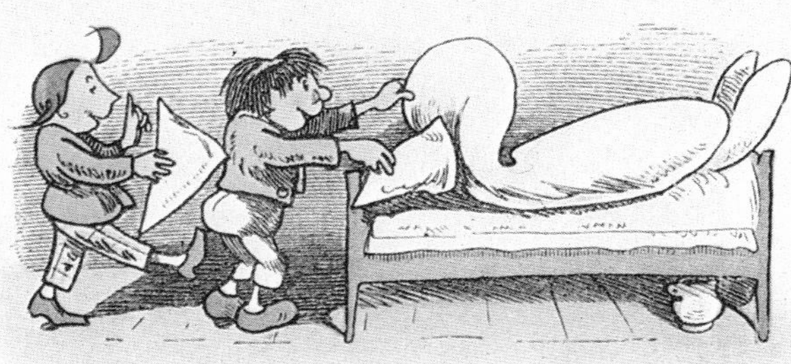

Quas immittunt scelerati
In cubiculum cognati.

papyrus = Papier(-Staude)

35 3*

FROM CHILDREN'S BOOKS TO COMIC STRIPS

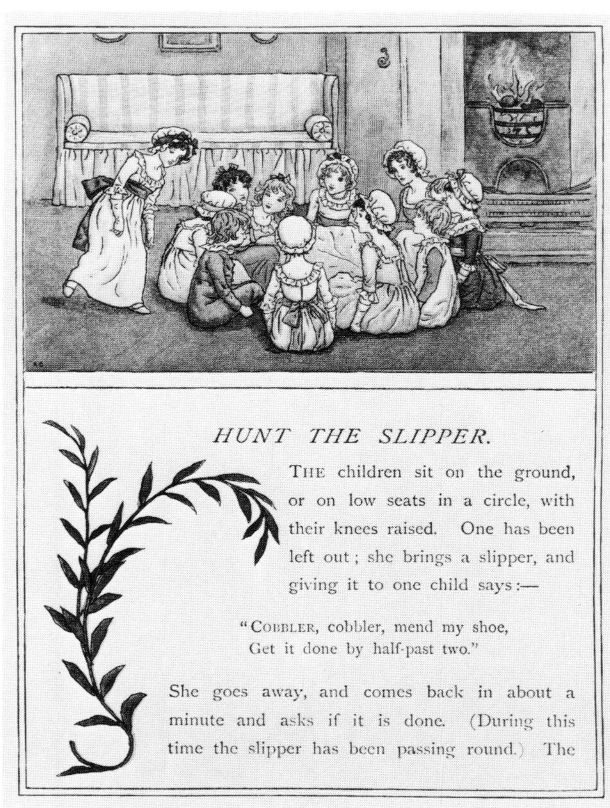

HUNT THE SLIPPER.

THE children sit on the ground, or on low seats in a circle, with their knees raised. One has been left out; she brings a slipper, and giving it to one child says:—

"COBBLER, cobbler, mend my shoe,
Get it done by half-past two."

She goes away, and comes back in about a minute and asks if it is done. (During this time the slipper has been passing round.) The

▲ Illustration by Kate Greenaway for *Book of Games*, London, 1889.

◀ Illustrations by Wilhelm Busch for *Max und Moritz, Eine Bubengeschichte in sieben Streichen*, 1865.

Children's literature, as distinct from primers and schoolbooks, was one of the points of least resistance in the front which language opposed to pictures: here the image easily made its inroads. This literature, in the nineteenth century, became an open field for the early diffusion of our system of knowledge and production, and the children's book was the intruder into this system. This can be seen clearly when one considers the two times and places where it flowered most remarkably: England during the Industrial Revolution, between 1740 and 1820, and the United States in the late nineteenth century. In England it benefited from the spread of private education, adapted to the needs of a middle class intent on utility and efficiency. From about the middle of the eighteenth century, publishers like John Newbery began specializing in illustrated books for children. Their origin goes back to the first children's adaptation of Aesop's *Fables* in 1692, one year before John Locke's *Some Thoughts Concerning Education.* Locke's little book went through nineteen editions up to 1761, when the famous *Tom Telescope* was published, a compilation of Locke's and Newton's views for the use of children. But well before this typical product of the age, several classics had appeared in England which were to fire the imagination of illustrators: *Robinson Crusoe* (1719), *Tom Thumb* (1721) and *Gulliver's Travels* (1726). After his *Little Pretty Pocket-Book* (1744), Newbery's list grew steadily, culminating about 1810 in his library of halfpenny books—at a time when France had gone no further than the *image d'Epinal.* But at its beginnings the *image d'Epinal* was intended for illiterate adults. The publishing of books for children called for the prior organization by adults of a market for children's products, such as costumes and toys. In their wake came the illustrated book, whose appeal extended even down to the lower middle classes. From England the fashion for such books spread to Boston, New York and Philadelphia, where schooling of a practical and accelerated kind, thought of as an economic necessity, was much more developed and less controlled than in Europe, and untrammelled by traditions.

In France too, as soon as the industrial production of books got underway, pictures invaded books destined for young people and made the fortune of big publishers like Hachette and Hetzel. By the mid-nineteenth century the Countess of Ségur's famous children's stories were issued

in the Bibliothèque Rose, illustrated by Gustave Doré, Bertall and Castelli, while Hetzel published Jules Verne illustrated by Férat, Bennet and Riou, in a series called "Magasin d'Education et de Récréation." These early illustrations of children's fiction left so strong a mark on the French imagination that "illustration," in France, automatically brings to mind these at once accurate and fantastic scenes which gave an echo of the marvellous to stories which, nevertheless, they faithfully reflected. For the distinctive thing about these pictures is their seriousness: the black and white gravity of the wood engraving, subtitled with a sober caption taken from the text. Child psychology was not then a matter of any great study. Children were not thought to require any specific style; Gustave Doré illustrated Perrault's fairy tales in the same style that he used for Dante and the Bible. Hence perhaps the evocative power of these pictures. It was not till the late nineteenth century, under the influence of historicizing styles (Pre-Raphaelites, Nazarenes), that English and German illustrators devised a style in which grown-ups could dream of childhood. Such in particular was the English school of Kate Greenaway, Randolph Caldecott and Walter Crane, followed in America by Howard Pyle. Line and colour here are idealized, while some German artists like Heinrich Hoffmann and Wilhelm Busch pointedly adopted a distorted line to suggest the light-heartedness of a puppet theatre or to imitate the style of children's drawings. In the early twentieth century the fairy-like illustrations of Arthur Rackham reached a degree of sophistication which at least made him very popular with grown-ups.

Frontispiece and title page of Kate Greenaway, *A Day in a Child's Life*, London, 1881.

Cover of Randolph Caldecott, *Sing a Song for Sixpence*, London, 1880.

HE found a door in a wall; but it was locked, and there was no room for a fat little rabbit to squeeze underneath.

An old mouse was running in and out over the stone door-step, carrying peas and beans to her family in the wood. Peter asked her the way to the gate, but she had such a large pea in her mouth that she could not answer. She only shook her head at him. Peter began to cry.

44

45

Double page from Beatrix Potter, *The Tale of Peter Rabbit*, London, n.d. (1902).

Double page from Maurice Boutet de Monvel, *Filles et Garçons*, Paris, 1900.

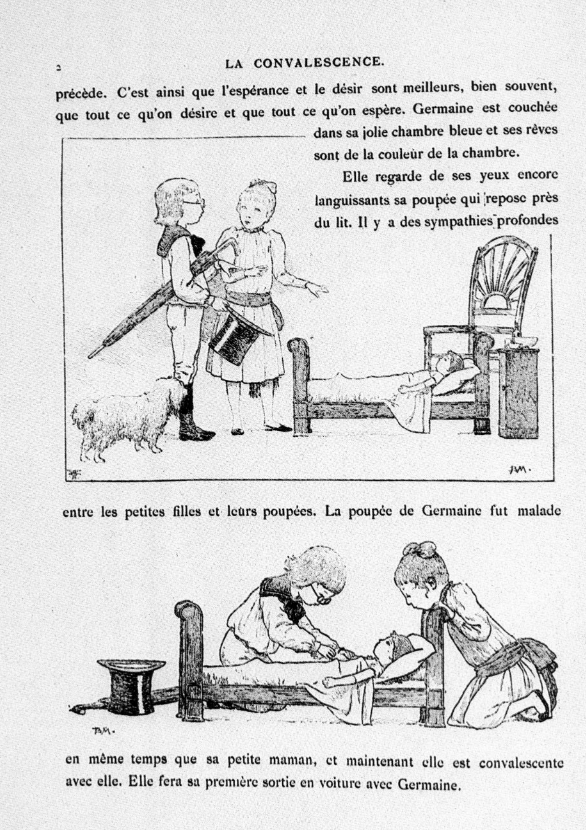

2 LA CONVALESCENCE.

précède. C'est ainsi que l'espérance et le désir sont meilleurs, bien souvent, que tout ce qu'on désire et que tout ce qu'on espère. Germaine est couchée dans sa jolie chambre bleue et ses rèves sont de la couleür de la chambre.

Elle regarde de ses yeux encore languissants sa poupée qui repose près du lit. Il y a des sympathies profondes entre les petites filles et leürs poupées. La poupée de Germaine fut malade en même temps que sa petite maman, et maintenant elle est convalescente avec elle. Elle fera sa première sortie en voiture avec Germaine.

LUCIE EST LA MEILLEURE DES SŒURS. PENDANT LES NEUF JOURS QU'A DURÉ LA MALADIE DE GERMAINE, LUCIE EST VENUE ÉTUDIER SES LEÇONS ET COUDRE DANS LA CHAMBRE BLEUE. ELLE A VOULU APPORTER ELLE-MÊME LA TISANE A LA PETITE MALADE.

From *Histoire de Mr. Jabot* by Rodolphe Toepffer, Geneva, 1833.

From *La Famille Fenouillard* by Christophe, published in *Le Petit Français Illustré*, Paris, from 1889 on.

Où l'on se retrouve.

Qu'ont donc mesdemoiselles Artémise et Cunégonde? Pourquoi leurs intelligentes figures expriment-elles un amer dégoût? Pourquoi ces intéressantes personnes, d'ordinaire si gracieuses, semblent-elles deux oies errant à l'aventure? C'est qu'elles éprouvent encore quelques révoltes d'estomac. Mais le devoir les appelle ! et, surmontant les défaillances de la nature, elles vont au poste réclamer leur famille.

Le commissaire. — Monsieur ! nous vous rendons à votre famille éplorée, mais tenez-vous prêt à répondre au premier appel... Quel exemple ! monsieur, vous donnez à vos jeunes filles !

Madame Fenouillard (dans un coin). — Qu'est-ce que vous faites là, mes filles?

Ces demoiselles. — Rien, maman, nous sommes malades !

Madame Fenouillard. — Pauvres petites, c'est l'émotion.

Libre, M. Fenouillard, homme têtu, revient à sa première idée, qui est de visiter un transatlantique. Oui, mais le tout est d'y pénétrer : ce qui n'est pas très commode quand on est obligé de passer sur une planche étroite et oscillante. M. Fenouillard s'en est bien tiré. « J'ai le pied marin », dit-il. Quant à ces demoiselles, prises du vertige à moitié chemin, elles restent en panne et y seraient peut-être encore si l'on n'était venu à leur aide.

Madame Fenouillard, ayant déclaré que « ni pour or ni pour argent elle ne se résoudra à prendre un pareil chemin, bon tout au plus pour des poules ou des chèvres », et M. Fenouillard ayant dépensé inutilement sa salive et son éloquence pour lui faire modifier son opinion, on se voit contraint d'employer les moyens perfectionnés de la mécanique moderne pour hisser à bord la mère d'Artémise et de Cunégonde.

Madame Fenouillard commence à craindre que la mécanique moderne soit par trop perfectionnée; mais les marins savent manier les colis : le mouvement ascensionnel ayant pris fin, madame Fenouillard se sent entraînée dans le sens horizontal. Puis un mouvement de descente s'opère et la mère d'Artémise est mollement déposée aux pieds de Cunégonde. M. Fenouillard admire les ressources et le moelleux de la mécanique moderne.

Là-bas, dit M. Fenouillard, c'est le gaillard d'arrière; ici, le gaillard d'avant ! Tiens ! qu'est-ce que ce trou pratiqué dans le pont sur le gaillard du milieu ?... Accourez, j'ai découvert la machine à vapeur... Mes filles, cette grosse barre de fer ça s'appelle la *bielle.* Cette grande roue s'appelle un *volant.* — Papa, est-ce qu'on ne peut pas voir de plus près ? — Si fait ! mes filles : qui m'aime me suive !

— 28 —

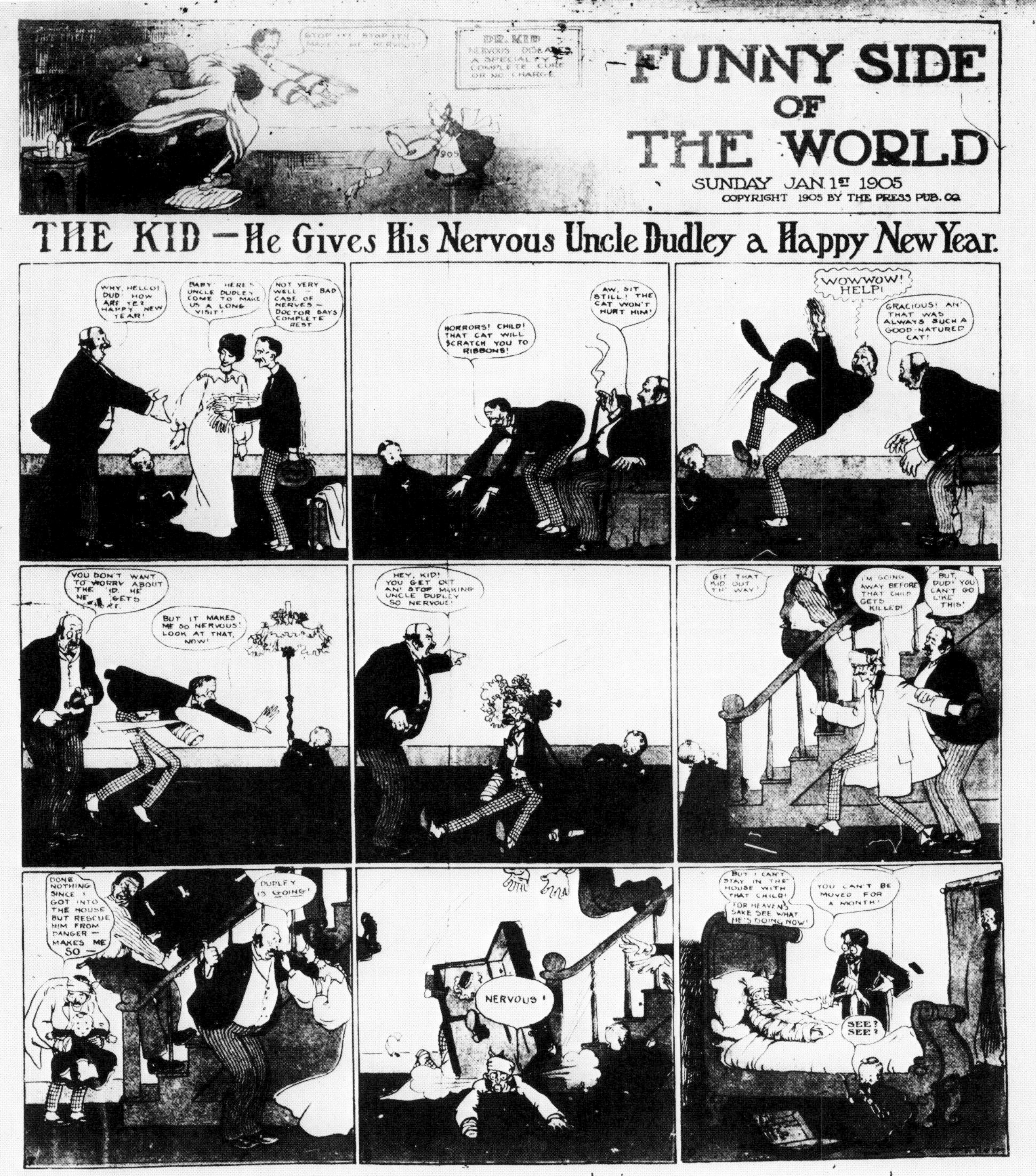

First appearance of R.F. Outcault's Yellow Kid in the *New York World*, January 1, 1905.

It was in the United States, chiefly in the periodical press, that children's illustration found its true dimension, in a superabundant production of pictorial papers which, from there, have now invaded the whole world. There were of course precedents, and comic strips originated in Europe, with what Rodolphe Toepffer called "literature in pictures," for Toepffer himself was first and foremost a writer. It seems an exaggeration to say that "Toepffer in fact invented a dead-born genre, different from the comic strip but anticipating its essence: a written and pictured story" (A. Rey). For Toepffer had translators, like Cham, who engraved his own books on wood blocks; he had plagiarists, like Cham again or Henri Emy; he had imitators, like Gustave Doré and his *Labours of Hercules* (1847), and one can easily follow the evolution of the genre by way of the drawings of Caran d'Ache or Wilhelm Busch, down to *La Famille Fenouillard* published by Christophe in *Le Petit Français Illustré* (from 1889). But it is certain that the originality of the comic strip lies in the inclusion of the text in the picture, thus giving the latter an overall, self-contained value, like a poster.

This inclusion was the work of American cartoonists, who deferred less to the written word than Europeans. It is significant that many French publishers were hostile to the "bubbles of text," and in diffusing American comics they at first reset the text outside the picture. These bubbles radically changed the notion of writing, for they are not in fact literature but a figured representation of the voice. This is quite clear in the early American cartoons, like Richard Outcault's *Yellow Kid*, which began appearing in the *New York World* in 1905, and even more in its rival the *Katzenjammer Kids* of Rudolph Dirks, where the words spoken by the characters are spelled phonetically, with all the looseness of popular American speech. The captions here are usually kept within the frame, forming a coherent whole with the picture either by means of bubbles or of onomatopoeic phrases expressly represented in the very heart of the picture, like concrete objects. So in this respect the incunables of the genre are not the works of Georges Colomb (Christophe) nor even *Bécassine* created in 1905 in the first number of *La Semaine de Suzette*, but perhaps *Les Pieds Nickelés* of Louis Forton in *L'Epatant* (No. 9, 9 April 1908). In the United States, where as with Forton the emphasis lay on popular speech and ways, the battle between the two great magnates of the press, Hearst and Pulitzer, had swept away at one blow the traditional barriers between text and picture as each was intent on reaching the widest possible audience. These early comics were aimed at a public of non-readers, not only at children. Since then America has set the pace, with the generation of Walt Disney first of all, who in 1928 invented Mickey Mouse and followed him up with innumerable animated cartoon creatures, sometimes used for overtly political purposes (as in a Chilean adaptation where the two unlovely crows are called Marx and Engels!); then with the generation of *Mad* in 1955, which launched the vogue of comics for adults, giving rise to a multitude of cartoon books sold in stations, barracks and prisons, and taken over as a postwar speciality by Italian printers who flooded the market with erotic, science fiction and horror comics. America set the pace, but the whole world capitalized on them, unabashedly taking them over and adapting them (except for the USSR, where comics are officially banned). Thus the Franco-Belgian cartoons of *Tintin* (1946), *Lucky Luke* (1947) and *Pilote* (1959), and for adults *Hara Kiri* (1960), triumphantly resisted the invasion of American cartoons organized by the Opera Mundi agency from 1930 on. Chinese comics, glorifying the revolution and proletarian values, are a remarkable social phenomenon in themselves, of noteworthy scope. The Italians too, with their sentimental photo-novels and parodies of westerns, have carved out a world market for themselves.

The cartoon landscape today is as vast and complex as the international political scene: one need do no more than scratch the surface to find the same values at stake. Comics open up a communications channel that works everywhere, being equally well adapted to the semiliterate public of the industrial countries and of the developing countries. Language is swallowed up by pictures and its role is secondary.

Yet language here, as in the poster, holds on; it even appears to be indispensable, judging by the spate of words in some comics and the total absence of any that are wordless. Comics, the most widespread and most radical mode of illustration of our time, are exactly contemporary with the cinema, with which indeed they are closely connected. The striking thing is that they are not an early form of cinema and that they were not superseded by films, despite the many adaptations as animated cartoons and the ever more abundant production of TV series. Comics were at the start and remain, against all comers, an independent medium of expression which, in contrast with the sound image of moving pictures, asserts and maintains intact the prestige of the written word and the static picture.

Envelope from Folon, Paris, to Giorgio Soavi, Milan, posted on 6 October 1967.

The Giant Sequoia

In volume of total wood, the giant sequoia *(Sequoiadendron giganteum)* stands alone as the largest living thing on Earth. One tree lives longer; one has a greater diameter. Three others grow taller. None is larger.

The age of the General Sherman tree, the largest of the sequoias, is estimated at 2,200 years. Coring devices used to date trees do not reach this big sequoia's heart. There is no record of a sequoia ever having lived more than 3,200 years. Some other statistics on the General Sherman: Estimated weight of trunk, 1,256 metric tons (1,385 tons); height above base 83.8 meters (274.9 feet); circumference at ground, 31.3 meters (102.6 feet); and diameter of largest branch, 2.1 meters (6.8 feet). Few records show mature sequoias ever having died from disease or insect attack. They usually die of toppling.

To appreciate the size of the General Sherman at Giant Forest and the General Grant tree at Grant Grove is difficult because neighboring trees are so large. The diameters of these trees at their bases exceed the width of many city streets.

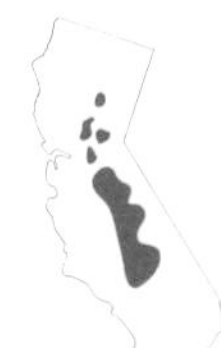

Range
The giant sequoia's early ancestors ranged over the entire Northern Hemisphere. As climate changed the giants retreated. Their natural range is now restricted to the western slope of California's Sierra Nevada, a strip about 580 kilometers (360 miles) long and 100-130 kilometers (60-80 miles) wide.

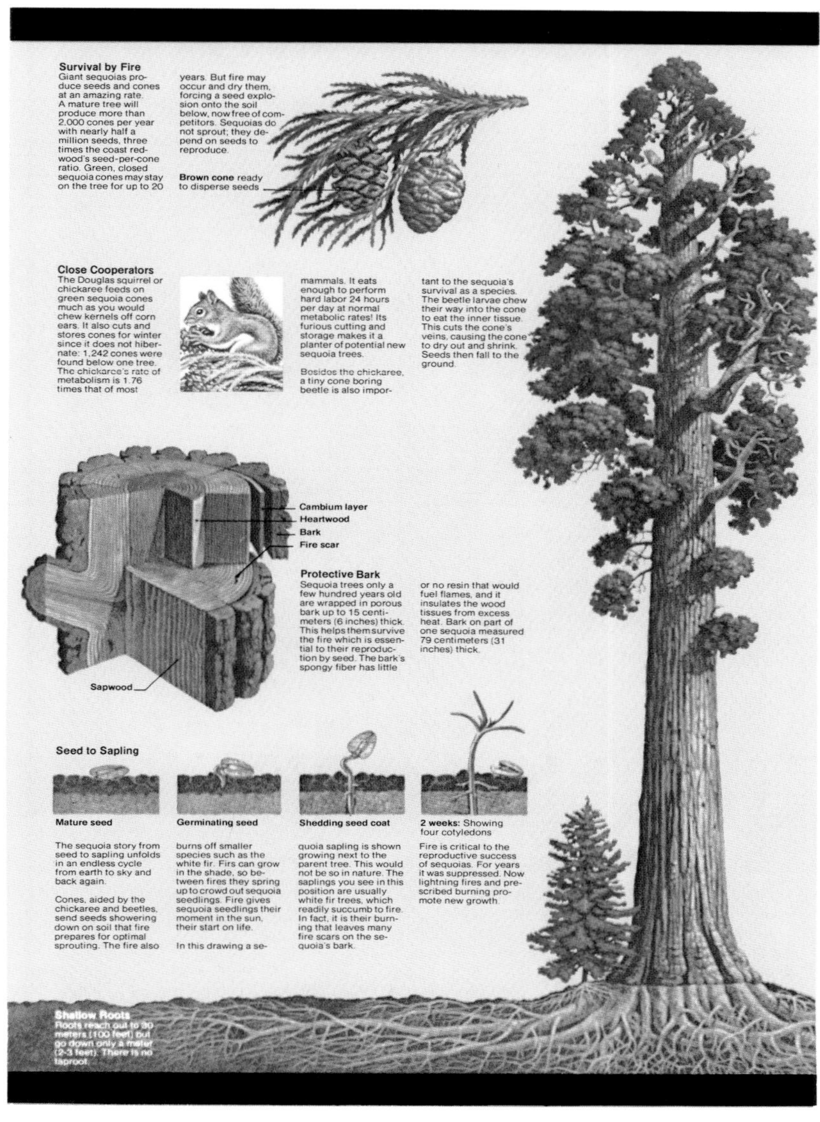

Publicity folder for
The National Park Service, California,
by Massimo Vignelli.

What is happening around us is not a change-over from written to audiovisual media of communications, but an overlapping of all known media, each being stimulated by and interacting with the others. From this complex phenomenon has arisen a new type of illustrator, the graphic designer. At home in every field, in advertising, in news reporting, in entertainment, he turns his hand not only to comic strips and children's books, but also to packaging, posters, covers, jackets, labels, ads, ornaments, etc.

One of the first of these versatile modern designers was Benjamin Rabier in France, who designed the now classic cheese-box image of *La Vache qui rit* (The Grinning Cow) and many publicity items, as well as cartoons, games, schoolbooks, and gadgets: Rabier, together with Emile Cohl, was a precursor of the animated cartoon (1908). From him, Walt Disney took over and gave to comics an industrial dimension.

Today the extraordinary interaction between different types of illustration has become in its turn a medium of significance, exploited by versatile illustrators who make the most of all the ambiguities of the genre: Saul Steinberg, a master organizer of many-faceted drawings; Tomi Ungerer, as resourceful in the apparent artlessness of his children's albums as in the sadism of his drawings for grown-ups; or Folon, a maker of posters, cartoons, book illustrations and prints, and also an actor. These "men of pictures" (to use the expression coined by Albert Plecy on the model of "men of letters") are not to be measured by the yardstick of illustration, which they overshoot on all sides, except in so far as the written word is, and remains, an integral part of their work.

Perrault's "Fairy Tales"

1

HISTOIRES
OU
CONTES
DU TEMPS PASSE'.
Avec des Moralitez.
Par le Fils de Monsieur Perreault de l'Academie François.

Suivant la Copie,
à PARIS.

M. D. CC.

2

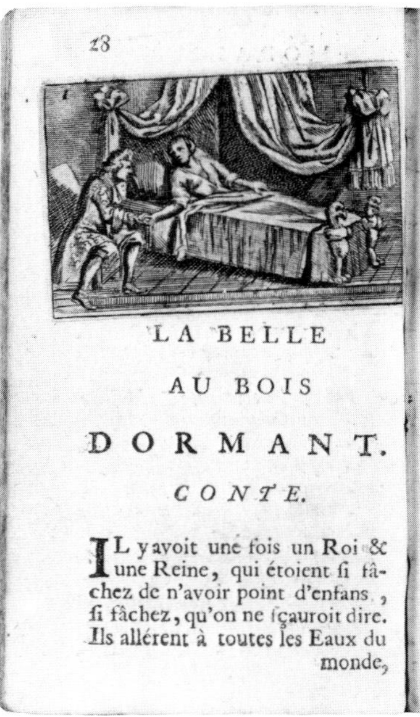

28

LA BELLE
AU BOIS
DORMANT.
CONTE.

IL y avoit une fois un Roi & une Reine, qui étoient si fâchez de n'avoir point d'enfans, si fâchez, qu'on ne sçauroit dire. Ils allérent à toutes les Eaux du monde,

au bois dormant. 29

monde, Vœux, Pélerinages, tout fut mis en œuvre, & rien n'y faisoit. Enfin pourtant la Reine devint grosse & accoucha d'une fille: on fit un beau Baptême; on donna pour Marraines à la petite Princesse toutes les Fées qu'on pût trouver dans le Païs (il s'en trouva sept,) afin que chacune d'elles lui faisant un don, comme c'étoit la coûtume des Fées en ce temps-là, la Princesse eut par ce moyen toutes les perfections imaginables. Après les Cérémonies du Baptême toute la Compagnie revint au Palais du Roi, où il y avoit un grand Festin pour les Fées. On mit devant chacune d'elles un couvert magnifique, avec un étui d'or massif, où il y avoit une cuiller, une fourchette, & un couteau de fin or, garni de diamans & de rubis. Mais comme chacun prenoit sa place à table, on vit entrer une vieille Fée qu'on

B 3 n'a-

3

1. *Frontispiece and title page of Perrault's "Mother Goose Stories," Paris, 1700.*
2. *Double page with headpiece of Perrault's "Sleeping Beauty," Amsterdam edition, 1721.*
3. *Illustration by Gustave Doré for "Sleeping Beauty," from Hetzel's edition of* Contes de Perrault, *Paris, 1862.*

The original French manuscript of the *Contes de ma mère l'Oye* ("Mother Goose Stories"), now in the Pierpont Morgan Library in New York, is already illustrated with seven anonymous gouaches. It contains four stories: *Sleeping Beauty, Little Red Riding Hood, Bluebeard* and *Tom Thumb.* The manuscript is dedicated to the Duchess Palatine Elisabeth Charlotte d'Orléans, sister-in-law of Louis XIV, a lady much respected for her wit and intelligence, and the dedication is signed "P. P." If this refers to Pierre Perrault, third son of the Academician Charles Perrault, he was then only sixteen years old, these stories having been written in 1695—no doubt by his father. They were not new or original, but tales handed down by the French oral tradition, now first given a literary form, and a definitive one, transmitted word for word to coming generations of children. They were also an inexhaustible source of illustrations, and indeed all the major illustrators felt called upon to try their hand at them. The anonymous gouaches of the original manuscript, very simple and straightforward, with an engaging touch of awkwardness, influenced the prints of the early illustrated editions. One of the earliest, of 1697, included a frontispiece and five full-page plates by a certain Clouzier, who merely copied the original gouaches, to which he added an engraved title reading as follows: *Histoires ou Contes du Temps passé, avec des moralités, par le fils de Monsieur Perrault de l'Académie Française, suivant la copie, à Paris.* One may infer from this that the original gouaches were also by Perrault (whether father or son) and originally intended to provide a model for the printed edition. The tales were translated into English in 1721 from an enlarged French edition again illustrated with prints copying the original gouaches. Since then, innumerable illustrated editions have appeared of these classic children's stories. One of the most famous is that published by Hetzel in 1862, illustrated by Gustave Doré with scenes at once so realistic and so fantastic that they remain a vivid memory for many children and grown-ups; another is the English edition of 1919 with Arthur Rackham's illustrations. ■

MAGAZINES AND REPORTING

LE MIROIR DU MONDE

6 Mai 1933 — 18, rue d'Enghien, Paris (10e) — Téléphone : Provence 15-21 — Le Numéro : 2 fr. 50

HITLER A FAIT DU 1er MAI BERLINOIS LA FÊTE NATIONALE DU TRAVAIL

Désireux d'accroître le prestige de son parti dans la classe ouvrière, le chancelier du Reich harangue les manifestants qui l'acclament.

▲ Cover of *Le Miroir du Monde*, Paris, 6 May 1933: "Hitler has made the First of May in Berlin the National Labour Holiday."

◀ Cover of *Vu*, Paris, 13 December 1933: "The coming war... friends and foes."

It is often assumed that the public at large calls for illustration. Judging by the press aimed at the working or the professional classes, so little or so poorly illustrated, this assumption seems unfounded. But the converse is true: illustration calls for a large public. Only a large print-run can bring a return on the expenses involved in the complex techniques of reproducing and printing pictures. Illustration therefore compelled the press, even more than the book trade, to appeal to a wide public. Now, in the last quarter of the twentieth century, the press has found in it a new meaning and dimension. Here, as in the poster and in certain fine art books, has occurred that reversal of forces in the relation between image and text, the latter gradually becoming subordinate to the former. But two obstacles had to be overcome in introducing pictures into newspapers: typography and censorship. There were two types of censorship based on a long tradition of suspicion and intolerance towards pictures. One was official censorship, which considered pictures more subversive than writing because the reader came more easily under their sway. This was the case in France when Louis-Philippe, called to the throne in 1830 to free the press, re-established censorship in 1835, but only for caricatures, on the ground that a caricature already amounted to an "act of violence," whereas a pamphlet was no more than a "violation of opinion." As if the caricaturist, over and above the picture, was attacking the model himself—a throwback to the primitive assimilation of the picture to the reality. The fight against censorship in France was a long and eventful one. In 1694 a man had been executed for representing Louis XIV fettered by his mistresses, and in 1832 Daumier was imprisoned. Liberalization only began with the revolution of 1848. But many pictures were banned by the censor during the Second Empire (1852-1870). It was not till 29 July 1881, with the Third Republic solidly established, that a law was passed guaranteeing freedom of expression in all its forms. Even this law, though genuinely democratic, left the censor free to act in the case of "immoral" pictures; so it is that Louis Legrand was convicted for an illustration entitled *Prostitution* published in *Le Courrier Français*. Still today, in the more serious French papers, there exists a self-censorship of pictures, reputedly less objective than for texts.

Technical obstacles also stood in the way of picture reproduction. Photography, for a long time, was difficult

L'ILLUSTRATION, 4 FÉVRIER 1854.

JOURNAL UNIVERSEL.

Ab. pour Paris, 3 mois, 9 fr. — 6 mois, 18 fr. — Un an, 36 fr. Prix de chaque N°, 75 c. — La collection mensuelle, br., 3 fr. N° 571. — VOL. XXIII. — Bureaux : rue Richelieu, 60. Ab. pour les dép. — 3 mois, 9 fr. — 6 mois, 18 fr. — Un an, 36 fr. Ab. pour l'étranger, — 10 fr. — 20 fr. — 40 fr.

SOMMAIRE.

Histoire de la semaine. — Courrier de Paris. — Chronique musicale. — La Saint-Vincent, fête des vignerons. — M. le capitaine d'état-major Monginot, à Constantinople. — Revue agricole. — L'Ame de la maison, nouvelle. — Excursion en Corse (suite et fin). — Causerie littéraire. — Vol d'un navire dans le grand Océan. — Costumes de Berne. — Revue scientifique. — Une question à l'ordre du jour. — Le couronnement de la Vierge, à Roubaix, etc., etc.

Gravures : Widdin. — Vue sous Kalafat. — Mad. Frezzolini. — La fête des vignerons, à Montreuil, près Paris. — Portrait de M. Monginot. — Un dessin de M. le capitaine Monginot. — Vue d'Ajaccio; forêt de chênes-lièges; laveuses dans le port d'Ajaccio; fontaine du Cours; marchande de figues, marchande de châtaignes, à Ajaccio. — Costumes de Berne : à la ville, à la campagne. — Le couronnement de la Vierge, peinture murale, à Roubaix. — Rebus.

Histoire de la semaine.

Viddin et Kalafat, situés à un quart de mille l'un de l'autre, en descendant le Danube sur la rive droite, ont été, du 15 au 20 janvier, le théâtre d'opérations dont le résultat paraît avoir été meurtrier de part et d'autre, sans avoir changé la position respective des deux armées opposées. Comme dans toutes les affaires de la guerre, tant qu'elles ne sont pas décisives, il faut rabattre, comme exagération, une bonne part des bulletins, et, si on veut absolument entendre le *Te Deum*, il faut se résigner à l'entendre deux fois. Ce n'est donc pas encore de l'histoire qui se publie sur les affai-

Widdin.

Vue sous Kalafat.

FRANK LESLIE'S ILLUSTRATED NEWSPAPER

NEW YORK — FOR THE WEEK ENDING FEBRUARY 18, 1888.

PENNSYLVANIA.—THE MINING TROUBLES IN THE SCHUYLKILL REGION—ATTACK ON THE COAL AND IRON POLICE BY A MOB OF POLISH STRIKERS, AT SHENANDOAH, FEBRUARY 3d.

FROM A SKETCH BY JOSEPH BECKER — SEE PAGE 7.

LESLIE'S WEEKLY

to combine with industrial printing. Gillot's process of "paniconography," for reducing lithographs to line blocks, was applied to photographs in *La Lumière* of 5 May 1855. But the line block here could give only a coarse rendering of the picture, and it took many years of experiment (1854-1880), by Berchtold, the Americans Frederick Ives and Stephen Horgan, and the Swede C.G.V. Carleman, to work out the half-tone process of reproducing the grey areas of a photograph. It is still imperfect and we are still living with it today. First used in the early 1880s in the United States, half-tone was taken up in France in the *Journal Illustré* (1 October 1886), for Nadar's photographic interview with the 100-year-old chemist Eugène Chevreul. This interview is memorable for the fact that it was also recorded by means of a new process invented by Charles Cros, so that it brought together three "firsts": sound recording, photographic reporting, and half-tone printing of a photograph on newsprint. About the same time, in Germany, Georg Meisenbach worked out a process of half-tone engraving which permitted photographs, by reducing the negative to a dotted screen, to be printed along with the letterpress; and such half-tone blocks were used, for example, in the *Illustrated London News* from 1885 onwards. It was this invention which led, in the 1890s, to the first photo-novels, which renewed the popular tradition of broadsheets and

LE NUMÉRO QUOTIDIEN 10 Cent.

DIMANCHE 2 AOUT 1914

EXCELSIOR

Journal Illustré Quotidien

Directeur : Pierre LAFITTE

88, Avenue des Champs-Élysées, PARIS

Informations - Littérature - Sciences - Arts - Sports - Théâtres - Élégances

LA FRANCE DÉCRÈTE LA MOBILISATION GÉNÉRALE

UNE MANIFESTATION PATRIOTIQUE A LA STATUE DE STRASBOURG

UN OFFICIER PORTÉ EN TRIOMPHE A LA GARE DE L'EST

LES PREMIÈRES AFFICHES DE MOBILISATION ONT ÉTÉ APPOSÉES HIER

Illustrirte Zeitung

Nr. 3600. 138. Bd. Leipzig, 27. Juni 1912.

Von der Kieler Woche 1912: Das gegenwärtig in Hamburg stationierte Zeppelin-Luftschiff „Viktoria Luise" begleitet die Regatta am 23. Juni auf der Kieler Förde.

Covers of illustrated magazines from 1850 to 1914.

romances. In Paris a "quality" newspaper like *L'Illustration* kept for a time to manual drawing after photographs and the first direct reproductions of photographs only began to appear in it in 1896. But already in the 1890s halftone was being used in American journals like *Collier's* and *Leslie's*. Shortly afterwards, the rotary printing press was introduced for the letterpress, and the problem of the quality of picture reproduction was raised anew—for it was always the pictures that were being sacrificed—until in 1910 the offset process permitted a lightening of the lead plate moulds which had become unbelievably heavy.

So in the United States and Europe one obstacle after another was overcome in the quest for efficient methods of printing drawings and photographs. The 1880s saw a renewal of the style of illustrated papers. They saw the rise of the American illustrated press, with, in 1876, the launching of *Puck*, the American counterpart (for a time) of the English *Punch*, followed by *The Judge* in October 1881 and *Life* in January 1883. The best-known pictorial weekly in the United States was *Harper's*, illustrated with wood engravings since the 1850s; in it Thomas Nast had made a remarkable career as a caricaturist from 1861 to 1886, and the satirical drawing was used with notable effectiveness in the pages of the *New York World* during the presidential election campaign of 1884. *Harper's* had a strong rival in *Frank Leslie's Illustrated Newspaper*.

The next generation of illustrated papers was that of rotogravure in the early 1900s. It was in Germany, in the *Freiburger Zeitung*, that in 1910 photographs were first printed from cylinders. It was quickly followed by the *New York Times*, the *Mid-Week Pictorial* and the *Berliner Illustrierte Zeitung*. This last, founded in 1890 by the editor Kurt Korff, began publishing in 1905 the work of photo-reporters like Erich Salomon and Felix H. Man. In France the publisher Pierre Lafitte, who already controlled some deluxe illustrated weeklies (like *Femina*, founded in 1901), launched in November 1910 a daily called *Excelsior*: profusely illustrated, it sold for 10 centimes and the first page was made up of a mosaic of photographs. From this period dates the spread of the photographic reportage and the first press agencies (the earliest photographs of the Meurisse Agency in France date from 1907). The first generation of photo-reporters included men like Kitrosser and Lucien Aigner.

The invention in 1907 of the telephotograph transmitted on the Belin system is a landmark in the history of illustration, for it opens the period of telecommunications whose later developments have been so spectacular. Here were the prerequisites for rapid and widespread news collecting, with pictures in the forefront: transmissible and transportable now, they had overcome their old handicap in relation to words.

1

2

A new generation of papers followed immediately after the First World War, with the *Münchner Illustrierte Presse,* run by the great "picture editor" Stefan Lorant; going into exile when Hitler came to power, he settled in London and there founded the *Weekly Illustrated* (1934) and, with Felix H. Man, the *Picture Post* (1938). The heyday of the photo-reporters came in the 1930s. They answered in fact to the demands of a new public—a very wide literate public, short of time (and often of money) and avid of cheap reading matter, and furthermore a public politicized by urbanization and the economic slump. The weekly magazine thus became, first of all in the United States, that banal product of prime necessity that one bought with one's groceries and leafed through at coffee time or while commuting to work. Pictures were the main attraction of such magazines. In November 1936 appeared the first number of *Life,* in 1937 the first number of *Look.* In France, on 28 March 1928, Lucien Vogel launched a weekly magazine with the revealing title of *Vu* ("Seen"): in its first year it published over three thousand photographs. The *USSR Under Construction* was published in Moscow in five languages from 1930 on, with constructivist layouts by El Lissitzky, Rodchenko and Stepanova. Then, in Nazi Germany, came Goebbels' paper called *Signal.* The status of the press photographer was assured. Salomon and Aigner were not originally professional photographers: the demand made them so. And henceforth the photographer, like the writer, signed his work, with signatures which are now famous, like that of André Kertesz. At the same time deluxe magazines like *L'Illustration* published "art photographs" by men like Emmanuel Sougez and Man Ray. The photographer stood on a par with the leading journalistic writers like Mac Orlan or Kessel. The page make-up recognized this, text and photos being treated on an equal footing (which all too often, in practice, meant with the same carelessness). Each number of magazines like *Vu* and *Life,* with editors like Vogel, Korff and Henry Luce, was focused on a photographic spread. Such was the case with another significantly named magazine, *Regards* ("Looking"), which from 1934 published the work of Robert Capa, David Seymour and Henri Cartier-Bresson. These three, with George Rodger, founded in 1947 an international picture co-operative called Magnum Photos: it confirmed the distinctive status won by the photo-journalist. The pictures he took were not only the record of a sensational event. They could also sum up a human or historical situation in the most telling and memorable way.

3

CETTE SEMAINE : Mme la Générale Weygand, André Maurois, de l'Académie française, le Comte Sforza, Léon-Paul Fargue, Luc Durtain, Fernand Gregh, Léon Werth, Georges de La Fouchardière

9e Année — N° 398 — "MARIANNE" 2 fr. 50 — Mercredi 5 Juin 1940

MARIANNE

L'HEBDOMADAIRE DE L'ÉLITE INTELLECTUELLE FRANÇAISE ET ÉTRANGÈRE

Rédaction, Administration : 44, avenue des Champs-Élysées (Élysées 49-26 et 27) — Publicité : 1, boulevard Haussmann (Provence 18-35 et 36)

Hitler historien

par le Comte SFORZA

L'OPPROBRE

(d'après Goya)

L'esprit et le cœur se refusent à accepter cette nouvelle.

C'est une trahison telle que l'histoire ne nous en donne pas d'exemple. C'est le sang allemand qui subitement s'est réveillé dans les veines du roi qui n'a plus de Belge que le nom.

Cette trahison était-elle préméditée, comme certaines circonstances permettaient de le supposer? Dans ce cas, ce qui reste inexplicable, c'est la stupidité de l'acte, stupidité égale à la bassesse.

Puisse l'armée belge ne pas suivre l'exemple abominable de celui qui fut un instant son chef par erreur. Le nom de Judas est encore trop beau pour qualifier un tel acte. Le Gouvernement belge par son attitude vient de sauver l'honneur du nom belge.

Maeterlinck

Carrefours de guerre

par Léon-Paul FARGUE

4

COMMENT
ILS
SONT TOMBÉS

LA GUERRE

Le jarret vif, la poitrine au vent, fusil au poing, ils dévalaient la pente couverte d'un chaume raide.. Soudain l'essor est brisé, une balle a sifflé — une balle fratricide — et leur sang est bu par la terre natale...

PHOTOS CAPA

N° 445 VU P. 1106

Lettre ouverte à PYRRHUS NON-INTERVENTIONNISTE 5

par André WURMSER

VOUS avez, cher Pyrrhus, dès la rébellion des généraux espagnols, formulé des vœux pour les Républicains — et préconisé leur désarmement par l'embargo sur les armes. A peine les avions de M. Mussolini tombaient-ils en Afrique du Nord que vous vous félicitiez du sang-froid de M. Delbos. Pour nous mieux accabler, vous avez baptisé ce bon tour et cette mauvaise politique de « non-intervention » et ceux qui refusaient de rompre avec le gouvernement régulier de l'Espagne d'interventionnistes, c'est-à-dire de bellicistes, et aussi de staliniens, et même d'énergumènes. Vous avez, hautement, proclamé votre sympathie envers ceux qui meurent pour la liberté du monde, puis, vous avez couru au plus pressé : vous avez protesté contre l'exécution de Zinoviev et — hier encore — rédigé une solennelle déclaration en faveur de ceux qui, en Catalogne, traitèrent la mobilisation de « trahison de la classe ouvrière » et suscitèrent ces troubles de Barcelone, qui ont coûté si cher à l'Espagne envahie.

Je vous ai rencontré plusieurs fois depuis que, pour la défense de la paix, nous ne nous rencontrons plus. Vous avez souri lorsque je vous ai dit : « La guerre que vous voulez éviter, Pyrrhus, est commencée, oui, la guerre que les fascismes se doivent de mener contre les démocraties, et cette guerre, je souhaite avant tout que les démocraties ne la perdent point! » « Allons donc! répondiez-vous, la guerre, cette guerilla! Mon cher, vous n'avez pas connu Verdun... » Et il était bien vrai que la guerre n'était pas encore la guerre totale qu'elle devient, lentement, sûrement. Comme elle n'était pas encore la guerre générale que peut-être elle deviendra — non-interventionnellement!

C'est que, cher Pyrrhus, nous ne sommes pas antifascistes de la même façon, vous et moi. Vous êtes antifasciste de cœur. Mais vous êtes plus intégralement pacifiste qu'antifasciste. Votre pacifisme est militant, et dussiez-vous déclancher demain un inéluctable cataclysme, vous refuseriez aujourd'hui d'en envisager l'éventualité. Votre pacifisme est militant. Votre antifascisme est platonique. Aussi bien êtes-vous moins antifasciste qu'anti-antifasciste. Vous avez moins peur, dans votre pacifisme intégralement aveugle, du fascisme que de notre refus du fascisme.

C'est pourquoi vous avez applaudi aux reculades de l'Europe démocratique; c'est pourquoi vous avez dénoncé, chaque fois que de nouveaux canons allemands débarquaient à Saint-Sébastien, chaque fois que de nouvelles troupes italiennes débarquaient à Cadix, le « bourrage de crâne » de la presse de gauche. Il n'est depuis un an qu'un acte contre la paix que vous ayez stigmatisé avec vigueur. Ce ne fut ni le bombardement d'Almeria, ni le discours de Mussolini (« ne les excitons pas, voyons! »), ce fut le cri d'alarme de « L'Œuvre » au sujet du Maroc espagnol. Car vous êtes vigilant, Pyrrhus, oh! combien vigilant!

Et votre politique aboutit à sa fin logique : les fascismes se moquent de vous — et de nous.

Vous voici victorieux... Pyrrhus!

◆◆

Que disions-nous, l'an passé? Que la rébellion n'avait été possible qu'avec le concours du fascisme international, que le général Sanjurjo revenait de Berlin, lorsqu'il s'envola de Lisbonne, que si nous hésitions à soutenir le gouvernement républicain, le gouvernement régulier de l'Espagne, les dangers de guerre se multiplieraient. Vous nous traitiez de déroulèdards. Il fallut, pour sauver Madrid, le discours de Maisky, à Londres, et que l'U. R. S. S. tînt parole. Aujourd'hui, M. Buré écrit : « J'ai été partisan de la non-intervention; je me demande si je ne me suis pas trompé. » Notre ami commun, Guéhenno, parle comme il se doit. Mais vous, Pyrrhus, vous, plus révolutionnaire que quiconque, quand prononcerez-vous votre « mea culpa »?

Que disions-nous l'an passé? La politique de non-intervention ne serait concevable qu'appliquée par tous, avec rigueur, mais comment espérer que le fascisme ne soutienne pas le mouvement qu'il a provoqué, si nous l'assurons qu'il ne court aucun risque à le faire? Ce n'est pas parce que les démocraties renonceront à leur solidarité que le fascime international perdra de sa virulence. Vous répondiez en nous accusant de manquer de confiance en Hitler; vous disiez : ce n'est pas question de confiance ou de méfiance... bien plutôt piquons-le d'honneur!

Nous disions : déplorable calcul que sacrifier l'Espagne à la paix du monde; le fascisme n'est pas un ogre dont la faim s'apaise; sacrifier l'Espagne, c'est perdre les chances de la démocratie française, et non sauver la paix. Vous répondiez : « Vous souhaitez la guerre, par haine du fascisme! »

Nous disions : quel terme fixer à ce jeu de dupes? Vous irez de reculade en rebuffade; chaque jour le danger s'accroît — et si vous devez un jour dire : non! ce non sera plus menaçant pour la paix qu'il ne l'eût été aujourd'hui... Vous répondiez : « Nous serons fermes, comptez-y. Il faut qu'aux yeux de tous les peuples le fascisme porte la responsabilité du conflit qu'il provoquerait. » Mais l'intervention ouverte, avouée, proclamée, de Mussolini vous laisse non-interventionniste. (Et quels moyens de faire entendre la vérité aux peuples asservis? Censure à Rome. Censure à Berlin. La presse allemande n'a pas publié les propositions franco-anglaises. Ceux qu'aveugle encore le hitlérisme ne savent rien, rien, rien.) Mais vous, votre logique linéaire vous satisfait, Pyrrhus : Chaque jour de paix, dites-vous, est une victoire sur la guerre. Ce qui serait vrai... si la guerre n'était commencée, Pyrrhus, encore que vous n'y participiez pas : désormais, chaque journée de guerre est une défaite de la paix. Sachez qu'en 1914, un quart d'heure avant le début des hostilités, il était trop tard pour éviter la guerre... une heure aussi... et deux jours... Dans toute agonie, un moment arrive — d'ailleurs indiscernable — où il est trop tard pour sauver le malade — ou la paix. Laisser venir ce moment, ce n'est pas « gagner du temps », c'est perdre la paix!

Lorsque nous disions : la politique qui mène à la guerre mondiale, c'est la vôtre, nous avions raison. La preuve en est faite!

Lorsque nous mettions le monde en garde contre une intervention de plus en plus grande des fascismes en Espagne, nous étions les vrais défenseurs de l'Espagne et de la démocratie.

Lorsque nous voulions interdire aux fascismes, alors que la défaite de Franco ne les eût pas compromis, de s'engager plus avant, nous étions les véritables frères des pacifistes allemands et italiens, nous étions les vrais défenseurs des peuples opprimés, qui ne se libéreront pas par l'apport de baïonnettes étrangères (nous sauvions la face au fascisme, peut-être, du moins nous sauvions la paix). Le vrai belliciste, le vrai aveugle, c'était vous, Pyrrhus.

Je suis sévère pour vous, qui êtes mon ami. Aussi, je veux ajouter que je vous sais de bonne foi. Non, Hitler ne vous paie pas. Pour qu'il vous paie **avant**, il faudrait que vous soyiez le traître que vous n'êtes pas; pour qu'il vous paie **après**, il faudrait qu'il ait le sens de l'ironie...

Que du moins cette affreuse année vous serve d'exemple. Soyez plus préoccupé de combattre la guerre — la guerre qui est là, à Bilbao, à Madrid — que nos alliés de la Paix, ou nos amis du Front Populaire. Et quand les assassins crient : « La parole est au canon! », ne soyez plus dupe de vos scrupules. Il ne s'agit pas de gagner le Paradis : il s'agit de ne pas perdre ce qui reste de liberté sur terre!

1. Cover of *Life*, New York, 23 November 1936.
2. Cover of *Weekly Illustrated*, London, 1930s.
3. Cover of *Marianne*, Paris, 5 June 1940, with photomontage by Marinus.

4.5. Robert Capa's famous Spanish Civil War photograph as published in two different layouts by *Vu* and *Regards*, Paris.

DIXIEME ANNEE. — N° 481. — JEUDI 1er JUIN 1933. — 18 pages, dont 4 pages humoristiques — Le numéro : 0 fr. 75

CANDIDE

Grand Hebdomadaire Parisien et Littéraire

18-20, rue du Saint-Gothard, XIVe

Il avait le jugement assez droit avec l'esprit le plus simple; c'est pour cette raison qu'on le nommait Candide. VOLTAIRE.

50% MOINS CHER A LA FABRIQUE
FAUTEUILS CUIR PATINÉ GRAND CONFORT FORMES NOUVELLES
DEPUIS... 175f
100 MODELES EN ATELIER
ASSISTEZ A LA FABRICATION
CONSTANT 62, RUE CHANZY PARIS - XIe
ROQ. 10-04. CATALOGUE C9 FRANCO SUR DEMANDE

L'ATELIER 75
SPECIALISTE DU MEUBLE MODERNE.
PRIX CRÉATION/ PRIX MODERÉS
DESSINS ET DEVIS GRACIEUSEMENT SUR DEMANDE
75 Bd du MONTPARNASSE. PARIS.

CEUX DE LA HAUTE

par DUBOUT

par DUBOUT

L'HERITAGE

— Le docteur prie ces messieurs, dames, de faire un peu moins de bruit. Monsieur le comte n'a pas encore rendu le dernier soupir.

— Deux heures de massage par jour ! Mon Dieu ! Si elle pouvait s'user !

— Et vous, Marquis. Jouez-vous au polo ?
— Presque. Je suis un fervent du croquet.

GRAND MARIAGE

— L'Académicien a l'air furieux.
— Parbleu ! Tout le monde le prend pour le suisse.

— Ce que j'admire, mon cher, c'est votre position à cheval.

VOIR LA SUITE PAGE DEUX

Rc 1085

THE NEW YORK TIMES, SATURDAY, JUNE 23, 1973

East Of the Ostpolitik

By C. L. Sulzberger

FOREIGN AFFAIRS

From the Bombmaster-General

By Russell Baker

OBSERVER

A Classmate Remembers...

By Kenneth Schlossberg

...And Others Share Their Later Thoughts on Mr. Buchanan

Cover of *Candide*, Paris, 1 June 1933, with drawings by Dubout: "Ceux de la haute" (The Upper Crust).

Cover of *Simplicissimus*, Stuttgart, 29 April 1929, with drawing by Karl Arnold: "Dawes Plan: Capital clamours for interest–so that was the rightful cause we died for."

Page from *The New York Times*, June 1973, with a Watergate drawing by Brad Holland.

The photograph by no means ousted the drawing or cartoon, which adapted itself to this new public and, becoming linear, to the rotary press. Thus arose a style which brought a radical change over the press cartoon. The taste for such comic or satirical drawings, commenting on current events or politics, spread through the press of Europe and the United States. In France *Le Rire* and *L'Assiette au Beurre* were followed during the First World War by *La Baïonnette*, which featured young illustrators like Gus Bofa, Falké and Vertès; then in 1915 by *Le Canard enchaîné*, with drawings by H. P. Gassier. The press cartoonist was not only a good artist, he was a picture writer, a man of ideas and, like Jean Effel, a poet. *The New Yorker*, with James Thurber and Charles Addams, set a new standard of humour and point. A comparable virtuoso in France was Dubout, whose cartoons are as significant of the age as Charlie Chaplin or Kafka, an age with a new sense of self-awareness and a new sense of anxiety.

This progressively less anecdotal conception of the press picture, whether photograph or cartoon, was fortified by the rise of the cinema news reel, then by television news broadcasts: it was there, on the screen, that the "brute image," direct and unvarnished, found its true place. It was left for the settled, considered image to single out and comment on events like an editorial. It did so with renewed effectiveness. Already in 1934 the French magazine *Marianne* had devoted its front page to a symbolic picture. In 1950, as a counterweight and comment to the editorial page, the *New York Times* introduced a cartoon in which all the great cartoonists were able to give their symbolic interpretation of topical events and social changes.

Today's photo-reporter, unless he has already gone over to television, seeks not so much the sensational as the symbolic image through which each reader may recognize his own idea and picture of the world.

Photomontage

1. *Lonely Metropolitan, photomontage by Herbert Bayer, 1932.*
2. *Never again!, photomontage by John Heartfield for the* Arbeiter Illustrierte Zeitung, *Berlin, 1932.*
3. *Goebbels, Hitler and Goering walking the Tightrope, photomontage by Marinus for* Marianne, *Paris, 3 April 1940.*
4. *Bonaparte to Hitler, Ribbentrop, Stalin and Goering: "Gentlemen, you're just a bunch of ninnies, and I don't mind telling you so," photomontage by Marinus for* Marianne, *Paris, 24 January 1940.*

1

2

Alongside the collages of the Surrealists, photographers took to piecing together fragments of pre-existing photographs, giving the combination some unity of theme or idea and reprinting it as an original whole: this was the photomontage. While the collage was usually a poetic evocation devised for artistic purposes, the photomontage was generally topical and political: it was like an allegory of the modern world, each element of it corresponding to actual facts. Developing out of journalism, it found its outlet in the photo-reporting magazines of the interwar years, like *Vu* in Paris, which in February 1931 published "The Coming War," a photomontage by A. Noël, then, in its special number of March 1933, a whole set of photomontages on the theme "End of a Civilization." To obtain a result uniform in subject and pictorially effective, great skill was needed with scissors, tonal transitions and retouching in gouache. The fresco-like image thus created out of disparate elements could convey a symbolic or premonitory message of great power. Another French magazine, *Marianne,* also made imaginative use of the photomontage to sum up the topical idea or trend of the week, as in a kind of pictured editorial. In its brief existence, from 1932 to 1940, it published over two hundred of them on its front page: all were the work of the Danish artist Marinus.

But the acknowledged master of the political photomontage was John Heartfield in Germany: his first, published on 4 August 1924, was followed by many others in communist periodicals waging a bitter campaign against Nazis and Social Democrats. The photomontage thus became a formidable satirical weapon, combining the techniques of caricature (symbolic attributes, grotesque situations) with those of photography. With Heartfield, it reached a disturbing degree of violence, acceptable only to the extreme left-wing press. Aragon paid tribute to his work in a lecture, "John Heartfield and Revolutionary Beauty," given on 2 May 1935 at the Maison de la Culture in Paris: "He speaks," said Aragon, "for the enormous host of the oppressed all over the world." Heartfield did indeed create a highly original art of his own, committed and militant, such as had not been seen since Daumier. ■

3

4

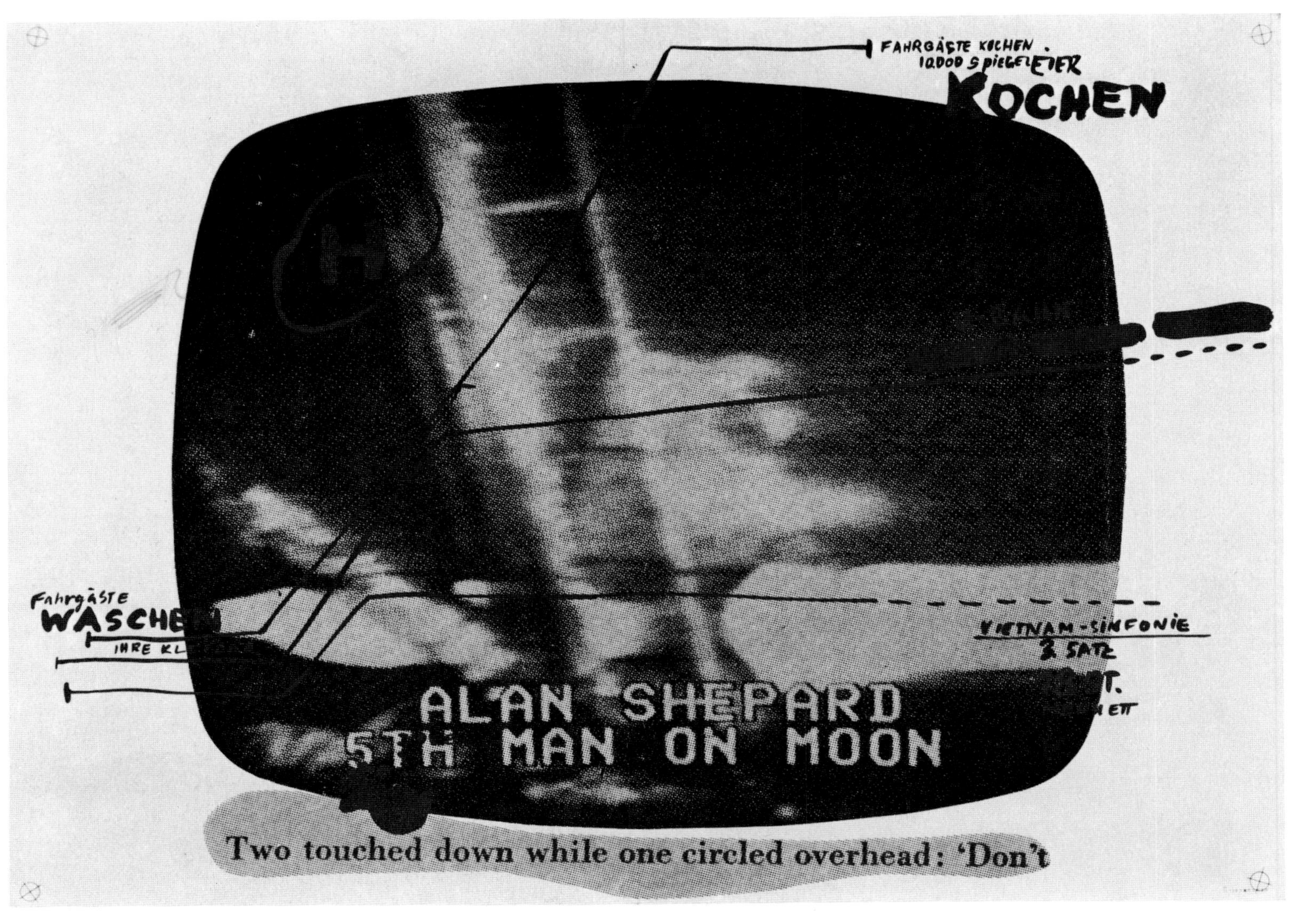
FAHRGÄSTE KOCHEN
KOCHEN
Fahrgäste
WASCHEN
VIETNAM-SINFONIE
ALAN SHEPARD
5TH MAN ON MOON
Two touched down while one circled overhead: 'Don't

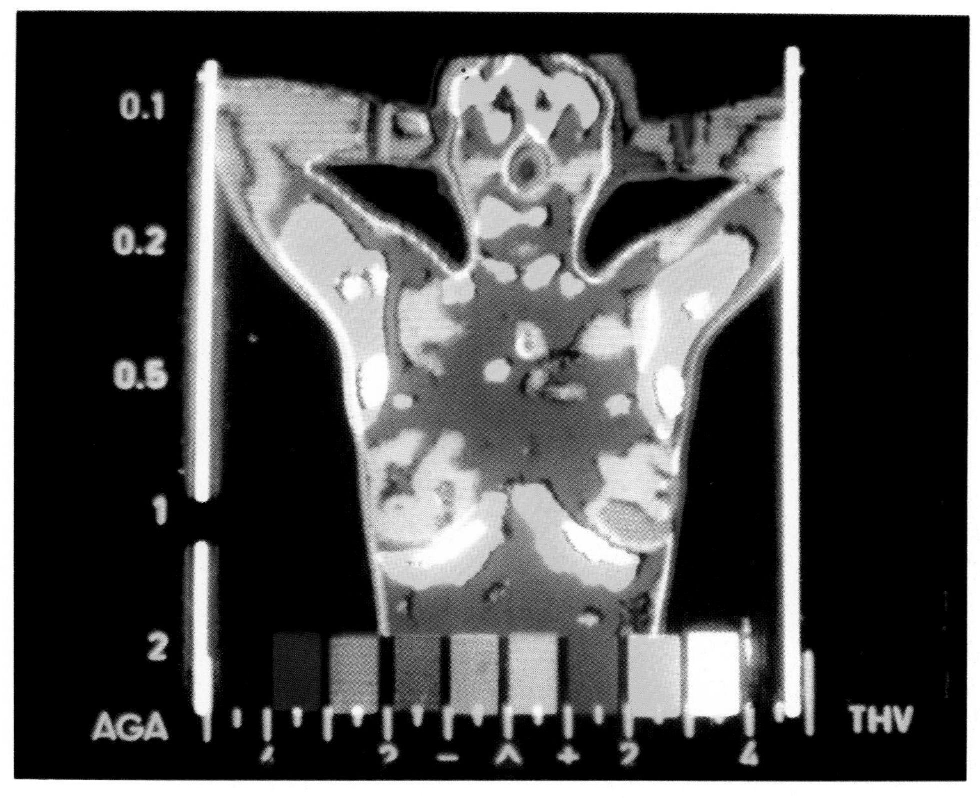

▲ Thermography of the human body.

◄ Wolf Vostell, Vietnam Symphony, two-colour silkscreen print, 1971.

CONCLUSION

From Illustration to Audiovisual Media

What about the relations today, in what we call "illustration," between those two terms so difficult to define and so restlessly variable: text and picture? Are we to see them as complementing each other in the happy way described in 1571 by Bartolomeo Taegio in *Il Liceo*: "Words and pictures separately have no meaning, but accompanying each other they manifest the secret of our soul"? Or is it an unrelenting rivalry between them and then the triumph today of the logic of the image prophesied by McLuhan? What appears from the foregoing chapters is that these varying relations between text and picture are not linked together in any linear sequence. A new relation neither cancels nor supersedes the previous one. It may safely be said that today they all overlap and co-exist. We know now that it is a mistake to suppose that the image has asserted itself at the expense of the written word. Not only because world publishing statistics, both of books and journals, prove the contrary (never has so much been printed and read since the advent of television, owing no doubt to the rising average standard of culture and more leisure time), but also because pictures cannot stand alone: far from dispensing with words, they call for them. One thinks of recordings, radio, telephone, which compete with writing for they play the same role. The silent film needed the crutch of writing to be understood, and foreign language films still need to be dubbed, the subtitling being a new form of "illustration." Television uses and often abuses texts which are awkwardly coupled with the pictures. What we find then is not the substitution of pictures for writing, but the addition and increase of them, not doing away with the typographic sector but on the contrary striking a new balance between the respective importance of these two media of communication, to the gain of pictures which for so long were frowned on or handicapped.

Just as printing, conceived for the text, imposed its frame on the picture for centuries, so today the picture in turn has a space of its own, the screen, which it imposes on the letter. But on the printed page and on the screen we meet both kinds of signs, in reverse proportions.

For no process exists by which text and picture together may be handled suitably and simultaneously. Typography requires relief, which reduces the image to uniform lines and surfaces. Photography, made for pictures, cannot give on the same exposure the strong contrast required by readable type-faces and the shaded modelling required by accurate pictures. The electronic image, riddling the screen with a multitude of dots, has by no means solved the problem. Electronic bombardment produces a scintillating image and forces a certain difformity upon letters. Till recently this problem may have seemed inescapable, and this strengthened the conviction of those who saw letter and picture as brotherly enemies. This is in fact a partisan position, its underlying assumption being that there is no defending the one without condemning the other. Technically speaking, scanners and lasers weaken this argument. The picture cannot be reproduced correctly—so the argument runs—since to do so it has necessarily to be broken down into dots. This is to forget that the cones and rods which apprehend light in our eye are just as discontinuous, and that the brain has to put them together again. Continuity does not exist in nature. Modern instruments are able to analyse an image, to break it down dot by dot, and with a resolution which defies the human eye. The image thus reduced to a multitude of figures (perfectly controlled by the computer) can be stored indefinitely, rapidly transmitted by signals and even printed out on argentic paper (for the sensitive surface of a photograph is not continuous either, it is the salt particles that register light intensities) with a resolution that may satisfy the keenest eye.

"Physically," then, texts and images can be reduced to a common denominator—that is, to figures, which permit both to be processed in the same way, on their most elementary level. The binary function, 1 and 0, which in the computer simulates our logic, can also, as positive

Joseph Beuys,
Heat Period Machine in the Economy,
colour offset postcard, 1975.

and negative, black and white, simulate any image. But it would be naive to assume that this fusion of image and text in the new recording and reproducing techniques produces an undifferentiated usage of both. Curiously enough, it is the image again that lags behind: being richer in data it requires a greater storage capacity and a longer and more costly transmission time than the text, whose letters, for the analyser and generator of forms, are merely poorer images. Moreover our civilization is still to a massive extent founded on coded language: the telematic screen displays mostly texts, occasionally diagrams and grids. The video disc, which can store over fifty thousand images on each side (12 inches in diameter), is a technology which has languished for ten years for lack of programmes. While the video disc is used to record films, it is no more than a substitute for the video tape: its real interest is that, connected with a microcomputer, it can store a hundred thousand static images (so that the fourteen thousand paintings in the Louvre would only take up a third of one side) in a variety of classifications permitting not only archival storage but interactive or thematic research in photo libraries or press agencies. But uncaptioned these images are of little use. They need a text to be placed and defined. They tell everything, except their name, and often it is the name that matters on a photograph. What is unnamable moreover can have no image: it is, as we say, abstract. But in every "abstract" photograph there is in fact a concrete subject: it is called abstract simply because it is not identifiable.

Today's superb technology of massive and varied picture reproduction is therefore dependent on the parallel reproduction of an accompanying text. Behind even the most perfected of modern high performance techniques, the functional duality of text and image remains intact, and so does their interdependence.

These are the two focal points of illustration at the present day: on the one hand, their resolution into a common technology of reproduction; on the other, a searching distinction between their specific functions. These two factors well sum up the vexed love-affair between these two types of signs. Text and picture are a couple, for the two of them together make up that category of artificial signs which might be designated as "figured" or "represented." They are distinguished from each other in this, that one is more directly bound up with language and so has its signifier necessarily connected with its signified, while in the other, in the picture, the signifier has only an occasional connection with its signified. There is no law obliging them to be coupled together, or to be coupled in one way or another. It would be pointless to list the particular relations they may arrive at: complementarity, competition, inclusion, etc.; tomorrow will add others to the forms already known. For this is not a history of those forms: they do not generate each other, and indeed each one springs from a particular situation. But at the moment in time when one such figure arises, the pictogram, the ornamental letter, the full-page plate or the caption, it answers to a historical demand, and the needs and notions behind it can be historically evaluated. Illustration has no history: it is an ideological manifestation of history. It is—as the etymology of the word "emblem" indicates—only a mosaic. Or rather a kaleidoscope. Various signs are thrown together in it. It is shaken and they are shifted about and seen in new combinations. The number of combinations is infinite and no one can foresee them. So long as it is believed that signs are in things and that it is things which make a sign to us, the ongoing manipulation will be forgotten and a vision of harmony will be assumed. It is this very "manipulation" that we have made a point of emphasizing here. We have seen the appearance of pictures in schoolbooks as denoting the rise of empirical methods as against dogmatism for a new public of schoolchildren in the later seventeenth century. We have seen the confusion maintained between the word and the image, to denote the divine nature of the Scriptures. We have seen the image assimilated to a vocabulary just as it was being drained of its transcendental significance; and then the photograph arriving just in time to substitute reality for divinity as the authority governing signs; and so on. These variations correspond to those of groups defending a power. But the power over signs is not wielded by any individual: it is a power necessarily shared, at least with him or her who is to receive the sign. The word is a conventional sign belonging to the educated classes. The picture permits a taking of chances, a capturing of meaning. Better than the text, the picture may seem to conceal some secret knowledge; one thinks of the aura of myth and mystery so long kept up around the Egyptian hieroglyphs. It may also serve to convey and divulge knowledge: books in the vernacular are more easily illustrated than scholarly books (the *Dream of Polyphilus* was not in Latin, and only the German language editions of the *Ship of Fools* were illustrated). The picture may be accepted and feared at the same time, according to the position of the authors. It is an extraordinary fact that of the three books which may be considered most important in the whole history of modern illustration (Horapollo's *Hieroglyphica*, Alciati's *Emblemata*, Ripa's *Iconologia*) not one was originally illustrated. The *Hieroglyphica* came to light in 1419 as an unillustrated Greek manuscript, probably deriving from an Alexandrian text; it was first given pictures when it was published in French in 1543. It has been shown that Alciati only intended to publish some epigrams, and that it was the publisher, no doubt for commercial reasons, who had the idea of combining pictures with them. The first edition of Ripa's book (1593) contained only a written description of its allegories; illustrations appeared with the third edition in 1611.

So there was some resistance to pictures, particularly in scholarly circles and among upholders of dogma and law. There was also some promotion of them, proportional to the development and needs of empirical knowledge, and also in religious circles where the image represented a sensuous approach to the divine. Thus considered, each conception of illustration was the outcome of a balance of forces and sometimes of historical contradictions. Illustration then, by its different uses and the agreements or conflicts it gave rise to, sheds light on the social implications and impact of theories of knowledge.

Today the apostles of the image think of themselves as apostles of modernism. They have gained a power which, however, still clings to letters and in the last resort is inseparable from them. In Brazil the number of television sets is greater than the number of literate persons. So for some Brazilians the TV image is their first experience of reading. A reading of pictures imposed to the same extent as the reading of words. Elsewhere some teachers remain hostile to "pictorial" teaching: the blackboard was not accepted in France till fifty years after it had been introduced in England. The text defends one order, the image another. When these two orders are confronted—that is, when we get illustration—there is necessarily a redoubling or a conflict.

Language has by no means yielded its privileged position: the role assigned to it in all modern philosophy amply confirms this. The image has not replaced it, but has added to it. Ours is not the civilization of the image, but it is certainly that of illustration.

Bibliography

List of Illustrations

Index

ɪnsulted and Bibliographical Guide

s of Illustration

e, son illustration, sa décoration, Paris, 1926.
ography of Book Illustration, London, 1955.
'llustration: the Illuminated Manuscript and the
ɔn, 1958.
ɪk Illustration, a Survey of its History and Develop-
nnessee), 1952.
ivers des livres, études d'histoire du livre depuis
IIe siècle, Paris, 1961.
Illustrated Book, London, 1981.
ᐣ, *The Illustrated Book*, Cambridge (England),

es

stern European Printed Books, Victoria and Albert
969.
Nationale, Paris, 1972.
cident, Bibliothèque Royale Albert Ier, Brussels,

Part One

ɪring

ɔvie et l'obtus, Essais critiques III, Paris, 1982
ticles on the arts).
ature du signe linguistique," in *Principes de lin-*
ɪris 1966, Ch. IV (1939).
Pour une sémiologie de la typographie, Docu-
1979.
Word as Image, London, 1970.
ɪts dans la peinture, Geneva, 1969.
se Calligraphers and their Art, Melbourne, 1966.
, "Rhétorique et typographie, la lettre et le sens,"
ɪtiques, Paris, 1979.
la grammatologie, Paris, 1967.
nce, Paris, 1967.
s mots et les choses, une archéologie des scien-
1966.
ng as Drawing, 1. Contour and Silhouette, 2. The
, 1970.
gage cet inconnu, une initiation à la linguistique,
ɪ 1981).
ɪtance de la lettre dans l'inconscient," in *Ecrits*,

it," in *Le Séminaire*, livre XX (1972-1973), pp.

ɪumber of *Littoral, Revue de psychanalyse*, No.

ɪD, *Discours, figure*, Paris, 1978.
ours de la figure," in *Critique*, XXV (1969), pp.

ɪtion," in *Critique*, XXVI (1970), pp. 928-929.
s, écriture, peinture, Paris, 1971.

MASSIN, *La lettre et l'image. La figuration dans l'alphabet latin du huitième siècle à nos jours*, Paris, 1970 (reprinted 1973).
Maurice MERLEAU-PONTY, *Signes*, Paris, 1960.
L'œil et l'esprit, Paris, 1964.
Le visible et l'invisible, Paris, 1964.
Edmond ORTIGUES, *Le discours et le symbole*, Paris, 1962.
Jérôme PEIGNOT, *De l'écriture à la typographie*, Paris, 1967.
Calligraphie latine, Paris, 1982.
Charles S. PEIRCE, *Ecrits sur le signe*, French translation, Paris, 1978 (chosen texts from *Collected Papers*, 8 vols., Harvard University Press, 1931-1958: see in particular Vol. 5, *Pragmatism and Pragmaticism*).
Semiotics and Significs, Bloomington, 1977.
Meyer SCHAPIRO, *Words and Picture, on the Literal and the Symbolic in the Illustration of a Text*, Paris-The Hague, 1973.
Paul ZUMTHOR, *Langue, texte, énigme*, Paris, 1975.

From Pictogram to Alphabet
(pages 17-25)

François CHENG, *Le vide et le plein, l'écriture poétique chinoise*, Paris, 1977.
Marcel COHEN, *La grande invention de l'écriture et son évolution*, 2 vols., Paris, 1958.
Ecritures, systèmes idéographiques et pratiques expressives, Actes du Colloque International de l'Université de Paris VII, Le Sycomore, 1982.
James G. FÉVRIER, *Histoire de l'écriture*, Paris, 1959.
Le déchiffrement des écritures et des langues, edited by Jean Leclant, L'Asiathèque, Paris, 1973.
L'écriture et la psychologie des peuples, Centre International de Synthèse, Paris, 1963.
André LEROI-GOURHAN, *Le geste et la parole*. Vol. 1, *Technique et langage*, Paris, 1964. Vol. 2, *La mémoire et les rythmes*, Paris, 1965.
L'espace et la lettre, Cahiers Jussieu 3, Paris, 1977 (articles by Jean-Marie Durand, Pascal Vernus, Alexandre Papadopoulo, Anne-Marie Christin, etc.).
Les pré-écritures et l'histoire des civilisations, Paris, 1974.
Eric S. THOMPSON, *Maya Hieroglyphic Writing*, University of Oklahoma Press, 1960.

Exhibition Catalogue

Naissance de l'écriture, cunéiformes et hiéroglyphes, Grand Palais, Paris, 1982.

The Appearance of the Diagram
(pages 27-35)

Kurt WEITZMANN, *The Joshua Roll, a Work of the Macedonian Renaissance*, Princeton University Press, 1948 (Studies in Manuscript Illuminations 3).
Ancient Book Illumination, Martin Classical Lecture, Vol. XVI, Harvard University Press, 1959.
Illustrations in Roll and Codex, a Study of the Origin and Method of Text Illustration, Princeton, 1949.
Studies in Classical and Byzantine Manuscript Illumination, Chicago, 1971.
Late Antique and Early Christian Book Illumination, London, 1977.
The Miniatures of the Sacra Parallela, Princeton University Press, 1979 (Studies in Manuscript Illuminations 8).

The Word Appears
(pages 37-45)

J.J.G. ALEXANDER, *The Decorated Letter*, London, 1978.
Mohamed AZIZA, *La calligraphie arabe*, Tunis, 1972.
L'image et l'Islam, l'image dans la société arabe contemporaine, Paris, 1978.
Richard ETTINGHAUSEN, *Arab Painting*, Geneva, 1977.
Bishr FARES, "La querelle des images en Islam," in *Mélanges Louis Massignon*, Institut Français de Damas, Damascus, 1957.
Essai sur l'esprit de la décoration islamique, Cairo, 1952.
S. FERBER, "Micrography, a Jewish art form," in *Journal of Jewish Art*, No. 3/4, 1977, pp. 12-24.
André GRABAR, *L'iconoclasme byzantin, dossier archéologique*, Paris, 1957.
Joseph GUTMANN, *Hebrew Manuscript Painting*, New York - London, 1979.
Françoise HENRY, *The Book of Kells*, London, 1974.
Abdekebir KHATIBI and Mohamed SIJELMASSI, *L'art calligraphique arabe*, Paris, 1976.
Alexandre PAPADOPOULO, *L'esthétique de l'art musulman, La peinture*, Paris - Lille, 1972.
Jérôme PEIGNOT, *Du Calligramme*, Paris, 1978.
Yasin Hamid SAFADI, *Islamic Calligraphy*, London, 1978.
Sir Edward SULLIVAN, *The Book of Kells*, London, 1952.

Illumination of the Text
(pages 47-57)

Myrtilla AVERY, *The Exultet Rolls of South Italy*, Princeton, 1936.
David DIRINGER, *The Illuminated Book, its History and Production*, London, 1967.
André GRABAR and Carl NORDENFALK, *Early Medieval Painting*, Geneva, 1957.
Romanesque Painting, Geneva, 1958.
Carl NORDENFALK, "The Beginning of Book Decoration," in *Essays in Honour of Georg Swarzenski*, Berlin - Chicago, 1951.
Henri STIERLIN, *Le Livre du feu: l'Apocalypse et l'art mozarabe*, Geneva, 1978.
O.K. WERKMEISTER, "Pain and Death in the Beatus of Saint Sever," in *Studi Medievali*, 3rd series, No. 14 (1973), pp. 565-626.
"The First Romanesque Beatus Manuscripts and the Liturgy of Death," in *Grupo de estudio Beato de Liebana, Actos del Simposio para el estudio de los codices del Comentario al Apocalipsis de Beato de Liebana*, 2 vols., Madrid, 1980.

Secularization of the Image
(pages 59-69)

François AVRIL, *L'enluminure à la cour de France au XIVe siècle*, Paris, 1978.
Robert BRANNER, *Manuscript Painting in Paris during the Reign of St Louis*, Berkeley, 1977.
Emile MÂLE, *L'Art religieux de la fin du moyen âge en France*, Paris, 1931.
L'Art religieux après le Concile de Trente, Paris, 1932.
L'Art religieux du XIIe siècle en France, étude sur les origines de l'iconographie du moyen âge, Paris, 1947 (5th edition).
L'Art religieux du XIIIe siècle en France, Paris, 1958 (9th edition).
Millard MEISS, *French Painting in the Time of Jean de Berry*, 3 vols., London - New York 1967-1968.
The Limbourgs and their Contemporaries, 2 vols., New York, 1974.
Mary Catherine O'CONNOR, *The Art of Dying Well*, New York, 1942.
Lilian M. RANDALL, *Images in the Margins of Gothic Manuscripts*, Berkeley, 1966.
Fritz SAXL, "A Spiritual Encyclopaedia of the Later Middle Ages," in *Journal of the Warburg and Courtauld Institute*, Vol. V, 1942, pp. 124-126.
Lectures, Oxford 1957 ("Illuminated Science Manuscripts in England," pp. 96-110; "Illustrated Medieval Encyclopedias," pp. 228-241).
Anne H. VAN BUREN and Sheila EDMUNDS, "Playing Cards and Manuscripts: Some widely disseminated fifteenth-century model sheets," in *Art Bulletin*, No. 1, 1974, pp. 12-30.
Henri ZERNER, "L'Art au Morier," in *Revue de l'Art*, No. 11 (1971), pp. 7-30.

The Image as Language
(pages 71-79)

Michael BAXANDALL, *Giotto and the Orators*, Oxford, 1971.
George BOAS, *The Hieroglyphics of Horapollo*, New York, 1950.
Peter M. DALY, "Trends and Problems in the Study of Emblematic Literature," in *Mosaic* (Winnipeg, Manitoba), No. 5 (1972), pp. 53-68.
Arthur HENCKEL and Albrecht SCHÖNE, *Emblemata, Handbuch zur Sinnbildkunst des XVI. und XVII. Jahrhunderts*, Stuttgart, 1967.
Robert KLEIN, *La forme et l'intelligible*, Paris, 1970.
John LANDWEHR, *Emblem Books in the Low Countries*, Utrecht, 1970.
Pierre L'ANGLOIS, *Discours des hiéroglyphes égyptiens*, Paris, 1583.
L'Emblème à la Renaissance (articles published by the Société Française des Seiziémistes), Paris, 1982.
Walter Jackson ONG, "From Allegory to the Diagram in the Renaissance Mind," in *The Journal of Aesthetics and Art Criticism*, XVII, No. 4 (June 1959).
Erwin PANOFSKY, *Studies in Iconology, Humanistic Themes in the Art of the Renaissance*, Oxford, 1939 (paperback reprint, New York, 1962).
Mario PRAZ, *Studies in Seventeenth Century Imagery*, Rome, 1964 (2nd edition).
Etienne TABOUROT, *Seigneur des Accords, Les Bigarrures et Torches... du Seigneur des Accords*, Paris, 1583 (reprint, Geneva, 1969).

Part Two

The Language of Technics
(pages 83-93)

Jurgis BALTRUSAITIS, *Le Miroir*, Paris, 1978.
Jacques-Louis BINET and Pierre DESCARGUES, *Dessins et Traités d'anatomie*, Paris, 1980.
Anthony BLUNT, *Artistic Theory in Italy, 1450-1600*, Oxford, 1940.
Robert BRUN, *Le livre illustré français de la Renaissance*, Paris, 1969 (new edition).
Yves DEFORGE, *Le graphisme technique, son histoire et son enseignement*, Seyssel, 1981.
Pierre DESCARGUES, *Traités de perspective*, Paris, 1976.
Philip HOFER, *Catalogue of Books and Manuscripts*; Part I, *French XVIth Century Books*, compiled by Ruth Mortimer under the supervision of Philip Hofer and William A. Jackson, 2 vols., Cambridge (Mass.), 1964.
George B. IVES, *Champfleury, Translated and Annotated*, New York, 1927.
Wenzel JAMNITZER, *Perspectiva Corporum Regularium* (1568), facsimile edition with a study by Albert Flocon, *Jamnitzer orfèvre de la rigueur sensible*, Paris, 1964.
Athanasius KIRCHER S.J., *Ars magnae lucis et umbrae*, Rome, 1646.
LEONARDO DA VINCI, *Carnets*, 2 vols., Paris, 1942.
Leonardo da Vinci's Notebooks, edited by Edward McCurdy, New York - London, 1908 (and later reprints).
J.P. RICHTER, *The Literary Works of Leonardo da Vinci*, 2 vols., London, 1939.
Marco ROSCI, *Il Trattato di architettura di Sebastiano Serlio*, Milan, 1967.

The Theatre of the World
(pages 95-105)

Bernadette BUCHER, *La sauvage aux seins pendants*, Paris, 1977.
Katherine van EERDE, *Wencelaus Hollar Delineator of His Time*, Charlottesville, 1970.
Amato FRUTAZ, *Le Piante di Roma*, Rome, 1962.
John LANDWEHR, *Romeyn de Hooghe as Book Illustrator*, Amsterdam, 1970.
Roberto WEISS, *The Renaissance Discovery of Classical Antiquity*, Oxford, 1969.

Silent Poetry
(pages 107-115)

Alain-Marie BASSY, "Iconographie et littérature, essai de réflexion critique et méthodologique," in *Revue Française d'Histoire du Livre*, tome III, nouvelle série, No. 5 (1973), pp. 3-34.
"Du texte à l'illustration, pour une sémiologie des étapes," in *Semiotica*, 1974, pp. 297-334.
René BENOIST, *Traicté catholique des images et du vray usage d'icelles*, Paris, 1564.
René BRAY, *La formation de la doctrine classique en France*, Paris, 1927.
Diane CANIVET, *L'illustration de la poésie et du roman français au XVIIe siècle*, Paris, 1957.
Robert John CLEMENTS, *Picta Poesis, Literary and Humanistic Theory in Renaissance Emblem Books*, Rome, 1960.
Jeanne DUPORTAL, *Etude sur les livres à figures édités en France de 1601 à 1660*, Paris, 1914.
André FONTAINE, *Les doctrines d'art en France*, Paris, 1909.
Rensselaer W. LEE, *Ut Pictura Poesis, the Humanistic Theory of Painting*, New York, 1967.

ɹveau illustrateur de Racine," in *Gazette des*

, the Parallel between Literature and the Visual

ɩome Problems in the Semiotics of Visual Art, ge-Signs," in *Semiotica*, I, 3 (1969), pp. 223-

ʀépertoire de livres à figures rares et précieux Ile siècle, contenant environ 1500 fac-similés figures, Paris, 1933.

enses

ı and his Place in European Art, London, 1962.
ɜux-Arts réduits à un même principe, Paris,

and Image, French Painting of the Ancient versity Press, 1981.
'amateur de livres à gravures du XVIIIe siècle,).
rigine des connaissances humaines, Amster-th an essay by Jacques Derrida, Paris, 1973.
débat sur les écritures et les hiéroglyphes au ɿuitième siècles, Paris, 1963.
:, *Essai sur les signes inconditionnels de l'art,*

s critiques sur la poésie et la peinture, Paris,

ı gravure originale dans l'illustration du livre — Die Original-Graphik in der französischen :htzehnten Jahrhunderts, Hamburg, 1975.
ɪnch Rococo Book Illustration, London, 1969.
G, *Laokoon, oder über die Grenzen der Male-*766. Extracts and bibliography in J. BIALOS-:IN, *Lessing, Laocoon...*, Paris, 1964.
ɜdie, presented by Roland Barthes, Robert Seguin, Paris, 1964.
'respondance des arts, Paris, 1969.

. *Jahrhundert*, Stadtgeschichtliches Museum,

ɪtion, The Hofer Collection, Harvard, 1980.

ɔn

n-Pierre SEGUIN, *Le livre romantique*, Paris,

*Ɔruikshank, the Artist, the Humorist and the ɪt of his Brother Robert: a Critico-Bibliogra-*n, New York, 1972 (reprint of the London

'ettes romantiques, 1825-1840, Paris, 1883.
:ngraved Book Illustration in England, Lon-

Book Design and Colour Printing, London,

raphy 1800-1850, London, 1970.
de l'amateur des livres du XIXe siècle, 1801- ·-1920.

), Cabinet des Estampes, Strasbourg, 1983.

ers

ɜrie vue par l'écrivain au siècle dernier," in ɘ *Vieux Papier*, XXVIII, fascicule 270 (Octo-

ı *France*, essays in honour of Jean Seznec,

ɟ Martin K. NURMI, *A Blake Bibliography*,

ttérature et Peinture en France, 1830-1900, : méthodologique," in *Revue d'Histoire litté-* 80th year (November-December 1980), pp.

ture et iconographie, Paris, 1973.
ke's Theory of Art, Princeton, 1982.
'ovelists and their Illustrators, London, 1970.
terature through Art, a New Approach to 'ork, 1952.

Louis HAUTECŒUR, *Littérature et peinture en France du XVIIe au XIXe siècle*, Paris, 1942.

Iconographie et littérature, d'un art à l'autre (articles published by the Centre d'études et de recherches d'histoire des idées et de la sensibilité), Paris, 1969.

M. MESPOULET, *Images et romans, parenté des estampes et du roman réaliste de 1815 à 1865*, Paris, 1939.

Revue de l'Art, special number on "Les écrivains dessinateurs," No. 44 (2nd quarter of 1979).

Romantisme, No. 43, 1984, special number on the relations between artists and writers, with in particular an article by Philippe Kaenel, "Autour de J.J. Grandville: les conditions de production socio-professionnelles du livre illustré romantique."

The Illustrated Papers

(pages 151-159)

Daumier et le dessin de presse, colloquy at Grenoble, Maison de la Culture, in special number of *Histoire et critique des arts*, No. 13/14, 1st semester, 1980.

Elisabeth and Michel DIXMIER, *L'Assiette au beurre: revue satirique illustrée 1901-1912*, Paris, 1974.

Pierre GEORGEL, preface to Vol. V of *Œuvres complètes de Victor Hugo*, Paris, 1967.
"Le Romantisme des années 60, correspondance Victor Hugo/ Philippe Burty," in *Revue de l'Art*, No. 20 (2nd quarter, 1973), pp. 37-64.

David KUNZLE, "L'Illustration, premier magazine illustré en France," in *Nouvelles de l'Estampe*, No. 43 (January-February 1979).

Léonée ORMOND, *George Du Maurier*, London, 1969.

Presse et caricature, in *Cahiers de l'Institut d'histoire de la presse et de l'opinion*, No. 7, Université de Tours, 1983.

Philip ROBERTS-JONES, *La presse satirique illustrée entre 1860 et 1890*, Paris, 1956.

Part Three

Photographic Illustration

(pages 163-171)

Roland BARTHES, *La chambre claire, note sur la photographie*, Paris, 1980.

Isabelle JAMMES, *Blanquart-Evrard et les origines de l'édition photographique française*, Geneva, 1981.

Les espaces photographiques: le livre, special number of *Les Cahiers de la photographie*, No. 6, 2nd quarter, 1982, with articles by Gilles Mora, Claude Nori, Alain Fleig, André Rouillé, Michel Wiedemann, Gabriel Bauret, Arnaud Claass et Denis Roche.

André ROUILLÉ, *L'empire de la photographie, 1839-1870*, Paris, 1982.

William Henry Fox TALBOT, *The Pencil of Nature*, new introduction by Beaumont Newhall, New York, 1969.

Illustrating Daily Life

(pages 173-181)

Jean ADHÉMAR, Jean-Pierre SEGUIN, Michèle HEBERT, *Imagerie populaire française*, Milan, 1968.

Jean ADHÉMAR, "L'enseignement par l'image," in *Gazette des Beaux-Arts*, February 1981, pp. 53-60 and September 1981, pp. 49-60.

Karen F. BEALL, *Kaufrufe und Strassenhändler, Cries and Itinerant Trades, a Bibliography*, Hamburg, 1974.

François-Marc GAGNON, *La conversion par l'image*, Montreal, 1975.

La carte postale illustrée, colloquy at the Musée Nicéphore Niepce, Chalon-sur-Saône, 1977.

Jean-Pierre SEGUIN, *Canards du siècle passé*, Paris, 1969.

Exhibition Catalogues

Le livre dans la vie quotidienne, Bibliothèque Nationale, Paris, 1975.

Le fait divers, Musée national des arts et traditions populaires, Paris, 1982.

Illustrating Street Life

(pages 183-193)

John BARNICOAT, *A Concise History of Posters*, London, 1975.

Das frühe Plakat in Europa und den U.S.A., ein Bestandskatalog.
1. *Grossbritannien, Vereinigte Staaten von Nordamerika*, Berlin, 1973.
2. *Frankreich und Belgien*, Berlin, 1977.

Françoise ENEL, *L'affiche, fonctions, langage, rhétorique*, Tours, 1973.

Max GALLO, *L'affiche, miroir de l'histoire, miroir de la vie*, Paris, 1974.

Alain GESGON, *Sur les murs de France, 2 siècles d'affiches politiques*, Paris, 1979.
Bevis HILLIER, *Posters*, London, 1969; *100 Years of Posters*, New York, 1972.
Walter KOSCHATZKY and Horst-Herbert KOSSATZ, *Ornamental Posters of the Vienna Secession*, London - New York, 1974.
Ernest MAINDRON, *Les affiches illustrées*, Paris, 1886.
Abraham A. MOLES, *L'affiche dans la société urbaine*, Paris, 1970.
Alain WEILL, *L'affiche française*, Paris, 1982.

The Illustrated Book
(pages 195-205)

Gérard BERTRAND, *L'illustration de la poésie à l'époque du cubisme*, Paris, 1971.
Jean-Paul BOUILLON, "La vogue des livres à gravures du XVIIIe siècle sous le Second Empire et au début de la IIIe République," in *L'illustration du livre et la littérature au XVIIIe siècle en France et en Pologne*, Cahiers de Varsovie, Vol. 9, Warsaw, 1982, pp. 247-288.
Roderick CAVE, *The Private Press*, London, 1971.
Walter CRANE, *On the Decorative Illustration of Books Old and New*, London, 1896.
R.W. ELLIS, *Book Illustration*, Kingsport (Tennessee), 1952.
Eleanor M. GARVEY and Peter A. WICK, *The Art of the French Book, 1900-1965, Illustrated Books of the School of Paris*, Dallas, 1967.
Una E. JOHNSON, *Ambroise Vollard éditeur*, New York, 1977.
Raymond MAHÉ, *Bibliographie des livres de luxe de 1900 à 1928*, 4 vols., Paris, 1931.
Pierre MORNAND, *L'art du livre et son illustration*, 2 vols., Paris, 1947.
Segolène SANSON-LEMEN, "Quant au livre illustré," in *Revue de l'Art*, No. 44 (2nd quarter, 1979), pp. 85-106.
Albert SKIRA, *Anthologie du livre illustré par les peintres et sculpteurs de l'Ecole de Paris*, Geneva, 1946.
Rolf SÖDERBERG, *French Book Illustration, 1880-1905*, Stockholm, 1977.
Walter John STRACHAN, *The Artist and the Book in France. The 20th Century Livre d'artiste*, London, 1969.

Exhibition Catalogues

50 ans d'éditions de D. H. Kahnweiler, Galerie Louise Leiris, Paris, 1959.
The Artist and the Book: 1860-1960 in Western Europe and the United States, Museum of Fine Arts, Boston, 1961.
Modern Artists as Illustrators, Museum of Modern Art, New York, 1981.

The "Livre d'artiste" in France
(pages 207-217)

Michel BUTOR, *Illustrations*, Paris, 1964.
"Le livre comme objet," in *Répertoire II*, Paris, 1964.
Antoine CORON, "Entretiens avec Michel Butor," in *Bulletin de la Bibliothèque Nationale*, 2nd year (1977), Nos. 3 and 4.
Pierre GARNIER, *Spatialisme et poésie concrète*, Paris, 1968.
Jacques SCHERER, *Le «Livre» de Mallarmé*, Paris, 1957.
Emmet WILLIAMS, *Anthology of Concrete Poetry*, New York, 1967.

Exhibition Catalogues

Livres de Pierre Lecuire, Centre National d'Art Contemporain, Paris, 1973.
Ecritures, graphies, notations, typographie, Fondation Nationale des Arts Graphiques, Paris, 1980.
Du livre, Musée des Beaux-Arts, Rouen, 1982.
Supports/Ecrits, plasticiens et écrivains contemporains, Bibliothèque municipale, Lyons, 1983.

From Children's Books to Comic Strips
(pages 219-229)

Christian ALBERELLI, *Benjamin Rabier*, Grenoble, 1981.
Gérard BLANCHARD, *La bande dessinée: histoire des histoires en images de la préhistoire à nos jours*, Verviers, 1969.
Wilhelm BUSCH, *Das Gesamtwerk des Zeichners und Dichters*, 6 vols., Stuttgart-Salzburg, 1959-1960.
François CARADEC, *Christophe Colomb, essai de biographie*, Paris, 1956.
Pierre COUPERIE, *Encyclopédie de la bande dessinée*, Paris, 1974.
F.J. Harvey DARTON, *Children's Books in England*, Cambridge, 1966 (2nd edition).
Pierre FRESNAULT-DERUELLE, *La chambre à bulle, essai sur l'image du quotidien dans la bande dessinée*, Paris, 1977.
GUMUCHIAN et Cie, *Les livres de l'enfance, du XVe au XIXe siècle*, 2 vols., Paris, 1921.
Derek HUDSON, *Arthur Rackham, his Life and Work*, London, 1974.
Bettina HÜRLIMAN, *Three Centuries of Children's Books in Europe*, London, 1967.
Wolfgang KEMPKES, *Bibliographie der internationalen Literatur über Comics – International Bibliography of Comics Literature*, Munich, 1974.
David KUNZLE, *Early Comic Strips...*, Berkeley, 1973.
La bande dessinée et son discours (Pierre Fresnault-Deruelle, Umberto Eco, Luc Routeau...), Paris, 1976 (*Communications*, No. 24).
Percy MUIR, *English Children's Books, 1600 to 1900*, London, 1954.
Alain REY, *Les spectres de la bande, essai sur la B. D.*, Paris, 1978.
Jerry ROBINSON, *The Comics, an Illustrated History of Comic Strip Art*, New York, 1974.
The World Encyclopedia of Comics, London, 1976.

Exhibition Catalogues

Early Children's Books and their Illustration, The Pierpont Morgan Library, New York, 1975.
Bandes dessinées chinoises, Centre Georges Pompidou, Paris, 1981.

Magazines and Reporting
(pages 231-239)

Louis ARAGON, *Ecrits sur l'art moderne*, preface by Jacques Leenhardt, Paris, 1981.
Raymond GAUDRIAULT, *La gravure de mode féminine en France*, Paris, 1983.
Nancy HALL-DUNCAN, *The History of Fashion Photography*, New York, 1979.
Michel MELOT, *Dubout*, preface by Frédéric Dard, Paris, 1979.
"Der Zeichner und die Massen, zur politischen Pressesatire in den dreissiger Jahren," in Klaus HERDING and Günter OTTO (editors), *Karikaturen*, Hamburg 1980, pp. 285-301.

Conclusion
From Illustration to Audiovisual Media
(pages 241-245)

Roland BARTHES, *L'empire des signes*, Geneva, 1970; English translation, *The Empire of Signs*, New York, 1983.
René BERGER, *La téléfission, alerte à la télévision*, Paris, 1976.
A. BIJAOUI, *Image et information, introduction au traitement numérique des images*, Paris, 1981.
Hubert DAMISH, "Huit thèses pour (ou contre) une sémiologie de l'image," in *Macula*, No. 2, 1977, pp. 17-23.
Umberto ECO, *Opera aperta*, Milan, 1962.
La structure absente: introduction à la recherche sémiotique, Paris, 1972.
Louis GOUSSOT, *La télévision monochrome et en couleur*, Paris, 1972.
Henri HUDRISIER, *L'Iconothèque*, Paris, 1982.
Image et Signification, actes du Colloque organisé par l'Ecole du Louvre, Paris, 1983.
L'Analyse des Images, No. 15 (1970) of *Communications*, with articles by Christian Metz, Umberto Eco, Eliseo Veron, Jacques Durand, Georges Péninou, Violette Morin, Sylvain Du Pasquier, Pierre Fresnault-Deruelle, Jacques Bertin, Louis Marin, Jean-Louis Schefer.
La révolution des images, special number of *La Recherche*, No. 144, May 1983.
Michel LUCAS and Pierre MORVAN, *Image et ordinateur*, Paris, 1976.
Marshall McLUHAN, *The Gutenberg Galaxy*, Toronto, 1962.
Marshall McLUHAN and Quentin FIORE, *The Medium is the Message*, London, 1967.
Albert PLECY, *Grammaire élémentaire de l'image*, Verviers, 1962.

List of Illustrations

Index

PRODUCED BY THE TECHNICAL STAFF OF
EDITIONS D'ART ALBERT SKIRA S.A., GENEVA

COLOUR AND BLACK AND WHITE,
FILMSETTING AND PRINTING BY
IRL IMPRIMERIES RÉUNIES LAUSANNE S.A.

BINDING BY MAYER & SOUTTER S.A.
RENENS/LAUSANNE

Printed in Switzerland